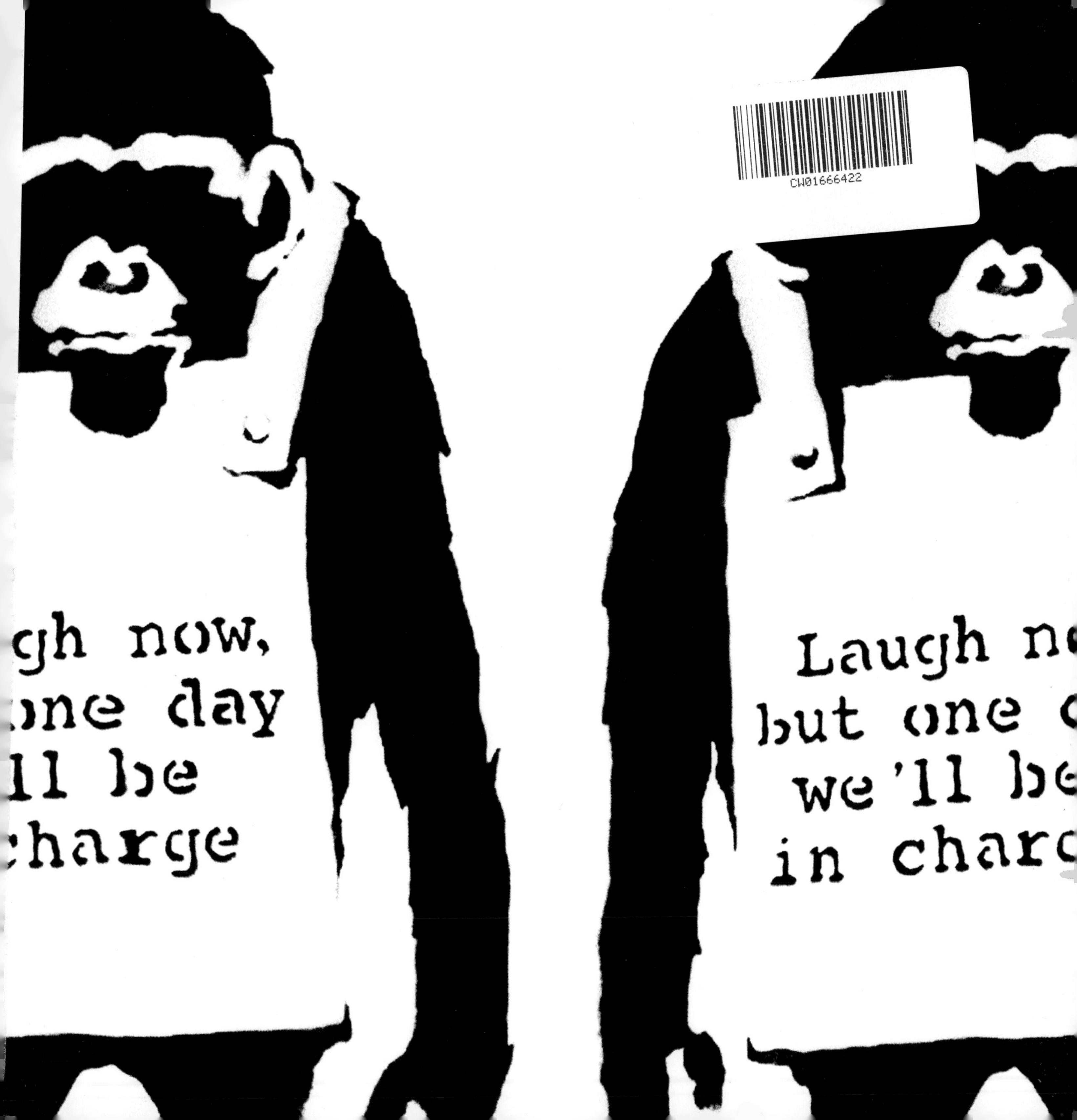
gh now,
one day
ll be
charge
Laugh n
but one
we'll be
in charg

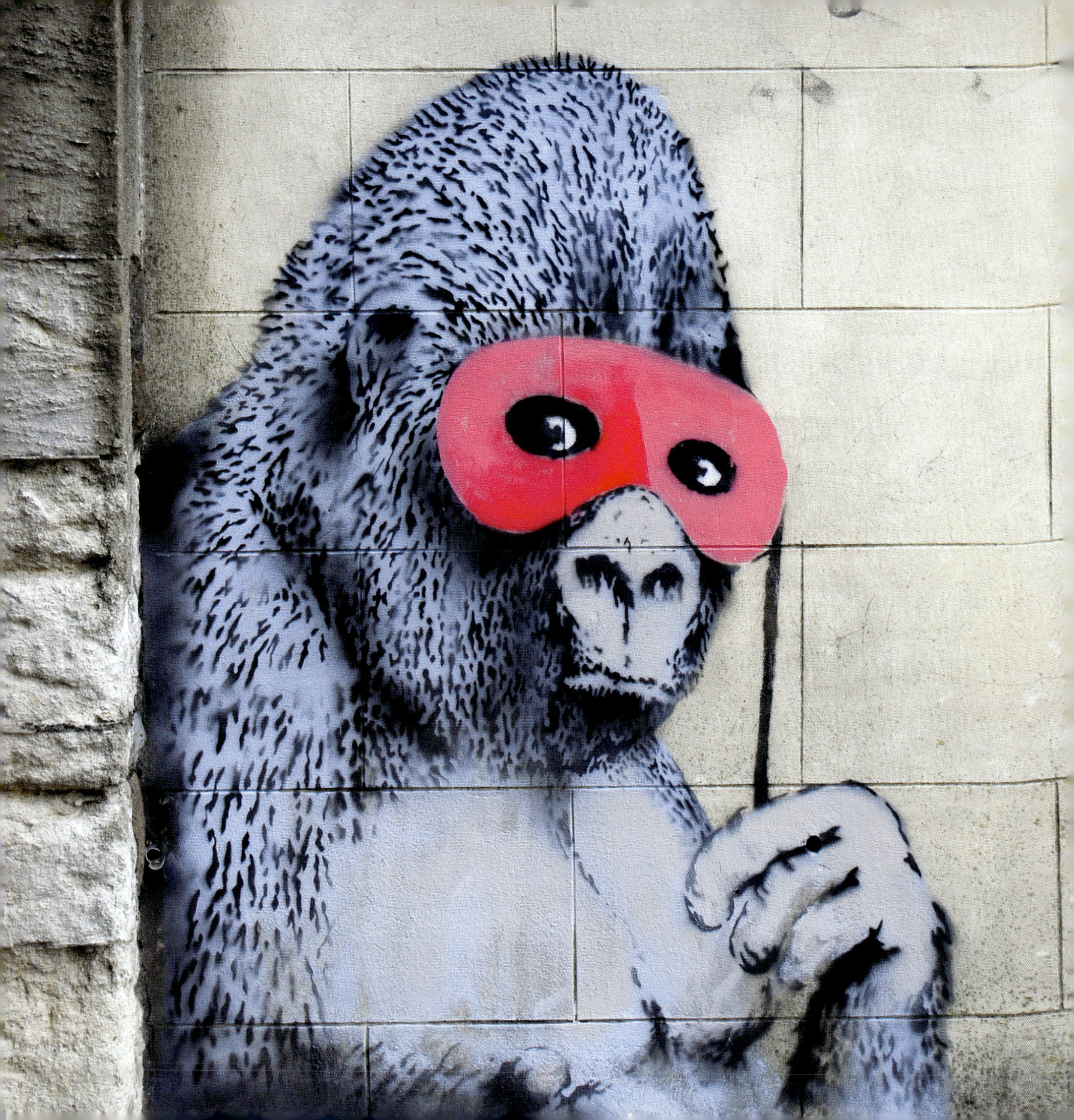

Banksy's Bristol

HOME SWEET HOME

By Steve Wright & Richard Jones

tangent books

Fifth Edition published 2020 by Tangent Books
ISBN 978-1-910089-93-4

Unit 5.16 Paintworks, Arnos Vale, Bristol, BS4 3EH
Tel 0117 972 0645
www.tangentbooks.co.uk
Publisher: Richard Jones richard@tangentbooks.co.uk
Production: Richard Jones, Anne Scott, Steve Faragher, Johanna Darque
Design: Cheba, Joe Burt

Photography: Mark Simmons, Pete Maginnis, Trevor Wyatt, Matt Harrison (MKWF), Zombizi, Sarah Connolly, Ikue Uyama (relaxamax), Doppelganger, Charlie Black, Jack, Rebekah Kortokraks, Alice Lowndes, Tristan Manco, Anne Scott, D. Neary, R. Boyle, Simon Ellis, Dan Jeffries, Richard Jones, Mena Telfer, Marc Leverton, Kevan Blackadder, John Nation, Lokey, R Grove, Anne Burt

Steve Wright thanks: Rach, my family, everyone at Tangent Books. This book is dedicated to Banksy and the people of Bristol
Thanks to: Mark Simmons, Cheba, Azlan, Charlie Backwell, Alan Bamberger, Petunia Begent, Naomi Berry, Robert Birse, Bristol Blogger, Ian Bone, Bristle magazine, Will Brown, Eugene Byrne, Chris (Illusive), Snoozie Claiden, Ghostboy, Gil Gillespie, Bear Hackenbush, Gary Hopkins, Beryl Jones, Feisal Khalif, Jon Lewis, John Mitchell, Stephen Morris, Jim Paine, Paris, Carlton Romaine, Gez Smith, Matt Smith, Steve Symons, Ralph Taylor, Will Wright, John Garrad

First published as a hardback in November 2007. Second edition (paperback) published January 2008, reprinted 2008, 2009, 2010, 2012, 2016, 2017. This edition published July 2020

Photographers: Inside covers: Sarah Connolly; title page: Richard Jones; P1: Ikue Uyama; P2: Lokey; P3: Mark Simmons; P4: Matt Harrison; P5: Jack (top), Unknown (bottom); P6: Mark Simmons; P7: Pete Maginnis; P8-9: Pete Maginnis; P11: Pete Maginnis; P12-13: Zombizi; P15: Pete Maginnis; P17: Matt Harrison (MKWF); P18-21: John Nation; P22-23: Pete Maginnis; P24: Pete Maginnis; P25: Iyue Uyama; P27: Top row (from left), Pete Maginnis, Jack, Mark Simmons. Second row, Matt Harrison, Rebekah Kortokraks. Middle row, Rebekah Kortokraks, Iyue Uyama. Fourth row, Mark Simmons, Pete Maginnis. Bottom row, Pete Maginnis; P28-29: Pete Maginnis; P30-31 Mark Simmons; P31 (top): Sarah Connolly; P32: Doppleganger, inset: Jack; p33: D Neary and R Boyle; P35: Mark Simmons; P37: Charlie Black; P40: Pete Maginnis; P42-43 Mark Simmons; P45: Mark Simmons; P46 Matt Harrison; P48: Pete Maginnis; P49: Ikue Uyama; P50 Pete Maginnis; P51: Ikue Uyama; P52-53 Trevor Wyatt; P54-55 Mark Simmons; P56: Matt Harrison; P57: Mark Simmons; P58-59: Pete Maginnis; P60: Mark Simmons; P57: Jack; P53: Pete Maginnis; P65: Jack; P67: Mark Simmons; P69: Pete Maginnis; P71: Pete Maginnis; P74-75: Rebekah Kortokraks; P77-81: R S Grove; P82: Pete Maginnis; P84: Pete Maginnis; P86: Ikue Uyama; P88: Doppleganger; P89: Sarah Connolly; P90, 91, 92, 93, 94-95, 96, 97, 99: Pete Maginnis; P100: Anne Smith; P101: Jack; P102-103: Mark Simmons; P104: Mark Simmons; P105: Pete Maginnis; P106-107: Mark Simmons; P108-109 Alice Lowndes; P110-115: Simon Ellis; P116-117: Paranoid Pictures; P118: Richard Jones; P119, 120: Marc Leverton; p122-123: Simon Ellis; P124, 125, 126: Mark Simmons; P127: Simon Ellis; P128, 129, 130: Mark Simmons; P131 Top row (from left): Richard Jones, Mena Telfer. Second row: Mark Simmons. Third Row: Mena Telfer, Simon Ellis. P132: Simon Ellis; P133: Richard Jones (left); Simon Ellis; P134-135: Dan Jeffries; P137: Matt Harrison (top); Mark Simmons; P138: Jack; P139: Richard Jones; p140: Richard Jones; P141: Marc Leverton; P142: Jack; P143: Richard Jones; P144-146: Richard Jones; P147: Kevan Blackadder; Anne Burt; P148-151: Richard Jones

Banksy

Contents

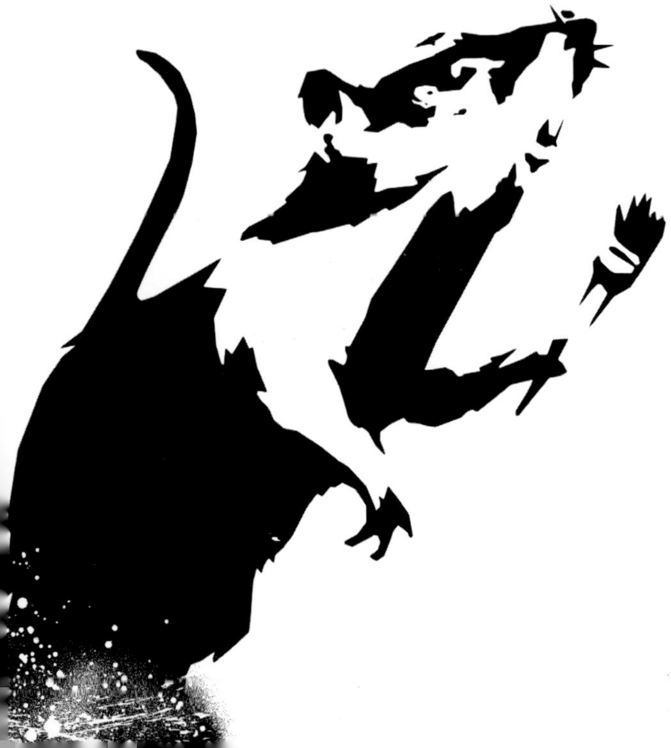

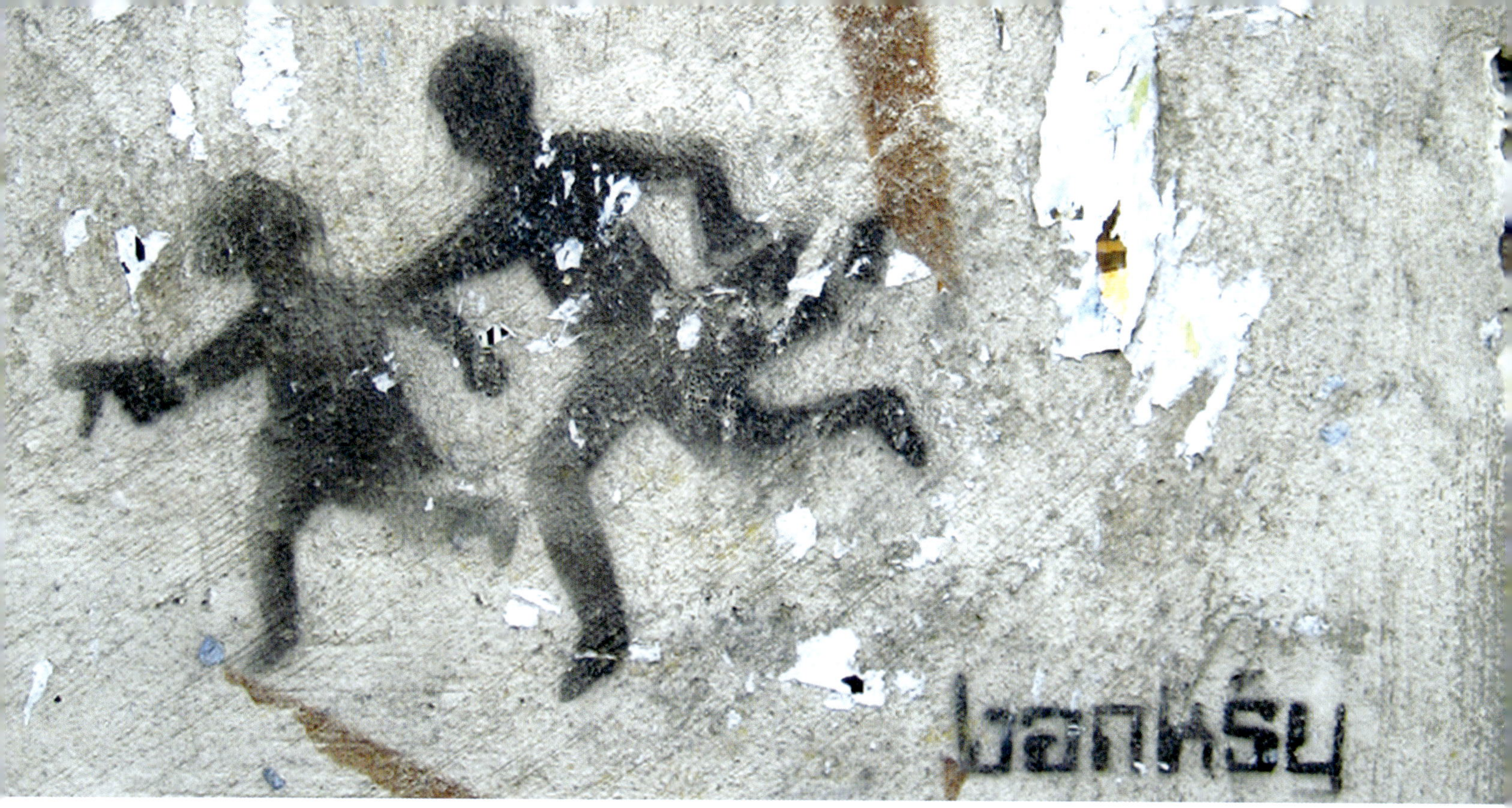

One of Banksy's early Bristol stencils. The tag soon changed into the one that is now recognised across the globe.

Introduction

So, why a book called 'Banksy's Bristol'? There's an awful lot of talk about the guy – he must be one of the most discussed, debated and acclaimed cultural figures of our age. A feat which is even more remarkable when you consider that his medium – visual art – is not usually one to grab the headlines.

And yet there is still very little known about where this all came from. Banksy's early graffiti career, and the amazingly fertile Bristol scene that nourished him, has not been given much attention. I wanted to understand a bit more about the Banksy phenomenon: how he has achieved what he has, where and when it originated and, finally, what it means – for the art world, for Bristol, for people that knew him then and know him now. I wanted, in short, to get to the bottom of his art, to understand where it came from and why it has taken him so far.

This book is an appreciation of Banksy's art, and explains why it has had such an immense impact; it looks at the targets Banksy chooses and how he nails them so effectively, with a mix of sharp humour and humanity; and it traces his roots back to Bristol's astonishingly rich graffiti and music landscape, looking at and hearing from some of the key protagonists in the scene.

Banksy enjoys an extraordinary, unique sort of fame. 30,000 people saw *Barely Legal*, his Los Angeles exhibition in September 2006, more than 300,000 people visited *Banksy vs Bristol Museum* in 2009 and more than 150,000 visited *Dismaland* in 2015.

So much intrigue surrounds the man: about his identity, for sure (for we all love a mystery), but also around his art, and a sharp strain of humour within it that speaks to people quickly and crisply.

"He's had the impact he has for many reasons," notes one (anonymous) friend and collaborator. "Being in the right place at the right time certainly comes into it, as does

This page: Banksy began writing freehand with the Bad Applez and DryBreadZ crews from the Kingswood area of Bristol. This is a rare photograph of Banksy's early work (1997) with Lokey (Lokea), Sorse (Soker), Kato, Verse and others.

That page: The shower curtain was one of several Banksy pieces at Dismaland.

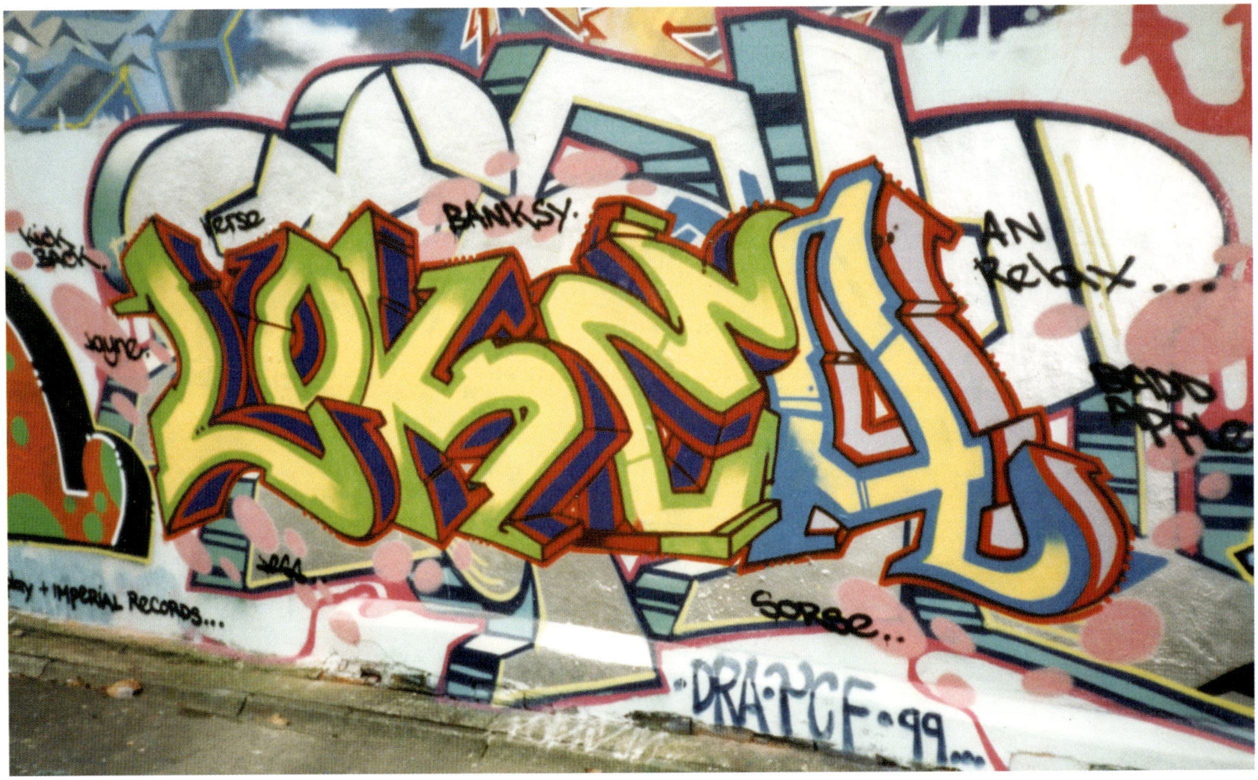

his sheer drive and work ethic. Chiefly, though, his style was simple enough for your average Joe to get. When he first started to become known outside his circle of artists and friends, it was people like builders and office workers that seemed to be picking up on his humour."

But some of the most striking parts of the Banksy story are the gaps, the bits that aren't known who he is, what he looks like, where he hangs out and with whom. In a celebrity-obsessed era, Banksy has created a universally-recognised brand without revealing his own identity – an extraordinary feat.

For many artists – particularly graffiti artists – art is ego-driven, all about getting your soul, your emotions or simply your name onto a wall or canvas. Not so for Banksy. What do we learn about him, as a person, from his pieces? Very little – which helps to feed the fires of intrigue. It's not just Banksy himself who's anonymous: his art somehow is, too.

Another part of the fascination with Banksy is that we don't yet know how he will be remembered, how much impact he will be judged to have had. It could be that he has changed the art scene massively by turning a whole new generation onto art. But where will the Banksy story take us next? Will he ever reveal himself? Will he eventually mellow, when he gets older and shinnying up a road bridge at 3am doesn't seem quite so appealing? Will he retire with a few goats to Cornwall? Of course, given his mystery, most of us will probably never know, although revealing himself and living off the interviews would be another option open to him. Probably not, you suspect, one he'll choose.

Finally, it was never our intention to reveal Banksy's true identity (though we could have published photographs of him) and I was impressed that it was only when I made this absolutely clear to the interviewees that they were prepared to talk about Banksy and his Bristol background. That loyalty seems to have been engendered by the fact that Banksy has never sold out. And because Bristol is very proud of him.

Steve Wright, Bristol

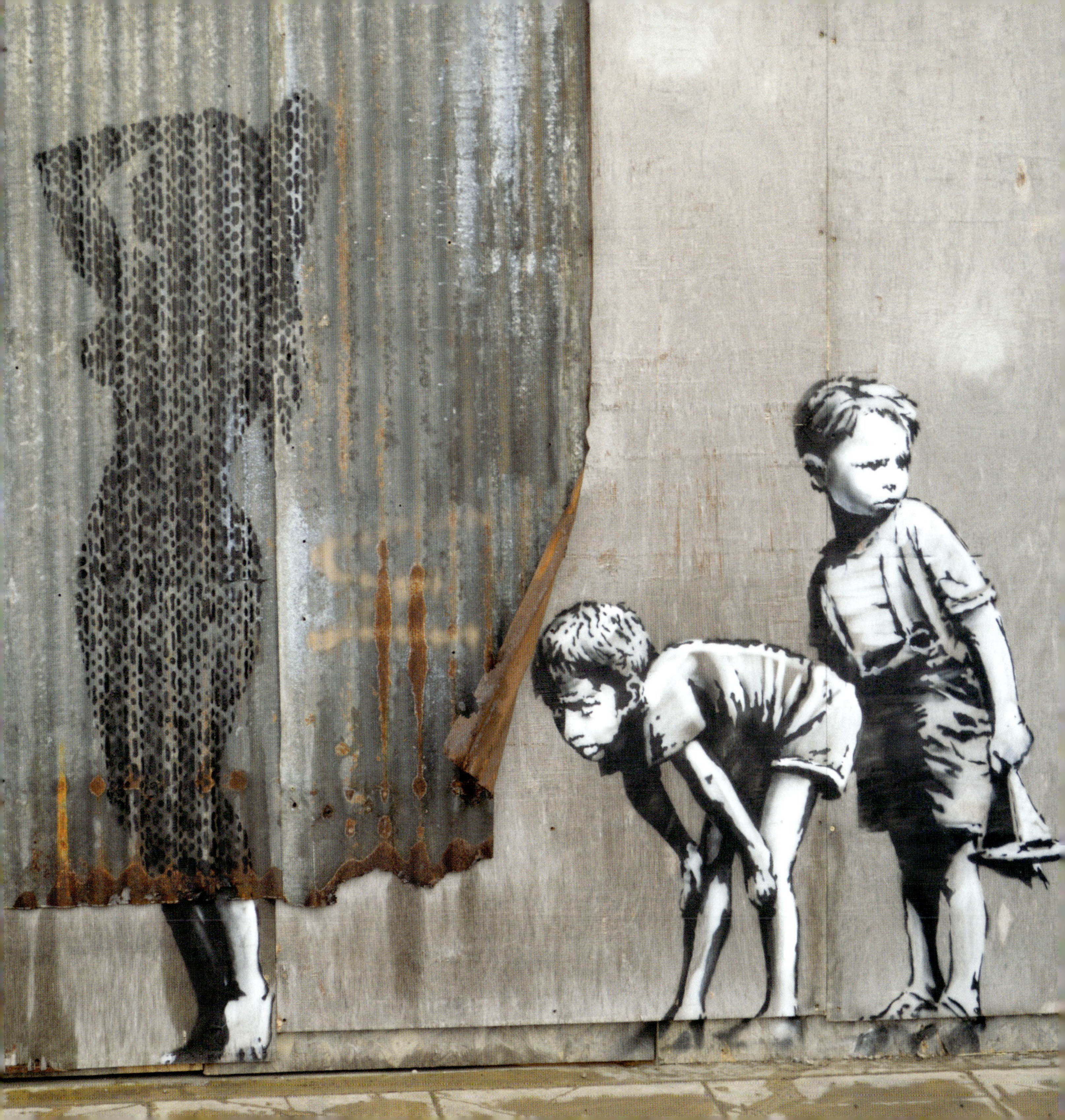

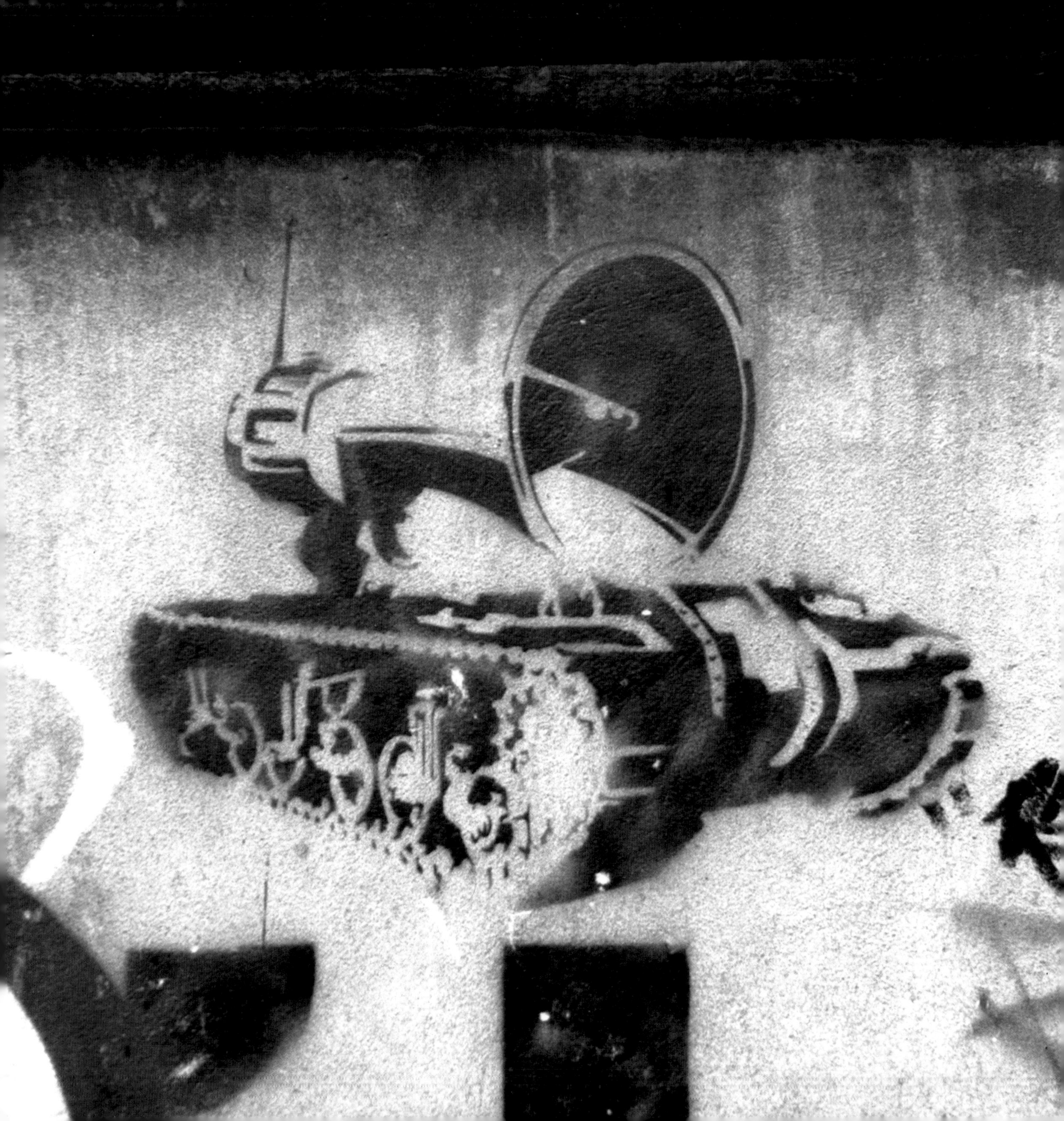

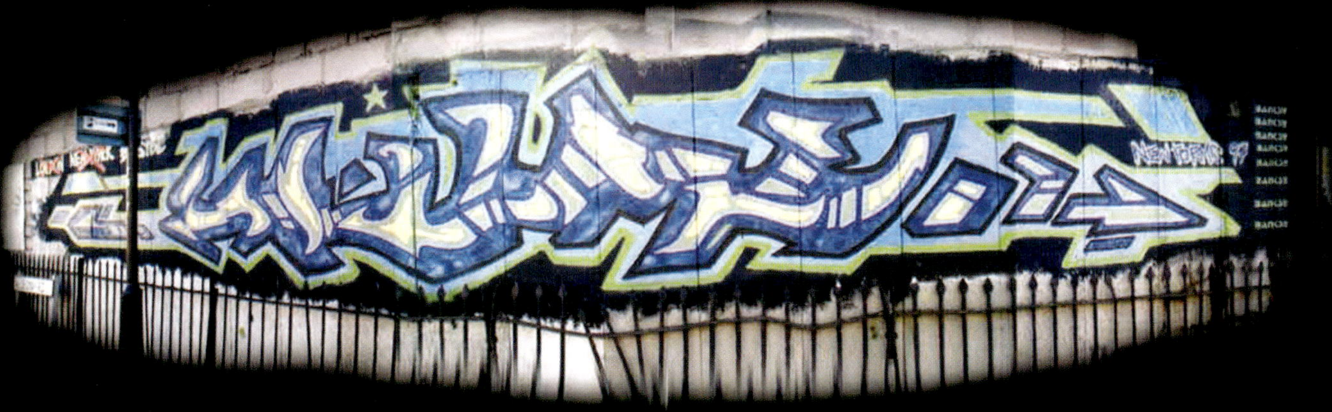

The Bristol Beat

"I come from a relatively small city in southern England. When I was about 10 years old, a kid called 3D was painting the streets hard. I think he'd been to New York and was the first to bring spray painting back to Bristol. I grew up seeing spray paint on the streets way before I ever saw it in a magazine or on a computer.

"3D quit painting and formed the band Massive Attack, which may have been good for him but was a big loss for the city. Graffiti was the thing we all loved at school – we all did it on the bus on the way home from school. Everyone was doing it."

Banksy, interview with *Swindle* magazine

Any account of Banksy's impact has to take in the larger context of street art in Bristol. For it's no coincidence that Banksy grew up, and made his first pieces, in a city with a rich graffiti and street art tradition from the early 1980s onward. In the early days of Bristol graffiti culture, four figures emerge as key. There right from the very start, as Banksy mentions above was Robert del Naja, aka 3D, who started out as a young graffiti artist spraying on Bristol walls in the very early 80s. More than that, 3D was responsible for importing some of the American hip hop and graffiti culture over to Bristol, bringing leading artists connected to the seminal NY hip hop/graff outfit Rock Steady Crew to paint over here. He went on, of course, to

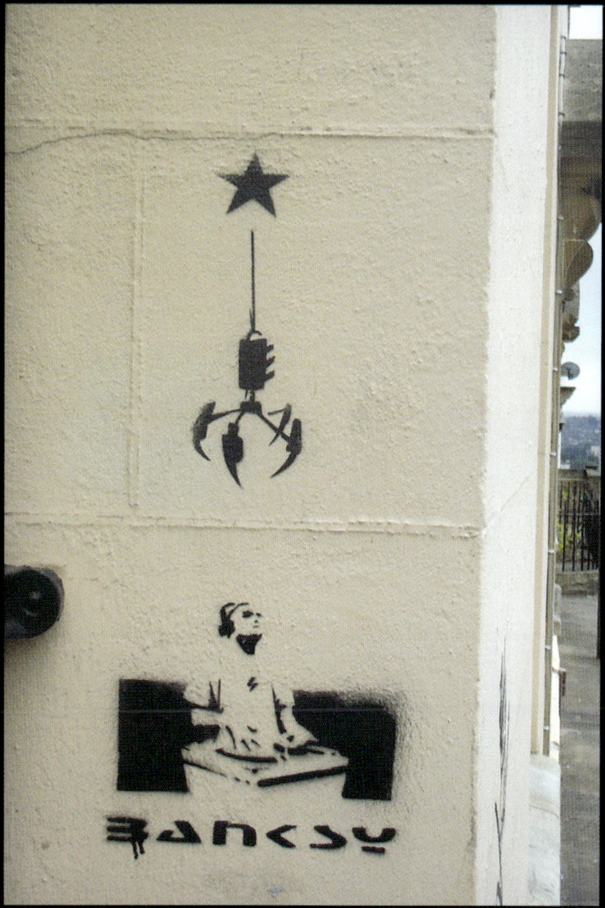

That page: The tank used to be on the wall in Frogmore Street where the Well-Hung Man is now.

This page: The freehand piece was in Albion Road, off St Mark's Road in Easton. The DJ was in Clifton.

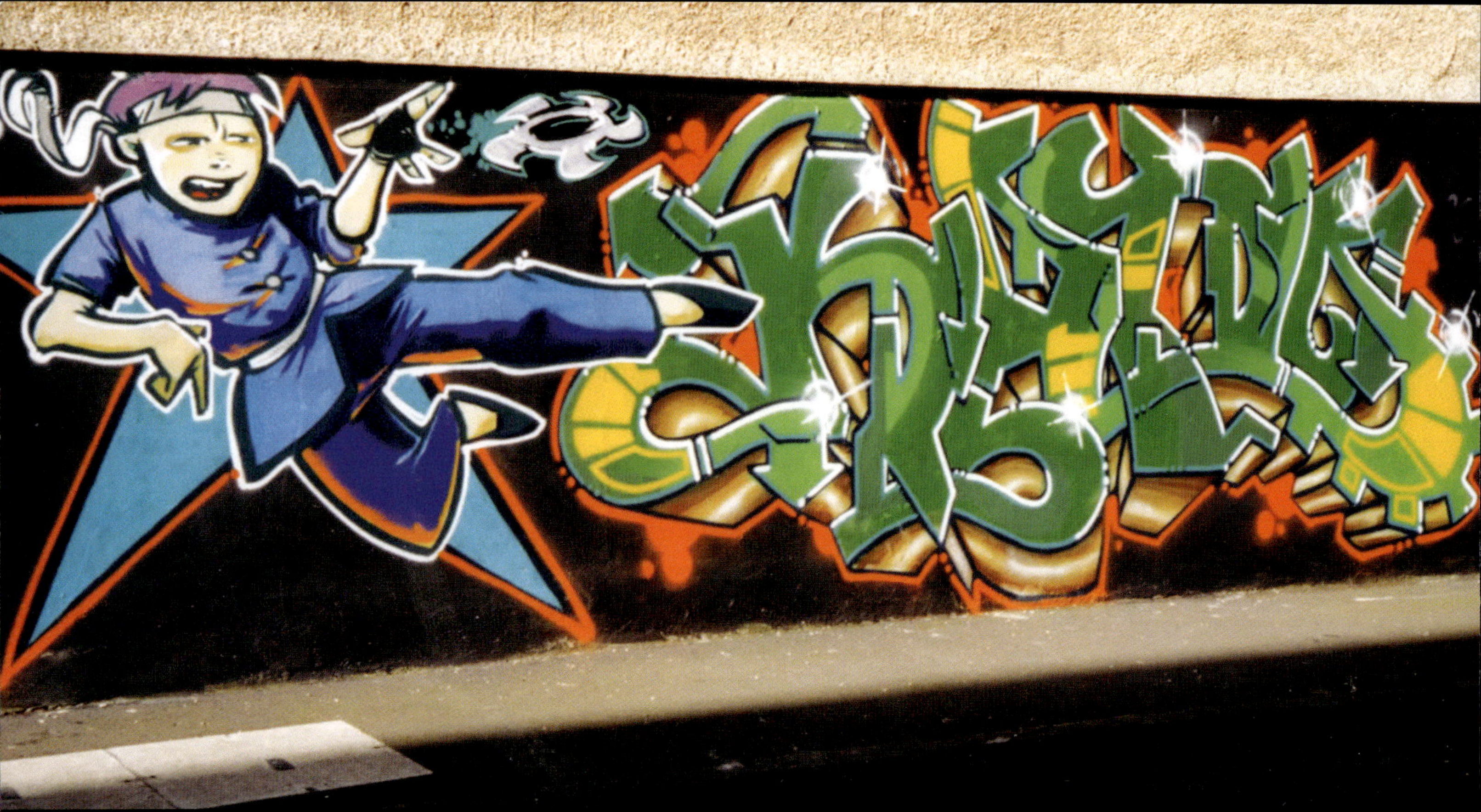

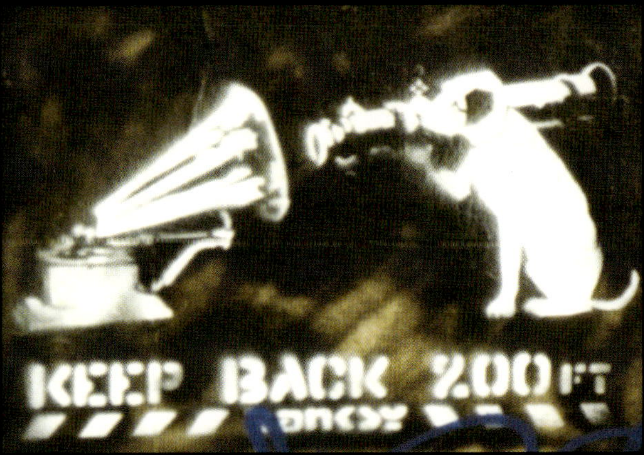

The original freehand piece in Cato Street, Easton – which was painted with Kato – was painted over by Banksy to create the piece that was put up for sale 'with house attached'.

form the hugely successful Bristol band Massive Attack, perhaps an even more prominent and distinctive part of Bristol's cultural profile than Banksy himself. Starting out painting alone around 1983, 3D soon hooked up with nascent graffiti crew The Z-Boys, Bristol's first major crew and an inspiration to all those that followed.

Second in the hall of fame is John Nation, who in the late 1980s was youth leader at the Barton Hill Youth Centre, in a densely populated area just east of central Bristol. Nation gave young artists wall space at the Centre and allowed them to express themselves – much of Bristol's best graffiti from the time was produced by young graffers cutting their teeth at BHYC. In fact, at this time, walls around town were being painted to such a high standard that a set of postcards by photographer Frank Drake was published by Arnolfini celebrating some of the city's best graffiti.

The third figure is linked to the last two. Inkie, a protégé of 3D's who also formed part of that Barton Hill

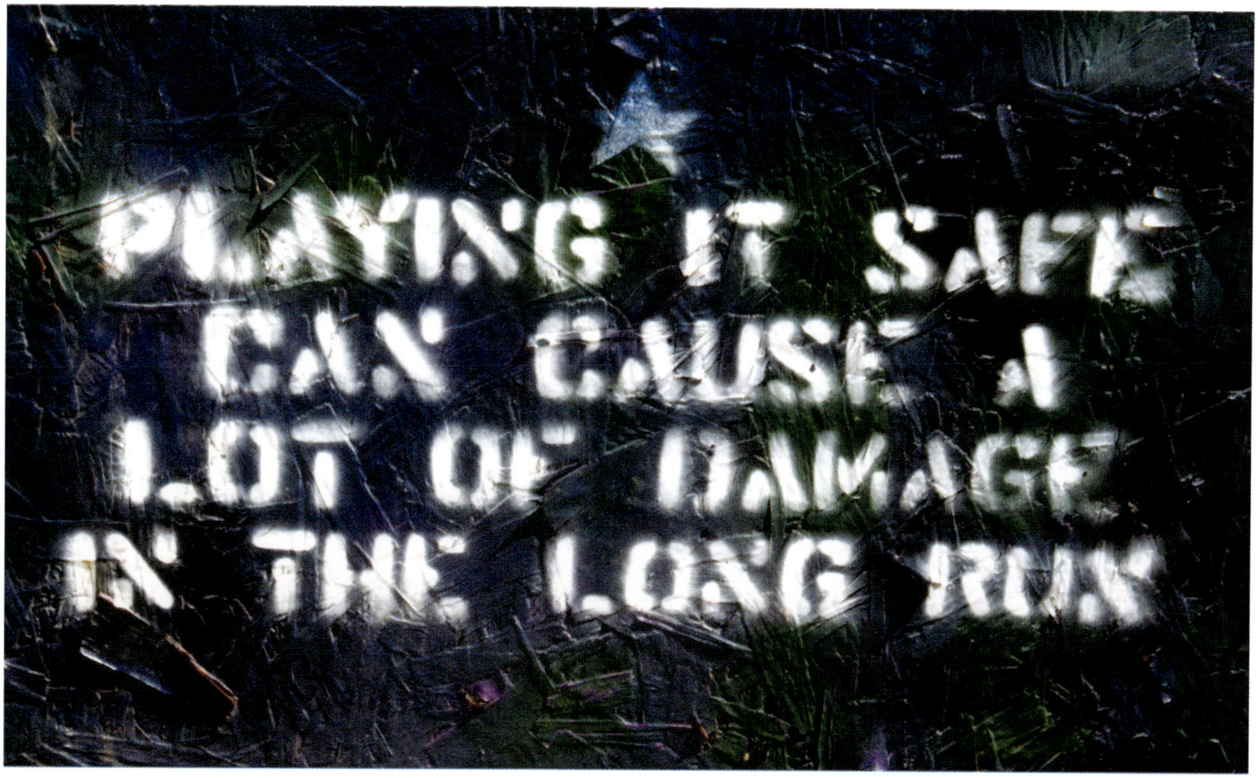

An early Banksy, heavily inspired by American artist Jenny Holzer.

group, is one of the most important figures on the Bristol scene. Inspired, like 3D, by 1982's seminal graffiti/hip hop film *Wild Style*, Inkie began painting freehand graffiti in around 1984, collaborating with our fourth key figure, Nick Walker, as part of the seminal 80s Bristol graffiti crew Crime Inc. These three (Walker, Inkie and 3D) became a huge influence on future generations of Bristol graffers. Inkie and Cheo were second in the World Street Art championships in 1989 and in the late Nineties, Inkie and Banksy collaborated on pieces in Bristol, most notably 1998's *Walls on Fire* graffiti festival in the centre of town.

3D was the first Bristol artist to use stencils in the mid 80s and Walker began experimenting with them in the mid 90s thus having a big influence on Banksy's career. He's now a high-profile artist and designer, working with fashion brands and on films such as *Eyes Wide Shut*, *Judge Dredd* and *Hackers*. He splits his time between Bristol and New York. His stencils, often with a provocative flavour similar to Banksy's, continue to sell across the globe.

Stephen Morris is a Bristol photographer who has documented some of the city's rich graffiti culture in a book, *Off The Wall* (Redcliffe Press). In his view, Bristol is the graffiti capital of Europe. "It is a striking feature of Bristol life," says Morris. "The city is the European leader in this form of art. Graffiti is by nature temporary. Taking the pictures for my book, I found I couldn't walk fast enough to keep up with the changes. Even the best is soon lost under fresh paint or to a demolition gang and some wears out and is replaced."

The city's art scene, too, has always been lively, with a huge number of art spaces from conventional galleries to more temporary spaces. In 2002, a Bristol City Council report on the City's Capital of Culture bid noted that 'Bristol has more working artists than any other city outside London.' Various theories have been put forward on just why Bristol has always fostered such a strong street art tradition. Inkie has noted, succinctly, that Bristol is: " A beautiful Georgian city with a very creative outlook and attitude tucked away from the rest of the UK… It also has a lot of good cider, weed and mushrooms."

Stencil artist Ghostboy, who's still doing his stuff around the city, puts the energy here down to various outside influences. "There's something about the place – an underground, anarchic quality, which is quite apparent in places like Easton [an inner-city area with a diverse racial makeup and a strongly alternative feel, where Banksy lived and painted prolifically]. There are a lot of activists here, and it's quite a liberal place. I think that influences the way that artists work – they don't toe the line as much. And it's not just the art, there's a general vibe about Bristol, which is all about doing what you want to do, not being beholden to others."

It's true that Bristol has a proud tradition of resistance – from the Queen Square riots of 1831, via some prominent suffragette activity, the Bristol Bus Boycott of 1963 to the 1980 St Paul's riots and, more recently the Stokes Croft 'Tesco Riots' of 2011. There's also *The Bristolian* scandal sheet, the Bristol Blogger, a strong subvertising culture and *The Bristol Cable* newspaper.

Ghostboy adds: "We've also had an influx of different cultures coming to Bristol, what with it being a historic port – for example, there's also a very strong performance poetry scene here which, like the street art, is a very American influence. We have a very varied mix of cultures, and that can only be enriching."

Fellow graffer Cheba says: "It was a lot to do with 3D going to and from New York, bringing back lots of graffiti writers. Bristol is such a small community, it's not hard to get your name around, everyone knows everyone on the scene. In London, there are graff communities, but they're much more scattered, less close-knit."

Banksy collector Gez Smith has another take on it all. "I remember seeing a programme on BBC4 about the 1950s, and how floods of cannabis came into Britain at the time, through two ports: Bristol and Liverpool. From Liverpool, it may have spread out across the north-west, but it seems as though it all just stopped in Bristol. Add to that the fact that the West Country has always been a somnolent place, everyone's very laid back and chilled out – that's why we've got movements like Slow Food and trip hop being

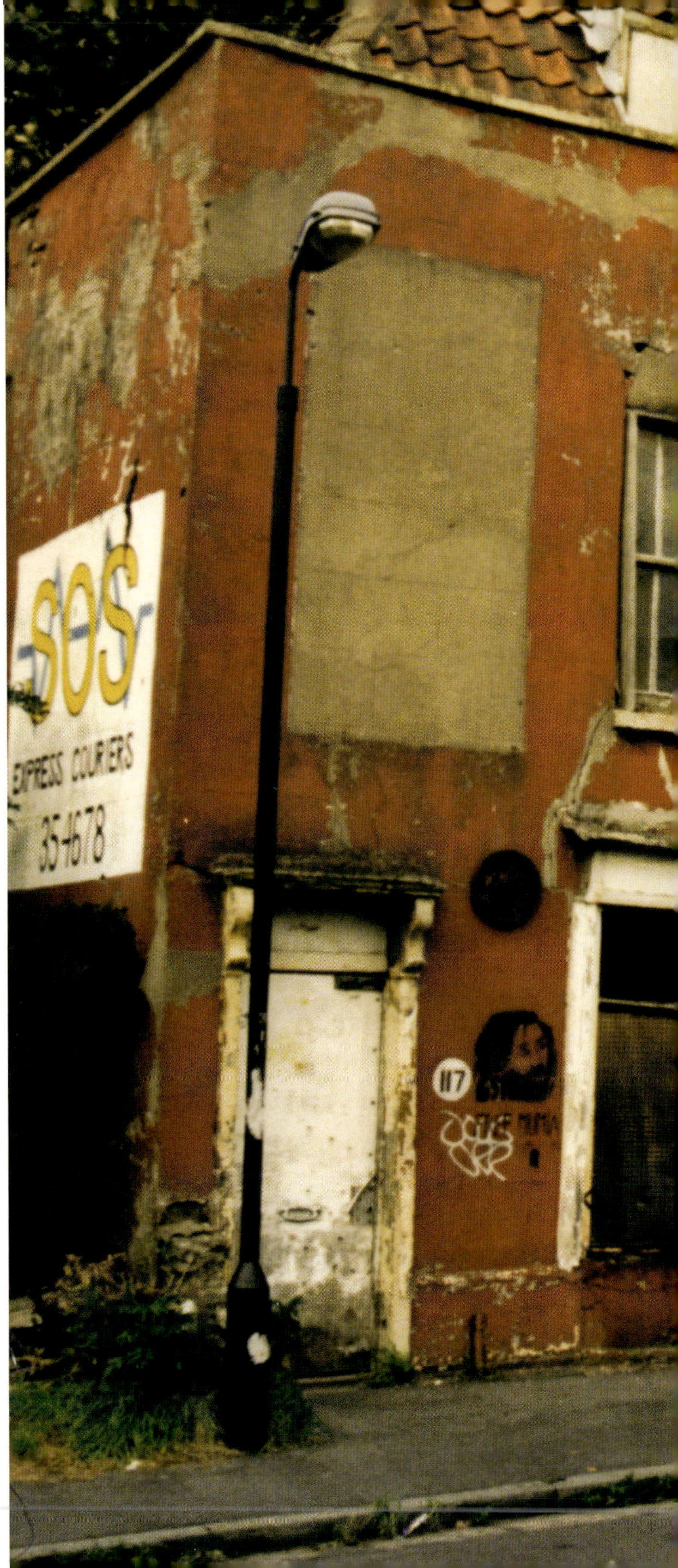

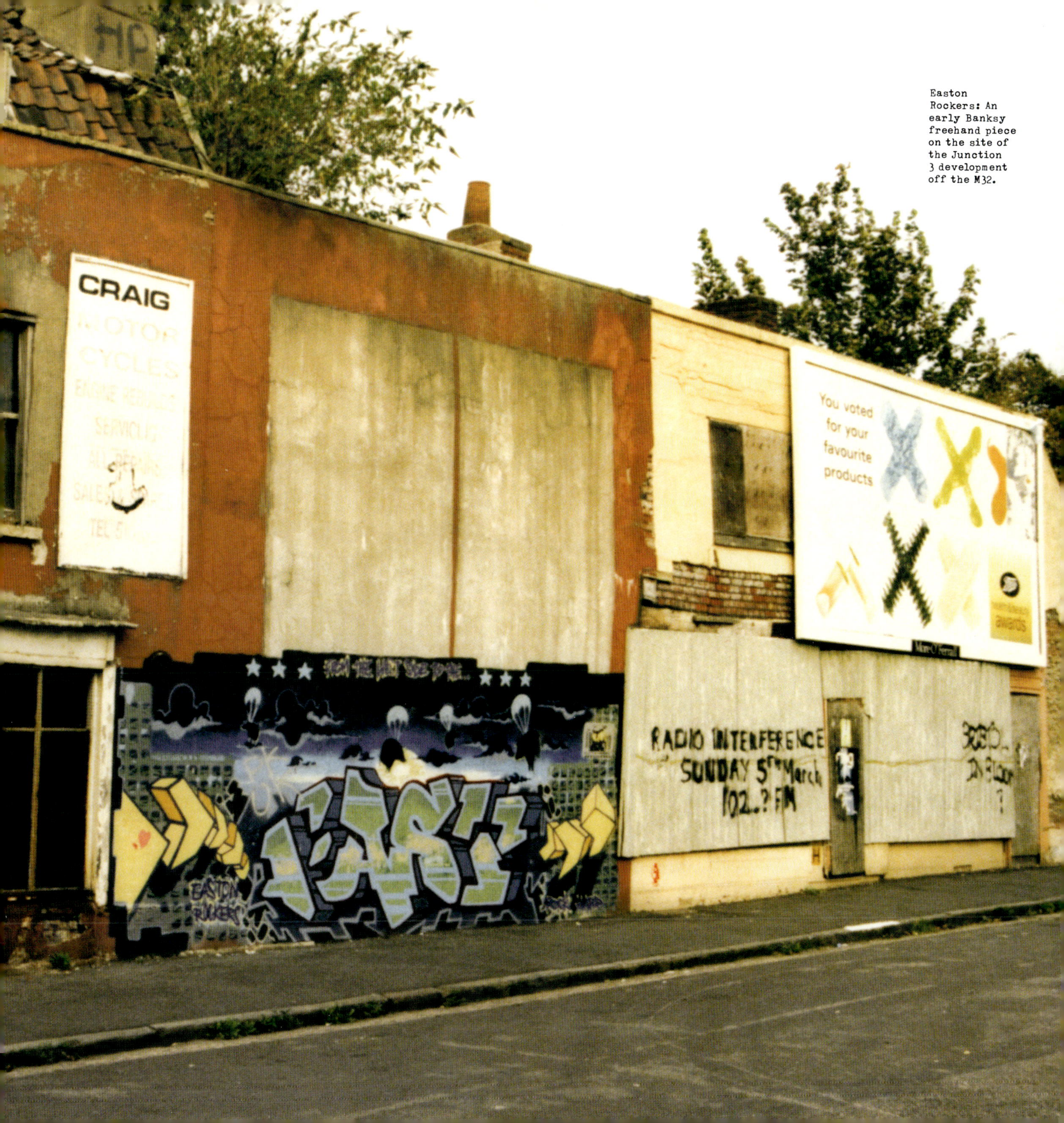

Easton Rockers: An early Banksy freehand piece on the site of the Junction 3 development off the M32.

3D from Massive Attack at the Graffiti Art in Bristol exhibition at Arnolfini in 1985.

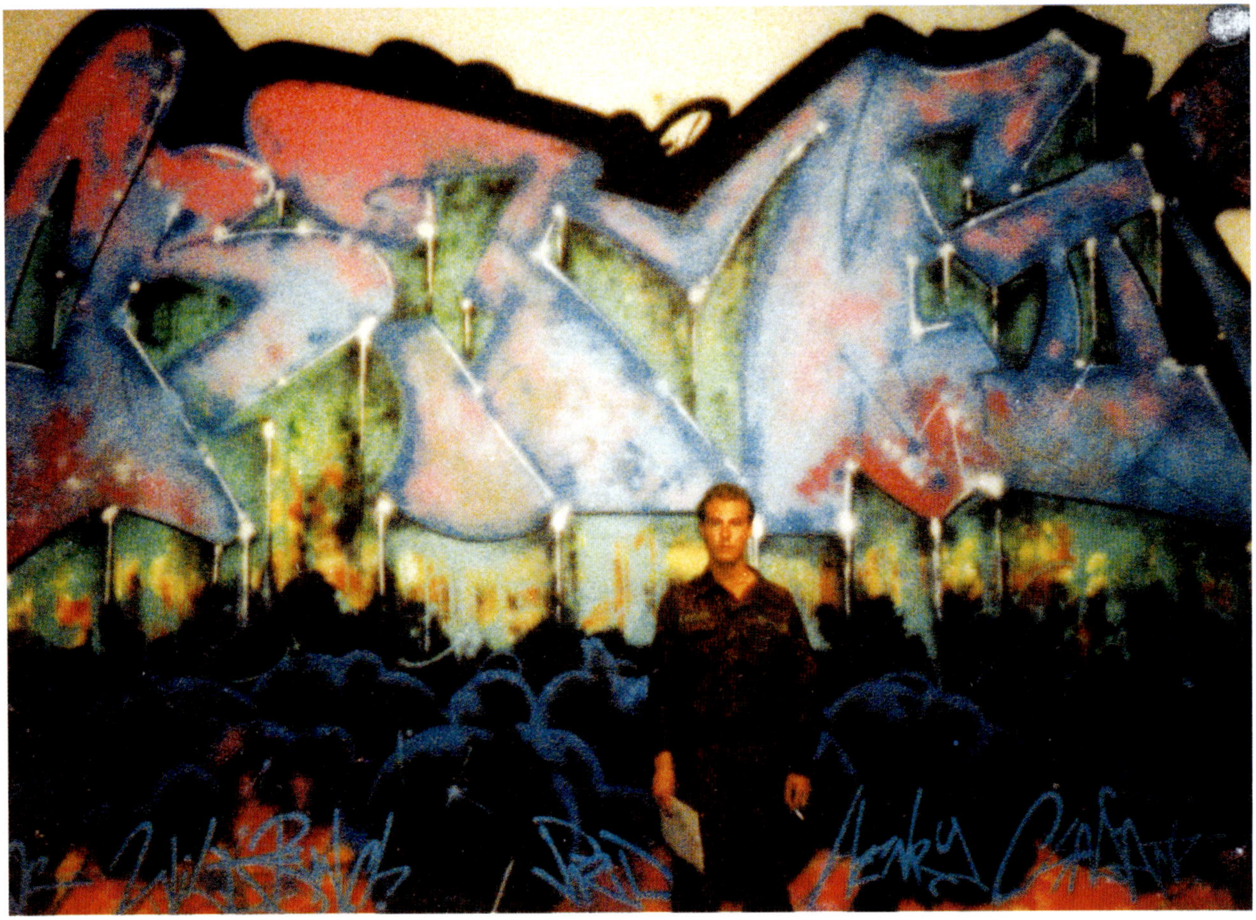

born here. All that stuff contributes to Bristol's creativity, people are more laid back, not so bothered about getting to work on time. And there's always been a strong left-wing thread in the city."

On a more practical level, there's the wealth of canvasses out there for street artists to use. According to the editors of *Bristle* magazine, who produced a book of Bristol political street art and subvertising: "Bristol has loads of empty buildings that are allowed to rot despite widespread homelessness and poverty; huge parts of the city are blighted by planning for cars, not people, and by provocative advertising hoardings. It's often about local people making their own mark on a dreary alienated urban environment."

One seminal moment early in the Bristol graffiti story was in July 1985, when the city's Arnolfini art gallery held an exhibition, *Graffiti Art in Bristol*, documenting the fledgling art form. Artists including 3D, Nick Walker, Z Boys, Bombsquad, Fade and Jaffa sprayed directly onto the gallery walls, and there was music from a young hip hop crew called The Wild Bunch, later to evolve into Massive Attack. Other future Bristol music luminaries – Tricky, Smith and Mighty – were in the audience. A teenage hip hop kid called Geoff Barrow also travelled in from his home town, a place called Portishead.

With the likes of Walker, 3D, FLX and Inkie spearheading the scene, the late 80s were an incredibly fertile time. In 1989, though, the scene was hit hard by Operation Anderson, a massive undercover police crackdown on graffiti. A total of 72 artists across the UK

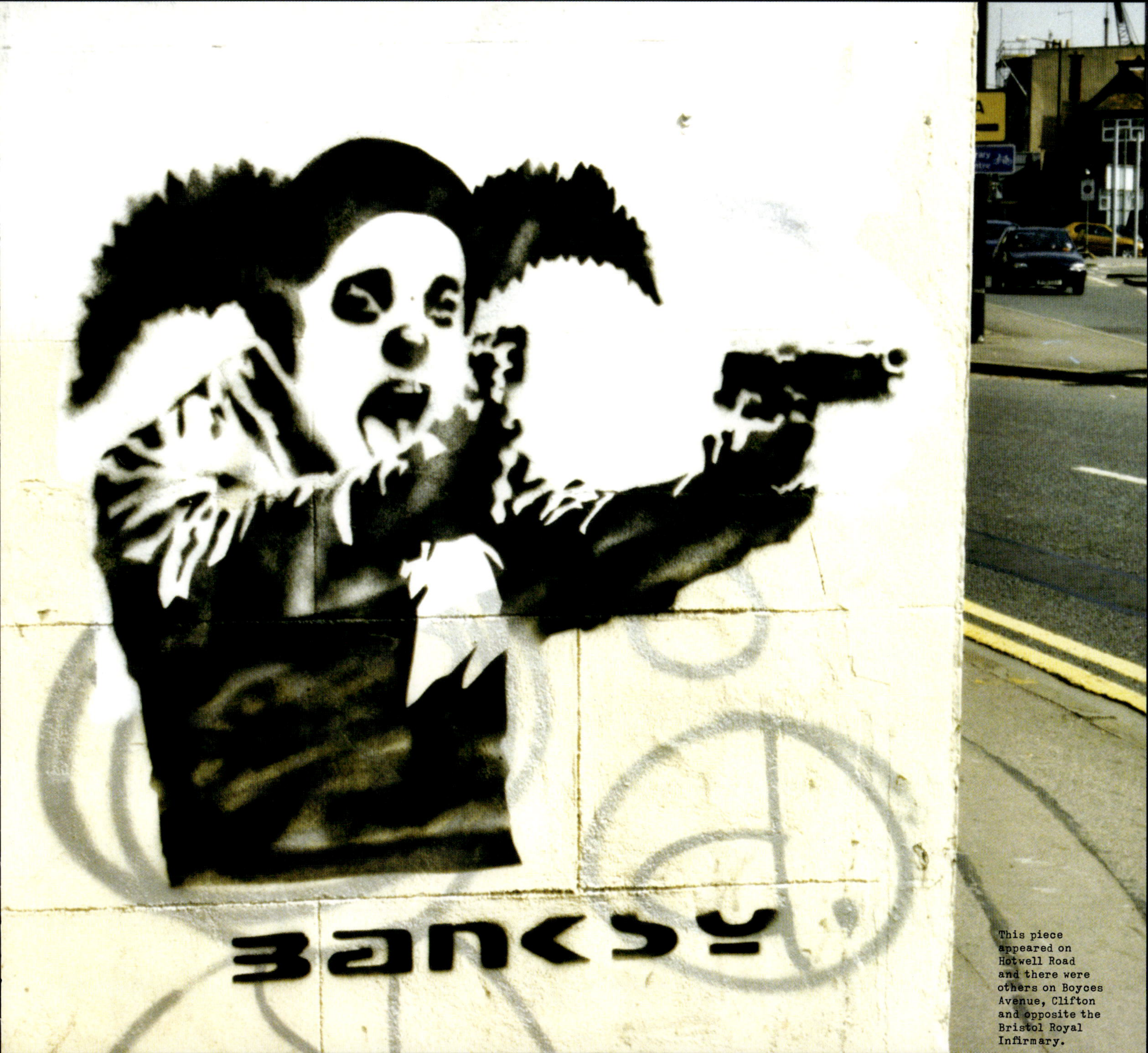

This piece appeared on Hotwell Road and there were others on Boyces Avenue, Clifton and opposite the Bristol Royal Infirmary.

(Inkie among them) were arrested on criminal damage charges. John Nation was also charged (though later acquitted) with incitement to commit criminal damage. The effect was to send graffiti back underground for several years. Recently, though, the Bristol graffiti scene has regained all of its original verve and inventiveness. It's also more populous than ever. Ghostboy, Kato, Mr Jago, Tristan Manco, Cheo, Lokey, Dicy, Xenz, FLX, Paris, SEPR, Deamz, Cheba and Sickboy are all prominent names in Bristol and far beyond: some are still doing their stuff here, others have beaten a path to London. Each of them, though, is a leading light on the global graffiti scene, and each of them honed their art right here in Bristol. For a city of its size, Bristol has made an awesome contribution to the art form.

Special K's and The Wild Bunch

"I remember meeting Inkie while he was doing a piece in Clifton in broad daylight… must have been 1985 or 1986," recalls Chris of music project Illusive. "I also remember Inkie and Crime Inc. Crew spraying up our school in around 1987 or 1988, they did the whole wall of our school gym. I even remember some of the teachers saying 'What an amazing piece of art!'

Nick Walker recalls: "We used to get together at a café called Special K's, at the bottom of St Michael's Hill. It was pretty much home to The Wild Bunch at the time, and it attracted a lot of like-minded people. Just a pool table and graffiti on the walls by 3D. And there were a lot of sound system parties. Bristol in the 80s, that was when the proper parties were. You'd turn up at a house, there'd be no furniture and it would just be rammed, wall to wall."

Nick Walker on the 1985 Arnolfini show

"I was 15, I just walked in off the street and suggested this graffiti exhibition to them. Jeremy Rees [Arnolfini founder] welcomed it with open arms. I spoke to 3D and the rest of The Wild Bunch, and some other graffiti crews who were around at the time. 3D took over the running of the show, and it was a great event. I don't think that would happen these days in any large art establishment. There was graffiti all over the walls; people were coming over

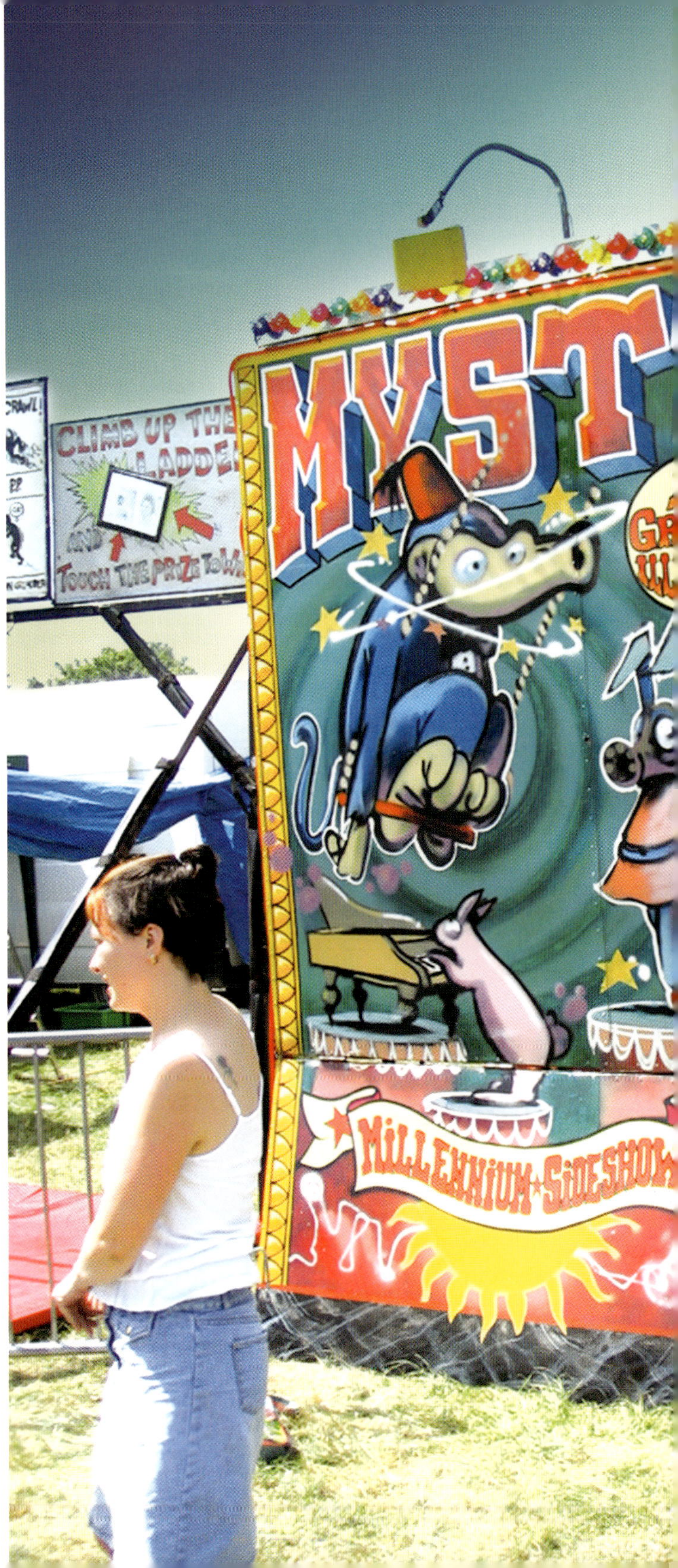

A Banksy piece at Ashton Court Festival, created in exchange for cider.

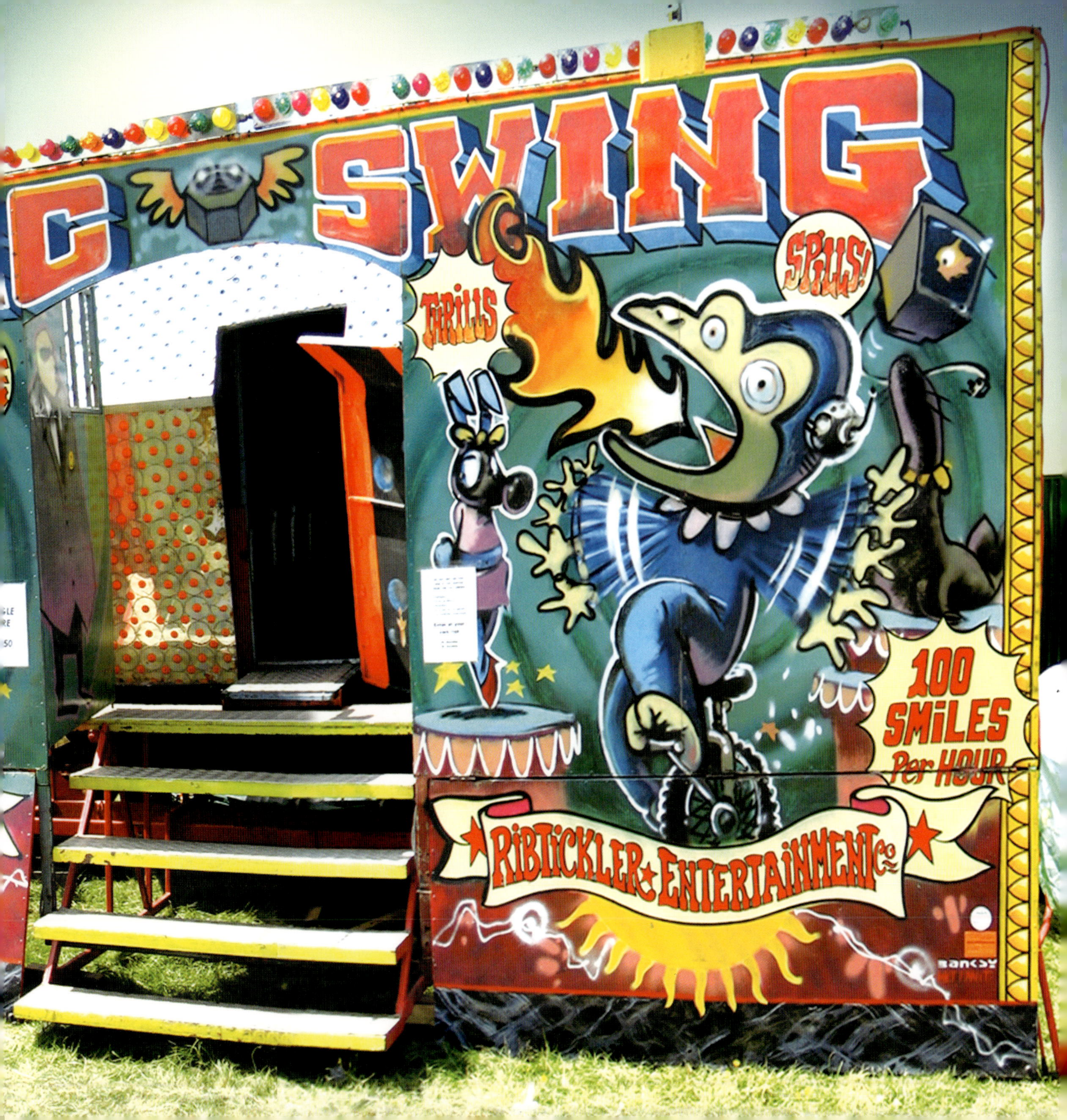
SWING
THRILLS
SPILLS!
100 SMILES Per HOUR
RIBTICKLER★ENTERTAINMENT Co
BANKSY

This page: The walls of Easton were the canvasses for much of Banksy's early freehand work.

That page: The girl with a bomb appeared on the Harbourside but only lasted a few days.

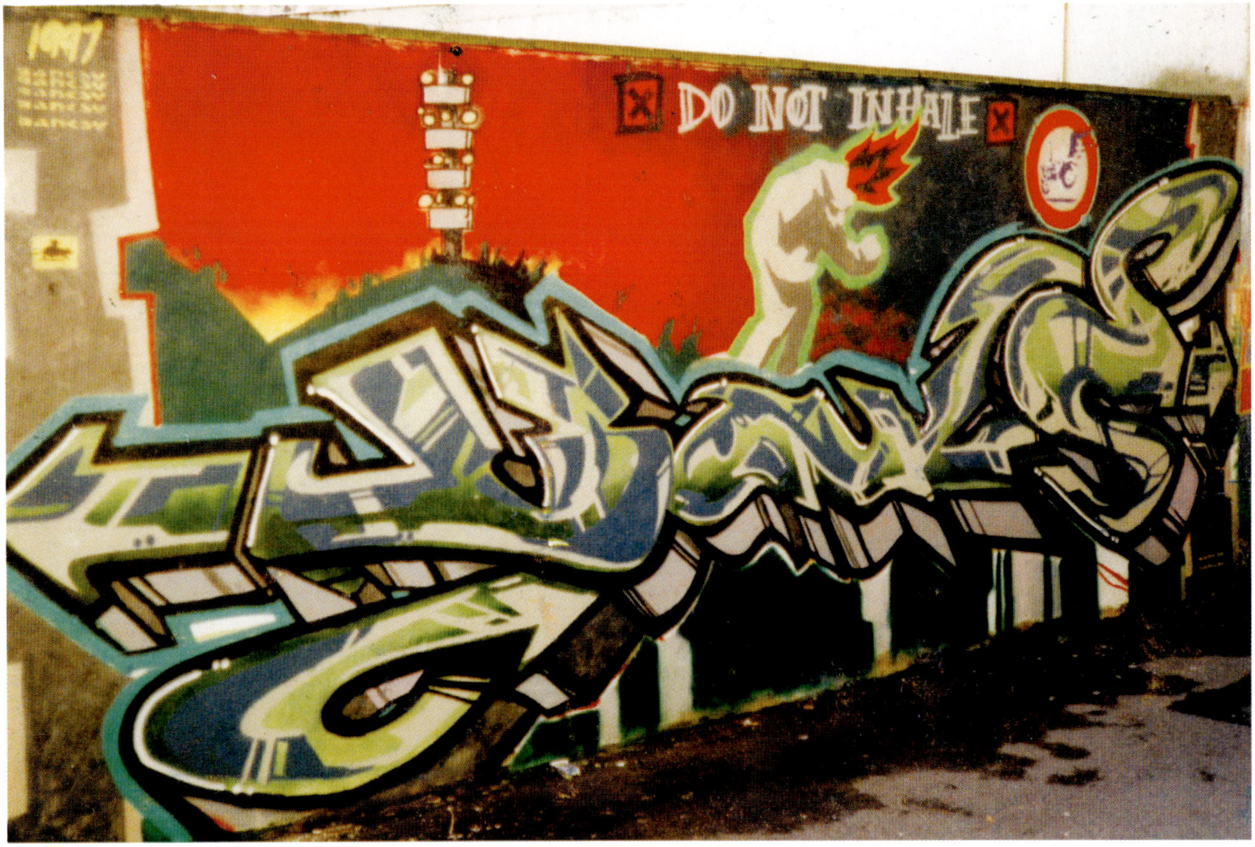

from New York and elsewhere. It felt like the beginning of something special."

Banksy and hip hop culture

Azlan was one of many people heavily involved in the late 90s music and graffiti scene in Bristol. He was a member of both Bristol hip hop group Aspects and Fantastic Super Heroes, a hip hop/graffiti crew which also included Paris, Dicy, Feek and Mantis.

"The Bristol art and graffiti scene has never been documented properly," he says. "Banksy was one small (yet successful) part of that scene." Instrumental to Banksy's development and the continued flourishing of the Bristol scene throughout the 1990s were a slew of writers infamous for changing their names more often than they changed their socks. Alongside artists Shim and Turoe was one crew comprising the artists Kato, Lokey (or Lokea), Juster, Soker and Tes. Originally known as MBA, they then became Bad Apples and finally DBS which stood for DryBreadZ – a reference to being so fiscally challenged they couldn't afford any spread for their toast.

"3D was never really a part of what happened in the mid to late 90s," says Azlan," although he may have been an inspirational figure through his early Bristol graffiti days and artwork for Massive.

The Bristol hip hop scene

"The main thing that brought everyone together in Bristol was the hip hop scene of the mid to late 90s. Forget Massive, Portishead and Tricky, I'm talking about the underground scene – Bristol's Hombre Records, special hip hop events and club nights run by the FSH (Fantastic Super

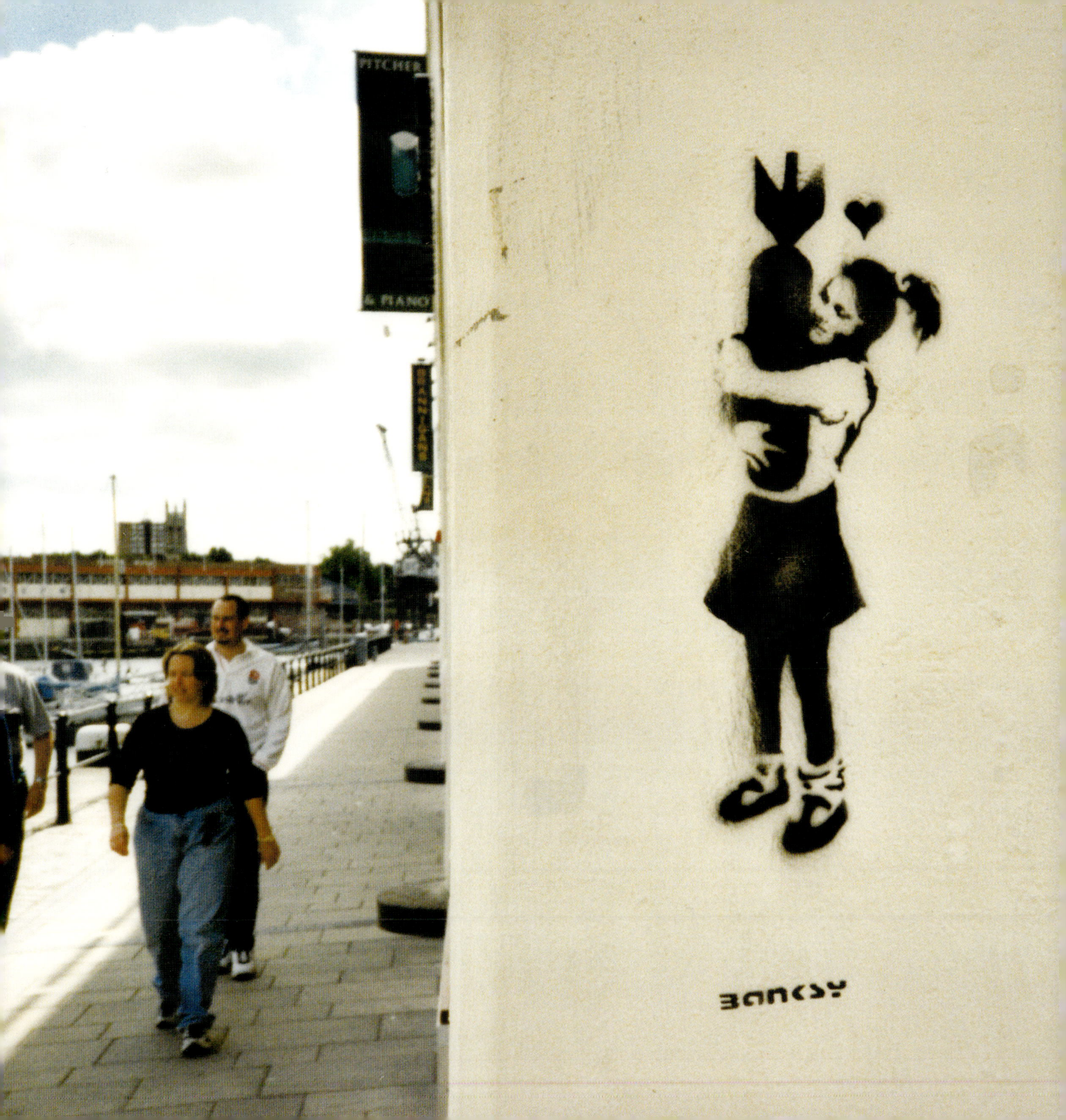
PITCHER
BANKSY

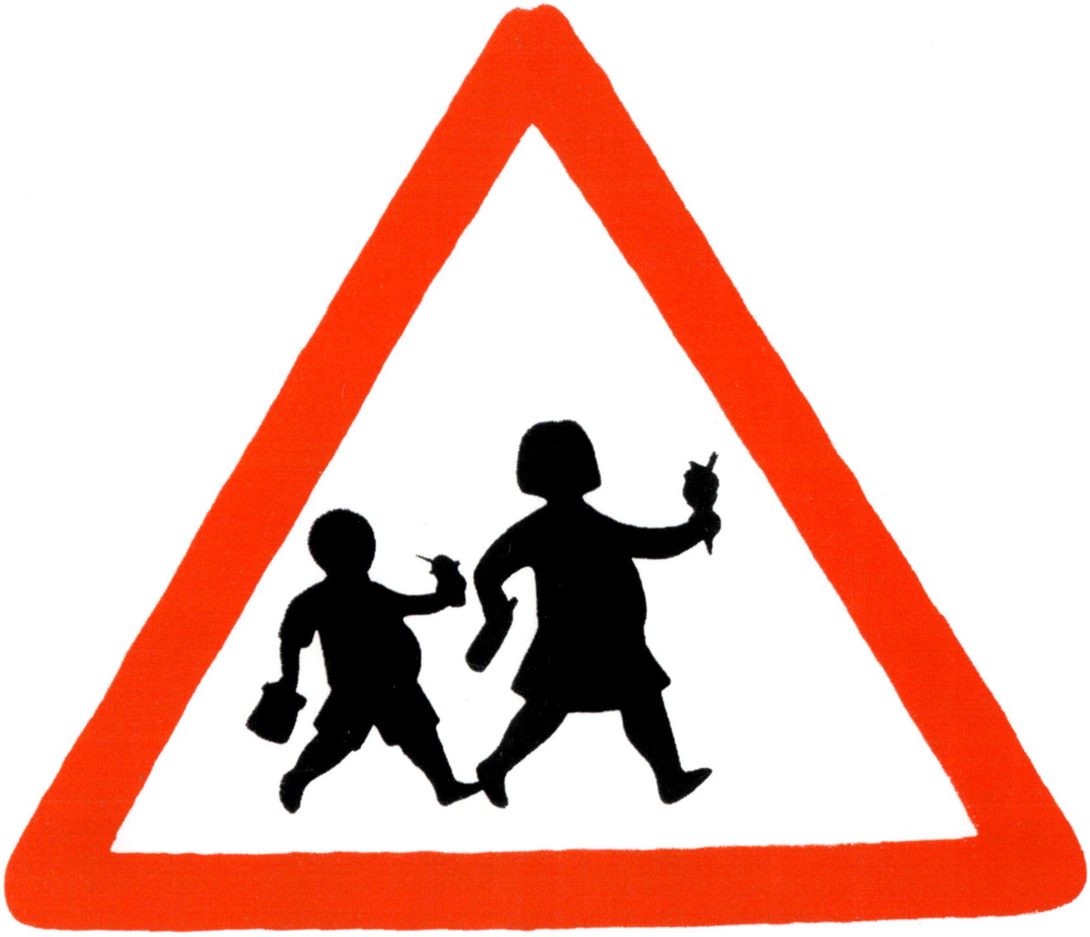

SLOW CHILDREN

BNK/5Y 021

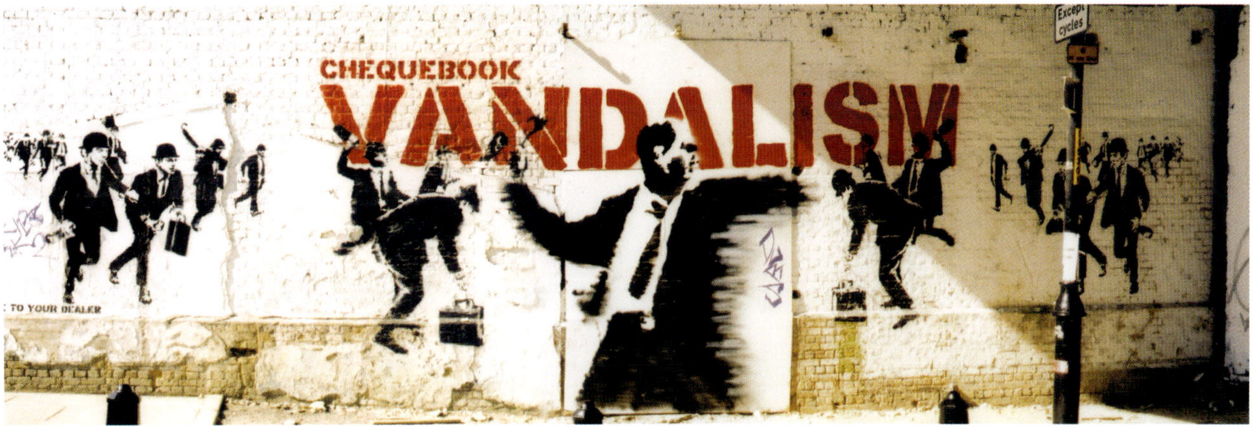

Banksy's sense of humour and anarchy came to the fore with the move to stencils.

Heroes) and Bristol bands Aspects, Parlour Talk, Numskullz and Onecut to name but a few.

"These were all groups of people brought together by the love of hip hop – not rap music or some chav gangster modern R&B tinged tosh – I mean underground, leftfield, creative, pioneering hip hop.

"Hip hop, is essentially about its 'Four Degrees': MCing, turntablism, breakdancing and, of course, graffiti, and that's exactly what we all did. Kept behind closed doors for years, bedroom DJs and covert graffiti artists now had a public forum. Local press and major record labels didn't really want to know, but UK hip hop and its strong visual identity was steadily crowbarred back into the media's gaze, locally and then nationally –most notably in magazines like *The Face* and *Sleazenation*.

Fantastic Super Heroes

"Hip hop is about one-upmanship," continues Azlan. "So, with all the talented artists and musicians who just happened to collide around the late 90s, Bristol became a creative hot spot with artists bouncing ideas off each other and striving to create the biggest and best 'piece'. Often artists worked together to paint walls in 'halls of fame' such as Bedminster skate park or under the M32 at Eastville.

"The Fantastic Super Heroes were a crew of people brought together by hip hop. Original members were myself (Azlan), El Eye, Mantis, Bubba, Nick Fury (all Aspects), Paris (TCF), Dicy (Kuldesac), Sir Beans OBE (Parlour Talk) and rapper/DJ Awkward. The idea for the crew was to be something like a Bristol version of The Rock Steady Crew and all those original 80s hip hop crews from New York. We combined all the elements: MCs, turntablists, graffiti artists. We even had a stab at breakdancing…

"From that core of people, the crew expanded so rapidly that identifying who really was an FSH member is virtually impossible. I think that, come the *Walls on Fire* graffiti event at the harbourside in 1998, we talked about having 60-odd members. The FSH was probably only active for about a year, as various people soon splintered off to do their own thing. Most of the graff artists became the TCF crew (Twentieth Century Frescoes). Bands emerged, too, like Aspects, Onecut, Numskullz, Parlour Talk.

The Bristol scene goes global

"As a graphic designer and original member of the FSH and Aspects, I worked with most of the street artists and illustrators, giving many their first break in print, from simple club flyers, to music magazine features and record sleeves. Most artists were either unemployed or in dead-end call centre jobs, but slowly, as things took off, they began to make their art pay the bills.

"The media and advertising companies began to take notice as the visual language of hip hop became something everyone wanted to be associated with. The result was that various artists were cherry-picked to work on bigger, higher-profile projects. Some artists from the scene have since been invited to paint and exhibit their work all over the world from Bristol, to LA to Japan."

That page: John Nation fills in an Inkie piece at Barton Hill Youth Club.

John Nation

John Nation has been a key figure in Bristol's underground art and music scenes over three decades. He ran his own rave production company Bristol Exposure, and programmed the club stage at Ashton Court Festival for four years in the 1990s. But it's as the key – and only – enabler of Bristol's very early graffiti scene that John is best known. As a youth worker at Barton Hill Youth Club for over a decade from 1980, John encouraged the likes of Inkie, FLX and Cheo to pick up a spraycan and experiment. This early wave of graffiti artists paved the way for the 1990s Bristol scene that spawned the likes of Lokey, Soker – and a certain Banksy.

I've got a lifelong passion for graffiti. I go to all the graffiti events, openings, launches and festivals in Bristol even now. I've kept in contact with lots of the lads who came to Barton Hill in the 1980s – Inkie, FLX, all those guys.

I started working at Barton Hill Youth Club in 1979/80, off the back of a Youth Training Scheme in electrical engineering. I was 17, 18, I had no focus, I was just pissing it up, getting in scrapes with the police, dabbling in football violence. The youth work gave me a focus. The Youth Club was pretty unruly at the time. A lot of the youth workers were from middle-class areas like Clifton and Redland and were met with negativity from the locals. They wanted people like them: local, working-class people who could relate to them and share their experiences – because it was fucking tough living on Barton Hill back then.

My passion for graff was awakened by a trip to Amsterdam in the early 1980s. Then, in around 1983 or 1984, a couple of local lads came to the club: one of them had been to New York, brought back a load of pictures of subway graffiti, and told me he wanted to paint the front wall of the Youth Club. He wanted to paint over the graffiti that was already there, which was racist, violent stuff – National Front logos, football hooligan stuff, 'fuck the police', that kind of thing.

I asked my line manager at the club if they could paint, and he said 'yes' without even seeing the designs. So this lad and a couple of others painted the front with a copy of a well-known New York piece of the time. After that they started painting the inner main hall of the club, then word got out that there was some good graff happening in Barton Hill so the likes of Inkie, FLX and Ian Dark from Z-Boys started coming over. Barton Hill had a rough reputation, but that broke down a lot of barriers.

The Youth Club was a big place. The inside of the club was the size of a sports hall, and the artists would paint it from top to bottom. They painted the ball court outside top to bottom, too. Pieces didn't stay up long – 48 hours max. Pieces on the showpiece wall at the front might stay up for two months or so. Soon enough, we started getting kids coming in from all over east and south Bristol, who were interested in graffiti, hip hop and breakin'.

At the time – the mid 1980s – Bristol had an epidemic of tagging. It was absolutely everywhere. So, because I knew the graffiti scene and lots of the young guys involved, the Council asked me to get out and try to persuade these guys to steer away from the illegal side, to do something legal, something positive, that would gain them some acceptance as artists: to work safely and legally, with someone like me facilitating the art. I got them paints and I found them places to paint all around Bristol – not just at the club.

I'd also organise events for them – like Ashton Court Festival in 1991, when a whole bunch of graffers painted at the festival. I also got commissions for them to do backdrops for club nights, and bands. They had their own bank account, in the name of Supreme Artists, and all profits went back into buying more paints.

For the first five years, I funded the project out of my own pocket, buying paints, finding legal spaces to paint, doing everything myself. There was one similar project going on in the UK, in Selly Oak, Birmingham. I had the passion and belief that this project had something to offer.

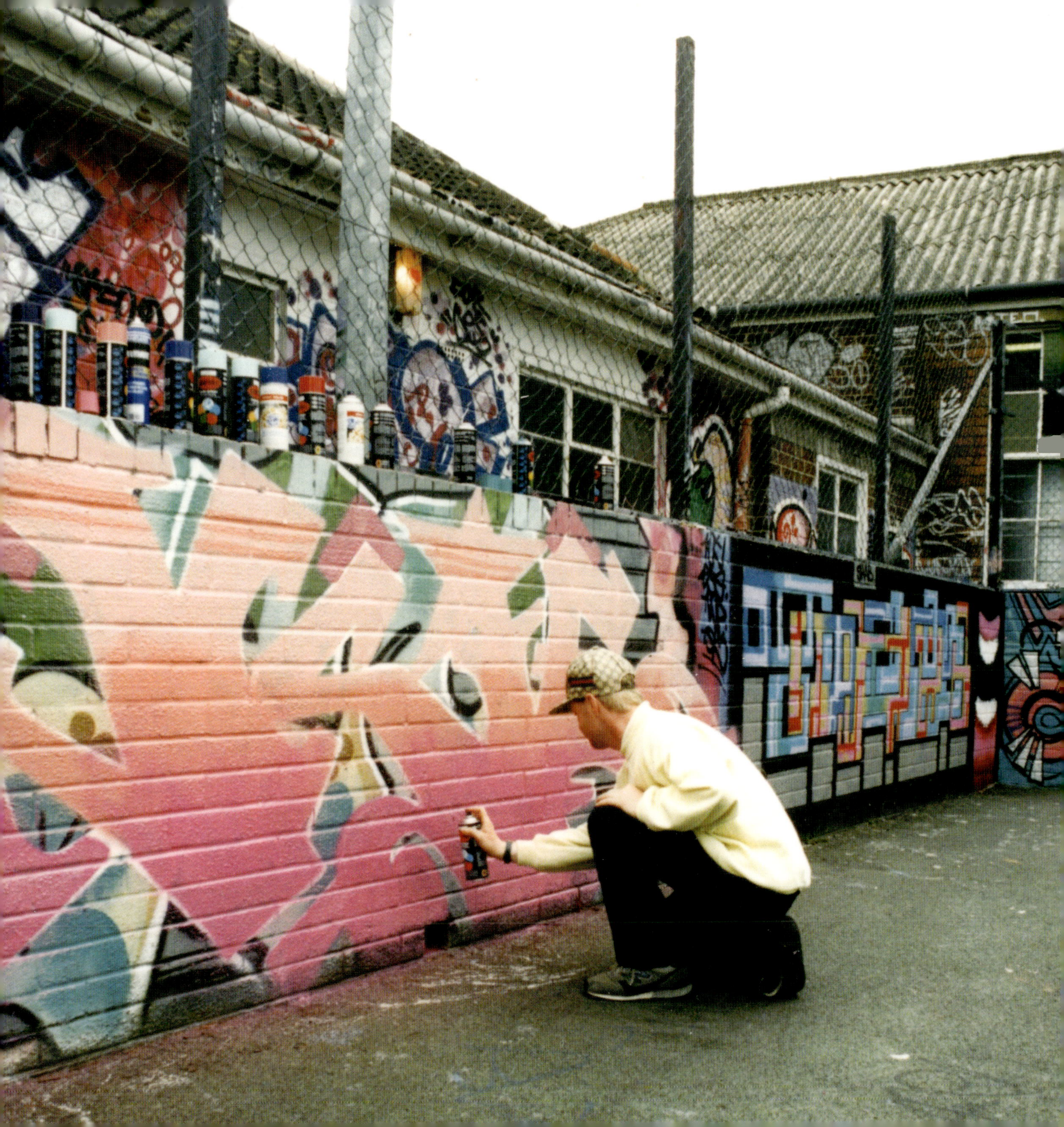

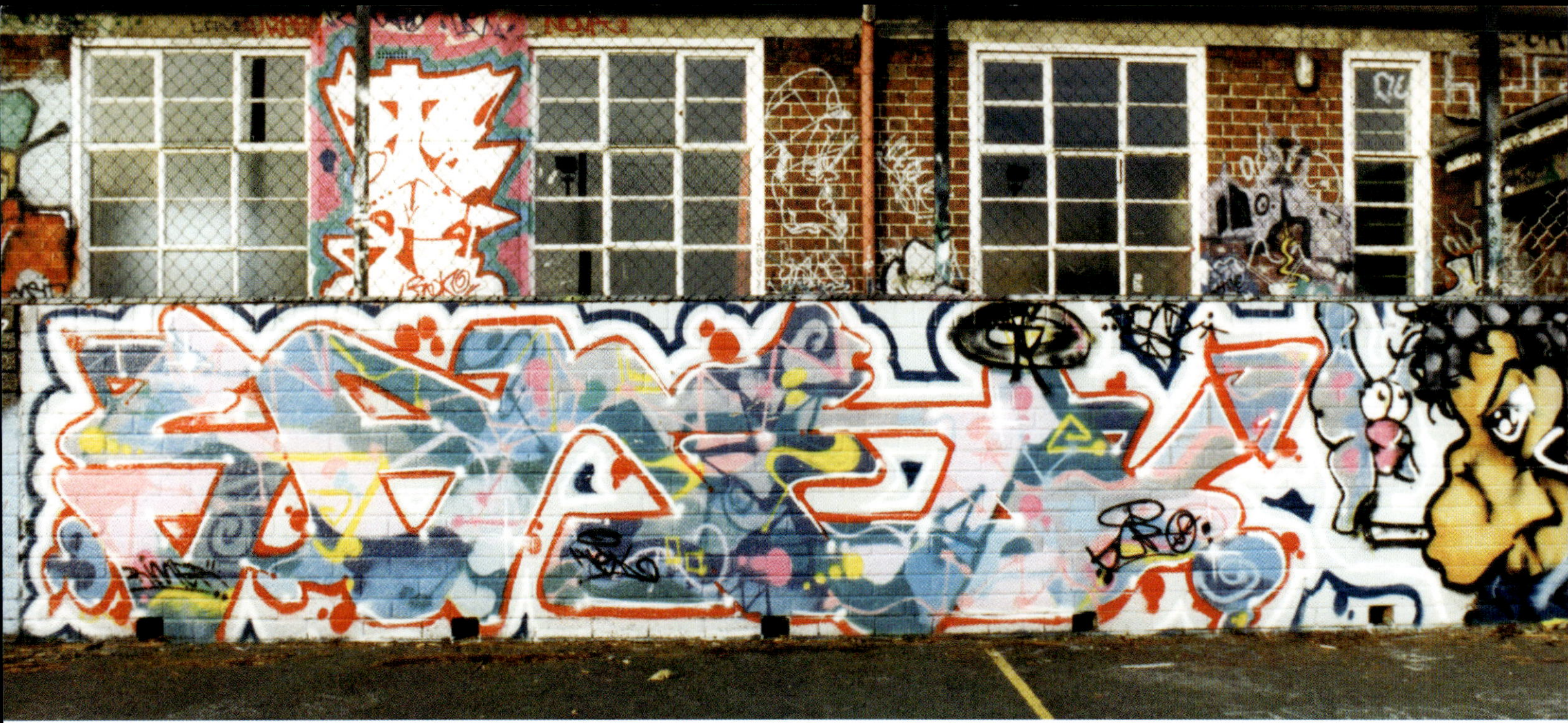

Pretty soon, Barton Hill graffiti started to get quite a reputation, and I began forging links with artists around Bristol, and then around the UK and later as far as the States, Europe and Australia. I was getting mail from all around the world, asking me to tell them what was going on in Barton Hill. By 1987-88, we were getting visitors from all over Europe and beyond – I've still got the visitor's books. New York graffiti magazines were writing about us, and I started corresponding with Henry Chalfant and James Prigoff, authors of the seminal *Spraycan Art*. Without that book and Chalfant and Martha Cooper's *Subway Art*, thousands of kids wouldn't have got into graff.

I approached Bristol City Council, Sustrans [Bristol-based cycling charity, who maintain various routes through the city] and many others to find legal wall space for the artists to paint. My argument was always, 'if you don't provide legal walls in this city, these guys will just work illegally, committing acts of criminal damage and destroying this city with illegal graff'.

Around the same time, the police were beginning an undercover operation to target Bristol graffiti artists. Their main focal points were myself and Barton Hill Youth Club, because they knew that 99 per cent of those working illegally in Bristol were also painting legally at BHYC. I was trying to channel those energies into legal stuff – but you cannot stop illegal graffiti in Bristol or any other city. But I do believe that we helped to lessen the illegal art.

The police's searches resulted, in 1989, in Operation Anderson, a series of dawn raids on graffiti artists and others – to this day the biggest police investigation into illegal graff in this country. 72 people were arrested. My mum's house and the Youth Club were both searched. The took all my work records, photos, paints and address books with contacts of people doing similar things in other cities.

I had 5,000 photos from all around the world, both legal and illegal. I wasn't just a facilitator: I was also documenting the art and sending out packages of photos all over Europe. The police saw me as a kind of Pied Piper: a linchpin of the graff scene across the UK, not just here in Bristol. They asked me to confirm the identity of all these graffiti artists working under pseudonyms, which of course I didn't do.

The case went to Bristol Crown Court: but on the day of

the trial, after spending half a million pursuing the case and using up countless man hours to build this huge case against me, the prosecution barrister stood up and offered no evidence for my charge. Basically, they were never going to prove that I criminally incited artists. They'd tried to make out that I was using books like *Subway Art* to incite these artists – but the fact was that anyone could walk into any bookshop and buy these books.

James Prigoff wrote a testimony for my court case, saying that this was a witch-hunt, a conspiracy against someone who was simply trying to harness the energies of these young people working illegally. And that if I was to be charged for inciting graffiti, then he and his publishers should be charged too.

The case against me was abandoned. That led to huge coverage in the national media. I made a graffiti documentary with BBC called *Drawing the Line*, I appeared on *Richard and Judy* and *Newsround*; me and Inkie went to the Hacienda in Manchester. We put out the message saying, 'this is what we do in Bristol and we're proud of it'. And all the time I carried on the work at the Youth Club.

However, there was a bit of a void in Bristol graffiti immediately after Operation Anderson, because lots of those graffers had been badly burned by the police. But soon enough the void was filled by the next generation of graffiti artists, who were just coming through when I left Barton Hill in '91. Foremost among them was the DryBreadZ Crew, which included Kato, Lokey, Soker, Tes… and Banksy. One piece of his, showing a poodle with a ram's head, and his signature, is still visible on the Ball Court at Barton Hill. Banksy seemed on the fringes of it all. He was one of those guys who would float into a crew and then float out again, which is hardy surprising when you look at the way he works.

In the book *Children of the Can*, Banksy referred to me as a "shouty, red-faced social worker who has had more impact on the shape of British culture over the past 20 years than anyone else to come from the city." Being called a social worker always used to get my goat – I was a youth worker, a very different thing – but for Banksy to say that of me… I was humbled. I have huge admiration for Banksy – I love his wit, his satire, the fact he's a piss-taker and a risk-taker.

That page: A piece by Cheo and SP27 at Barton Hill Youth Club circa 1989/90, about the time a young Banksy began visiting the Club.

There's been a sequence of seminal events in Bristol's graffiti history, beginning with 3D, who kicked the whole thing off. He was an absolutely crucial figure, not just in the future of Bristol music but of graffiti too. Then came Inkie, FLX and Nick Walker, a.k.a. Crime Inc and the Arnolfini exhibition in 1985, which was an absolutely massive event. After that you've got Barton Hill and, in 1989, two events: Operation Anderson and the World Graffiti Art Championships in Bridlington, where Inkie and Cheo were selected by me to represent Bristol and came second. Through the '90s the big events were Banksy's solo shows, at Severnshed and Greenleaf Bookshop, and then of course Walls on Fire. Since the millennium we've had Crimes of Passion, Upfest and See No Evil.

I think that Mild Mild West is Banksy's best piece. It's his most iconic piece and the most representative of what he stands for because of the connotations and the reference to civil unrest. It's significant that it's on the edge of St Paul's where there were riots and on the site of the Stokes Croft riots, but it's also saying that we're all cuddly people down here as well. Mild Mild West shouldn't be protected. Who decides which pieces are protected and which ones aren't? I'd hate to see it go and I was really pissed off when the sniper opposite the BRI got painted over, but the nature of graffiti is that it's temporary and Mild Mild West has had a good run.

People call me a legend. Am I really? I'm just a normal geezer with a passion for graffiti and for anything to do with Bristol. I facilitated something that laid the foundations for where we are now. I have a lot of respect from graffers in Bristol for that – and also for the fact that I didn't sell them down the river back in '89!

Inkie on Banksy

Inkie has always been one of the best-known and most inventive artists on the UK street art scene, blending a huge variety of styles – he cites Inca art, Egyptology, William Morris, Art Nouveau and even children's illustrator Richard Scarry among his influences.

He started painting around Bristol in 1983 alongside Massive Attack's 3D, Nick Walker, FLX and Goldie, the future drum 'n' bass legend who started out as a graffiti artist in his native West Midlands. In 1989, Inkie and fellow Bristol graffer Cheo came second in the World Street Art Championships, beating off competition from Los Angeles, New York and various European countries.

Earlier that year, Inkie hit the national headlines when he was arrested as 'the Kingpin' in Operation Anderson, the UK's biggest-ever graffiti bust. British Transport Police and Avon and Somerset Constabulary raided the homes of 72 suspected graffiti writers in and around Bristol and Inkie was accused of causing £250,000 worth of damage to Clifton Down Railway station. His arrest, court case and subsequent acquittal were recounted in a BBC2 documentary *Drawing The Line*.

Almost a decade later in 1998 he and Banksy organised the UK's largest graffiti event to date in Bristol. *Walls On Fire* pulled together the UK's finest street artists to create a 400-metre painting on hoardings around the Harbourside.

Inkie went on to become a leading designer for the video-game industry, and now travels the world painting and promoting street art events.

Why do you think Banksy has had the impact he has?
Because of the PR and press backing for his work done by the team he has built up around him. He attacked the scene with a military precision, choosing key events and locations and transport hubs to bomb with his work and releasing images to the press afterwards. No-one had done this as well before him.

How would you class his style?
Iconic. Political. Ballsy.

London artist Mode2 worked with Inkie and Banksy on Take The Money and Run opposite the Old England pub in Montpelier.

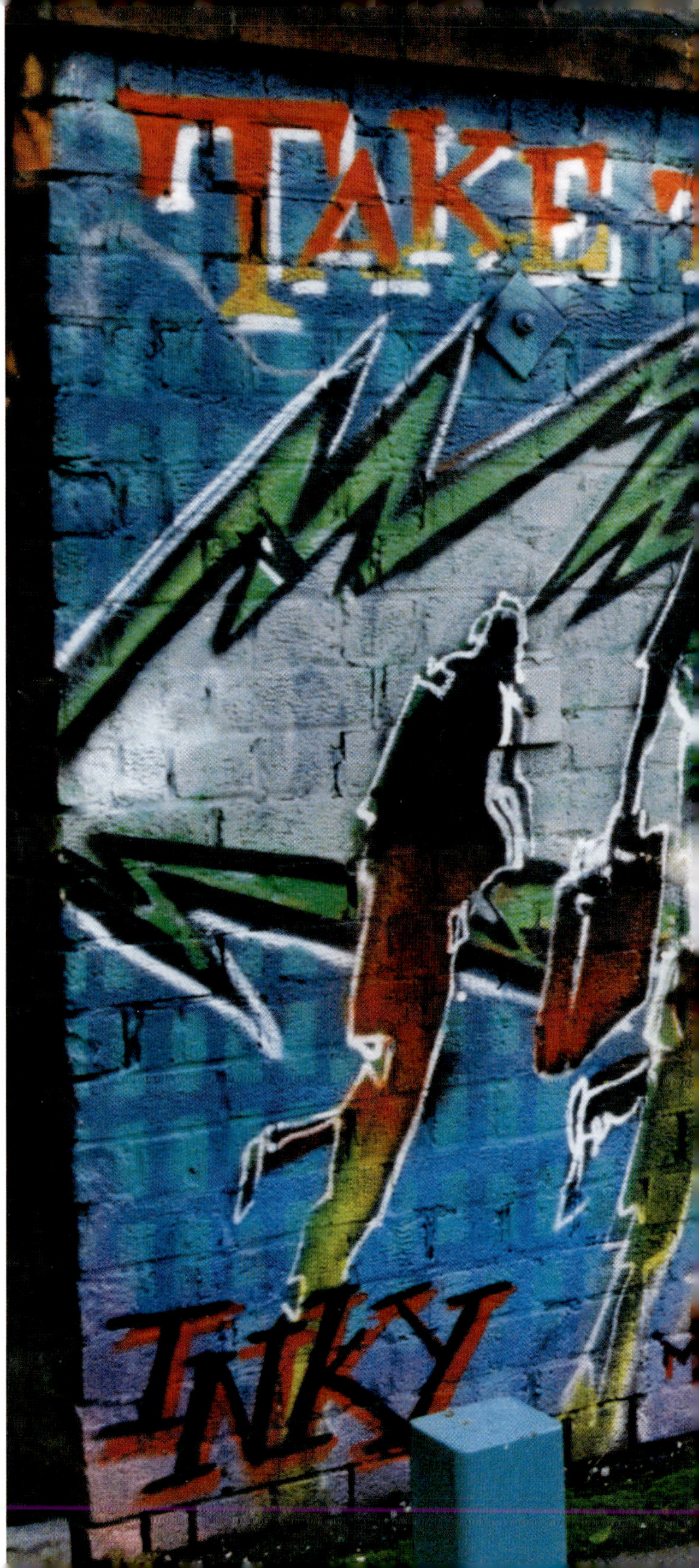

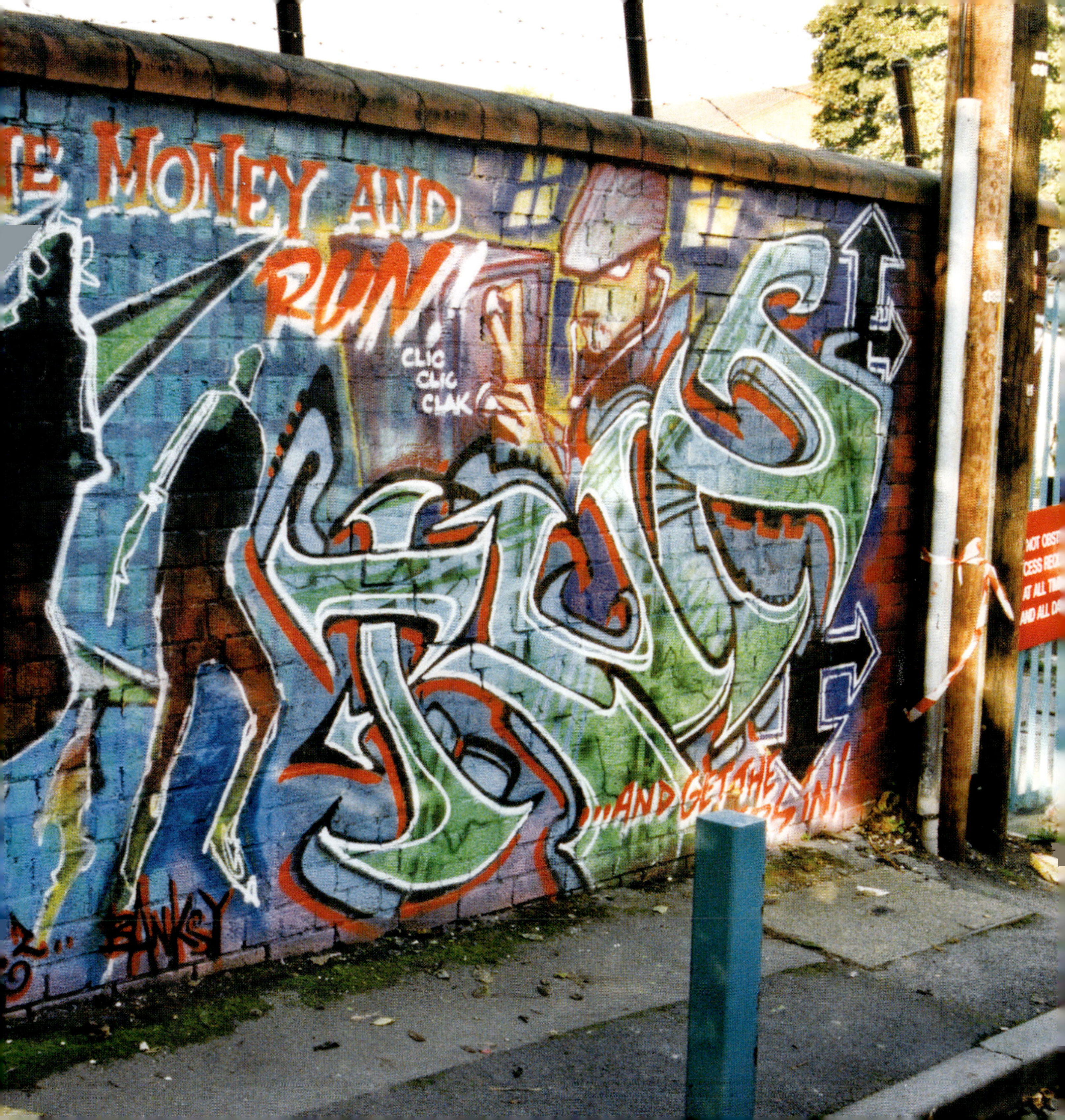
MONEY AND
RUN!
CLIC
CLIC
CLAK
...AND GET THE
BANKSY

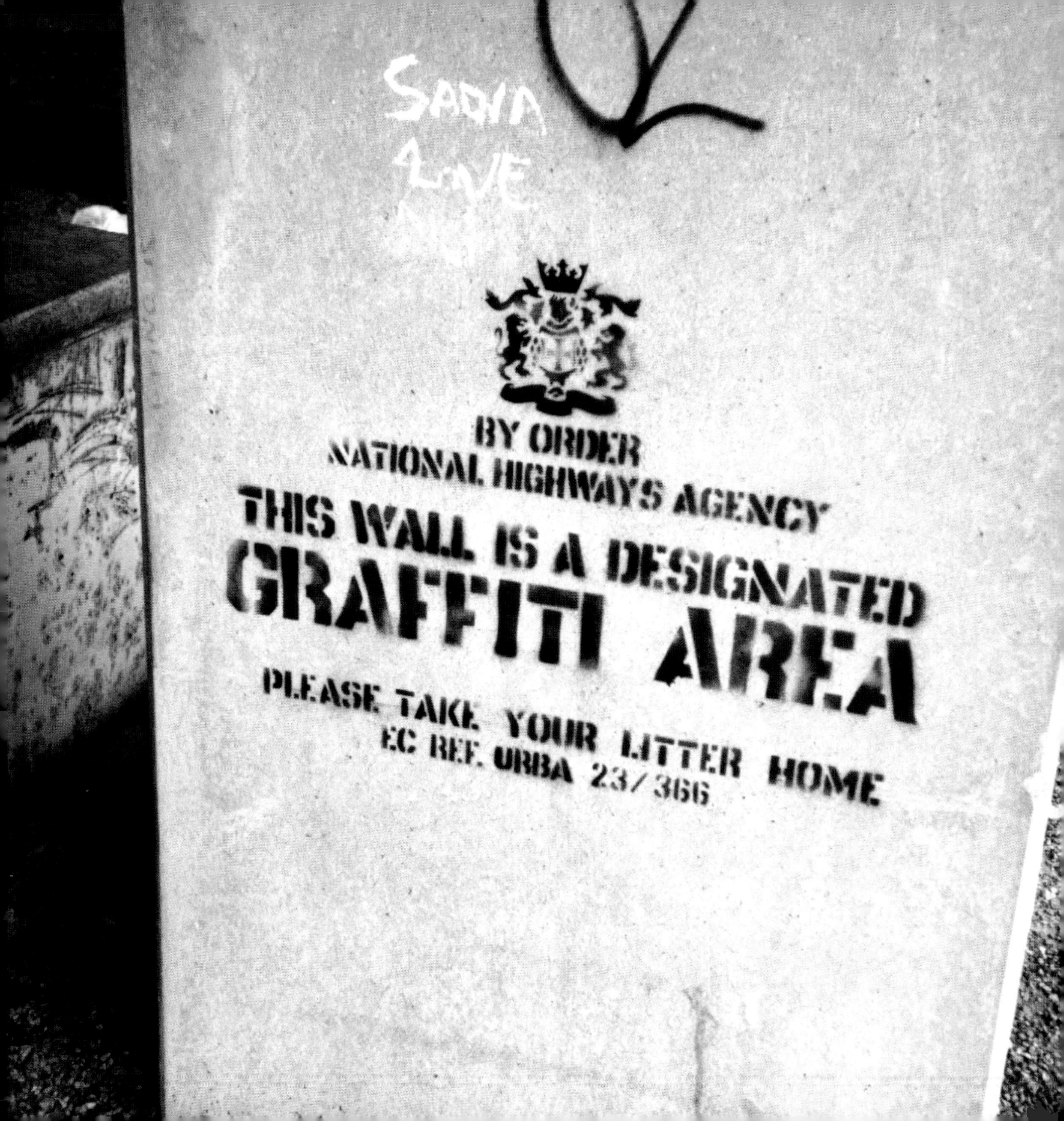
BY ORDER
NATIONAL HIGHWAYS AGENCY
THIS WALL IS A DESIGNATED
GRAFFITI AREA
PLEASE TAKE YOUR LITTER HOME
EC REF. URBA 23/366

What are your memories of painting in 1983 alongside 3D and Nick Walker?
Myself, 3D and Nick were definitely there at the forefront of the Bristol graffiti scene, but there were many others: Jinx, FLX, Fade, Jaffa, Toots, Tarzan, the Z-Boys and the Barton Hill crew. We were all driving each other forward on the buzz of doing illegal work in the mid Eighties to early Nineties.

Does Banksy follow on directly from the likes of you, 3D and Nick Walker? Or has he developed in a different direction?
3D and Jody, an artist from the Barton Hill Youth Centre, were doing stencil work in the late Eighties. But for most graffiti writers back then, using a stencil was seen as taboo. We all worked freehand.

I was well aware of the Parisian stencil scene, but in Bristol, we were all about large-scale 'bombing'. Banksy used stencils to his advantage to get up a lot more stuff, and faster, with less risk of being caught. Nick's work has evolved and he is using more stencils now than before.

Memories of Operation Anderson?
I'd been nicked quite a few times before, but on that occasion I was up in Liverpool and got a phone call from my brother saying that my parents' house had been raided and that they'd arrested 70 other people. It was all over the local news and was covered in the national news.
I went back down to Bristol to turn myself in and found out that they'd nicked nearly everyone that I'd painted with. The police had found someone's diary and gone through it, matching the numbers to the writers.

***Walls on Fire* seemed like a renaissance for the Bristol scene...**
It brought a lot of writers together who hadn't spoken or had contact in a long time and helped to create a resurgence of the UK scene. I helped Banksy organise the event but took a bit of a back seat and got pretty drunk on the day if I remember rightly.

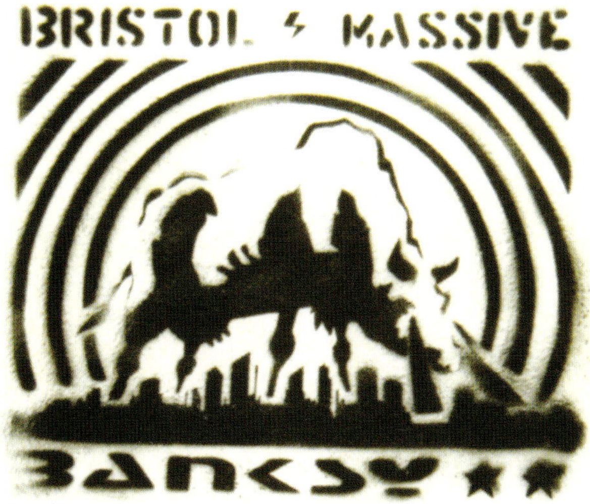

That page: Banksy authorises a Designated Graffiti Area under the M32 in Eastville.

This page: Bristol Massive from a series of images for Blowpop Records in 1999.

Why did such a strong scene grow up in Bristol?
Geographically, Bristol was cut off, so we developed our own styles. Also there was no internet back then, so it was all about exchanging photos. You had London up the M4 where people used to go every couple of months and take photos of graffiti and buy trainers, and you also have a big Jamaican community in Bristol, so people would bring music over from New York and Jamaica.

There aren't really any other major cities around, it was its own city and that's why it developed its own scene. But we still managed to create a worldwide network of writers and had several trips around Europe and the States.

Did the music and graffiti go together?
About six months after I started doing graffiti, I gradually got into hip hop. The Wild Bunch were doing a lot of parties. Everyone wanted to put on the best hip hop shows. It was like this small corner of south-west England consumed by New York.

Is Banksy well-respected among the graffiti crowd because he avoids commercial work?
He sticks to his guns, and that is something to be admired in anyone. He's no sell-out.

Cheba on Banksy

Cheba is a Bristol-based graffiti artist who has been painting around the city since he was at school. Unlike Banksy's later work, he favours a freehand graffiti style rather than stencils.

When did you first get the graffiti bug?
I first got into graffiti when I started seeing pieces by Inkie around town. I'd always been a keen drawer from childhood. I'd never considered myself as a graffiti writer because I wouldn't do the traditional tags and letterforms, but I seemed to be thrown into that category. I got into stencils around 2000 but I lost the love of stencils pretty quickly.

Why? Because Banksy was dominating the scene?
Basically, yes. But I also realised it wasn't the route I wanted to go down. I moved on to posters then I got more into freehand stuff. I guess I was experimenting with what I could do and what I could get away with.

How do the two forms compare?
Stencil graffiti is hard to get right. Many view it as a bit of a cheat, though, because it can all be done beforehand, whereas with traditional graffiti you've got to spend a lot more time actually up there doing the piece. With the stencils, you can do all your preparation at home – which is a lot more painstaking, but the risk levels are less. Stencil, though, is a lot harder to make look like your own, to achieve an individual style.

Was Banksy an inspiration?
He inspired me to start doing it in a way (as well as just being in a city such as Bristol) not through his art, but by being so prolific. He'd 'bomb' a part of town and you'd suddenly be seeing his work everywhere. For me, he's more about the message than the art – I don't think he cares too much about what the art really looks like, I think he's more about taking the piss. It's more about getting across a visual joke than the quality of the art.

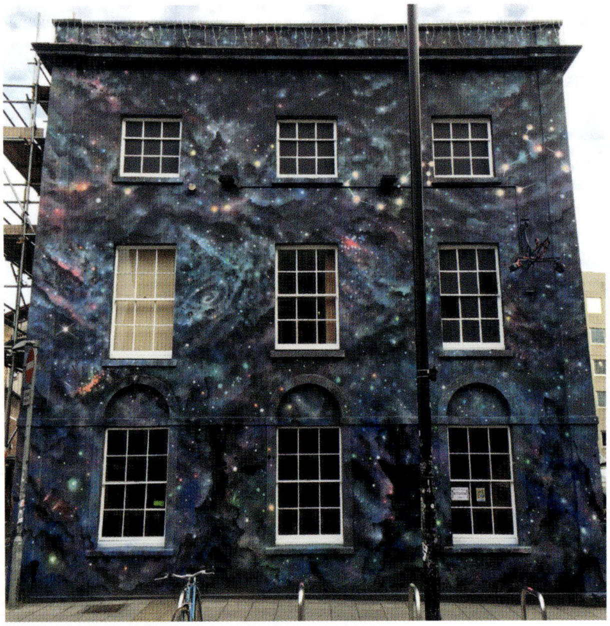

Top: Cheba's treatment of the Full Moon in Stokes Croft.

Mild Mild West

Bristol writer and publisher Richard Jones on Banksy's 'Welcome to Bristol' sign...
"Some of Banksy's fellow artists from outside Bristol are said to be dismissive of his iconic Mild Mild West mural. Apparently, the font Banksy uses for the Mild Mild West wording has been singled out for particular criticism.

"Yet for many Bristolians, this is Banksy's signature piece – it's like an alternative 'Welcome to Bristol' sign, and its impact has as much to do with its position as its content. It's impossible for anyone who has lived in Bristol for a long time not to see Mild Mild West as a reference to the St Paul's riots of 1980 which started with a police raid on the Black and White cafe on nearby Grosvenor Road. I've always thought it's like a Blue Plaque for the rioters.

"The riots had an immense cultural resonance in Bristol as they came at the height of the reggae movement coming out of St Paul's with bands such as Black Roots and Talisman; Barton Hill scaffolder Gary Clail was teaming up with Adrian Sherwood at On-U-Sounds to produce a fearsome bass-heavy form of dub with warped up

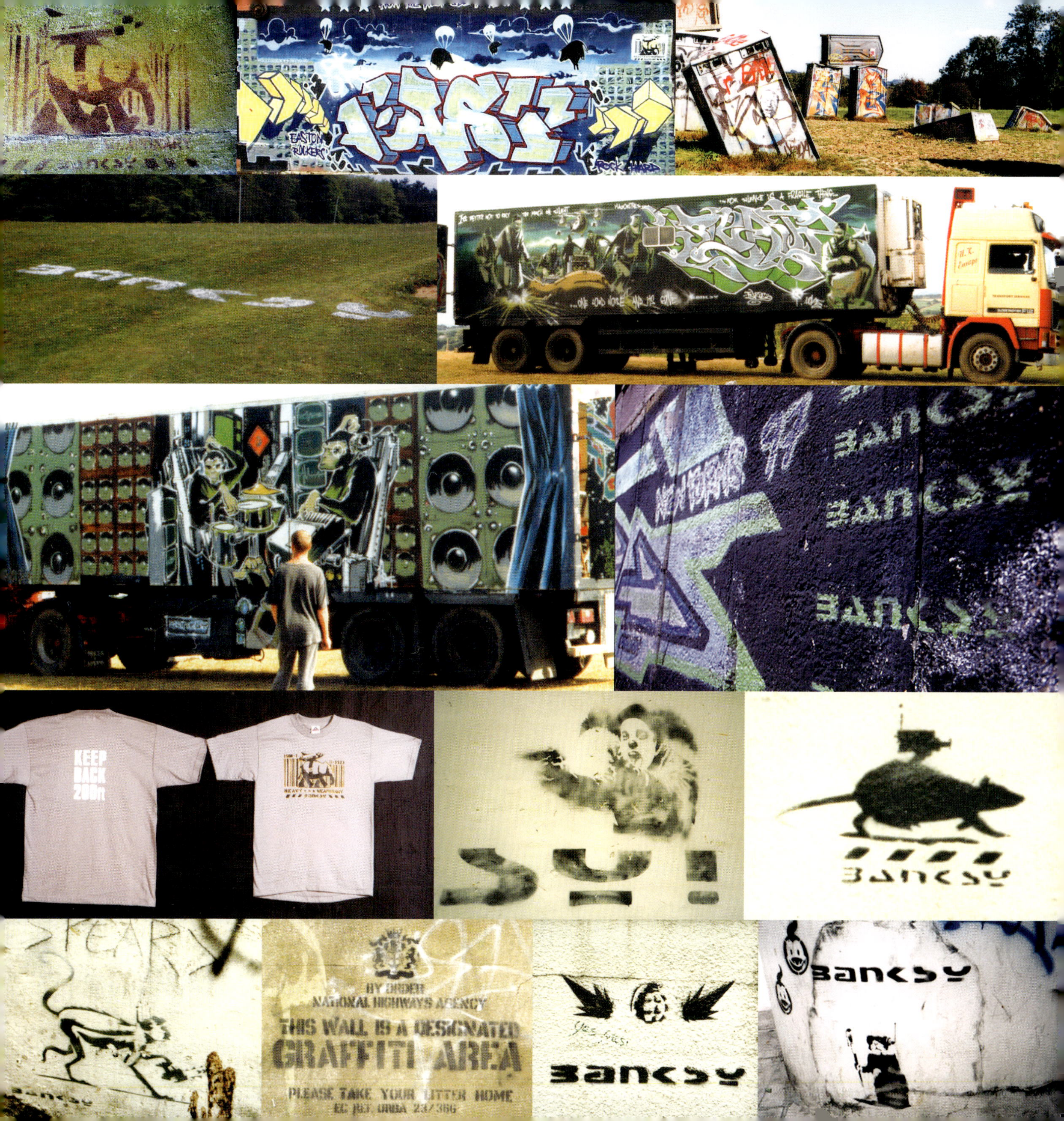
EASTON ROCKERS
KEEP BACK 200ft
BANKSY
BY ORDER
NATIONAL HIGHWAYS AGENCY
THIS WALL IS A DESIGNATED
GRAFFITI AREA
PLEASE TAKE YOUR LITTER HOME
BANKSY
BANKSY

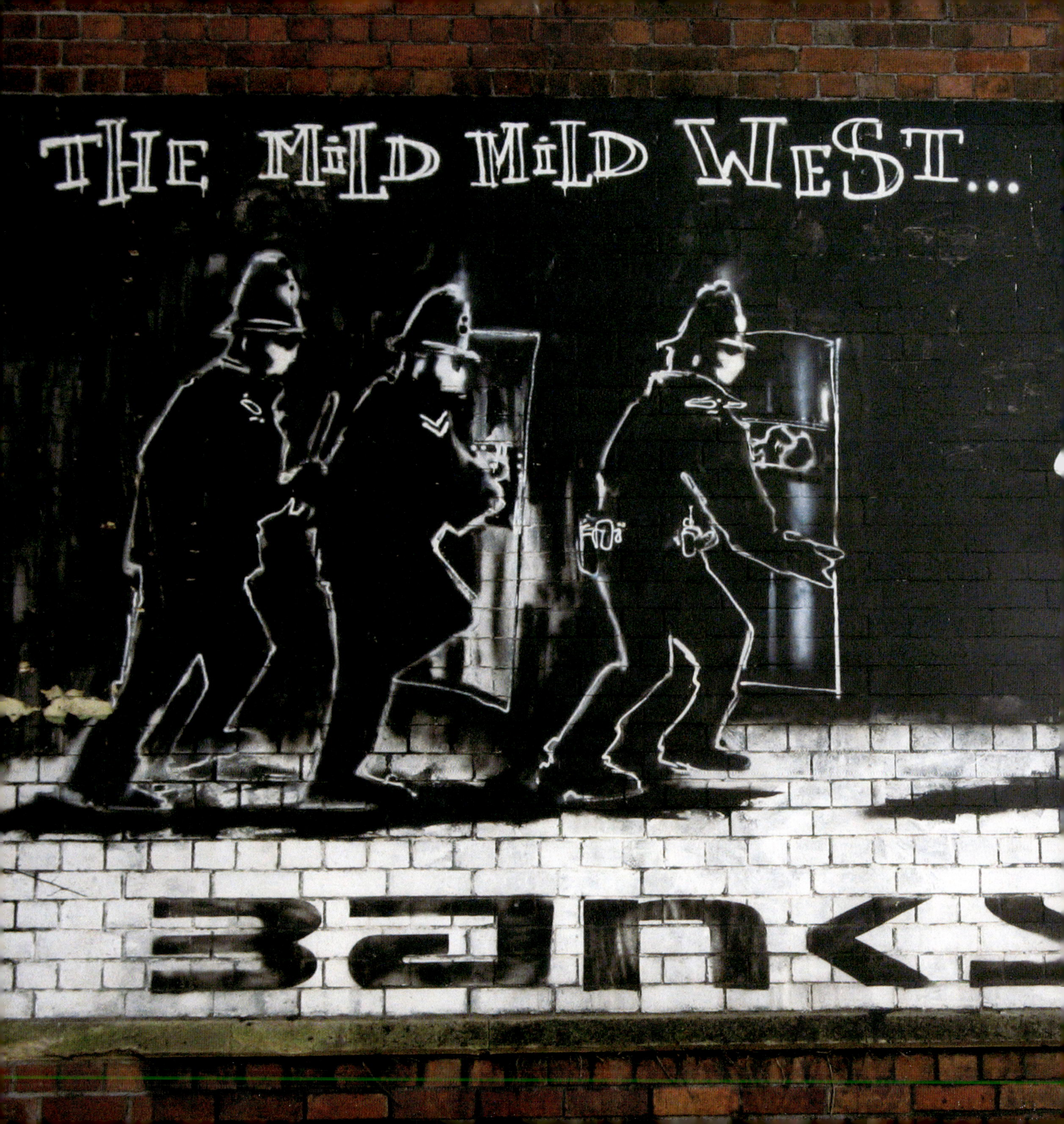
THE MILD MILD WEST...

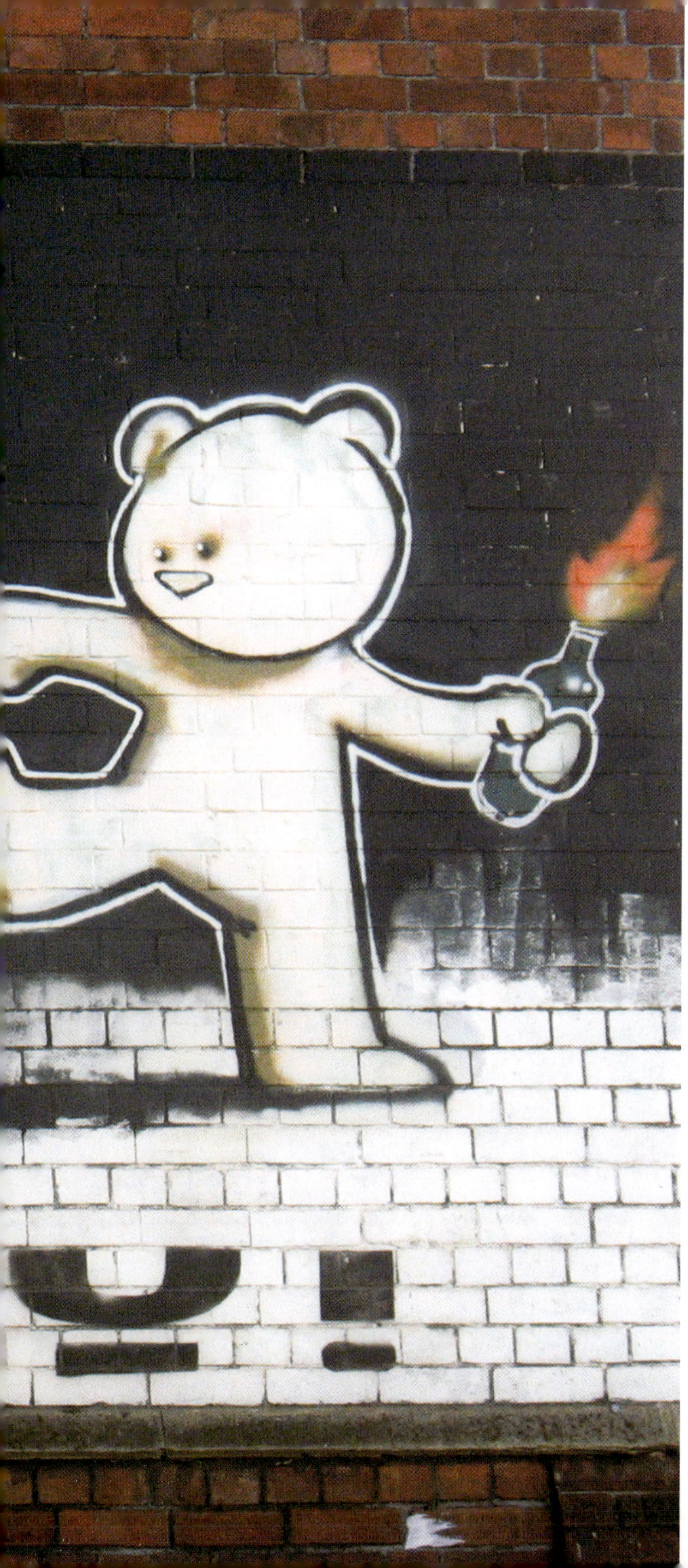

psychedelic references; punk was rising up in East Bristol's working class suburbs with the likes of Vice Squad and Onslaught, while the Cortinas put a more middle-class spin on it, and the boho-funk adventurists, led by Mark Stewart and the Pop Group, were holding court at the Lion pub in Cliftonwood. It would be an overly romantic notion to think that there was any great fusion between all these diverse expressions of urban culture, but there was certainly cross-over on a social level mainly between Stewart and The Wild Bunch who had a regular night at a club called the Dug Out on Park Row.

"So how does all this relate to the Mild Mild West? Who knows? But for people familiar with the Bristol scene at the time of the riots, it kinda makes sense."

Bear essentials

The real story behind Mild Mild West, by Jim Paine – the man who got Banksy to do it

Jim Paine started out with a shop, Subway Records in Walcot Street, Bath, selling techno and hip hop records. He got that one decorated by Bristol graffer Feek. He opened a second Subway Records on Stokes Croft, Bristol in 1998. The shop also sold spray paint, and Jim later had the shop front decorated by TCF (Twentieth Century Frescoes, aka Paris, Eco, Xenz and Feek). He was also involved in the Bristol free party scene from 1993 to 2004.

"I knew Banksy from a while back, from the mid to late Nineties when he was sharing a house in Easton, a couple of streets from me. I was at a free party at a warehouse on Winterstoke Road, Ashton – the old HMSO building. This must have been New Year's Eve 1997/98. Free parties were basically unlicensed events where we broke in to a disused building. There were a lot of them at the time, in warehouses in Feeder Road, St Philips Marsh and Whitby Road in St Annes. But we also did legal club nights at Easton Community Centre, the Trinity, the Lakota, Club Loco and the old Leadworks [demolished to make way for the At-Bristol complex].

"Many of the crowd that night at Winterstoke Road were assaulted by the police, along with members of the sound system who were playing. That party, in fact, marked the beginning of a more hardline approach from the police, using violence as a method of breaking up the parties. We were also getting chased and harassed a lot by the police at the time.

"Anyway, soon after I opened up the Bristol Subway shop, I told Banksy about this massive space on the wall of the building next door. The building was unoccupied at the time – it had been squatted, set fire to, abandoned and boarded up. I had access to the wall, and it just seemed like a great place for a big graffiti piece. He was really up for it. I got the ladder, we bought the paints between us.

"We discussed what the piece should be for about a fortnight. His first sketches had an anti-consumerist message. Banksy's first design had a building in flames, with a looter fleeing the inferno with a loaded shopping trolley. But then I started talking to him about the episode on Winterstoke Road. That was what gave him the idea for the piece.

"I said that, as far as social expression went, we felt pretty oppressed. We were pretty ordinary, fluffy, party people, and we were being bullied by police with riot shields and truncheons. The teddy bear was his idea. The idea of a teddy bear with a Molotov cocktail in his hand – it was showing that mix of hard and fluffy that, basically, was the free party scene. We were a pretty laid-back scene, but at the same time we were involved in things like the Poll Tax demos, Reclaim The Streets… it was a mixture of laid-back and quite fervent. We were also involved in the demos against the Criminal Justice Act. The free party scene in Bristol had a strong New-Age Traveller element, and they also had a history with the police. With the teddy and the Molotov motif, Banksy was saying, 'we could be one or the other. We'd prefer to be mellow, but…'

"I was surprised that there wasn't more reaction to the piece – police attention, angry letters to the *Evening Post*. After all, it's someone (OK, a teddy bear) chucking a petrol bomb at the police! I expected there to be all sorts of complaints of incitement to violence. Instead, it's been accepted into mainstream culture. And yet they complain about him writing his name on a bridge…

"Is it a reference to the St Paul's riots? I don't think so,

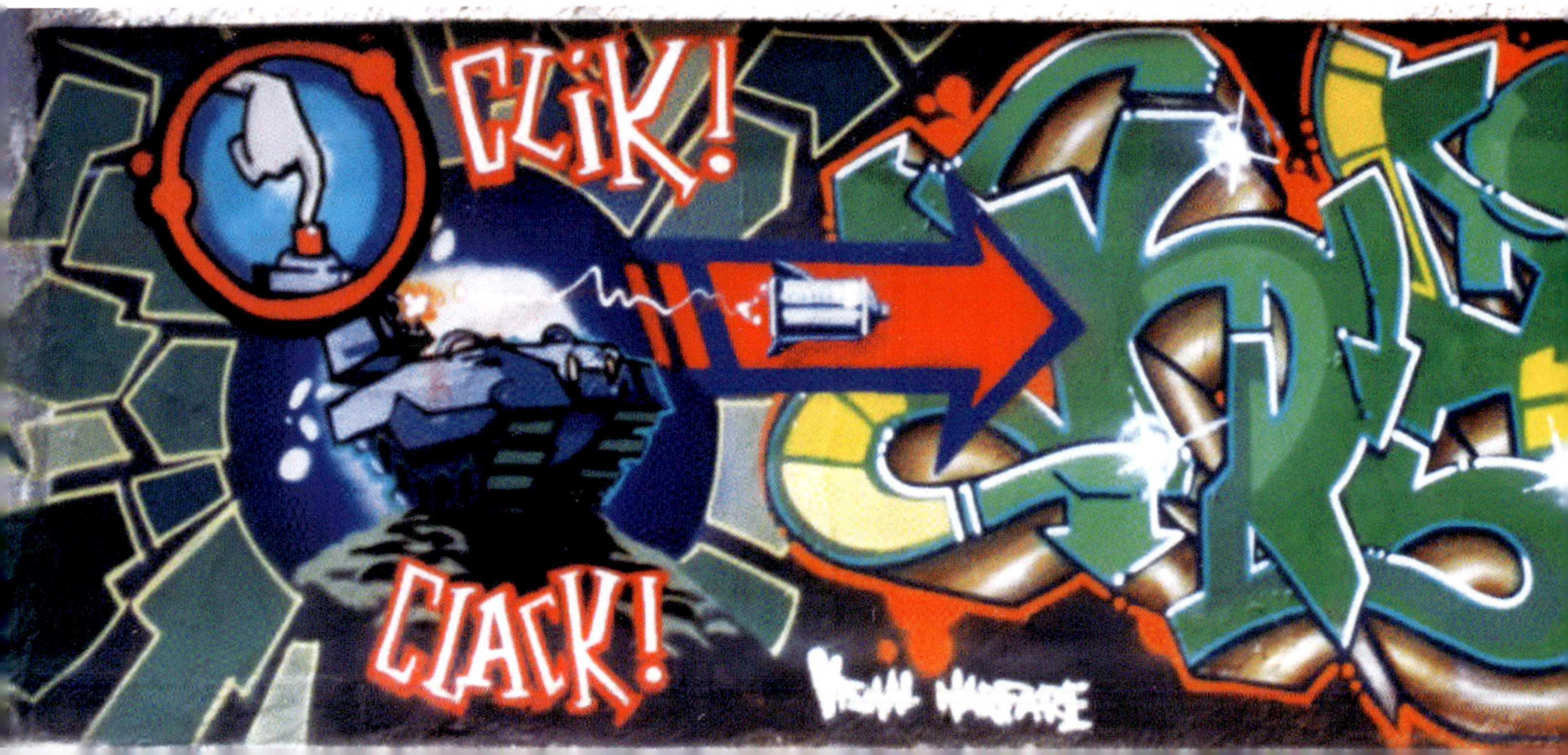

particularly. We certainly never mentioned it while we were talking about the piece. And the riots were a long, long time before that. So no, I don't think they were an inspiration – but then again, I'm sure he was thinking in a much wider context than I was.

How the West was done

"We did it in daylight, over three days. I held the ladder for him and kept lookout. The first day, he painted the wall black. Banksy used car paints – he had a deal with a guy who ran an auto shop. The next day he put the teddy bear in, and then the police. We did the cops last thing that day because that was the most provocative part. The third day, I think, he did the lettering. He wasn't happy with the coppers after doing his first draft, and if you look closely you'll see he's adjusted the outlines of the policemen. Banksy's a perfectionist. I love the way the teddy looks slightly wobbly, slightly ungainly… he looks kinda docile. It's a simple piece, but there's so much to read into it."

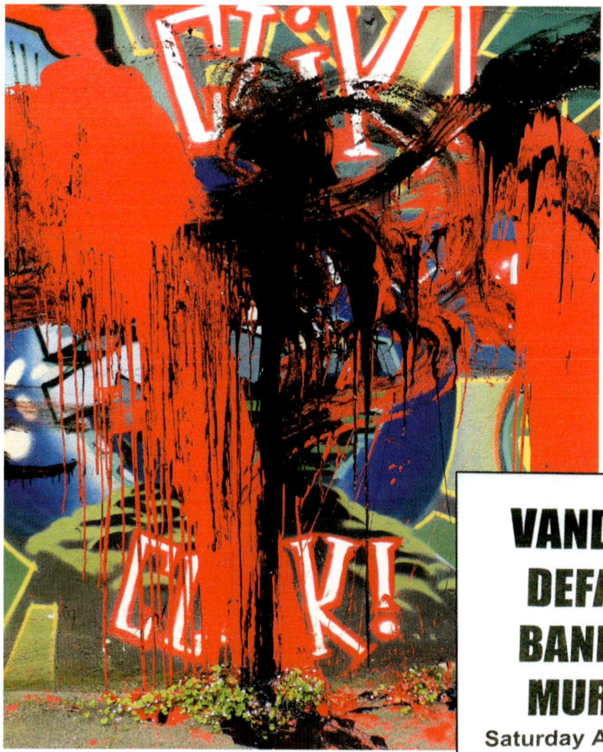

Below: Banksy's mural in Cato Street, Easton

Left: the mural after being defaced before the adjoining house was put up for sale. See over page for more.

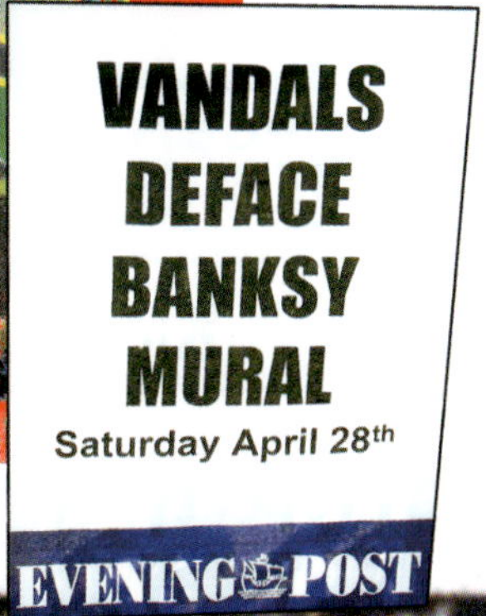

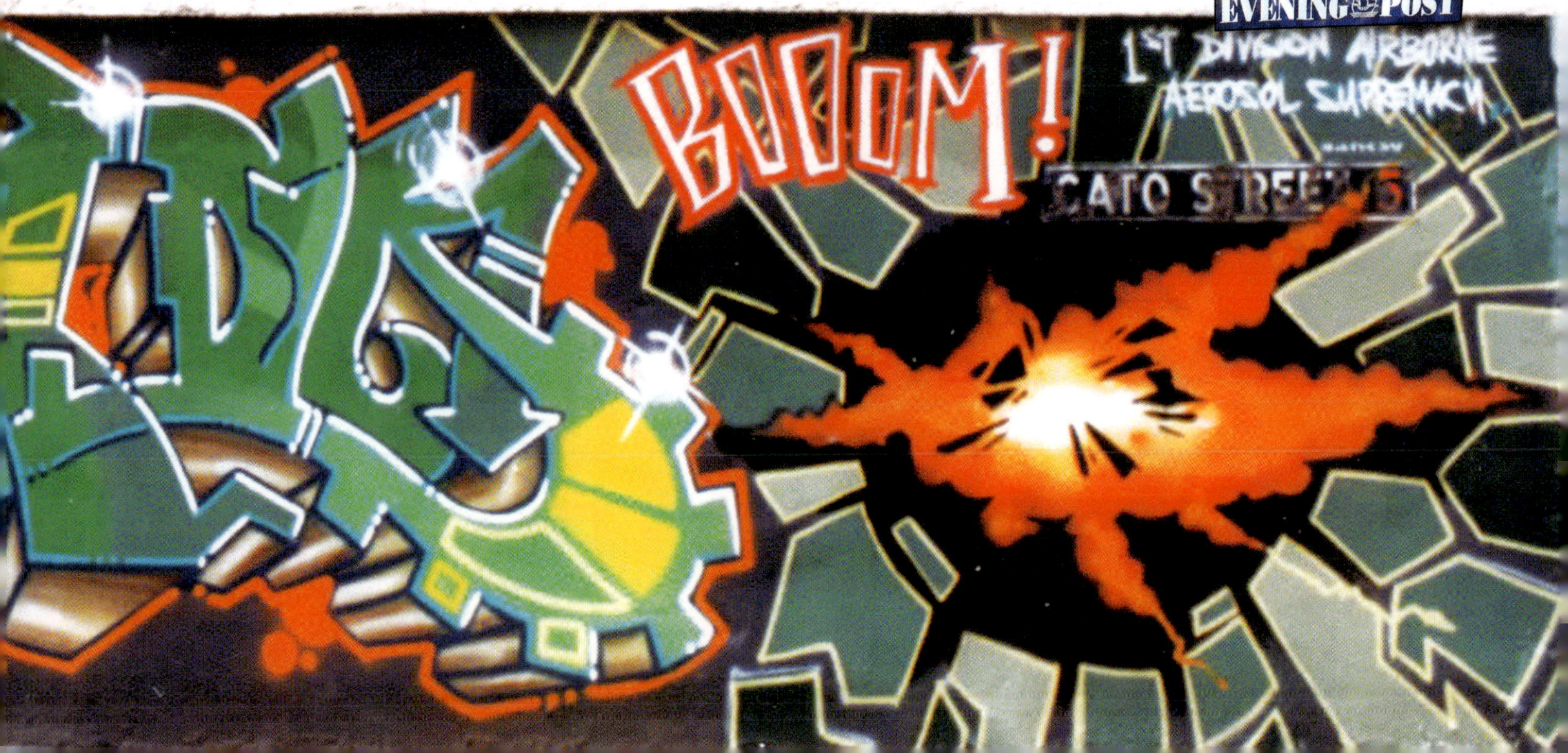

The original tag (which was removed by the Harbourmaster) and the Grim Reaper that replaced it on the side of the Thekla.

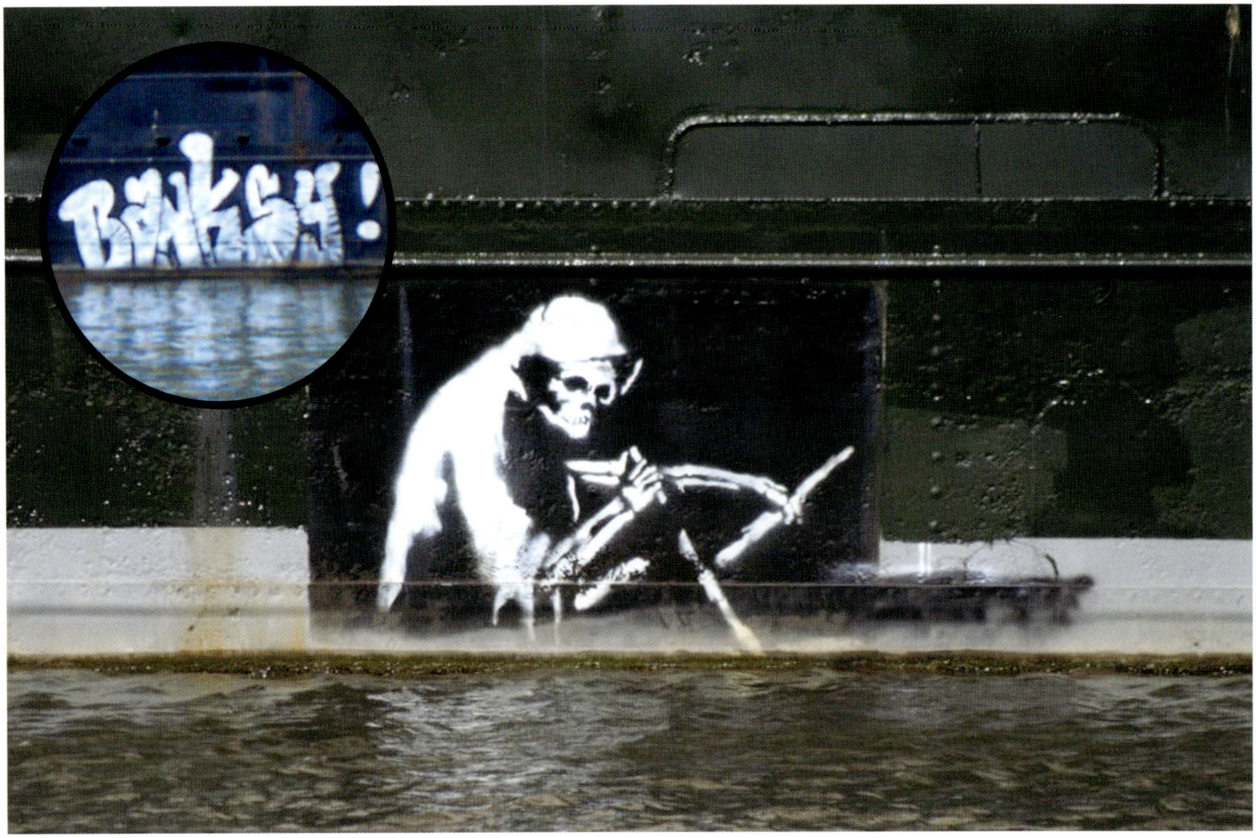

Banksy – not for sale

A Banksy mural on a house in Easton was deemed so valuable that it was advertised for sale as a Banksy piece with a house thrown in. The owners of 21 Mivart Street instructed an art gallery as well as the usual estate agents to seek buyers for the house. The owners were determined that the artwork should stay, and refused offers from buyers who planned to clean it off. The house was taken off the market after 'vandals' threw red and black paint over the artwork. A rumour even went around that Banksy himself might have defaced the piece – but we haven't found any confirmation for that one.

All in the same boat?

Banksy originally tagged the side of the Thekla floating nightclub in spring 2003. The Thekla owners posted a photo of the tag on their website and asked punters whether it should stay. Back came the response: keep it. But even as the votes were coming in, Bristol City Council ordered its removal. It was an interesting decision given that, later that summer, art installations were introduced around Bristol's docks as part of *Dialogue*, a public art event and part of Bristol's 2008 Capital of Culture bid. Thekla manager Joanna Jackson said the decision "Suggests that if it's an official installation it's art, but if it's unofficial it's not." Unperturbed, Banksy returned to paint the Grim Reaper in the same spot. The image was removed when the Thekla went into dry dock in 2014 and has been on display in the nearby M Shed museum since 2015.

TCF Crew

If Nick Walker, FLX and Inkie's Crime Inc. were among the first major graffiti crews to hit Bristol, a decade and a half later another crew began to make a huge impact in the city. TCF (Twentieth Century Frescoes) was actually formed in Hull in 1987 by graffers Xenz, Paris and Eko, who had all been painting together since leaving school in the city (the story behind the name is that Xenz had just returned from a trip to Venice and Florence, full of ideas for painting on walls). From 1996-98 the trio took root in Bristol, drawn by the city's already famous graffiti scene. By 2004, the crew was 10-strong, having added the likes of Feek, Ponk, Dicy and Ziml to its number. "I've always thought that crews need to be formed on friendships rather than similar painting practices," said Eko at the time. "I count my crew as some of my best friends."

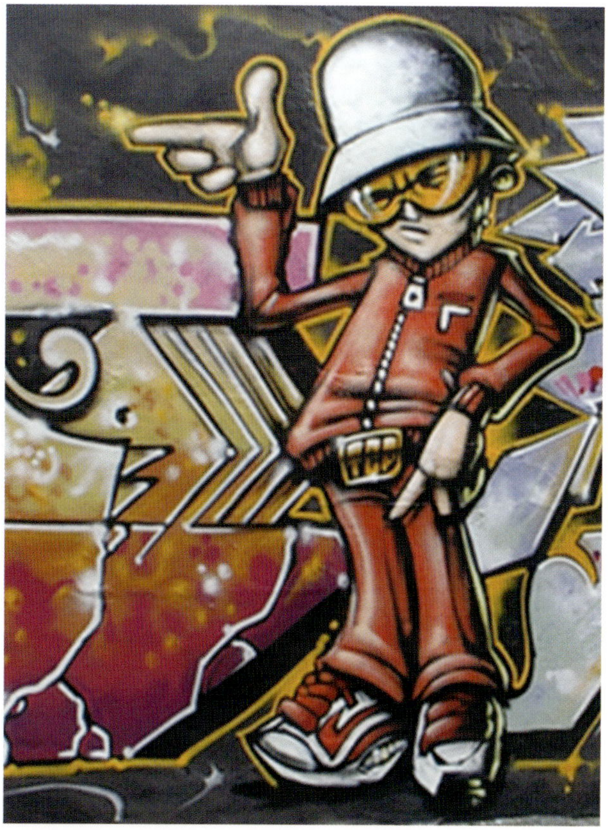

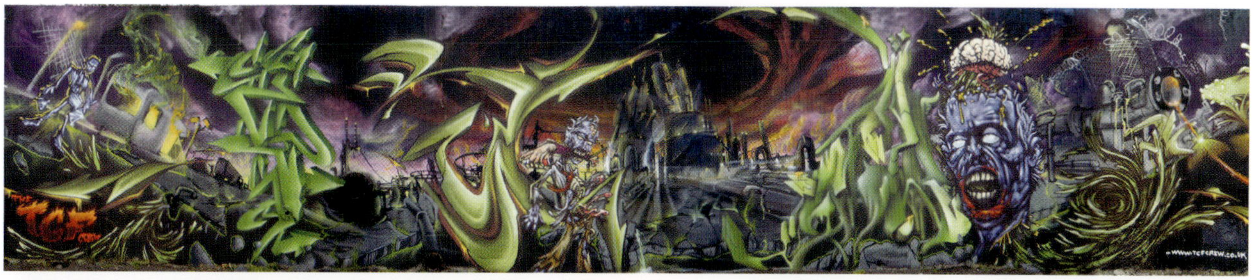

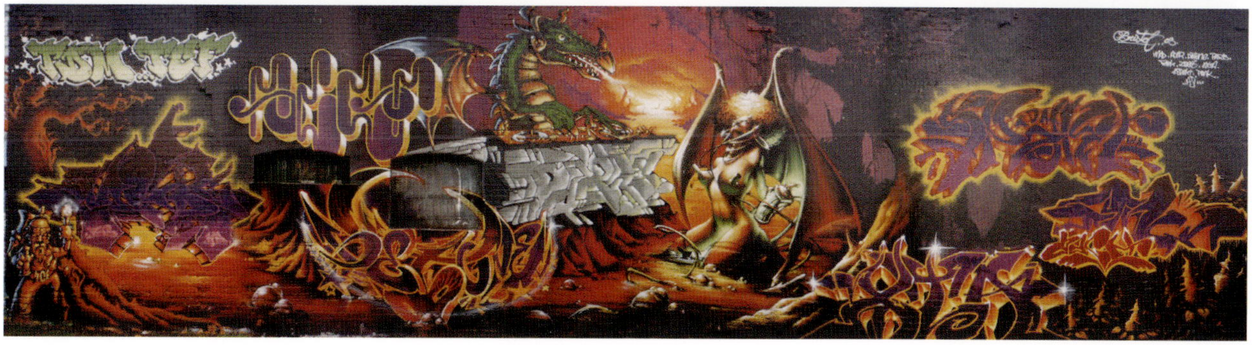

Production of The TCF Crew's work. Bottom pic: Production with The TDM Crew from Montpelier, France.

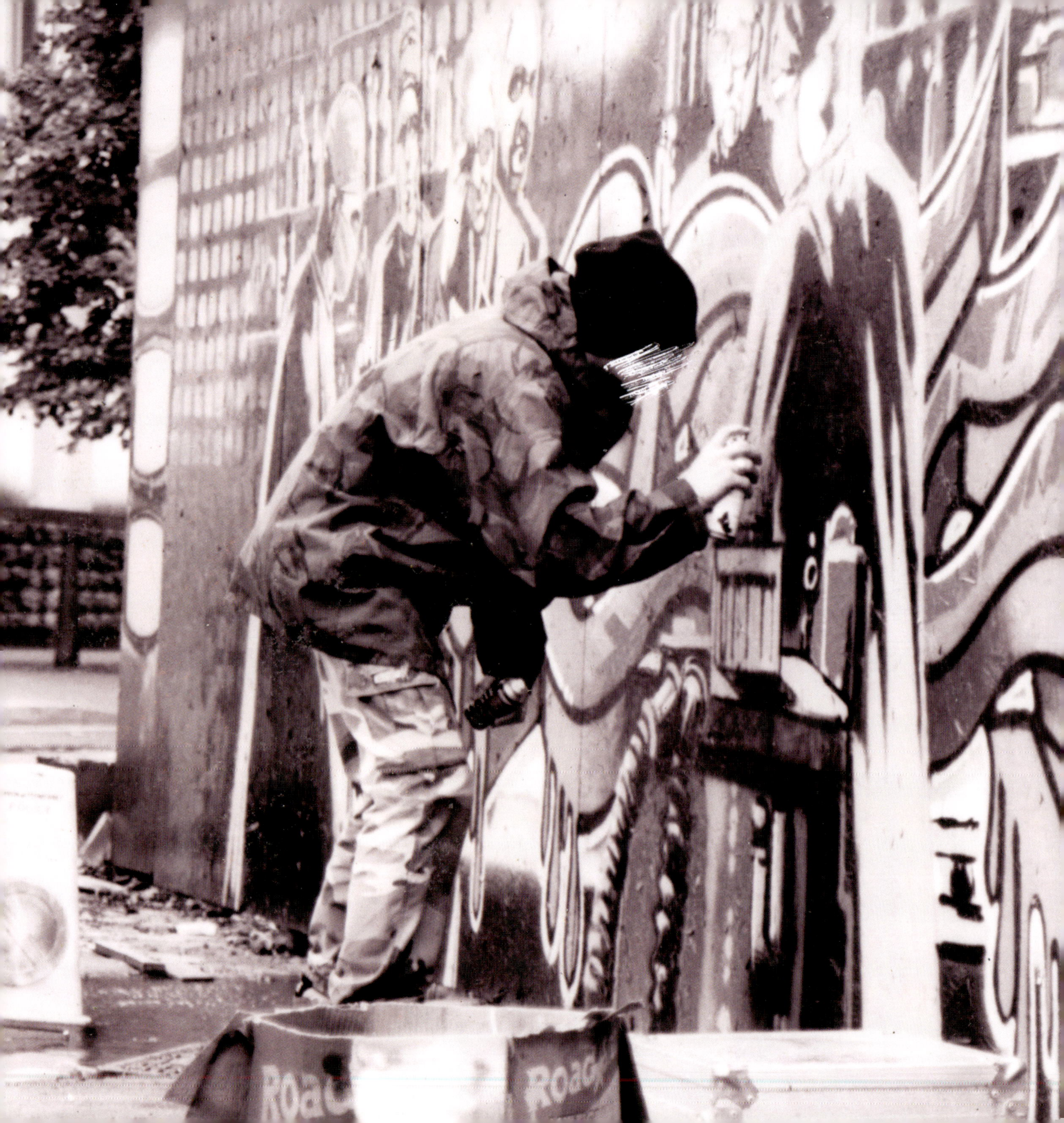

Who Is Banksy?

We all love a mystery, and the swirl of myth and rumour that surrounds Banksy is actually far more exciting than a CV and a bald set of facts would be. Who was it that said that you should never meet your heroes, after all?

That said, what is Banksy actually like? "Down-to-earth, working-class, quite direct," says photographer Mark Simmons, who has worked with Banksy on several occasions. "Confident, cheeky, mischievous, maybe a little arrogant… but with a good heart."

Steve Symons worked at Time Bomb, a DJ and record promotion agency on Stokes Croft. "Banksy used to pop down to the office a lot. He was doing stuff in Bristol perhaps as far back as the Dug Out days in the mid-80s, and was friends with Inkie and 3D. He was just a really ordinary, working-class geezer. Totally solid bloke. The kind of anonymity that was necessary because of what he did – less so what he does now – suits him fine, because he likes to keep a low profile. He's got a very low threshold for bullshit from anyone. But he's a great game-player – he loves that whole mystique thing, but he also likes being ring-fenced from journalists and the media."

Gez Smith arrived at Bristol University in autumn 1997, and started seeing Banksys around Clifton that autumn. "I lived by the student union on Queens Road, and a couple of months after I arrived, I started seeing these huge Banksy logos – just his tag – all around that area. Then, over the next year, I started seeing his pictures all around town – Nipper the HMV dog in Park Place by the barbers, the clown with two guns down on Hotwell Road." He took dozens of photos of Banksys all around the centre, Clifton, Stokes Croft and Easton in 1999-2000, almost all of which have now disappeared.

Gez also worked, in 2000-2001, for Time Bomb. "I wish I'd asked them to pay me in Banksys, because there were quite a few around the office at the time." He remembers Banksy coming into the offices regularly. "He just seemed like a lot of other people at the time – easygoing, liked his clubbing, wore baggy jeans and T-shirts, he was quite tall."

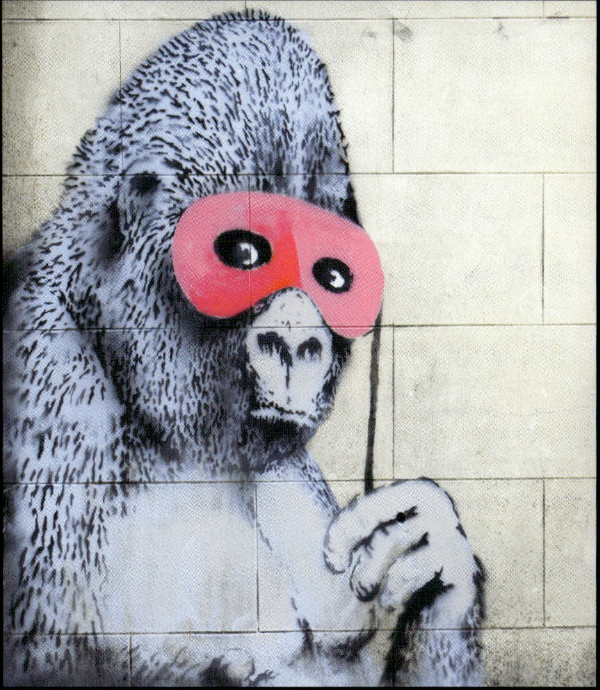

That page: Banksy at work.

This page: The unsigned masked gorilla is on the wall of the North Bristol Social Club at the junction of Fishponds Road and Sandy Lane near Eastville Park.

"I've bumped into him a couple of times," says Ghostboy, another Bristol street artist and contemporary of Banksy. "We've been painting in the same place a couple of times, coincidentally. I was asked by a mutual friend if I wanted to meet him, but it just felt a bit peculiar, a bit forced… we're in the same line, I appreciate his work.

"He's extremely focused and driven. A friend of mine has been out and worked with him in the past, and he says that Banksy doesn't hang out with the other graff artists, it's purely business to him. He's always had a very strong sense of his direction, knows exactly where he wants to go. That's unusual, in that other graff artists generally hang out together quite a lot."

"He's incredibly gifted and very observant," agrees Jim Paine, who held the ladder when Banksy painted Mild Mild West. "And sharp's just not the word for it! He's great at satire, in a real British tradition. He always sees the satirical side of things. His output's phenomenal – and, what's more amazing, everything he does is good. He's hugely influential and successful. And very hard working."

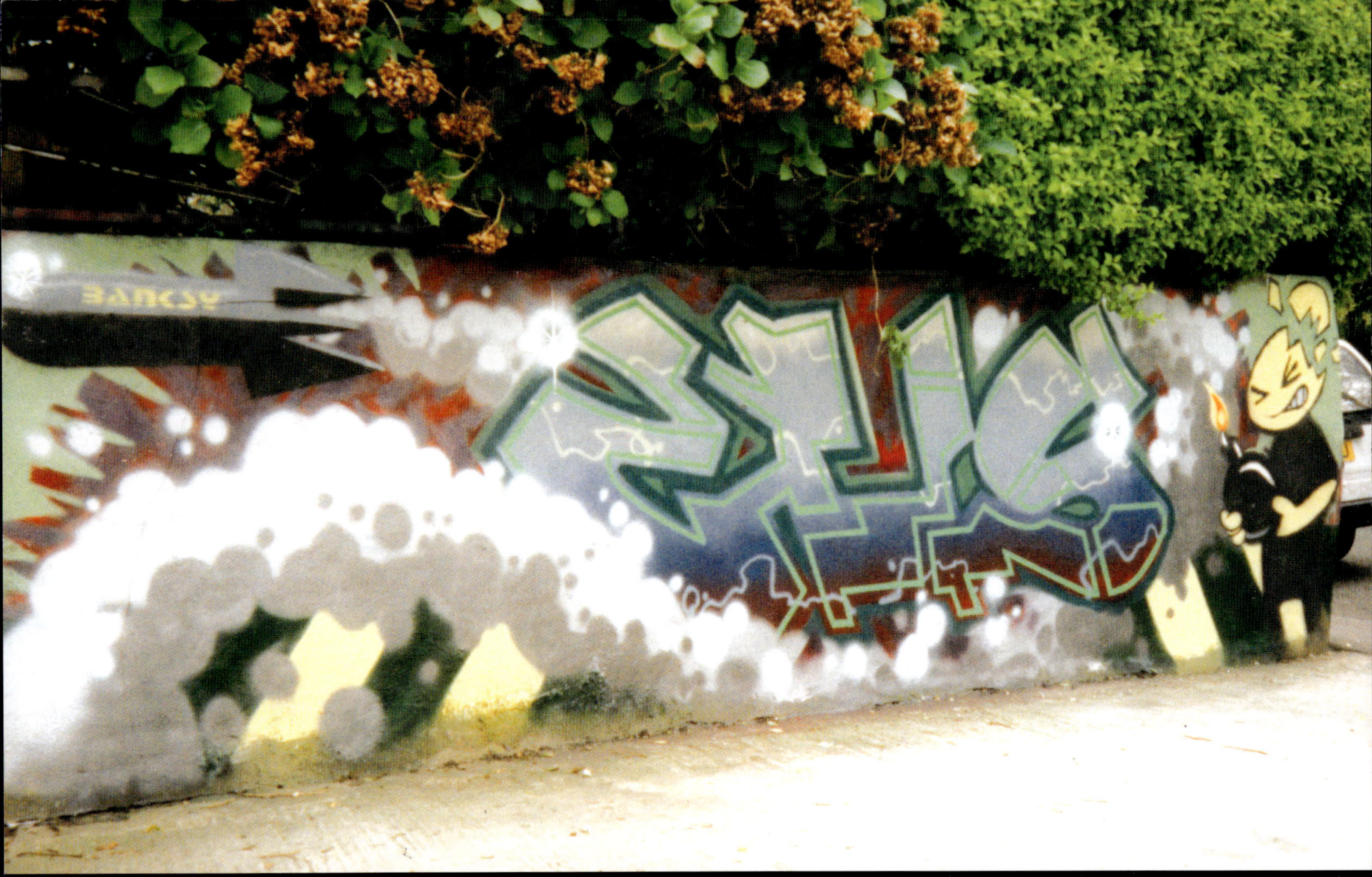

Banksy's first full colour piece: St Werburgh's, 1996.

So, what of Banksy's early life? According to the original (now deleted) Wikipedia entry: *Banksy is a well-known yet pseudo-anonymous English graffiti artist, possibly named Robert Banks. It is believed that Banksy is a native of Yate (near Bristol) who was born in 1974 but there is substantial public uncertainty about his identity and basic personal and biographical details.*

The name is wrong for a start. And Yate? Really?

Bear Hackenbush is a long-standing Bristol artist and illustrator, and a prominent figure on the 1980s skateboarding scene at Dame Emily Park, Bedminster. "I just remember skating down at Bedminster in the late 1980s, and having this kid called Banksy pointed out to me… I seem to remember he was tall. Then later, in the early to mid Nineties, I remember covering up quite a lot of his stuff when I was flyposting and promoting club and gig nights. He'd be painting a lot at places like the Tropic Club on Stokes Croft and the Old England in Montpelier, and we'd go down sticking flyers over his stuff. I remember thinking, 'I like this guy's work a lot', but stuff on the street never had a very long shelf life!"

"When I first met him, which was probably in 1993, even then he was very driven," recalls one prominent Bristol graffer, friend and former collaborator of Banksy's. "He wasn't concerned much about what anyone else was doing – even though he was, back then, up for getting together and collaborating on projects and pieces, something he seems less likely to do these days. But he already had that 'goal' then – wanting to get his message across, have that dig at the system, make that point. It seemed obvious then that he was going to become big or well known, he just had that air about him."

In an interview with the *Sunday Times* in October 2006, Banksy seemed to claim having achieved an E in GCSE art. A lack of inspiration, asked the interviewer? "That, plus I had also discovered cannabis." Another rumour runs that he was expelled from school and went to prison.

He seems to have been inspired by the street on which he grew up. "At the end was a giant billboard, and underneath it girls were doing tricks and cars were dumped. The billboard showed a toothpaste tube three times bigger than the houses, and none of the money from those adverts went back into the street," he said in the *Sunday Times* interview.

In 2005, Banksy told *Wired* magazine: "I always wanted to be a fireman, do something good for the world" and that he wanted to "show that money hasn't crushed the humanity out of everything." When asked by Bristol's *Venue* magazine when he had first picked up a spraycan, he answered: "The day someone ram-raided the Halfords round the corner from our house about ten years ago."

And, lastly, why the move to stencilling? Banksy started out as a freehand graffiti artist, but – he tells the tale in his book *Wall and Piece* (Century) – had something of an epiphany one night while painting trains with a group of other artists.

When I was eighteen, I spent one night trying to paint 'LATE AGAIN' in big silver bubble letters on the side of a passenger train. British transport police showed up and I got ripped to shreds running away through a thorny bush. The rest of my mates made it to the car and disappeared so I spent more than an hour hidden under a dumper truck with engine oil leaking all over me.

As I lay there listening to the cops on the tracks, I realised I had to cut my painting time in half or give up altogether. I was staring straight up at the stencilled plate on the bottom of a fuel tank when I realised I could just copy that style and make each letter three feet high.

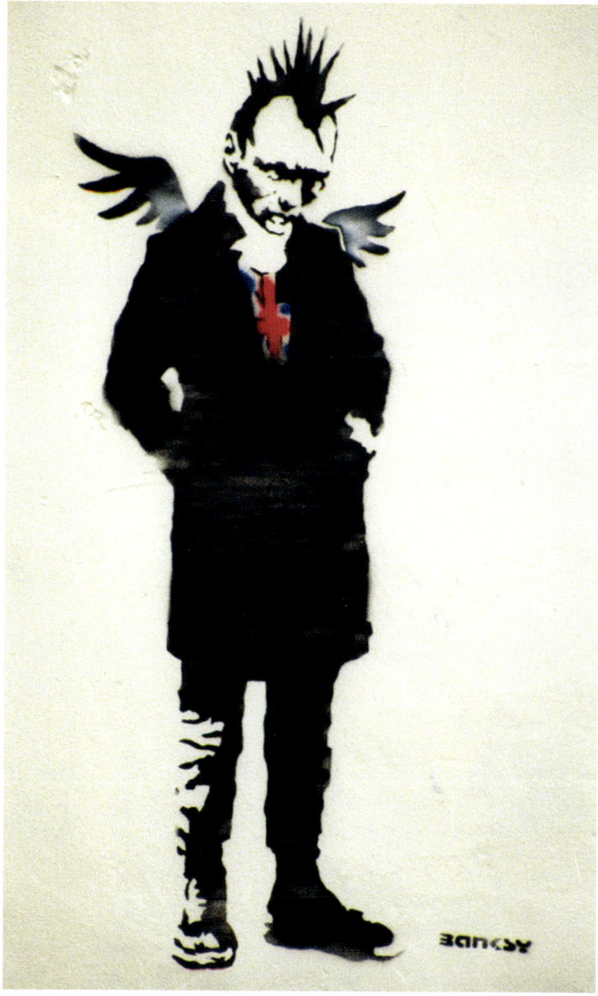

This piece above the phone boxes on the Hippodrome side of the Centre only lasted three days.

Fire starter

Feisal Khalif helped organise the 1998 *Walls on Fire* festival with Banksy and others

"The graffiti festival was commissioned by At-Bristol following lengthy proposals by Banksy and his colleagues. I was the temporary public art project manager during the planning stage, as well as being At-Bristol's marketing manager. The project was partly designed to enable At-Bristol to communicate the ethos of the future millennium project (a fusion of science, art and nature) and partly as a practical way of decorating the

Banksy's work at the Walls on Fire event.

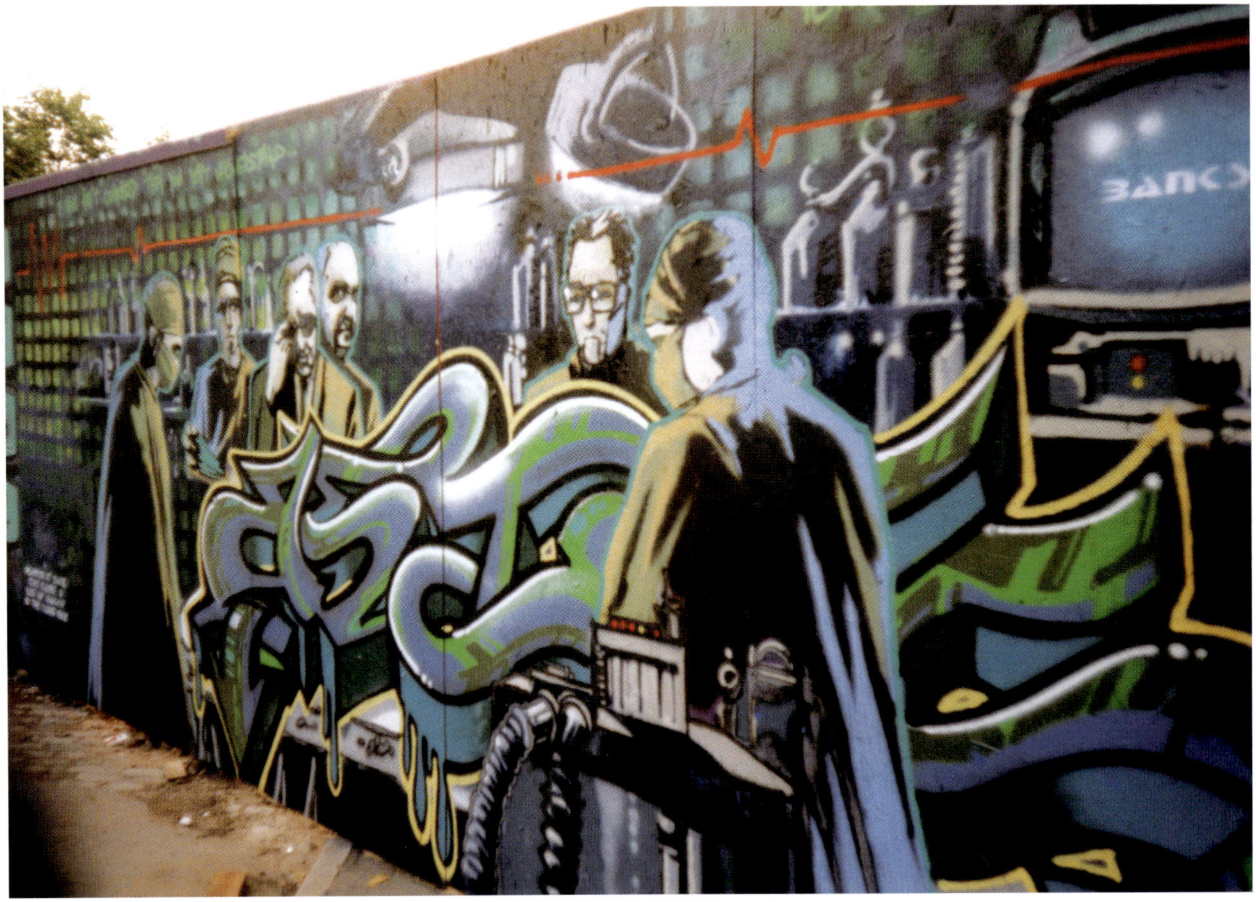

hoardings that surrounded the building work. The basic principle guiding the graffiti was that any work displayed must adhere to the themes of 'science, nature and art'. As, frankly, these are themes that govern virtually all known human activity, it meant pretty much anything was allowed. This therefore neatly avoided having to attempt to square the philosophy of most graffiti writers (certainly at the time) with the idea that their work might be prescribed, edited or censored.

"Banksy and all the graffiti artists I encountered were fantastic to deal with – committed, personable and streetwise. This was particularly evident in the early planning stages when the event was by no means guaranteed to happen. The event itself was pretty much self-regulating and a huge success."

Inkie and Banksy were among the stars of the show; *Venue* magazine put Banksy on the cover to trail the festival. "If you want to say something, you have to put your message up where people can see it," he tells *Venue's* John Mitchell. "It's about putting your neck on the line and putting the effort in to create something; about having the energy and guts to see it through. Easton's an area which is on the way up and my work celebrates that. I paint hard for Easton and if every area had someone painting hard for it, the country would be a far more colourful place."

Jim Paine of Subway Records adds: "Banksy organised the whole event: the artists' roster, who was painting where and when, but also the sound system and DJs. His piece was the best, and was nicked days later."

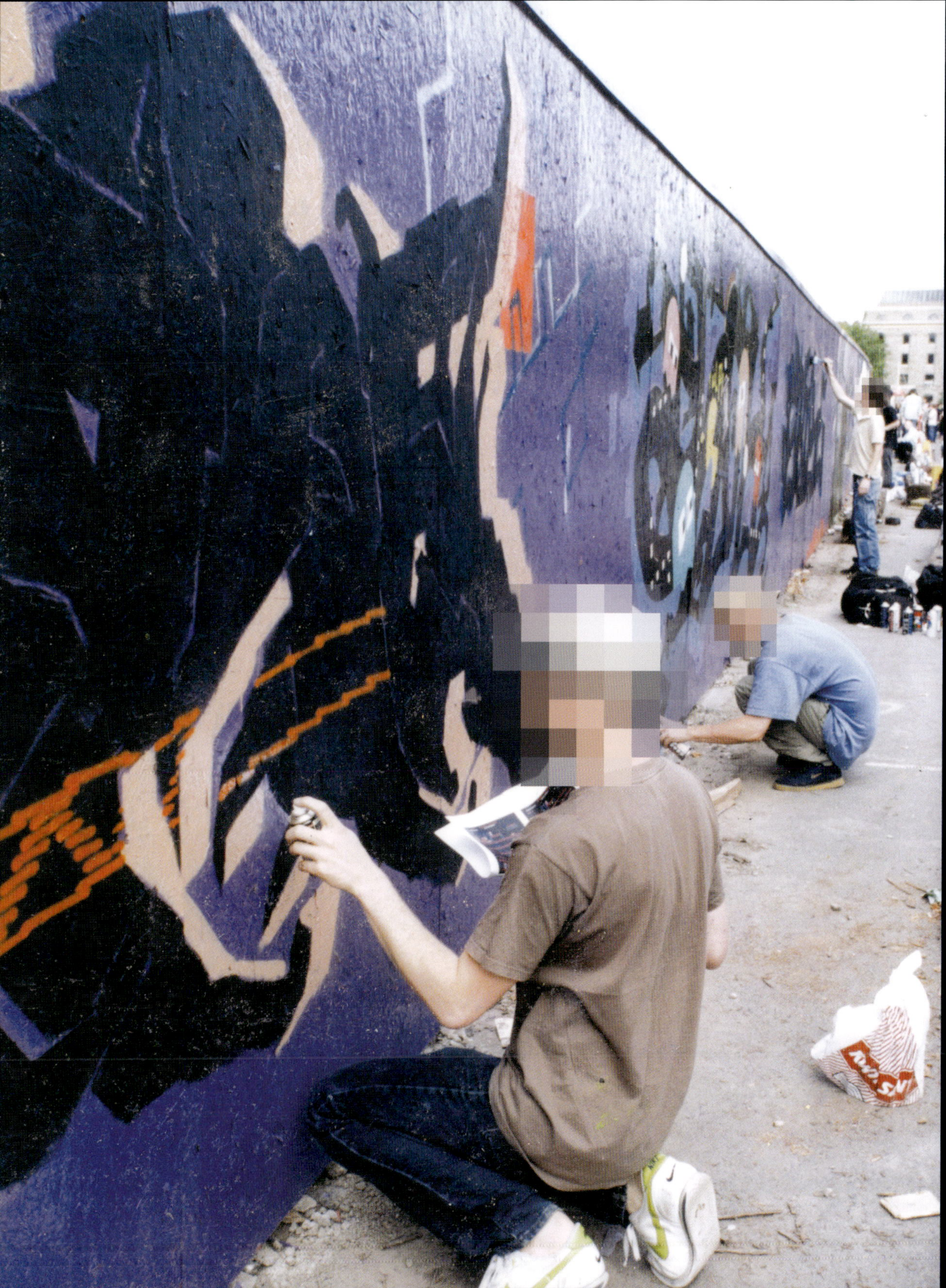

Writers and artists from all over Bristol and the UK took part in Walls on Fire.

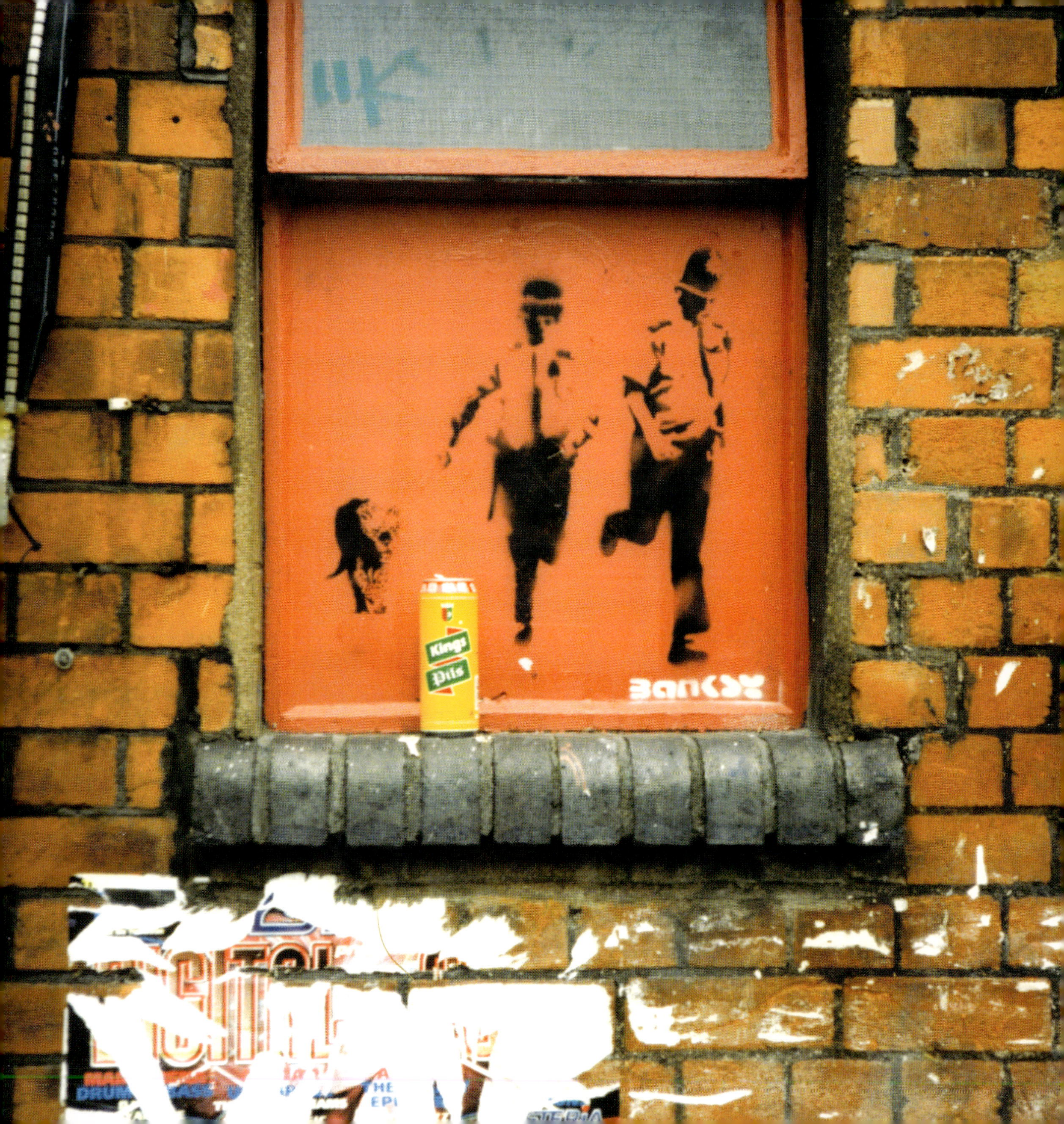
Kings
Pils
BANKSY

Severnshed, 2000

Banksy put on his first major solo show at Severnshed restaurant in Bristol from February to April 2000. He had recently left the city for London, but returned with a variety of designs including his Self Portrait (with chimp's head) and the flower-toting rioter. Artist and designer Robert Birse curated the Severnshed show with Banksy.

"I had been curating shows at Severnshed for a while, and leapt at the chance of doing a show of his work. I'd been a massive fan since first seeing his work when I came to art college in Bristol in 1995. I remember seeing his rats on Park Street and being hugely intrigued, both by the art and the guerrilla tactics of whoever was doing it. He took a strong role in all aspects of the show – he's a man who knows what he wants. He had very strong ideas of how pieces should be hung, what the feel of the exhibition was to be. He also did all his own flyering for the show. He's a very strong-willed guy – not in an overpowering, aggressive sense , he just knew exactly what he wanted. And because of that he was a pleasure to work with.

"I was never in any doubt that, as soon as he made the decision to start exhibiting in a saleable format as well as on the street, he would go a long way. It was clear he had the intelligence and the ability to be huge in the art world. And he's a great self-publicist, there's no one else like him. The work sold out on opening night. I did not buy any, but I was given one of an edition of ten as a 'thank you'. It was one-in-one-out at the venue pretty much from opening time. During the day before the opening night, we had a sort of preview. Lots of people came down and wanted to buy a piece, but we were both adamant that nothing was going on sale until the exhibition started, that we wanted it to be completely democratic, first-come-first-served. I had to say no to [Massive Attack's] Daddy G who wanted to buy one before opening – he was not chuffed! We had a call during that day from the head of Avon and Somerset Police, who asked me if I would approach Banksy for a get-together with the police. They just wanted to have a nice chat with Banksy, and encourage him to move away from the street graffiti, maybe take a different tack. When I told Banksy about the call he just laughed his head off."

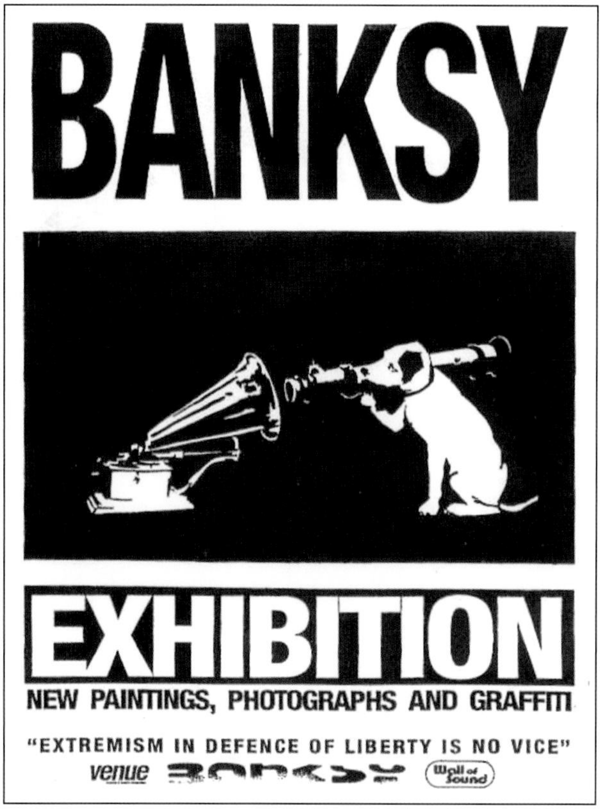

That page: Police near the Centrespace Gallery in Leonard Lane.

This page: Poster advertising Banksy's seminal Severnshed show. Nipper the Dog is from Bristol as well.

Paul Kelly

Paul Kelly is a seminal, if elusive, figure in the Banksy story. A 'representative' for the emerging artist, he pushed his protégé hard in the early years. He was also a peripatetic but vital part of the 1990s Bristol scene – and something of a character. Carlton Romaine recalls that Kelly and Banksy approached him when Romaine was one of the organisers of the St Paul's Carnival, in 1998, to arrange for the artist to do a large freestyle graffiti piece on the side of Valentine's, a late night music bar, for that year's Carnival.

"Paul was pushing Banksy everywhere, trying to get him involved in whatever was going on in Bristol. Paul was quite an elusive person, you wouldn't see him for months at a time, but every time I'd run into him, he'd mention Banksy to me, and try to push Banksy at every opportunity. He was always trying to flog a Banksy to me, too…"

Friends with Massive Attack's Daddy G and others,

Mark Simmons was invited to an early Banksy exhibition in a flat in Easton where he shot these canvases.

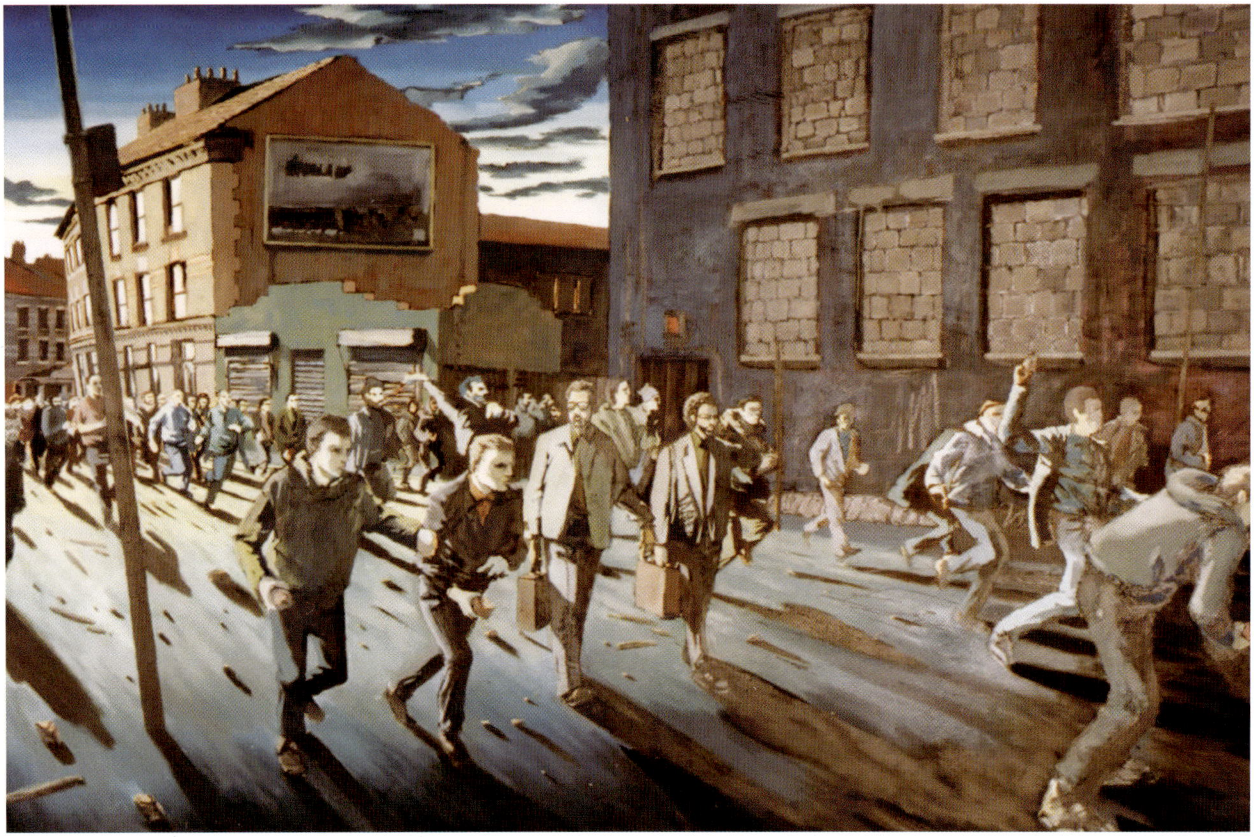

Kelly was, as Romaine puts it, "a kind of freelance promoter/hermit/maverick" on Bristol's music, club and art scenes.

"He took up Banksy's cause right at the beginning, and was definitely partly responsible for getting his name around Bristol. But with Paul, it was always about the art, the street, and freedom of expression. Art had to stay true to the street. In a way, he's more real than Banksy, in that he has always kept it real. It was always about the art and the music and never about the money, to the point where he was living hand-to-mouth, crashing on people's floors, trying to do his stuff. He's real. He believes in it all the way, in ways that perhaps Banksy doesn't, or doesn't anymore."

Richard Jones, who was the *Bristol Evening Post's* music writer at the time remembers: "Paul ran a barber's shop on Stapleton Road called *Kelly's*, and was well-known for cutting Batman logos and the likes into kids' hair, so it usually had loads of kids in there getting some street cred logo on their bonces. He did a mean flat top as well. It was a real characterful place with a few old West Indian guys hanging out and loads of banter.

"Paul always claimed he had interest from EMI for a band he looked after called The Spasmodics, but EMI signed a band from Oxford called Radiohead instead. The last time I saw Paul, he was going on about this artist called Banksy he was helping out and how Banksy was going to paint something on the side of his house in Chapel Road in Easton in a special paint that only showed up with UV light or something. It was probably nonsense, but raises the question of whether there is an invisible Banksy in Easton."

Paul returned to Bristol in 2010 after studying photography in Newcastle.

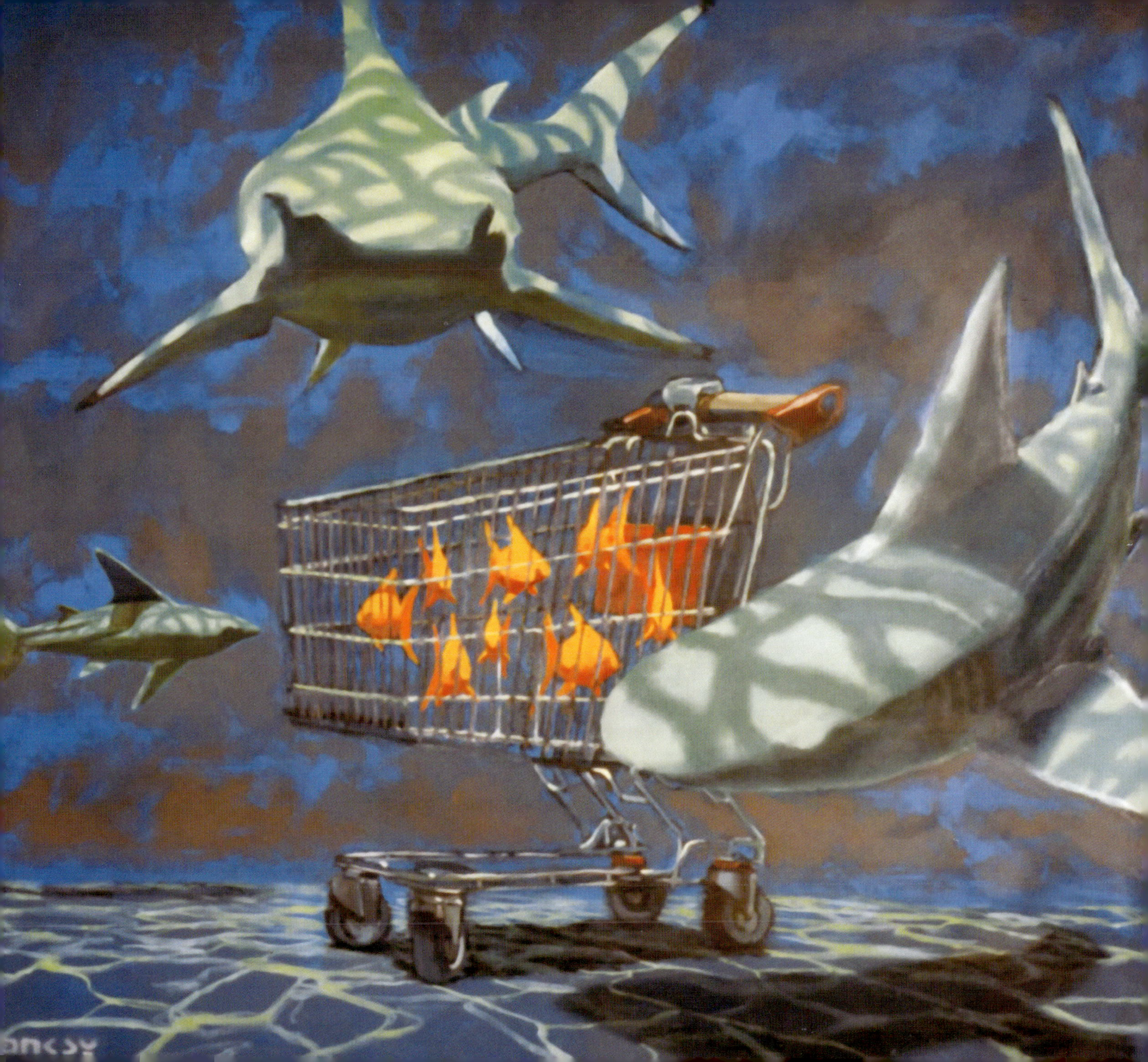

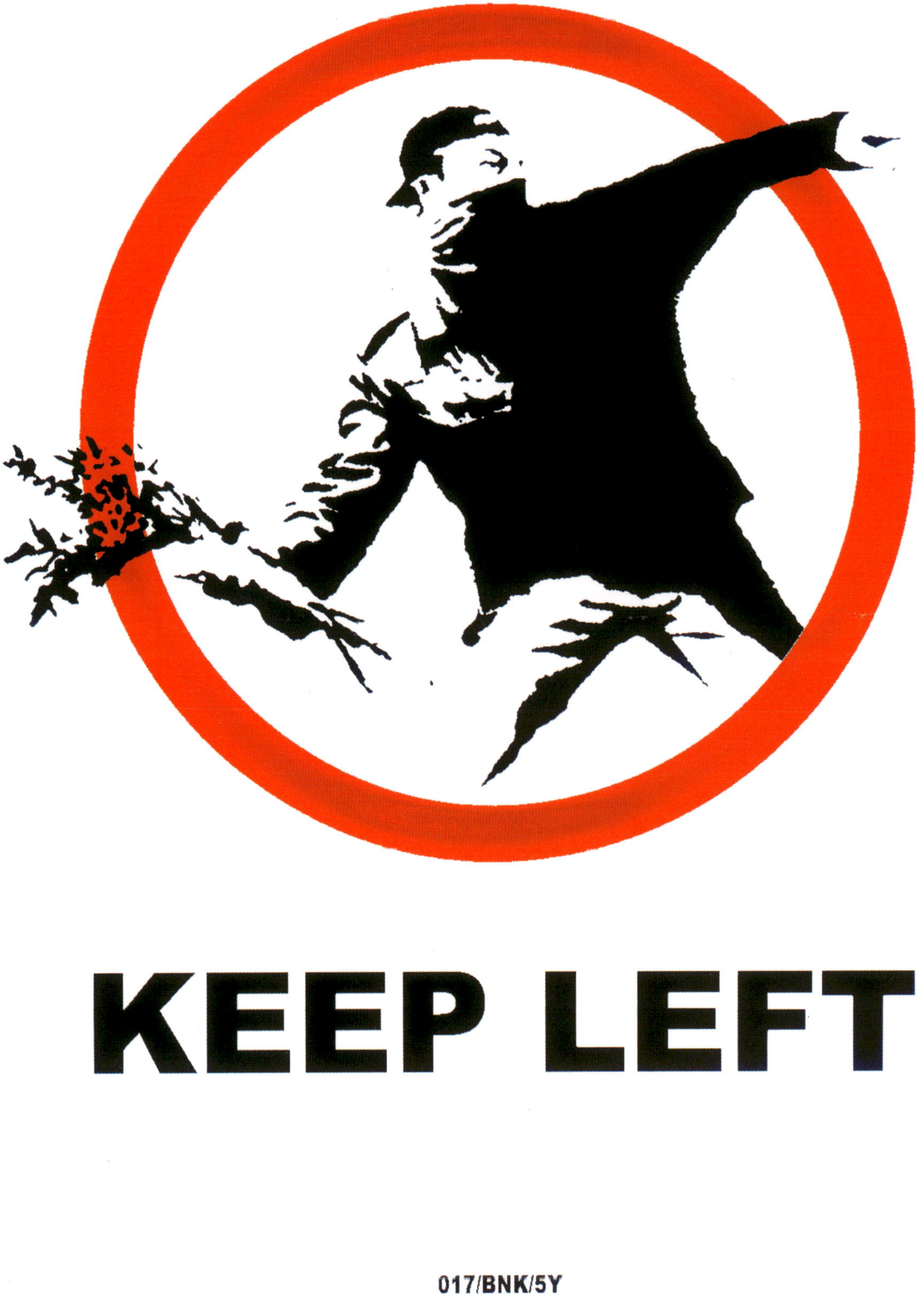
KEEP LEFT
017/BNK/5Y

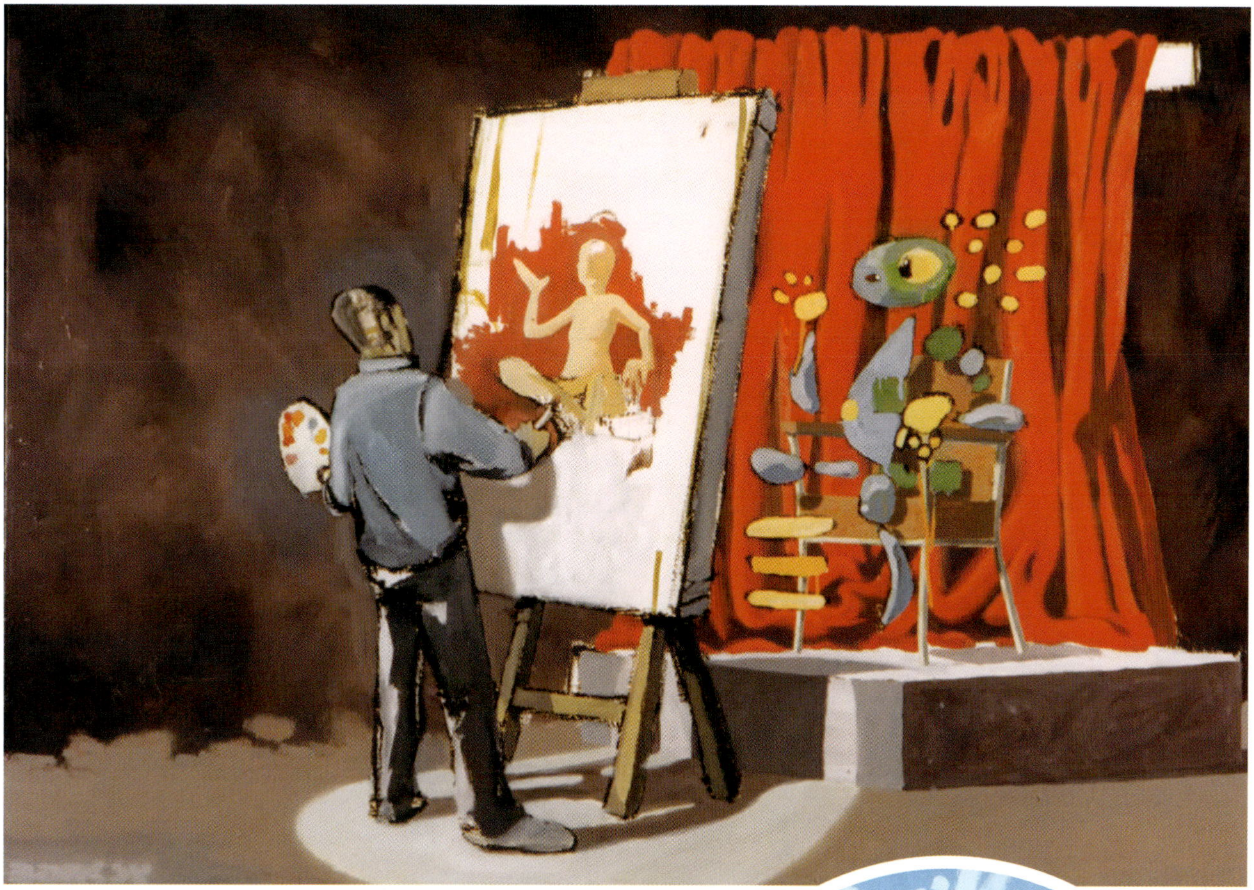

More shots from the Easton exhibition and a Banksy sticker.

Sweet charity

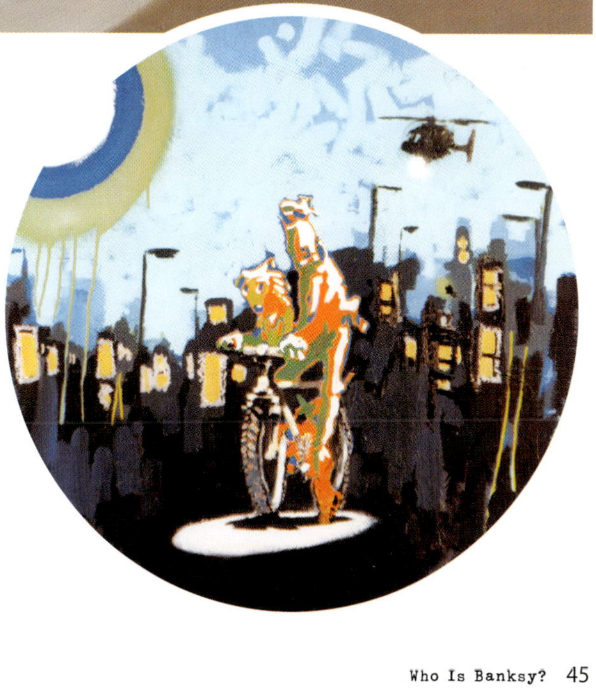

In 2006, Banksy fans queued for three hours outside the Workshop store in Perry Road, Bristol. The reason? His new print, Flag, went on sale at £100. Proceeds were given to Sightsavers International, a charity working to combat blindness in developing countries, restoring sight through specialist treatment and eye care.

"There was a note on the back of them encouraging anyone re-selling the print to contribute a proportion of the revenue to Sightsavers. The print went on sale in the Workshop store in Bristol and at Santa's Grotto, a temporary exhibition of his work in London," said Ann Noon, Sightsavers' Media Manager. The prints sold out at Workshop within two hours.

This one got removed so quickly, nobody is entirely sure where it appeared.

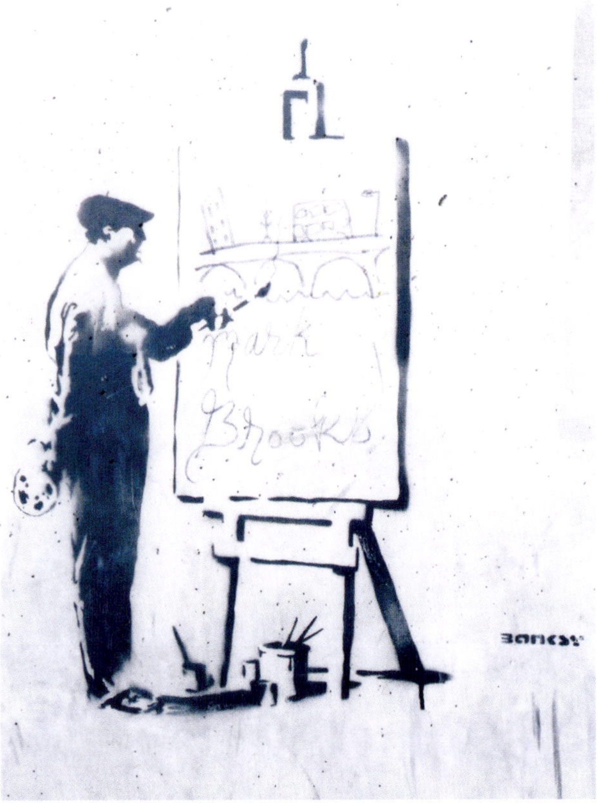

My Banksy

Gez Smith went to the Severnshed show in Feb 2000 and picked up a Banksy with his student loan

"I was first through the door, so I went around taking my pick. I ended up paying £300 of my student loan for Riot Green. There were other pieces there, including his Self Portrait [with a chimp's head that subsequently sold at Bonhams for £198,000]. Nothing there was selling for over £1,000, and most of it was around £150-£500.

"When I decided to see how much it was now worth. Sotheby's quoted me £30,000 – it ended up selling for £78,000. I drove it up to London in a Pieminister van.

"The current prices are bonkers. The bubble will burst. The contemporary art market is in a massive bubble at the minute. Generally that bubble collapses about two years after the housing market collapses. What is a shame is that there's such a culture of competitiveness, people paying ever higher prices for the cachet of owning a Banksy, which stops real people owning one."

Yes, Banksy's left Bristol – but he's left a lot of random people with a nice little nest egg – people that have been given sketches or bought a print for £60 at Greenleaf Bookshop or at various small shows around town over the years. That's a very Banksy kind of thing to do.

Bristol Artist Will Brown was one of the early admirers of Banksy's art

"I saw an early Banksy stencil [Heavy Weaponary] in Stokes Croft in 1998 and was so intrigued, I started systematically photographing graffiti – I have a collection of about 2,000 images. I went to Banksy's exhibition at the Severnshed when he left for London and bought one of the limited edition of 10 canvasses of Heavy Weaponry for £100. I sold it in 2007 for £24,000.

"Banksy is interesting to me because he has become a successful artist without interesting or appealing to the art intelligentsia or academy. His pictures rarely refer to other art or the art world. They are not complex or difficult to 'get' so they don't confer on the viewer the pleasure of being in a select club of the artistically literate who are able to 'read' them.

"Banksy's work is always political and his political concerns reflect those of contemporary British counter culture (animal rights and exploitation, hi-tech policing and surveillance etc) which interest me. Banksy's persona takes further the 20th century concern with the life and spectacle of the artist in relation to his own work – this strand goes through Van Gogh, Jackson Pollock, Warhol etc. Banksy is the artist who is so famous he is unknown."

A woman from Totterdown, who refers to herself as 'Lucky Bugger' was also at the Severnshed show

"The title of the piece I bought is Heavy Weaponary (yeah, that's how it's spelt on the piece). It's an elephant with a nuclear missile on its back and over-stencilled with the words London, New York and Bristol. London and New

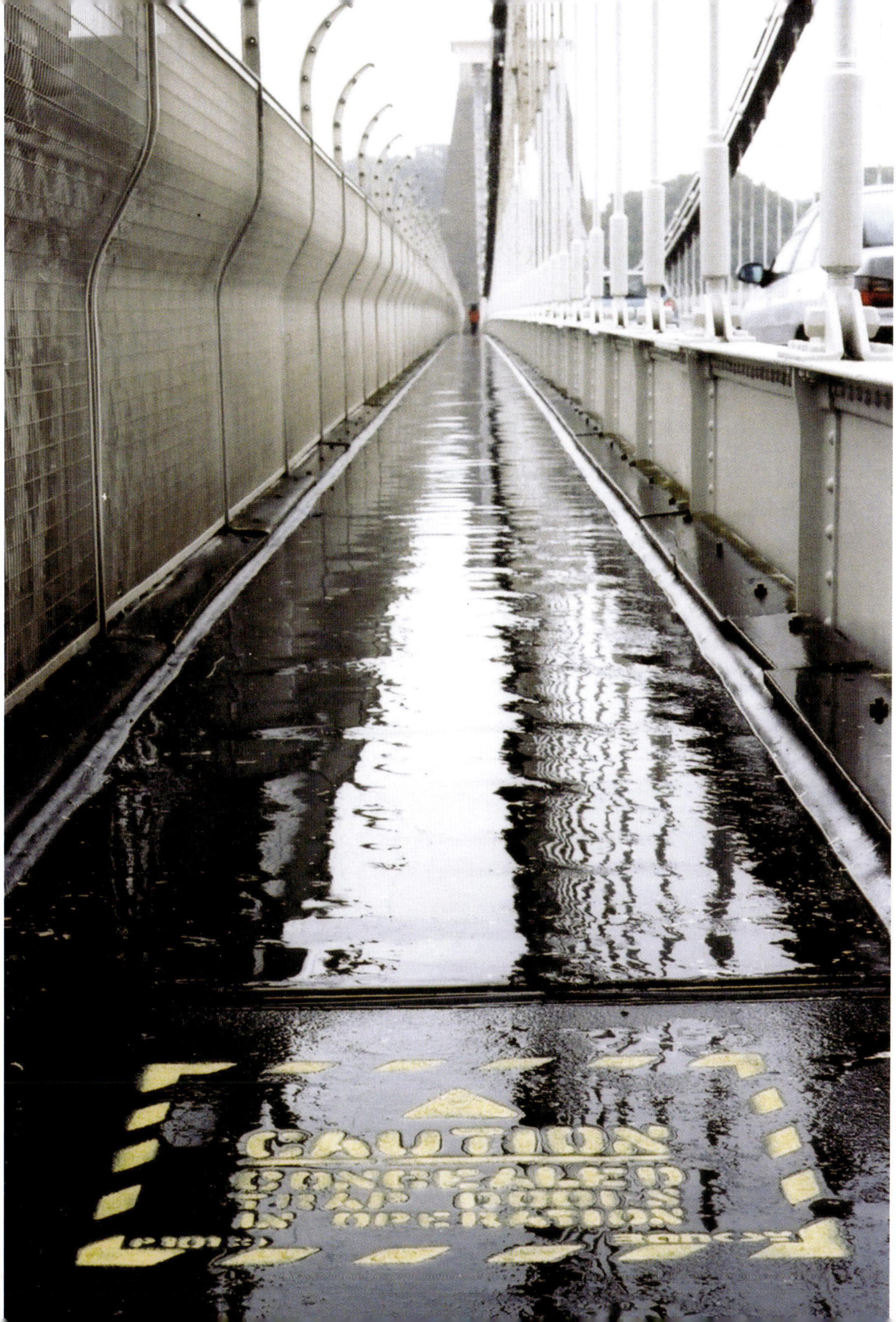

Banksy
meets Brunel
at Clifton
Suspension
Bridge.

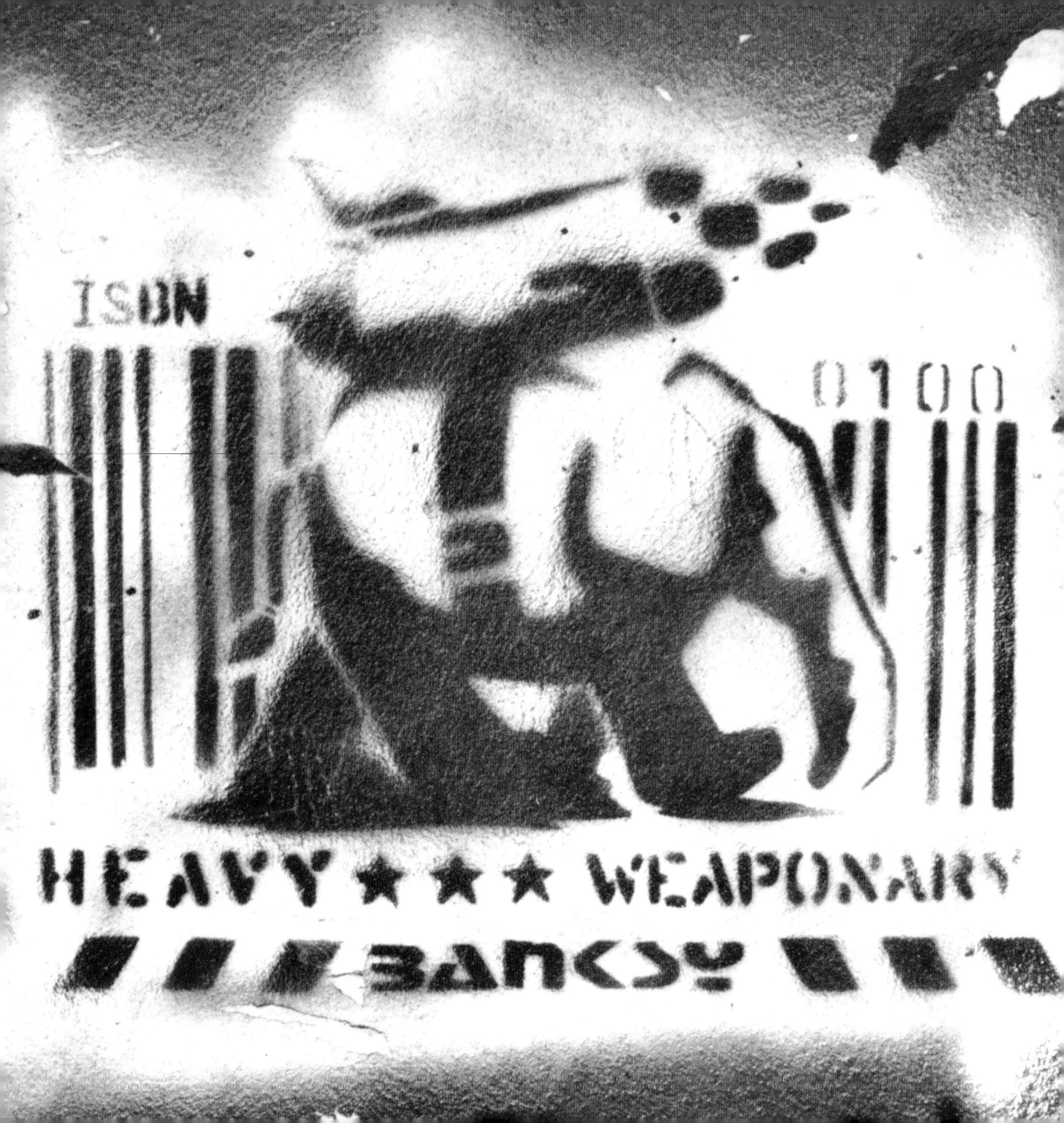
ISBN
0100
HEAVY ★★★ WEAPONARY
BANKSY

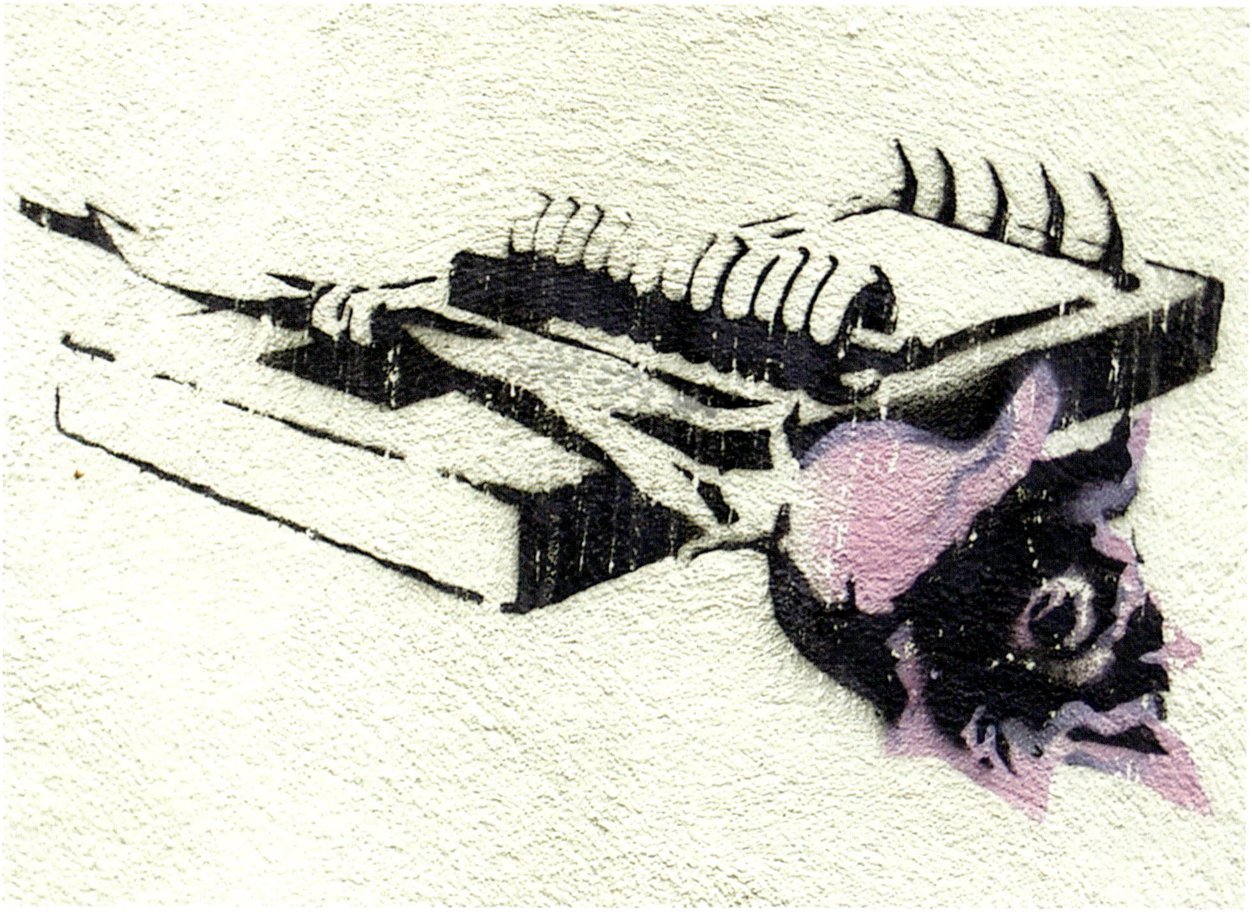

That page: Heavy Weaponary stencil in Stokes Croft.

This page: Banksy the Romantic in Kingsdown.

York are heavily crossed out in crayon. It's paint on board with an unfinished oil piece on the reverse. I bought it at the Severnshed exhibition for £150 and sold it in 2007 for more than £30,000

"I'd seen Banksy's stuff on walls all over Bristol in the late Nineties and they'd always made me grin. So when he had his first exhibition at the Severnshed I wanted to support him and also buy a bit of the city I love.

"I liked the flower-flinging rioters pieces but chose this one because it seemed to say you don't have to move to capital cities to get creative recognition and that basically Bristol rocks! I interpreted the lumbering elephant carrying a bomb as a wake up call to slow down.

"The reverse had a strange unfinished oil painting with a character sitting in a hanging cage wistfully staring at an out-of-reach key – it was really dark and used to give me goose bumps. I decided to sell the piece when I heard of the crazy figures being paid for his work in LA (there's a reason they call it lala land)… and I'm just as happy now to have a digital copy hanging on my wall.

"All power to Banksy and the madness of fashionistas!"

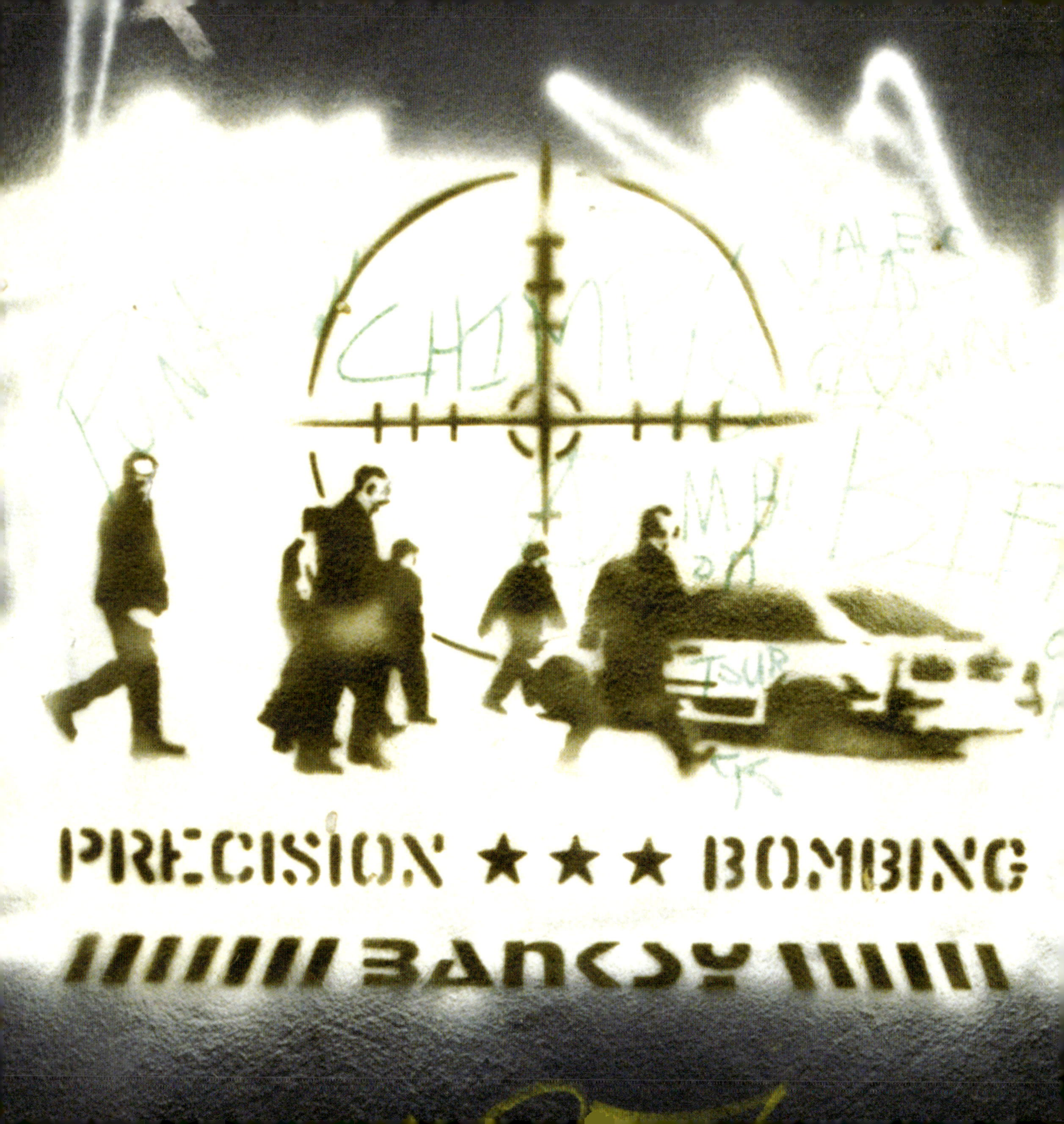
PRECISION ★★★ BOMBING
BANKSY

Crest Of A Rave

Bristol photographer Matthew Smith was heavily involved in the early Nineties rave culture, and events such as the huge demos against the 1994 Criminal Justice and Public Order Bill – introduced, as he puts it, "to outlaw dancing together in the open air and to criminalise the travelling lifestyle."

"I first met Banksy (although he wasn't using that name then) in Bristol in 1995, when we were part of the organisation behind a huge free festival called *The Mother* which was meant to happen in Devon. The festival was to mark the first anniversary of opposition to the 1994 Criminal Justice Bill.

"I was part of Sunnyside, a sound system which we'd taken on the huge and peaceful demos against the Criminal Justice Act on Mayday and on 23rd July 1994. We'd also been part of a nationwide tour called *The Velvet Revolution*, to mark the passing of the Criminal Justice Act and to raise awareness about its implications for civil liberties. It was funded by Liberty, Charter 88 and The Levellers. We were doing a lot of free parties around that time from a warehouse under Feeder Road – I remember a crowd of about 15,000 from all over the country coming to one of them. I shared a house with a few of the people involved in our crew in Bruton Place, Clifton, and while we were waiting to head down to Devon for the festival a sound system came down in their truck and parked up outside. I remember a Banksy stencil going up in Bruton Place then – and I think it was one of Nipper the HMV dog with the 'keep back 200 feet' thing going on, but it may have been later...

"Banksy just hit all the DIY social and political ideals of that time right on the head – the idea of music as a social weapon, music crossing boundaries and creating communities in a way that felt threatening to those in power at the time. NVDA (or non-violent direct action) was one of the buzz words of the time, and graffiti is just that: creative peaceful protest. It's about one person's voice being able to make a difference, especially if you

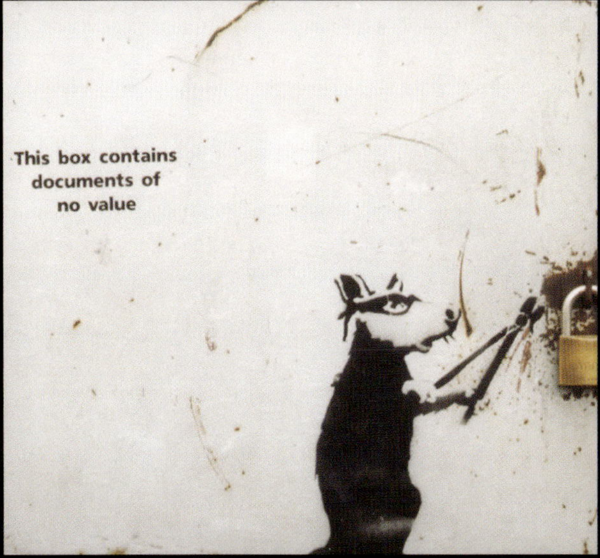

Humour, subversi
politics
rats.

are visually literate and incisive enough to catch the public imagination. Banksy is at his most successful as an interventionist and his sense of place and situation is brilliant. That said, I do think part of his contemporary success is down in no small way to some very clever niche networking when he moved to London – and the help of some highly commercial and cynical art marketeers.

"The whole London thing is crucial. It's sad, but he would never have become the success he has if he hadn't left Bristol and got his work on the walls of the city that houses all the creative heads of state, most of whom are far too complacent to leave the capital for any length of time. Spraying around Soho, Hoxton and the East End is a great way to become instantly trendy, as long as you have the product. If the mountain won't go to Mohammed...

"The dance music and festival scene wasn't the huge in-house industry it is now. It was all about word of mouth, people deciding to be in the same place at the same time, and to take the consequences if necessary. Festivals and free parties were funding and publicising the traveller lifestyle in a massive way, and the government was desperate to prevent this.

"Early rave culture was hugely democratic. It also had a tremendous sense of community, far more than there is now, and it was regarded by the authorities as

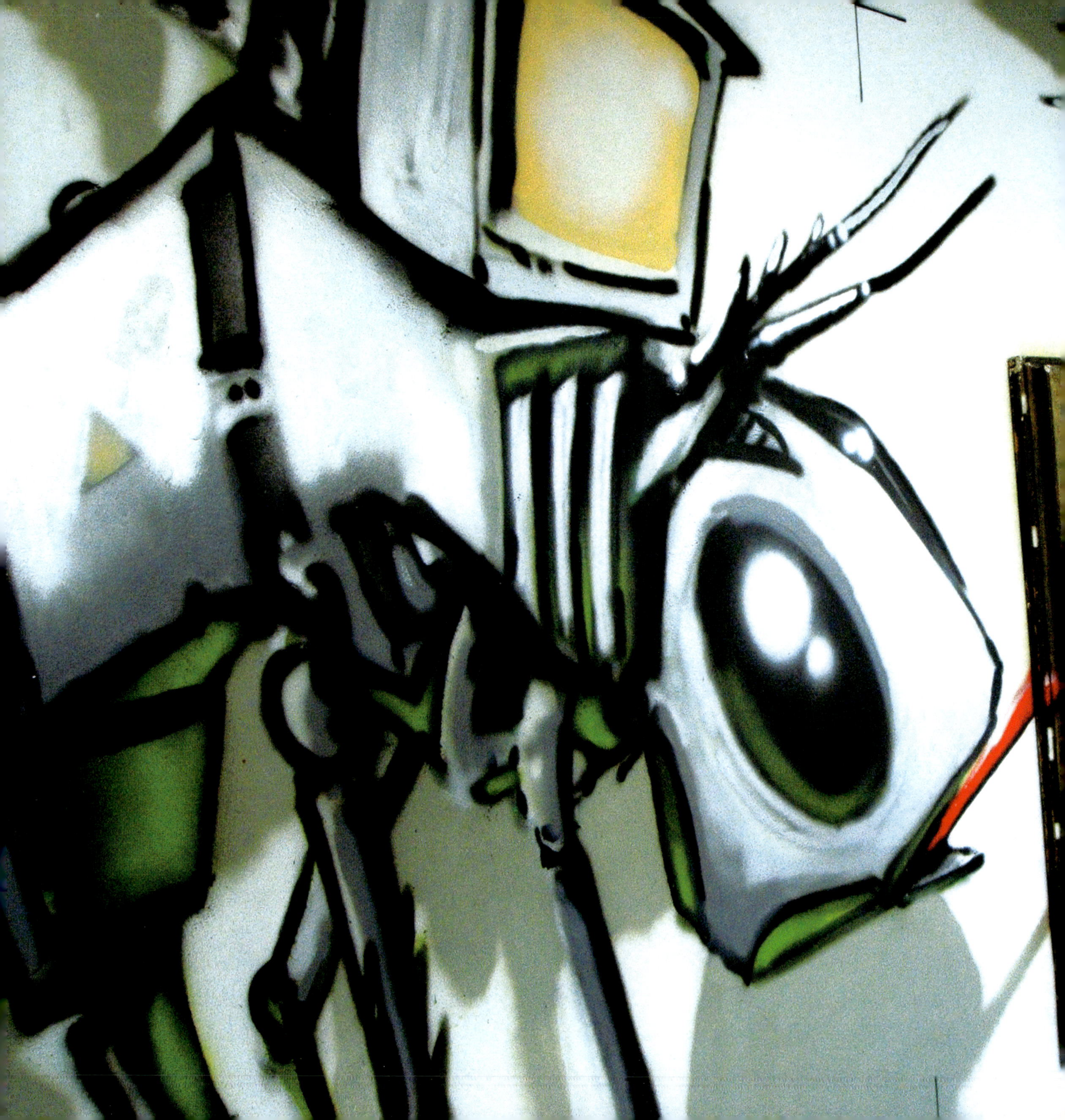

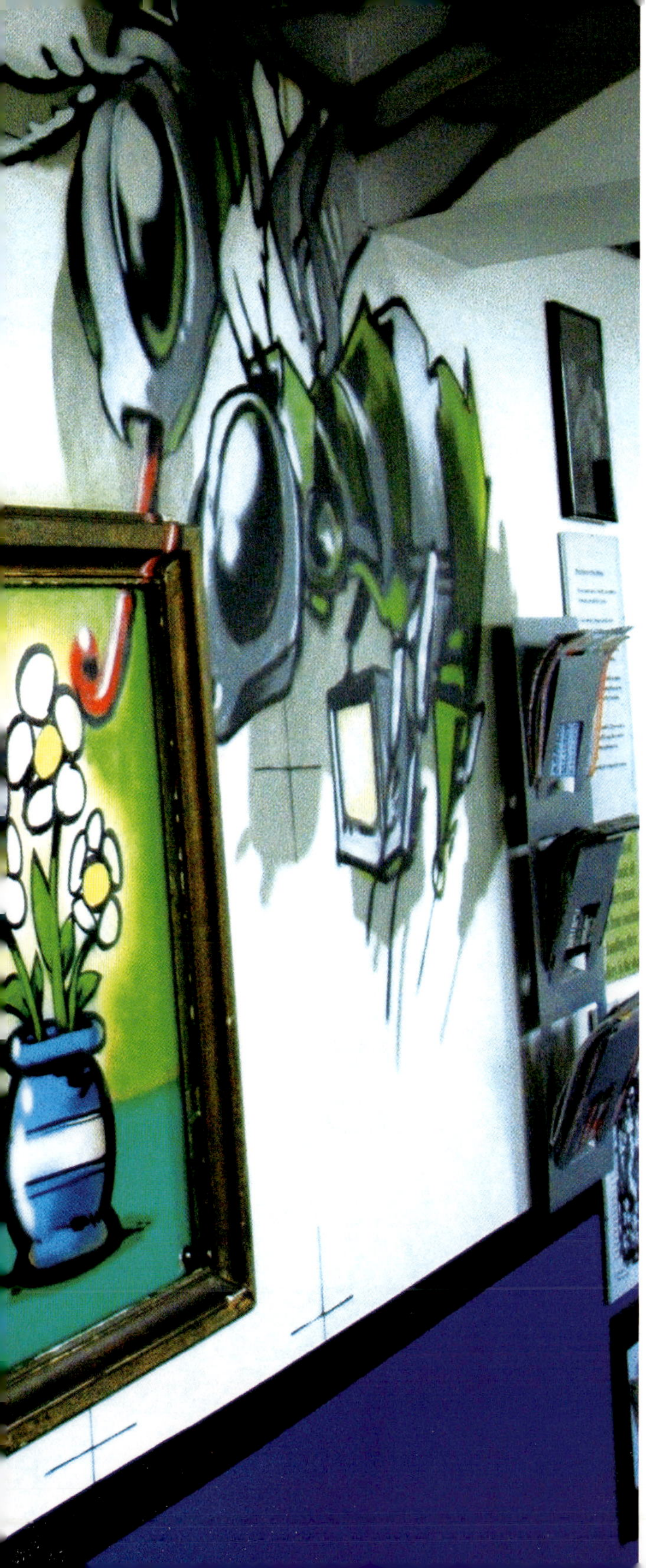

A Banksy original in the Pierced Up tattoo parlour.

extremely dangerous. Even punk, which was the first mass music subculture to really challenge and say 'fuck you' to authority, never aroused the interest of the government to such an extent that it actually got off its arse to find an excuse to legislate against it.

"Operation Snapshot was set up around that time: an intelligence-gathering exercise on raves and Travellers, designed to establish a database of personal details, names, nicknames, vehicle registration numbers, Traveller sites and movements. It was basically an initiative to stop people meeting in public places, to stop them building any kind of community – however temporary. It was the beginning of our surveillance society – a lot of people working with us had their phones bugged, some people working with us in London had been busted by MI5.

"Lots of people were realising that an independent media was the only way to get real social messages across. I think that's one of the great beauties of graffiti: it's public information, unedited and straight from the heart – something that never happens in the conventional mass media. I think that's where a lot of Banksy's anti-authoritarian politics may have come from."

Many of Banksy's pieces are cheeky and defiant – they thumb their noses at authority and urge us not to swallow the usual lines fed us by politicians and big business. And it may be that this wised-up defiance simply rings truer with people in today's more guarded, cynical society than it might have done ten years ago.

"His ideas are striking a real chord with people now," adds Smith. "Five or ten tears ago, it sounded naive to talk about conspiracy theories, to suggest that the government might not necessarily have your best interests at heart. But ever since the Iraq War, the fudged justification for that war and the charade it's been ever since, I think a lot of Banksy's messages are having a lot more resonance. People are more receptive to his ideas."

There's All This Noise...

A particularly thought-provoking Banksy piece (painted with Lokey) commenting on the media was There's All This Noise which was on the side of a building at the Redcliffe end of Welsh Back, but has long-since gone. "It's one of my favourite Banksys – it pretty much sums up most of TV and the media," says Mark Simmons. "The endless, vacuous chatter, how it sucks you in and drains your spirit. It reminds me of a quote I once heard, that as long as you provide the people with enough well-produced light entertainment as a distraction, they won't rebel.

"The thing about Banksy is that he's taken something accessible to all – street art, and with his flair and determination and imagination, has taken it to another level. He's democratised art, made it more accessible – but the irony is that the art world, by pushing up his prices, has hi-jacked that accessibility."

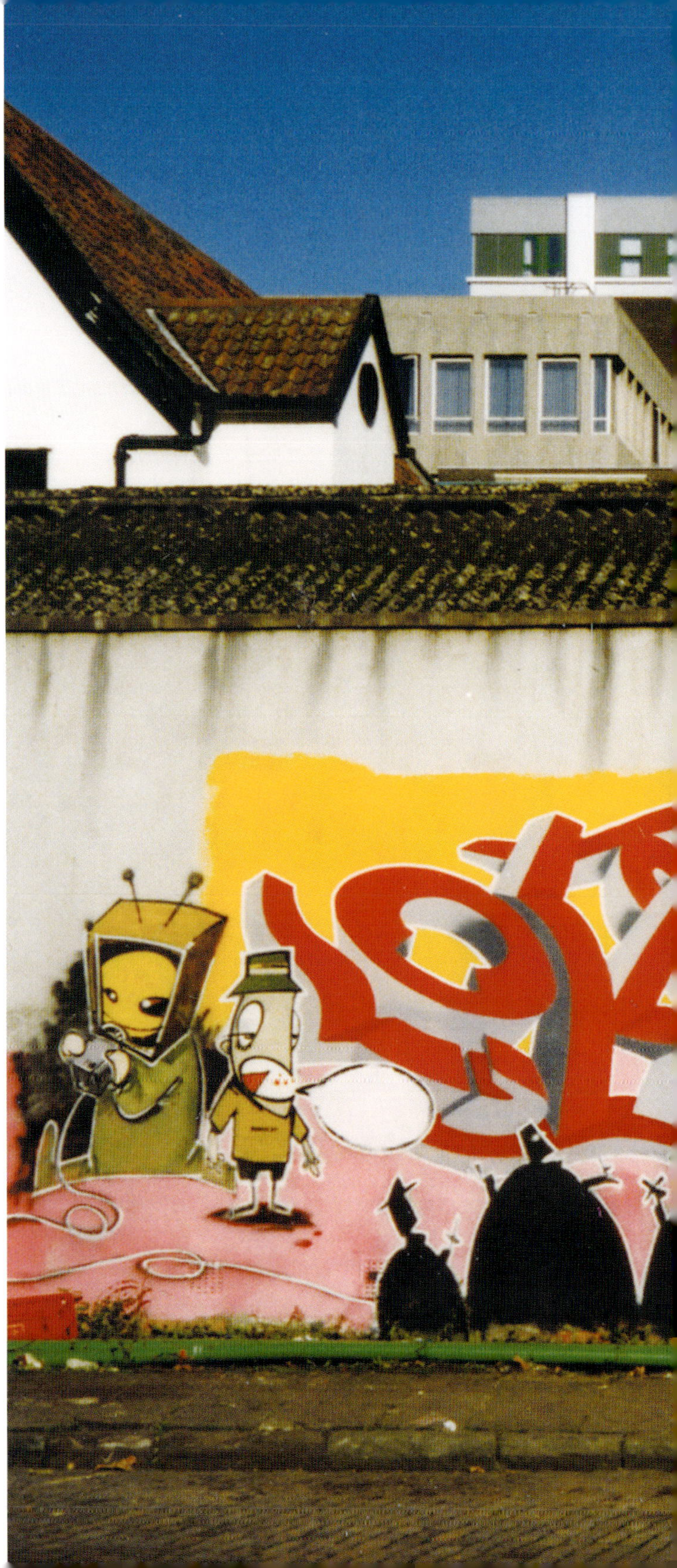

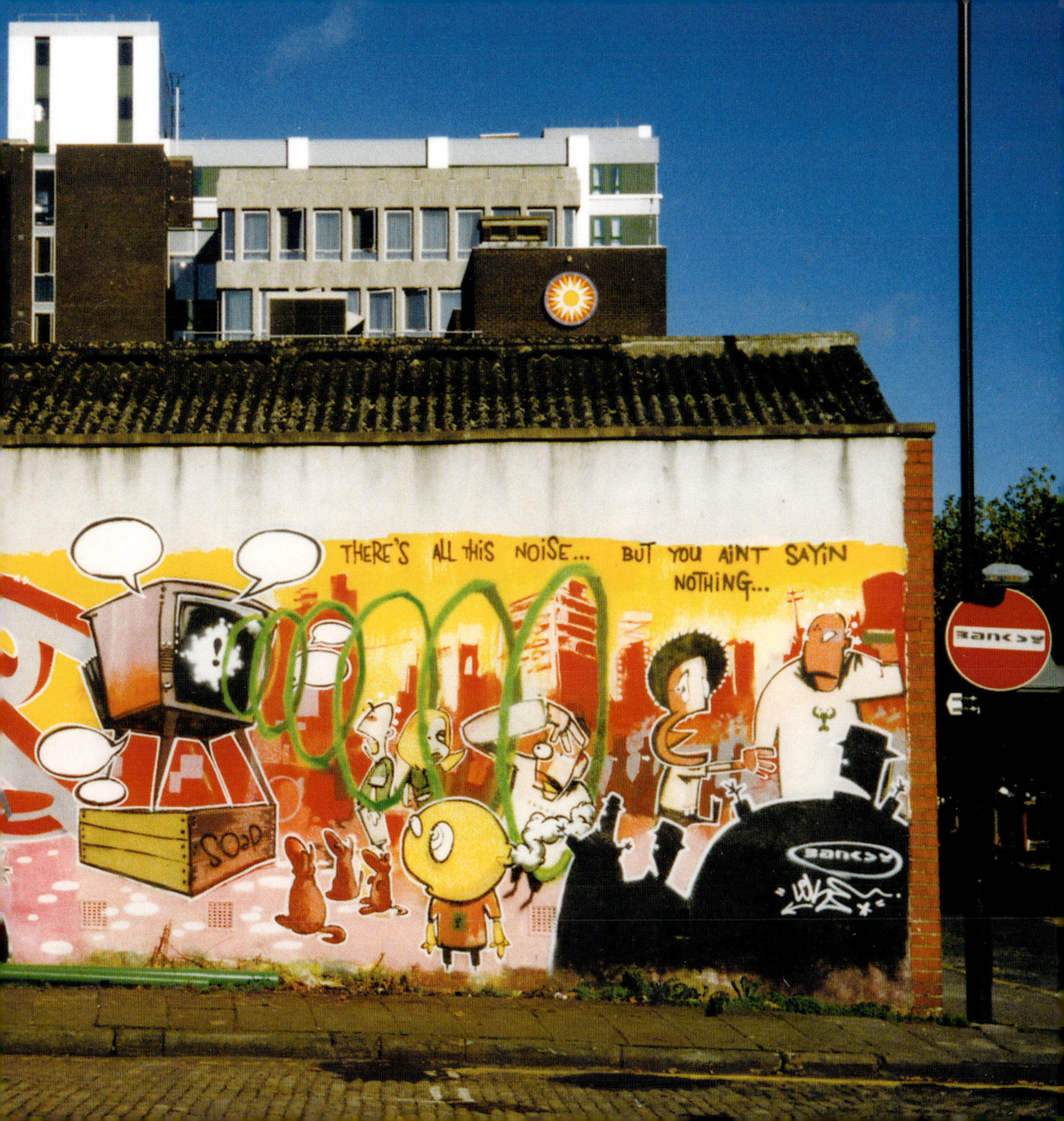
THERE'S ALL THIS NOISE... BUT YOU AINT SAYIN NOTHING...
SOaP

Christmas spirit?

December 2003: Phone giants Orange sponsor a Christmas show in which artists' work is projected onto London's landmarks at night. But Orange censor two pieces of work – one a depiction of the Virgin Mary, her face replaced with a globe and her halo replaced with a peace sign. The other is Banksy's depiction of Jesus, with arms outstretched and weighed down with bags of shopping. "This could have been the most poignant and relevant representation of Christmas for our modern times," laments one observer.

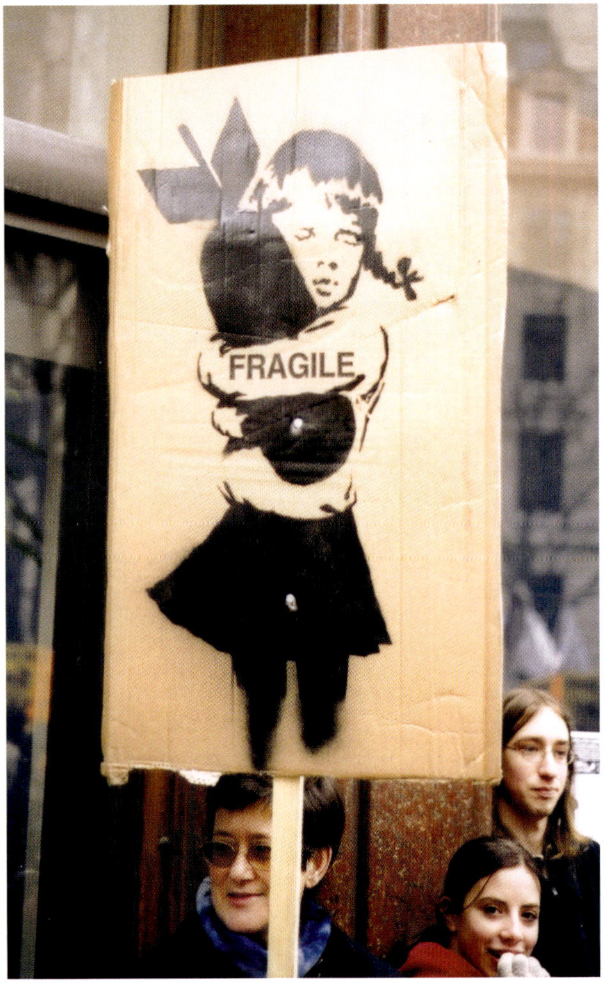

This page: Protestors at an anti-war demo in London with Banksy placards.

That page: Banksy's home-made Christmas card.

The subvertisers

Bristol is the spiritual home of subvertising, a movement with which Banksy has much in common. Subvertising is the practice of altering billboard adverts with often witty, often angry slogans (anti-war, anti-capitalism and, of course, anti-advertising itself). This form shares a lot, of course, with street art, with stencil art especially, and with Banksy's own particular brand perhaps most of all.

Like the stencillers, the subvertisers meticulously prepare their artwork before spending a few minutes mounting it over the billboard; also, like some of Banksy's pastiches of classic pieces from the canon of Western art (his wilting take on Van Gogh's Sunflowers, for example), the message they place is usually designed to be cleverly at odds with the ad they've doctored.

Subvertisers' response to questions about criminal damage is also remarkably similar. "I see it as a right to reply," one subvertiser told *Venue* magazine. "Why should I passively receive these marketing messages but not have a right to respond? Advertising is eating into more and more of our public space, with adverts on the side of buildings, lasers in the sky, on pavements, advertising in schools and hospitals. We have no say in these billboards going up, and some are downright offensive.

"They put adverts for posh, expensive cars up in poor neighbourhoods where people have no chance of ever affording them. I also want people to see that there is resistance, that people are attempting to engage and have a dialogue instead of accepting being mindwashed."

The subverts, like Banksy, have the benefit of universality. "You could hire gallery space and maybe 500 people would see your pictures. With this, thousands of car drivers and pedestrians see it each day." The two forms also share a reliance on humour. "The humorous ones get the best reaction, you get people honking and cheering as they drive by," the subvertiser told *Venue*.

Researching a piece about Bristol's subvertising culture, I asked the editors of south west anarchist magazine *Bristle* why people do this stuff. "A famous subvert from the Eighties comes to mind," came the reply. "The advert read 'If this car was a woman you'd pinch its

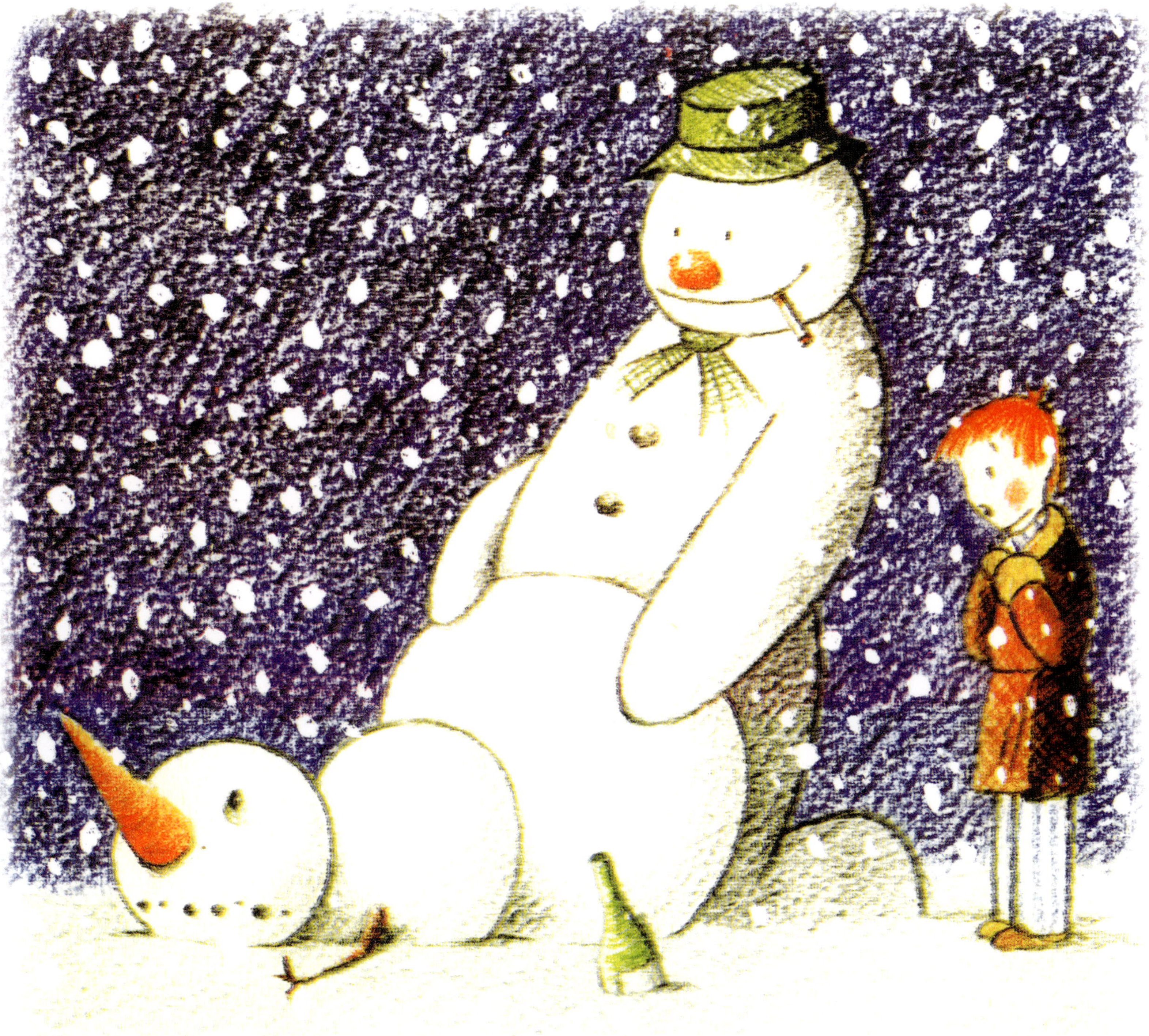

bottom' and the response was 'If this woman was a car she'd run you down'. It's a way of thinking that mocks authority, surveillance and consumerism." Sound familiar?

It all fits in, more generally, with a certain Bristol tradition of subversion, of people doing things their own way, refusing to be led by the prevailing fashions and truisms. *Bristle* itself, for example (in its own words "an anti/post-capitalist magazine which challenges the idea that capitalism is sustainable") spread its leftfield gospel around the city from the mid Nineties until 2007 and in 2005 published a collection of the region's finest subvertising images in *Political Street Expressions in Bristol and the South West.* It all chimes with the points Banksy makes in a short essay called *Brandalism* in *Cut It Out*, the third and final of his 'little black books'. He too clearly feels bombarded, harangued by advertising – or, as he calls, it 'chequebook vandalism':

"They [the advertisers] make flippant comments from buses that imply that you're not sexy enough and that all the fun is happening somewhere else. They are on TV making your girlfriend feel inadequate. They have access to the most sophisticated technology the world has ever seen and they bully you with it. They are The Advertisers and they are laughing at you."

Bristol graffiti artist Rowdy put it this way: "You've got billboards everywhere, people driving too fast with their mobile phone stuck to their ear. Then, when you get home, the television is either trying to sell you stuff or is just bombarding you with trivia or violence. I know graffiti is sometimes offensive too, but that's because it's trying to get a message across. For those of us who are never going to own some two hundred grand property, this is a way of saying that we own this environment too. Some people go out and start a fight in the Centre, this is at least a different way of venting frustration."

This one first appeared on a wall in Clifton before becoming a best-selling print at the old Greenleaf bookshop.

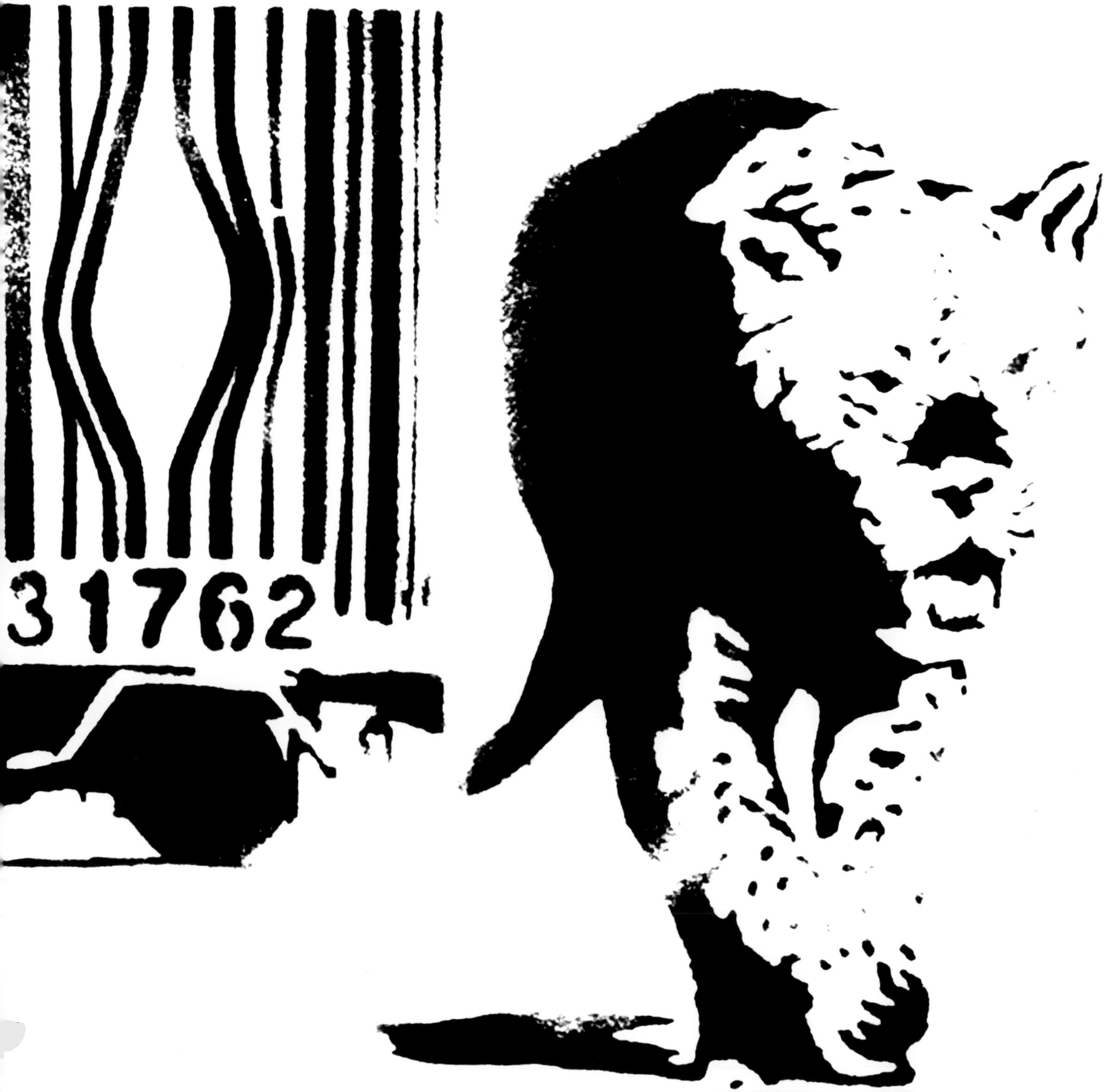
31762

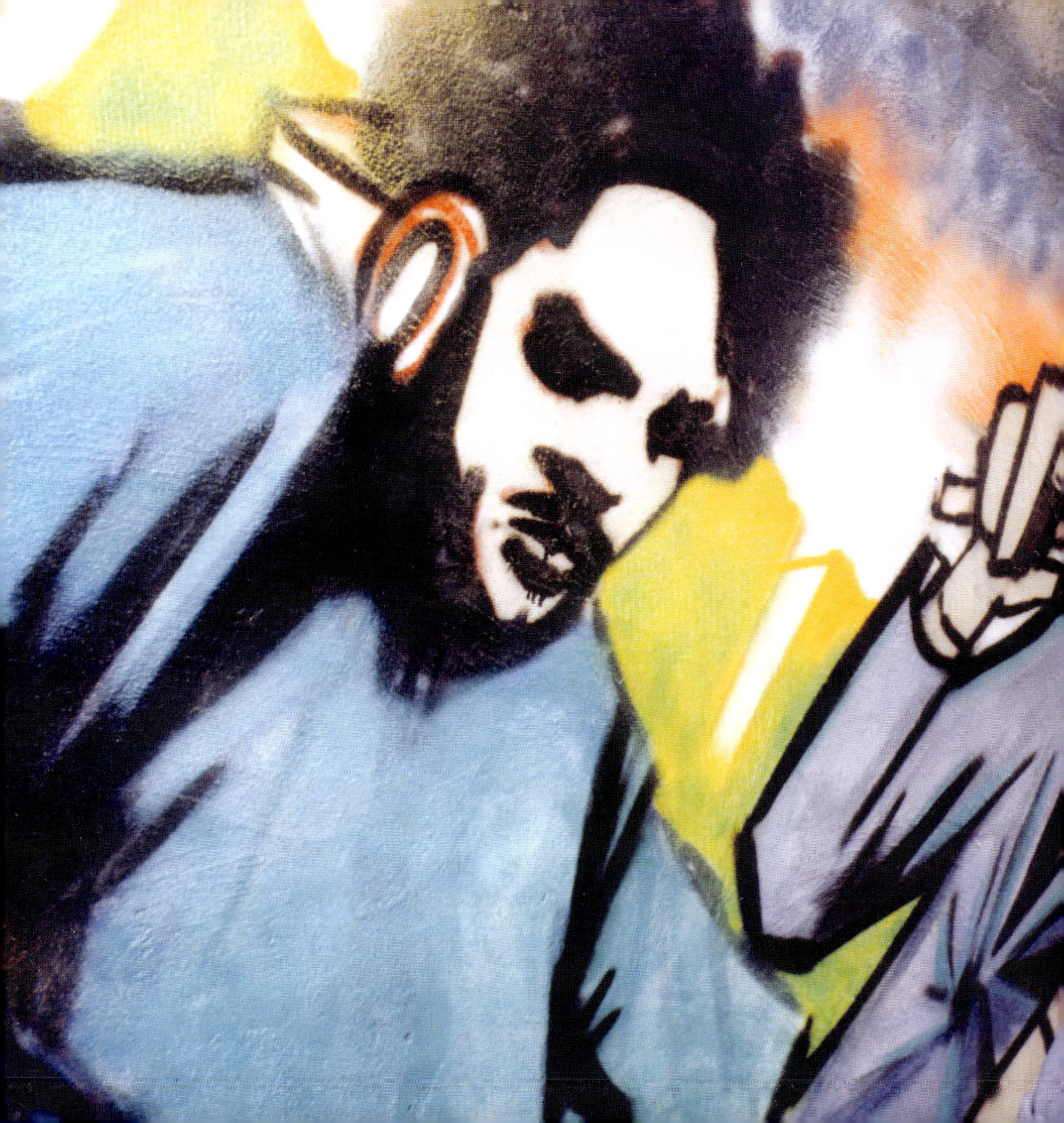

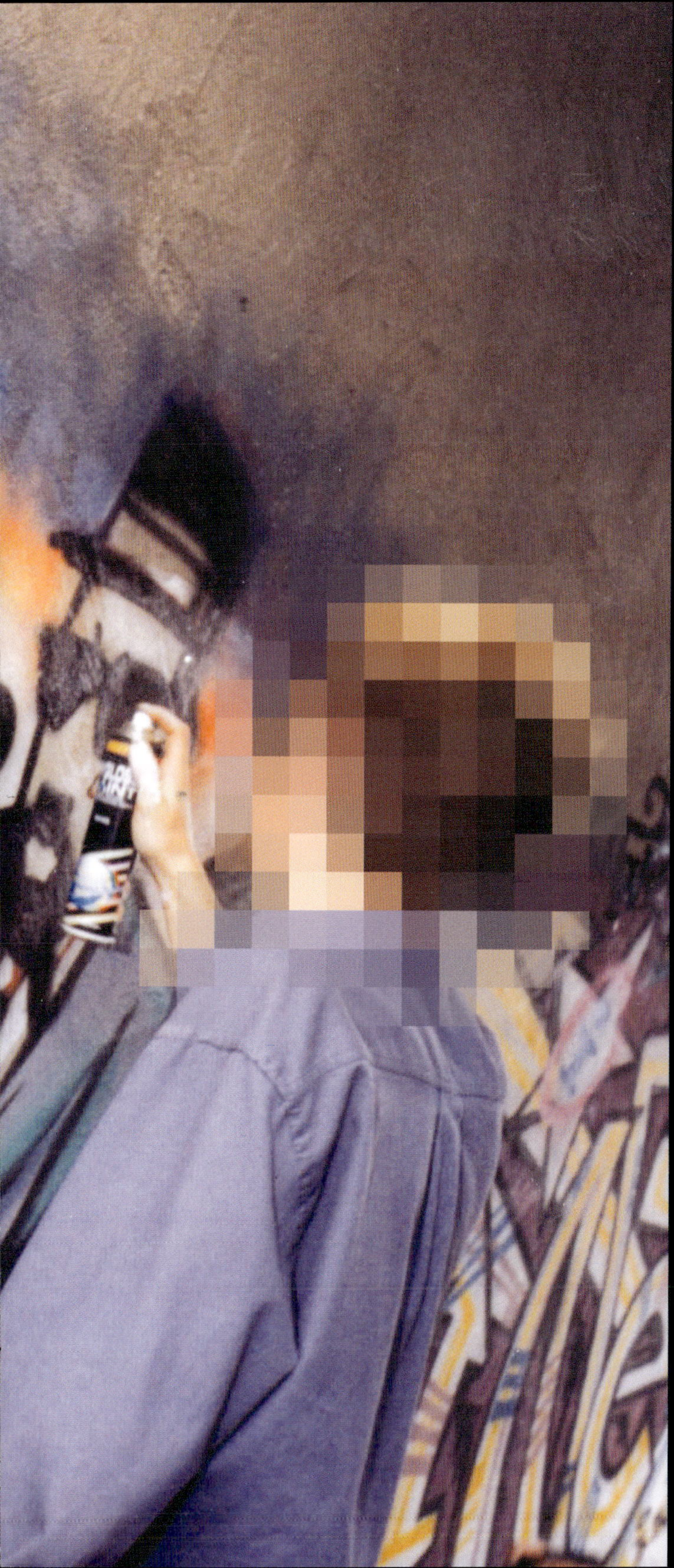

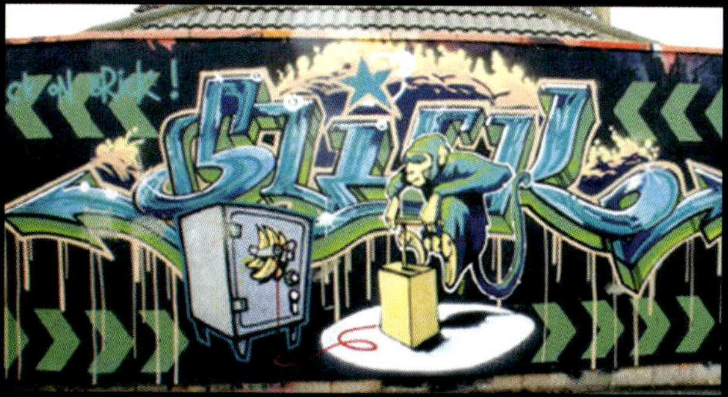

That page: Using a jerk chicken stand as cover, Inkie and Banksy paint an illegal on Grosvenor Road in the middle of the day at St Paul's Carnival.

This page: An Easton freehand piece.

Artist At Work

"The craft is finding a decent drainpipe to get access to the site as much as it is in the art, and that's interesting to people… Van Gogh used short, stumpy brush strokes to convey his insanity – I use short, thin ledges above mainline train tracks."

Banksy quoted in *Bristol Evening Post*, **February 2004**

What can easily be forgotten, among all the froth about Banksy and the glamorous mystery surrounding him, is that the physical realities of doing what he does are almost always far from glamorous. Illegally painting on public spaces takes a hefty amount of resourcefulness, patience, physical fitness and stamina; it often involves heading out at the dead of night, shinnying up buildings or hanging from bridges, knowing exactly which CCTV cameras to dodge and police shift changes to profit from.

Some of Banksy's stunts have amazed and impressed because of the sheer bravery of the event. Walking into some of London and New York's most venerable cultural institutions and sticking his art up on the walls; working in secret, at night, often in dangerous environments. Check out the stories he tells, in *Wall and Piece*, of infiltrating Barcelona Royal Palace, surrounded by armed police. Or, more comically, of being stuck in the same city's Zoo, in the kangaroo enclosure, at midnight. Banksy associate Steve Symons recalls the stunt at London Zoo (where Banksy climbed into the penguin enclosure, daubing 'We're bored of fish' in seven-foot high letters) was one

This page: Banksy's first ever stencil appeared in Windmill Hill in the mid Nineties.

That page: Battling surveillance cameras in Battersea Road, Easton.

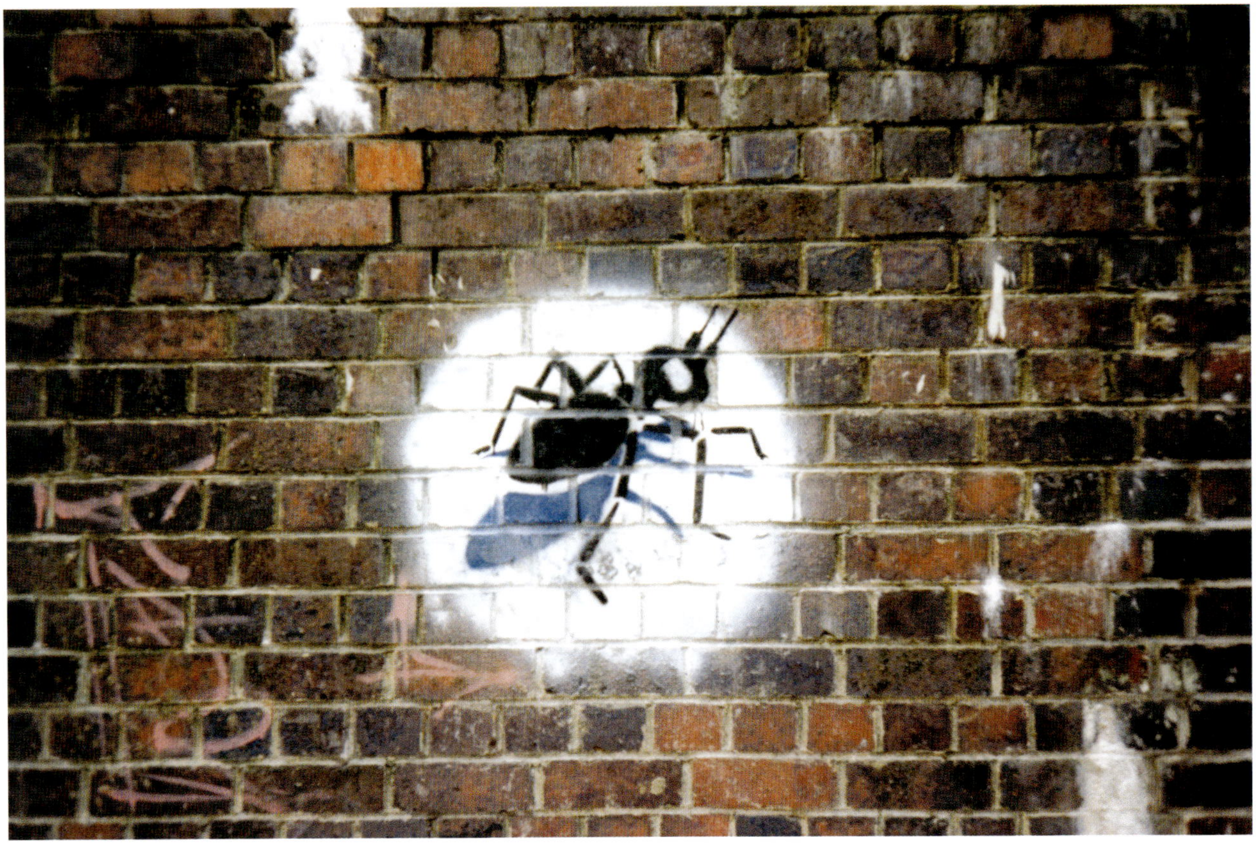

that gave its creator a few nightmares. "He was convinced that the graffiti he did in the penguin enclosure at London Zoo was the one that had wound the police up the most, and that they were really wanted to catch him for."

We know that on one night in Bristol, Banksy painted both Pero's Bridge and the Thekla floating nightclub, because he tells us about it in his book *Cut It Out:*

One night I painted the side of Bristol's new harbour bridge with a message about the slave trade which got painted over within six hours of daybreak. Afterwards, I made the slowest getaway in criminal history splashing through the darkness in a tiny rowing boat before stopping off to paint my name on the side of the Thekla.

"I heard he got chased by the harbour master," adds one Bristol graffer and friend of Banksy's.

Perhaps the most notable trip, even on Banksy's itinerary, was to paint the Palestine Segregation Wall in 2005. During the visit to Ramallah, Banksy reports some tense moments. His spokeswoman Jo Brooks said: "The Israeli security forces did shoot in the air threateningly and there were quite a few guns pointed at him."

Caution – artist at work

"It is incredibly exhilarating going out at night," says Bristol graffer Ghostboy. "It's the adrenaline buzz. And also the response you get: I can get my work up straight away and within days I'll be getting emails from people, the majority very positive.

"It's the cheekiness, getting away with it, living on your nerves. Sometimes you have to be really cheeky and do it in broad daylight. Rush hour is a good time to do it, because police responses are slower."

Banksy talks about his art in pragmatic, not highfalutin' language. He often cites the 'efficiency' of stencil art as

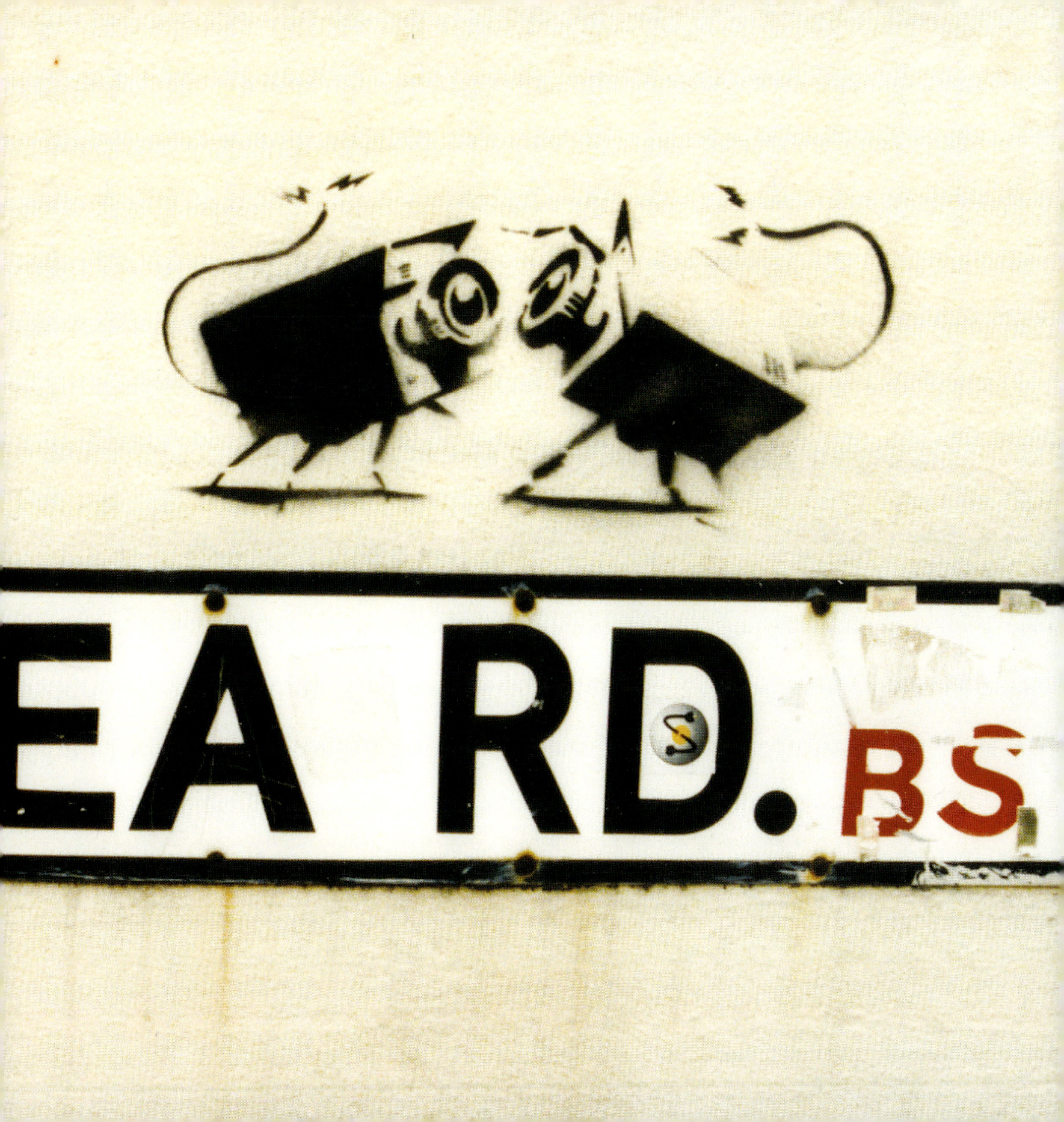
EA RD. BS

the thing that most excites him, as he told *Guardian* interviewer Simon Hattenstone in 2003:

I ask him if you need to be nimble to be a good graffiti artist. "Yeah, it's all part of the job description. Any idiot can get caught. The art to it is not getting picked up for it, and that's the biggest buzz at the end of the day because you could stick all my shit in Tate Modern and have an opening with Tony Blair and Kate Moss on roller blades handing out vol-au-vents and it wouldn't be as exciting as it is when you go out and you paint something big where you shouldn't do. The feeling you get when you sit at home on the sofa at the end of that, having a fag and thinking, there's no way they're going to rumble me, it's amazing... better than sex, better than drugs, the buzz."

How not to get caught

From the early Eighties, one of Bristol's original street artists Nick Walker was heading out to create his urban canvases at 4am to coincide with police shift changes: "You're always nervous about being caught, but, after you've had a few pints you get Dutch courage, and you feel like a superhero," he told *Venue* magazine in March 2006. "We're brought up in a society where everywhere you look, there's some billboard telling you to buy this or vote for that. If their views are up there in massive letters, why shouldn't yours be? So you find that wall you've always wanted to paint, and just go and do it. Daytime was best: no-one expects you to do it then, and no-one does anything about it either: they're too wrapped up in their own little worlds."

On his website, Banksy once told the story of how he was standing in a shallow switched-off fountain in the small hours, spraying a piece, when his low-slung jeans (no belt, in the hip hop style) began creeping down his legs. Needing one hand to spray and the other to hold the stencil in place, he couldn't pull his jeans up, and needed to finish the piece fast to avoid arrest. He finished it "standing in a kind of Led Zeppelin rock pose to keep my sodden, beltless jeans from falling into the water. There was no way I was going to let go of the stencil before it was done, so eventually I lost the trousers all together."

His tip? "Fuck hip hop – wear a belt."

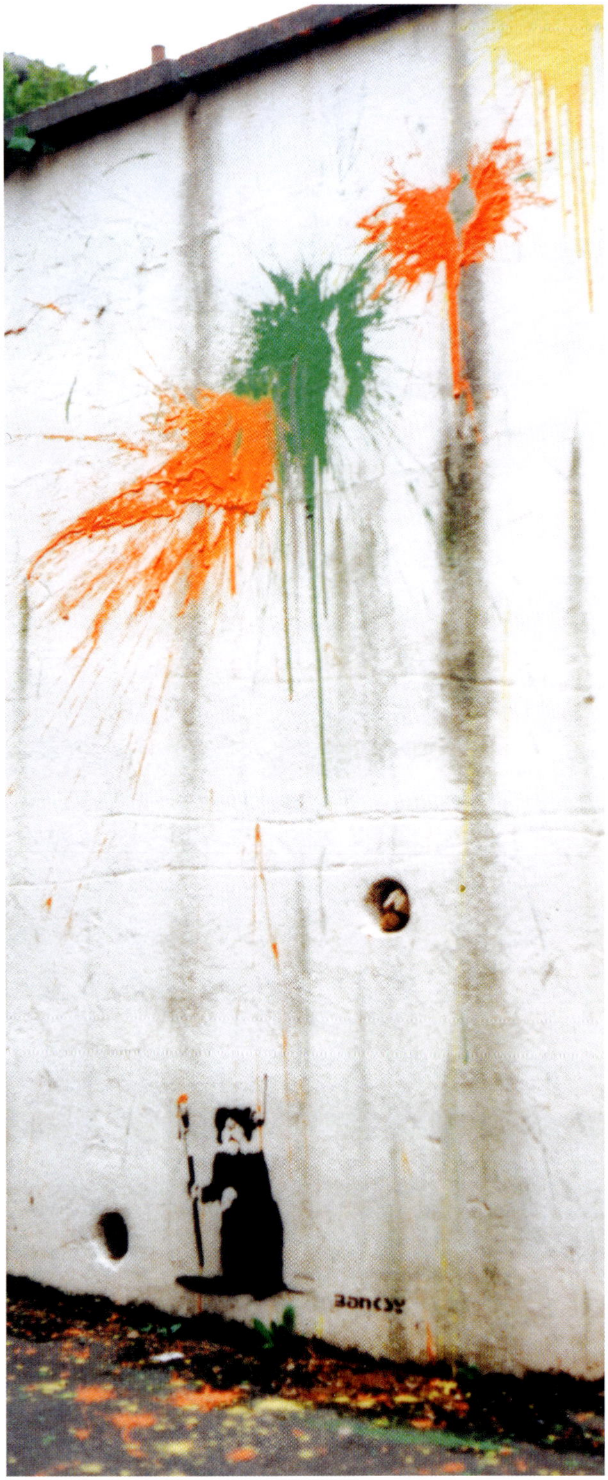

Banksy and stencils

From where we see it now, Banksy's career seems to have taken off from the moment he ditched freehand graffiti and picked up a stencil. But, as this close friend and collaborator tells us, Banksy's use of stencils goes back a lot further.

"The very first time I met him, probably 1992-94 time, he was down Bedminster skate park hanging around as we were painting, and he'd been doing these 'ant' stencils everywhere. I had seen them before and wondered what they were. We got chatting, and started to hook up every now and then. When we first went to his house/studio, what struck me straight away was that it was a hive of creativity. His conversation was full of plans for different projects and ideas for putting up work around the city.

"The first time we painted pieces together, he mixed freehand graff with stencils. I think it was just easier to put work out on the streets with stencils, rather than freehand stuff... a more instant, prominent hit.

"You have to realise that stencilling had been around already, not particularly in Bristol (although Nick Walker was already using stencils in his work), but definitely in Paris and a bit in London. Banksy was just very prolific, so before long his stencils started to appear all around, and people started making out it was a new thing."

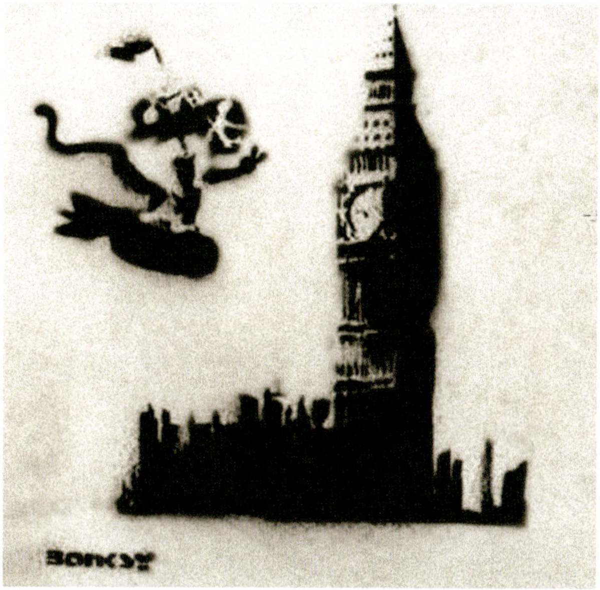

Animals feature strongly in Banksy's work, particularly rats. Rat is an anagram of art...

Ghostboy on stencils

"I did a bit of freehand stuff when I was about 18 for a year or two, but back then I think most graffiti only appealed to other graffers. I started placing sculptural stuff on the streets as well as stencils, but the stencils just seemed to resonate with other people more (maybe it's because they are less cartoon-like). I also think that less is more, and the punchiness of stencils works better if you are trying to get something across. The hard work goes on in the studio and the convenience of banging a stencil up means you can get them in more appropriate places.

"Banksy's career did take off when he went from freehand to stencil. That was partly because it was still relatively unusual to see street stencils in this country when he started doing them, so they had the curiosity value. Also, you can put up 20-30 stencils in the time that it takes to do a decent freehand piece, which means you can get them seen by more people. The more people see your work, the better. Political activists have used stencils for years in other countries, and so have the army (to label their ammunition crates and vehicles), so the form was begging to be used – and subverted – by artists."

This page: Death wears a smile...

That page: A canvas from Banksy's early Easton exhibition.

Bristol Zoo

"I remember the night Banksy did Bristol Zoo," recalls photographer and Banksy acquaintance Matthew Smith. "The evening before, I was at the Black Swan in Easton, and he was there too, along with a bunch of mutual friends. At 4am, I got this call from him, saying he was down at the zoo and would I come and take some pictures the next morning because he was about to do the seal sanctuary and a couple of other places.

"The next morning, around 9.30, having been up all night and quite the worse for wear, I got to the zoo. I found the seal sanctuary and shot a few pictures of Banksy's work. It was a big 'We demand more fish now!' slogan with an A for anarchy, on the wall at the back of the sanctuary.

"I was snapping away when I was rudely interrupted by the arrival of a group of about ten police, who must have been alerted by the Zoo. I just kept my eye on my camera and pretended to be photographing the seals."

Banksy elaborated on his philosophy in an interview with *Swindle* magazine: "Ultimately, I just want to make the right piece at the right time in the right place. Anything that stands in the way of achieving that piece is the enemy, whether it's your mum, the cops, someone telling you that you sold out, or someone saying, 'Let's just stay in tonight and get pizza'."

On several occasions, Banksy has used plain cheek and ingenuity to do what he does. This graffer and close friend of Banksy's spilled the beans on how Banksy's iconic Well-Hung Man on Frogmore Street in central Bristol was achieved.

"Banksy organised for some scaffolding to be put up on the building, with full covering over it, like when they're taking off render and the cover keeps debris from flying everywhere. On a Sunday, once the scaffolding and covering was up, the piece was painted pretty much under cover from anyone on the street. When he'd finished, he just had to phone the scaffold company to take it down... job done!

"He will have taken a lot of care designing that one, studying the surroundings to make sure it fits, even taking measurements. Take a close look and you'll see that the window has been drawn to exactly replicate those just around the corner of the building; and its base is on exactly the same level as the other windows. As for the naked man hanging down, you can see his muscles stretching and straining as he hangs. You can feel the gravity pulling him downward. That's why that piece works so well and is so popular – for a few seconds it will deceive any onlooker."

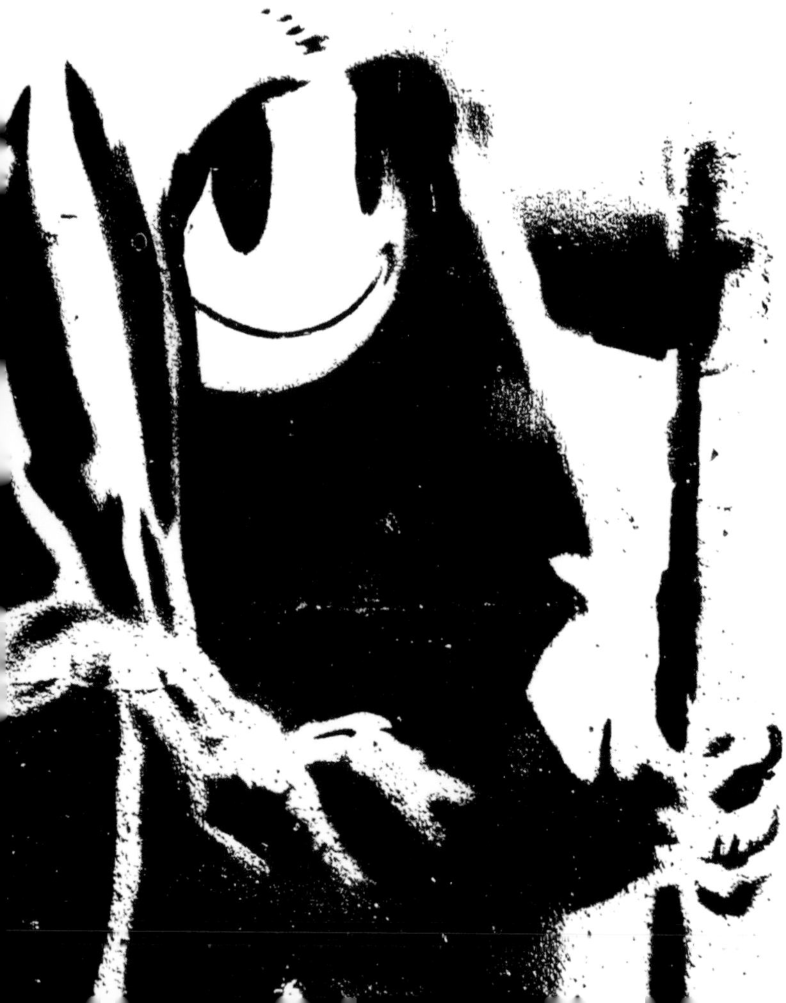

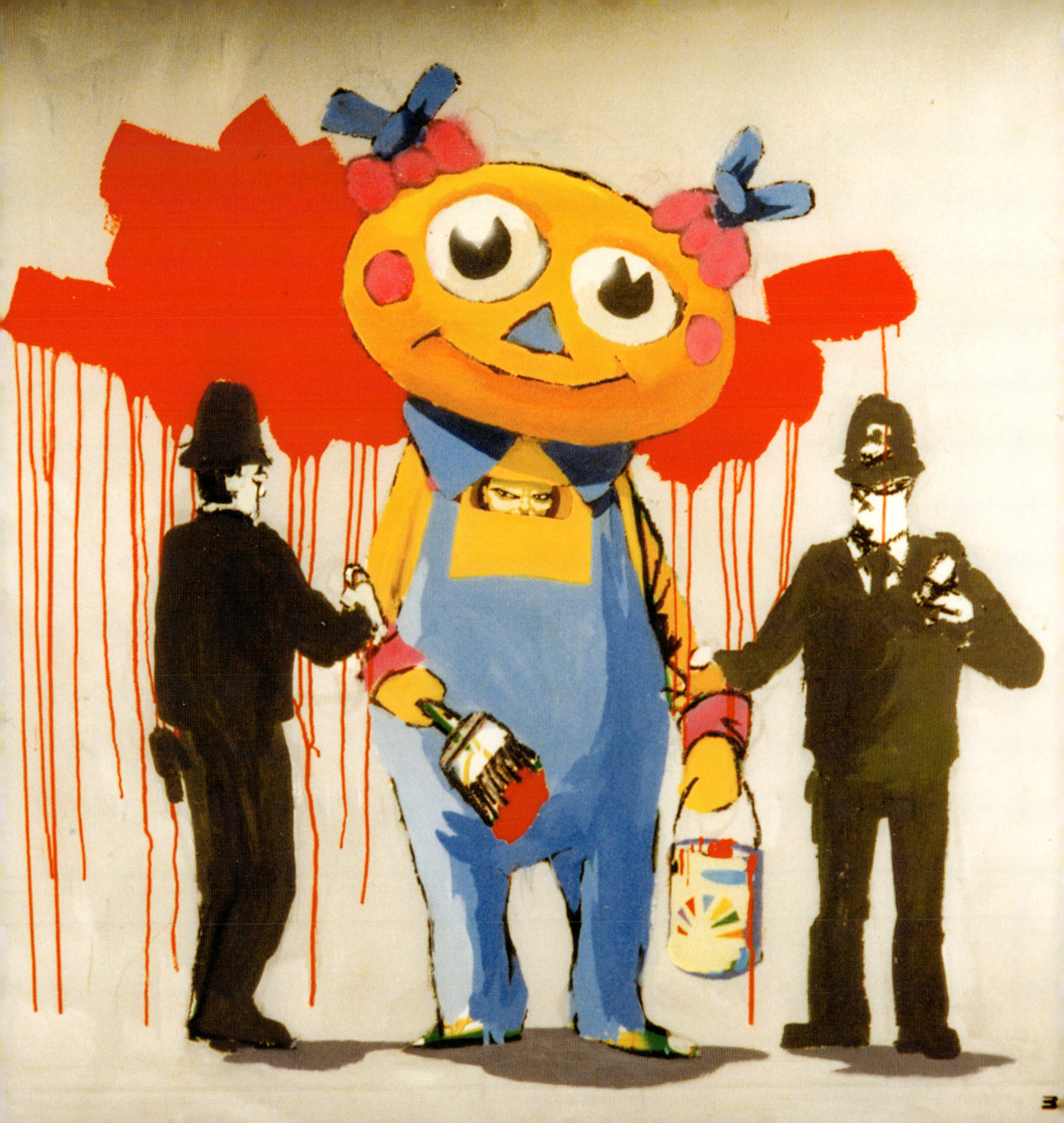

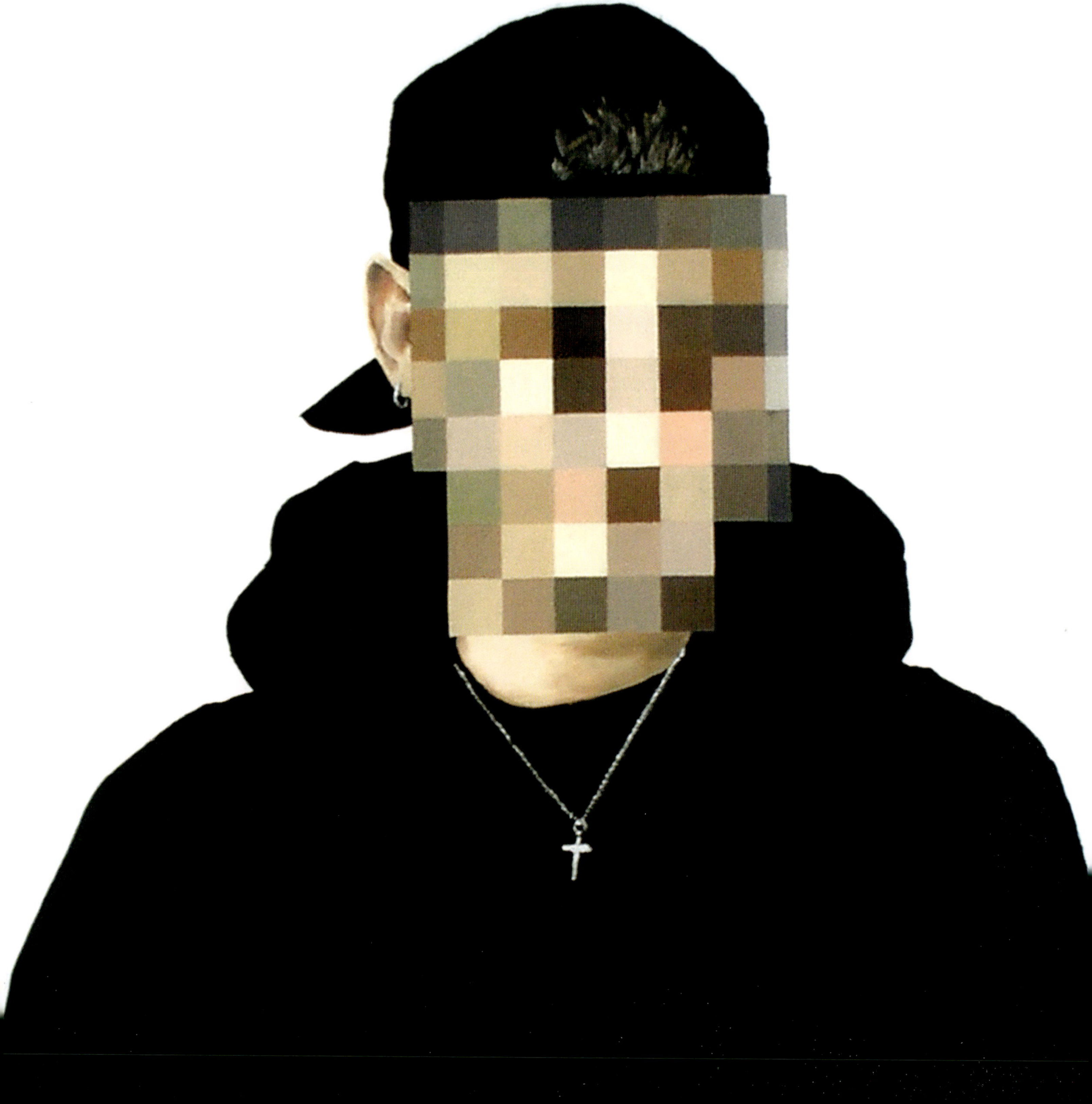

That page: A Banksy self-portrait

Anonymity Rules

"I have no interest in ever coming out. I figure there are enough self-opinionated assholes trying to get their ugly little faces in front of you as it is."
Banksy in *Swindle* magazine, Issue 08

It's quite a thing to maintain anonymity – especially when you're having the impact Banksy is. In many ways Banksy is one of the most recognisable brands on the planet, but no one outside his social circle knows what he's called, or what he looks like. How does he manage this? Part of his continued anonymity comes down to the amount of loyalty he commands from his friends – so much so that people will steadfastly refuse to give away clues about him. His mix of extremely prominent, attention-grabbing stunts and near-complete personal mystery is unique, an impressive kind of reverse exhibitionism.

Why has he maintained this anonymity? To elude the police, of course – but is it not also an attempt to construct a powerful aura, a cult of Banksy? He might well scoff at that notion, but it has undeniably been the main consequence of his anonymity. Would we value him as much if we knew his identity? The fact is that the myths and the Banksy 'brand' are more interesting than a few bald facts abut him.

"The anonymity is a very useful device, quite apart from the sheer necessity of not getting caught: because it gives Banksy's art a longer shelf life," says Martin Roberts (not his real name), a friend from the free party scene. "It's much more interesting to be able to look at his art work without getting too involved in his personality, without trying to project his personality on it. He's famous but somehow non-famous, because no one knows who he is. And that's the best situation to be in: he's made a lot of money doing

Banksy originally started painting graffiti with the DBS crew from east Bristol. DBS included Kato, Lokey, Juster, Soker and Tes – most of whom are still painting in Bristol today.

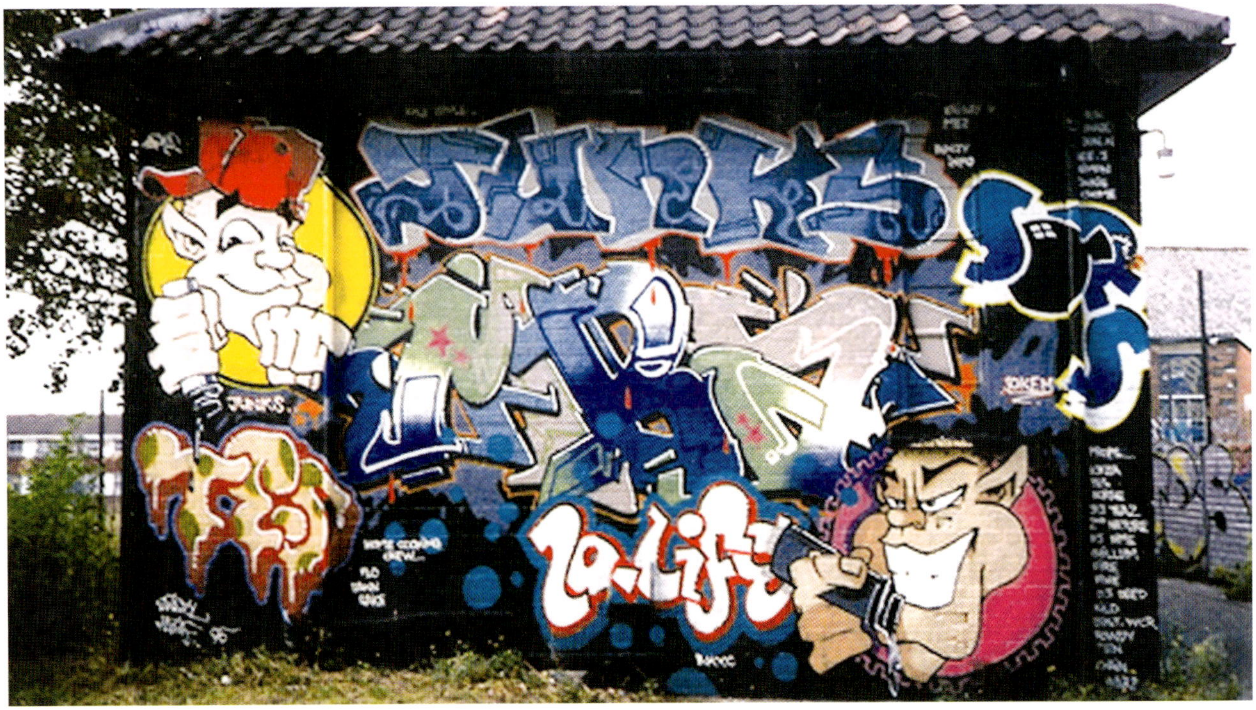

something he loves, and yet still has complete control over his image – he isn't public property at all. Also, people like to build people up and then knock them down – as we've done with Beckham, Barrymore, Britney, whoever. But it's quite hard to knock someone down without even knowing who they are.

"When Banksy makes statements, it's more potent because it's just the statement that we hear – it doesn't get mixed up in our perception of who he is. Contrast that with, for example, David Hockney fulminating about his right to smoke in public, or, worse, Madonna or David Beckham getting into the Kabbalah. It's difficult to take them seriously, to listen purely to what they have to say on the subject, because you're basically just thinking, 'Yeah, come off it! This is David Hockney or David Beckham talking here!' You can't divorce what they say from what you know about them. Banksy's mystery makes his views somehow more authentic. Part of the appeal is that we don't know who he is, so we can engage with his art without having that dulled by our knowledge of him, or by a celebrity obsession with him."

Banksy seems to agree with this view himself. As he notes in his book *Existencilism*:

You find that people who know you rarely listen to a word you say, even though they'll happily take as gospel the word of a man they've never met if it's on a record or in a book. If you want to say something and have people listen then you have to wear a mask. If you want to be honest then you have to live a lie.

Being yourself is overrated

In the words of one Banksy acquaintance: "Banksy's a clever guy, but keeping your mouth shut can make you seem much more intelligent than you really are."

The anonymity, though, seems to be purely pragmatic, with the mystique being a (fortunate?) by-product. "You've got to have a degree of anonymity as a graffiti artist," says Ghostboy. "You don't want to go giving out your name, address and telephone number if you're committing crimes. It's risky work. How can you concentrate on the work if you're answering the door to the police? But yes, it does help keep the intrigue alive. You have this bizarre ongoing 'who is he?', intrigue, which is also propped up by the media, because they get so many column inches from it. Once that anonymity ends, it's kind of game over as far as they're concerned."

Banksy, again: "Being yourself is overrated anyway. It doesn't help. People say 'I'm just being myself' as if that's some kind of fucking achievement. That's not an achievement, that's not honesty, it's lack of imagination and cowardice."

Steve Symons met the artist regularly when he shared a Stokes Croft office with Banksy's former manager. "I once got a call from a friend on the *Observer* saying he was going to email me a picture of Banksy, and would I say if it was him or not. I was like, 'well, no, because he wants to retain his anonymity'. He sent me the picture anyway, and it was a picture that's been used in the media quite a few times, and claimed to be 'Banksy'. So I said, 'well, I don't know if you'll believe me after all I've said, but that's not him'. My friend was like, 'brilliant, that's exactly what we thought. The *Daily Mail* printed this a couple of weeks ago, so we've got one over on them'. And then I noticed, a few weeks later, the photo appeared, captioned as Banksy, in the *Guardian*. It just seems to go around and around. So he does very well at maintaining his anonymity."

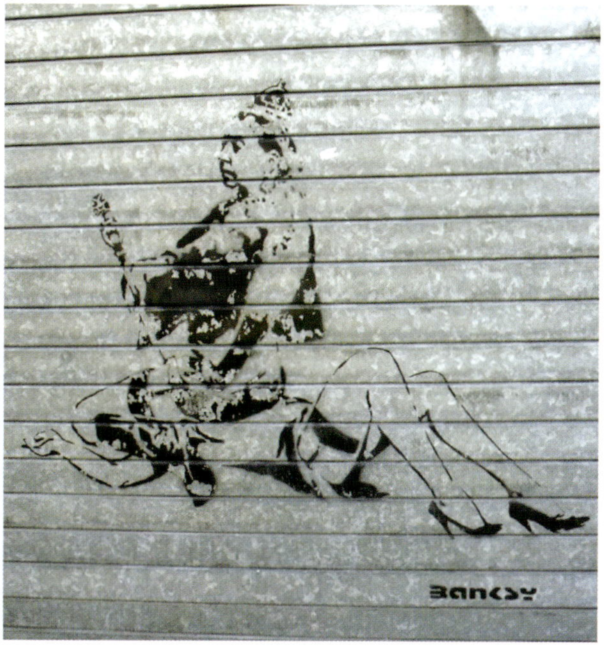

The Queen Victoria pieces were removed pretty quickly. This one survived longest because it was on the shutter of a shop that stayed open until 9pm.

Banksy and me: MsBehaviour

Helen Baxter, aka MsBehaviour, lived in Bristol in the 1990s, when she was Helen Rees. She is now a DJ in New Zealand

"Banksy's art was part of my urban landscape. You never knew what might lie around the next corner. He made my walk to work a little more bearable. His ode to Free Party Abi, teddy bears in the Mild Mild West, monkeys, rats, clowns. Disturbing, political, or laugh-out-loud.

"We met a few times at The Farm (a pub in St Werburgh's) over a pint or three, and I saw him in action once at Glastonbury. He was intelligent, softly spoken, and always taking the piss out of everything and everyone – including himself. He loved doing pieces for the kids, and hated any celebrity shit. I live in New Zealand now but felt a glow of Bristol pride when I saw his art on walls in Palestine. I laughed my ass off when I saw his pink elephant in LA. He still makes me smile. He still makes me think. Is Banksy for real? Definitely."

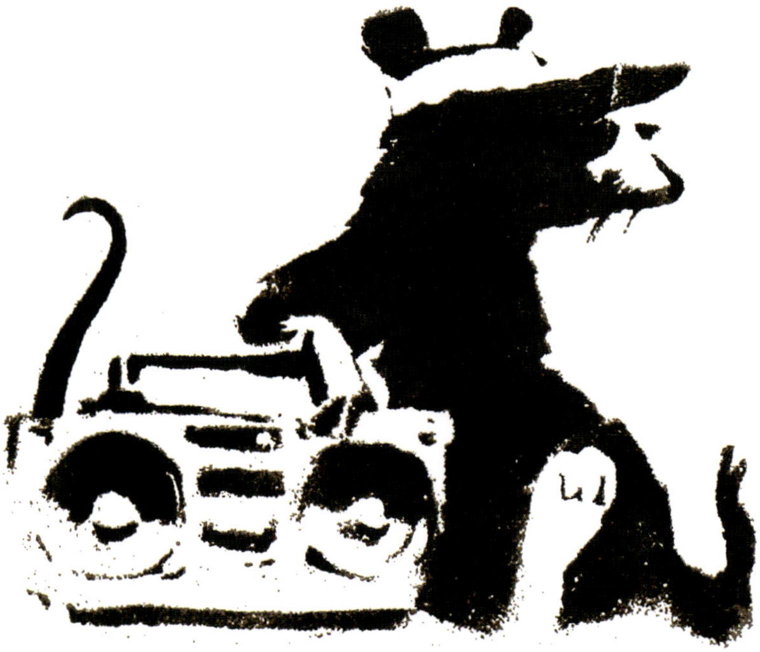

John Mitchell

John Mitchell was *Venue* editor from 1998-99, during which time he interviewed Banksy and put him on the cover of the magazine

"I got to know Banksy through Inkie, who I knew well at the time, and what I liked about both of their work was that they were taking spray art out of its self-ordained Wildstyle* ghetto and into all sorts of new areas. I worked with them in 1998, when they decorated the Glastonbury Dance Tent together.

"At the time, Banksy and Inkie were doing a huge range of styles – everything from gothic lettering to big clown figures. Then Banksy moved away to concentrate much more on the stencilling. He wasn't a national name in those days – he was quite well-known around Bristol and he was quite enjoying his anonymous notoriety, but it was a long time before he sprang onto the national stage. He was enjoying the attention he got from women, and doing his own particular innovative flavour of art.

"*Wild Style* was a phenomenally influential film on the original Bristol pioneers, and it continues to exert a great (I would argue an undue) influence over artists. Banksy's art was just so much more intelligent than the fairly repetitive, tag-based stuff you were seeing around town until then. It was taking graffiti into a whole new arena where no one had gone before. It was more politically engaged, funnier, more provocative. I remember there was another graffiti crew in Bristol at the time who had completely the opposite perspective: for them, *Wild Style* was the beginning and the end. Their mission was simply to repeat what was all around the New York subways, all around Bristol. Inkie and Banksy, who were kind of a duo in those days, took a far more individualistic outlook.

"He struck me as being a thoroughly nice guy – very thoughtful, not particularly on a mission to change the world or raise political awareness. He just wanted to do his art and produce stuff that made people think a little. His work was still developing at the time – his recent stuff is much more technically and creatively advanced. He was getting the stencil thing going, mainly because it allowed him to operate faster.

"He came into the *Venue* offices before an interview. He didn't seem that bothered about being recognised – but this was before things took off for him. I never thought that Banksy's anonymity was a pretentious thing, it was for self-protection. If you're spraying all over public property, you need to be anonymous. But I was a bit concerned when my 12-year-old daughter developed a crush on him, and I asked why and she said, 'he's sooo mysterious'."

** Wildstyle is a highly expressive, intricate freehand graffiti style, which uses interwoven and overlapping letters and shapes. It had its roots in 1970s New York City and has been hugely popular and influential ever since.* Wild Style *is also the name of a seminal 1982 film about old-school hip hop and graffiti culture.*

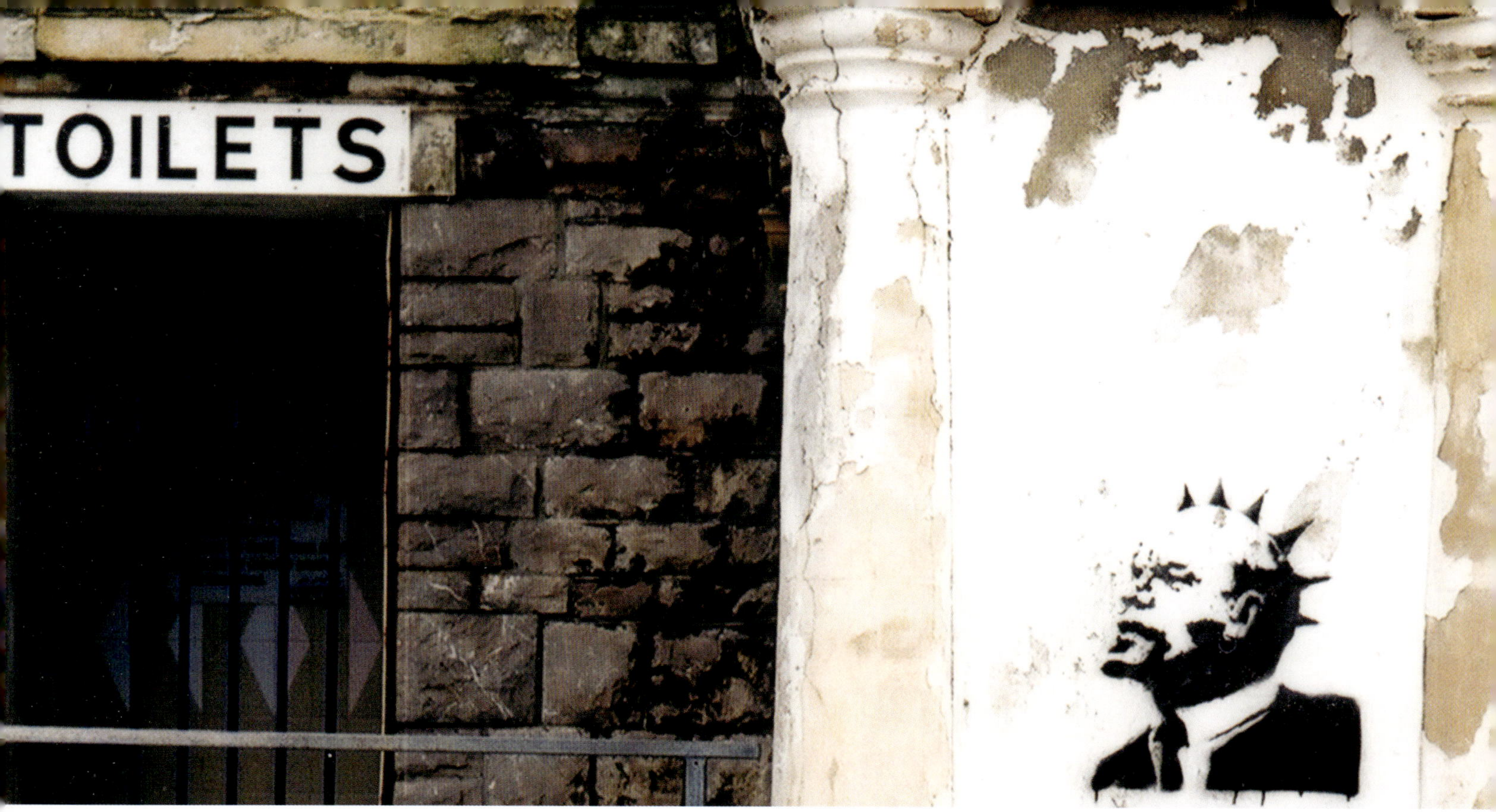

A 1997 stencil outside public toilets in Weston-super-Mare.

In the picture

Bristol graphic designer Azlan took a rare official shot of Banksy

"Like most graffiti artists, Banksy preferred to remain anonymous, and felt cagey revealing his identity to the press for fear of prosecution by the police. I remember taking a portrait photograph of him for an early artist feature in a drum 'n' bass magazine in 1997. We decided to have him move in the shot to blur his identity. As far as I know, it was the first and only official image taken of him. In later press photographs, his old housemate would pose for the cameras wearing a mask.

"The whole thing about his anonymity was really created by the media for the media. They seemed to latch onto a shred of information they thought unusual and slowly re-invented Banksy as a mythical artist, not a person. Now it seems that the more mythical his identity, the more notorious his artwork/stunts have become."

Lizard kings

Petunia Begent went to the Lizard Festival, during the total solar eclipse of 1999, with Banksy

"I remember we were all sitting around, the three of us – Banksy, Sally, my friend who knew Banksy well, and me. I didn't know him that well. We'd heard about this festival down on The Lizard in Cornwall to coincide with the solar eclipse, and we all really wanted to go, but we needed to do something to get some money together while we were there. We'd all been to a few festivals that summer and were pretty skint.

"We decided to do a stall at the festival. I suggested selling these Chinese fortune sticks, and Sally wanted to do a jewellery stand, but Banksy was up for something a bit different. He said, 'let's do a coconut shy!' I asked him how he planned to do that, and within five minutes he'd sketched out exactly how the stall would look. He was like that – completely focussed and sure of what he wanted to

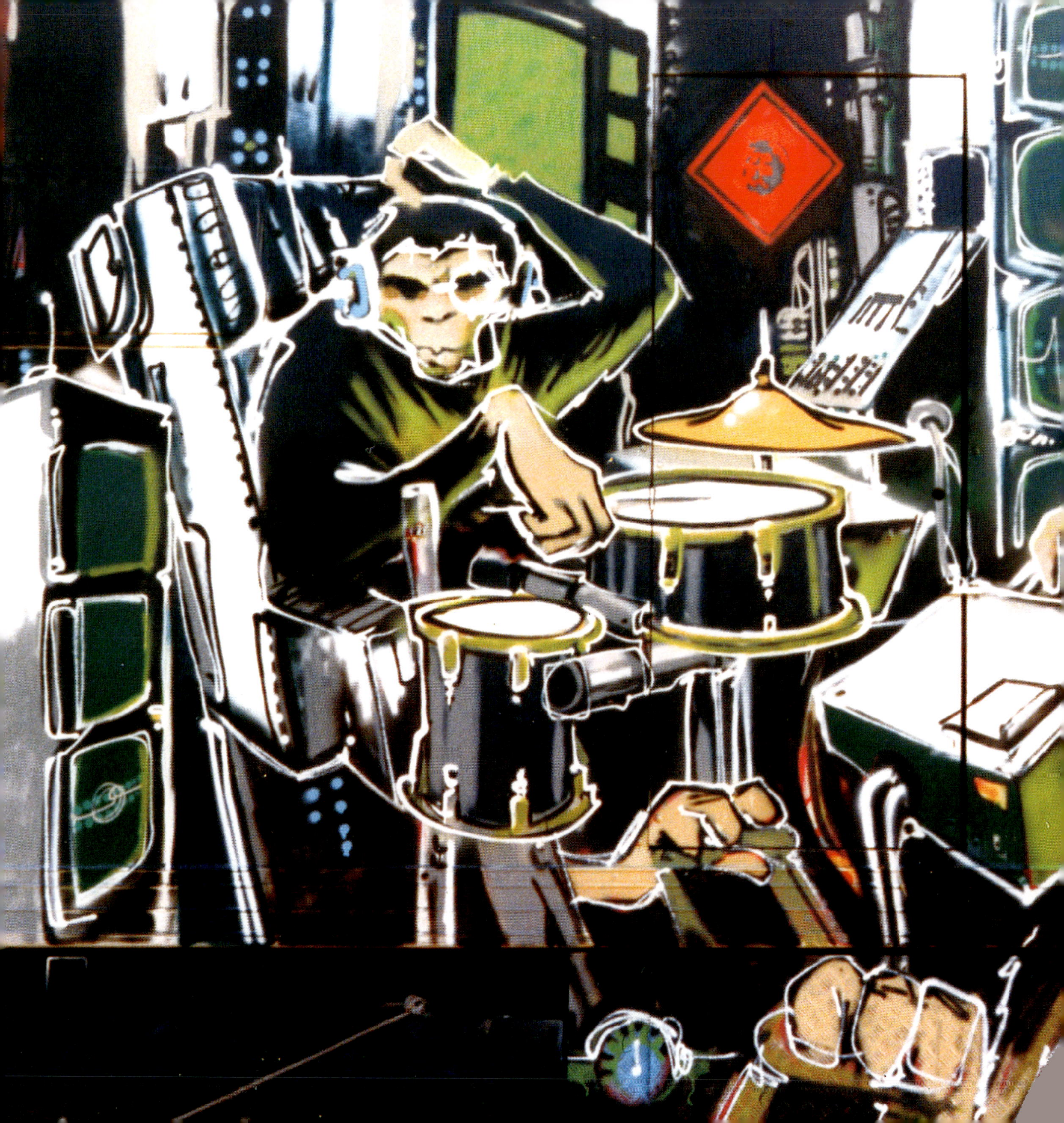

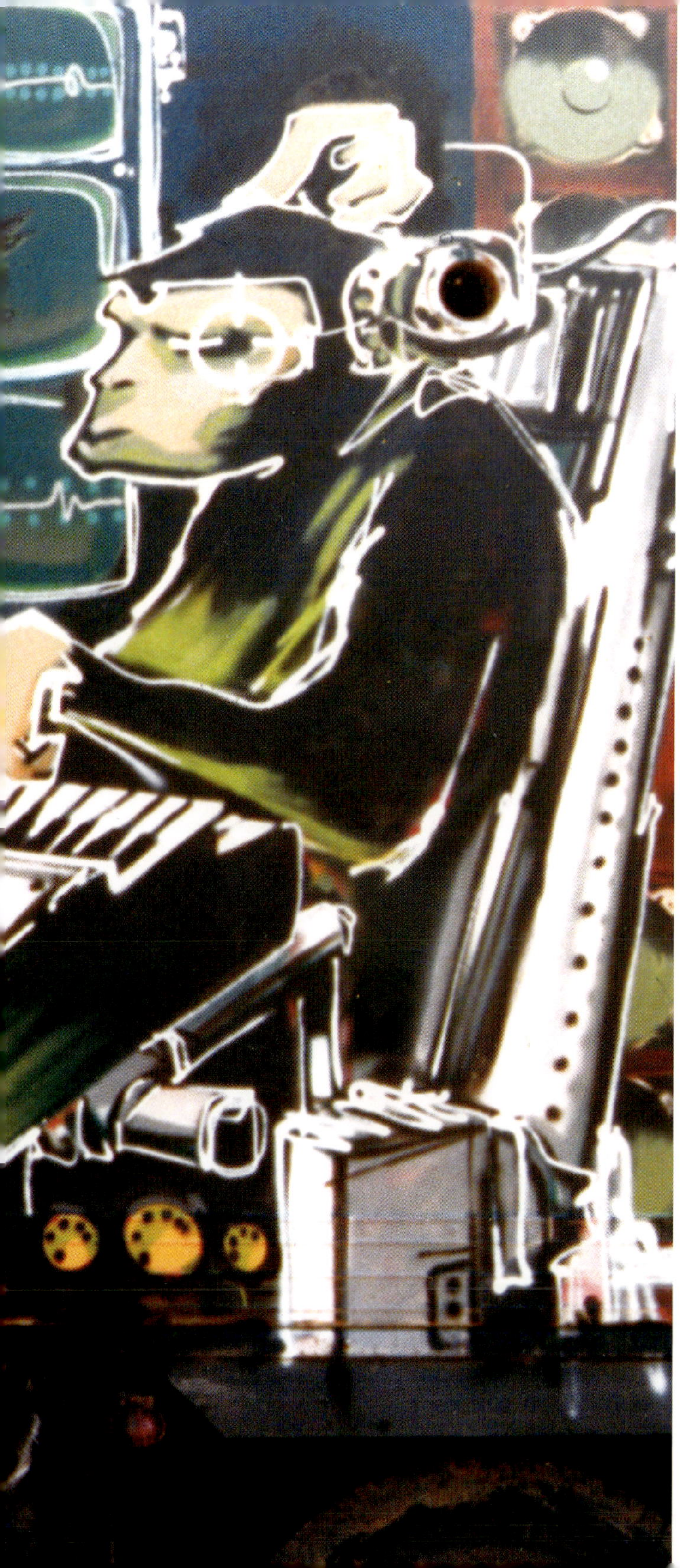

do. Basically, we were going to have a coconut shy and lots of rum and pineapple juice and serve pina coladas.

"He knew this guy who could get us a few sacks of coconuts, and we got hold of very strong rum and served pina coladas in the coconuts. We just used scaffolding poles with nuts on the top for the shies, and tennis balls and netting. Banksy painted a 'Coconut Shy' sign as well. We did the stall only at night, so that everyone was so trashed they couldn't see straight. I remember Banksy rushing behind the stall to pick up the tennis balls all the time. He also painted one whole side of this articulated lorry near the stall, with all these monkeys on DJ decks.

"The festival was a bit anarchic in the end, because the security guards all left because they weren't being paid enough. It was a bit of a free-for-all – the best festival I've ever been to. I also remember Howard Marks came over and tried our pina coladas. He liked them so much, he said he'd be endorsing them all through the festival.

"I was just amazed that Banksy was so up for anything, any way to make a bit of money. He just had this incredible energy and made you feel anything was possible."

Detail from a lorry that Banksy sprayed at the Solar Eclipse Festival in Cornwall.

Stickers handed out at anti-war demos in Bristol and London.

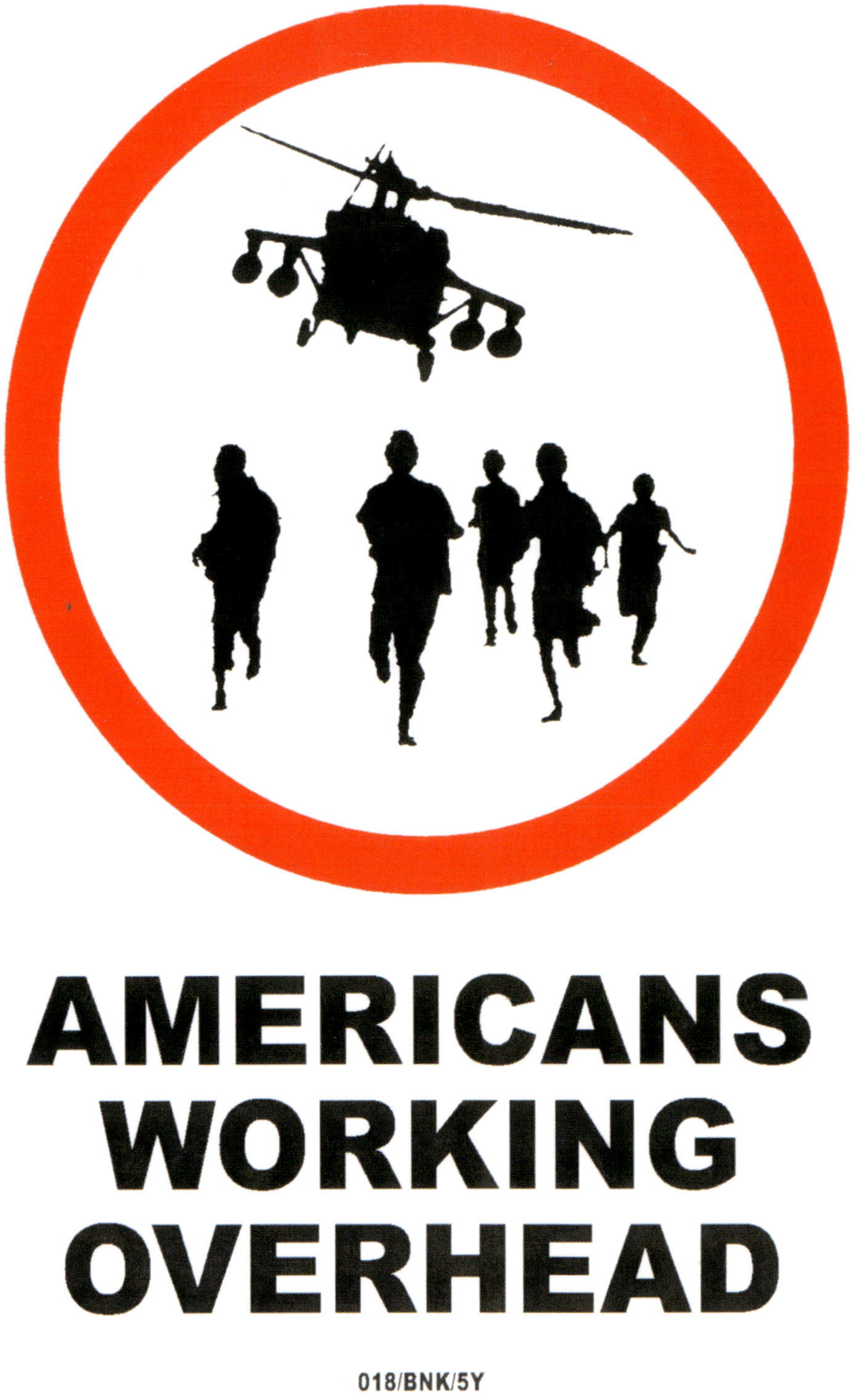

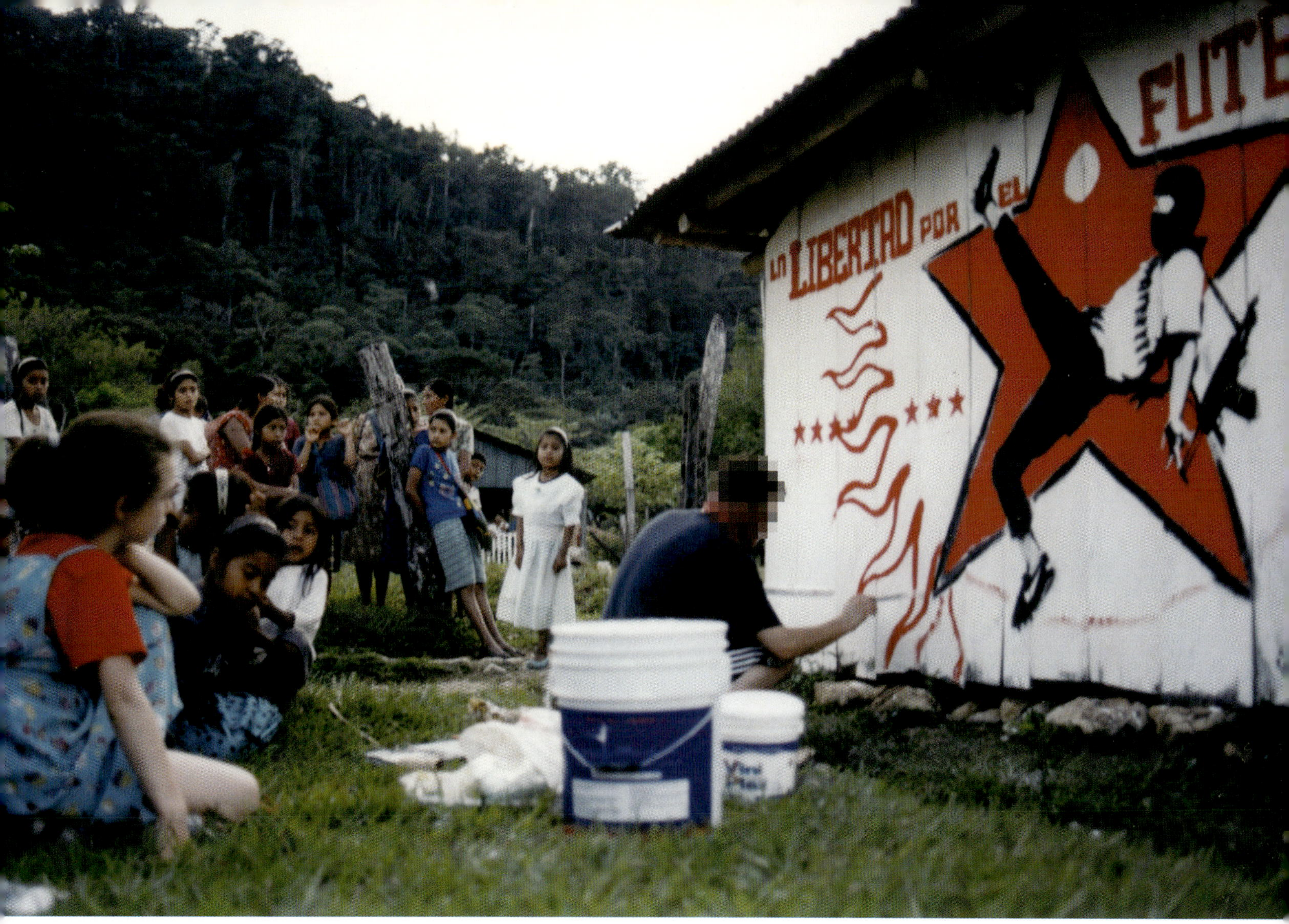

This page: Banksy at work in the Chiapas region of Mexico.

Easton Cowboys

Banksy joined Bristol's radical football team the Easton Cowboys on tour in 2001 to play against teams from the Zapatista Army of National Liberation (Ejército Zapatista de Liberación Nacional, EZLN) a revolutionary leftist group based in Chiapas, the southernmost state of Mexico.

It was the second time that the Cowboys had sent a team to play the Zapatistas and Banksy joined the squad as a goalkeeper. He'd been training with the Cowboys and turning out occasionally up to this point and had also supported them by displaying a number of canvasses at a fundraising event at the Thekla nightclub in Bristol and allowing the Cowboys to use an image on a T-Shirt sold to raise funds for a water project in Chiapas. The image depicted a Zapatista player in a balaclava and with a machine gun over his shoulder performing an overhead kick.

This was one of the images that Banksy painted on the side of a building in Chiapas in 2001. At the time of writing it was still there.

Banksy donated the original canvas to the Cowboys on the understanding that it would be raffled off. So the

Not a stencil in sight as Banksy paints for the Zapatistas.

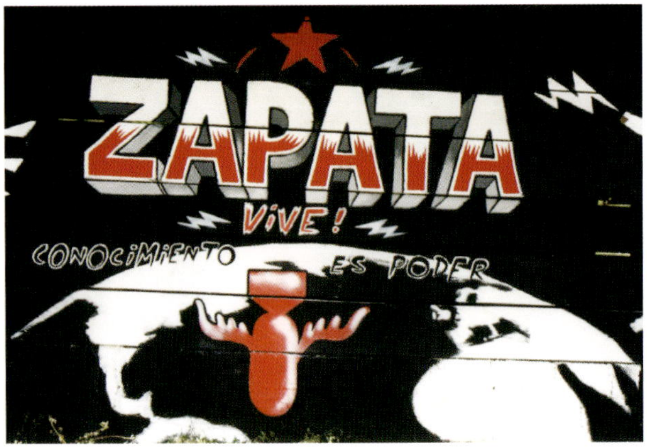

Cowboys arranged a Spot the Ball competition with Eat the Beat, a local record shop and café. Tickets cost £1 each. But some of the Cowboys thought the canvas was worth far more than that because Banksy was starting to make a name for himself. The dilemma was that Banksy had only donated the canvas to the Cowboys on condition that it was raffled.

So it was decided that £300 would be taken out of the water project fund and two Cowgirls agreed to go to Eat the Beat and buy 300 Spot the Ball stickers meaning that they were almost bound to win the canvas. The Cowgirls set off but had a guilt attack half way to Eat the Beat and never bought the tickets.

The raffle raised about £300 and a woman from Knowle who had bought just one ticket for £1 won the canvas. She sold it a few years later for £20,000.

The pictures here were taken by Richard Grove with Banksy's permission. They are the only authentic pictures of Banksy at work that have been published so far.

Banksy: a view from across the Pond

Bio is a member of the veteran New York graffiti crew TATS CRU.

Banksy has taken street art to another level. He wasn't the first and he won't be the last – but his ideas are that much cleverer and sharper than other artists'. He has led the way to a stronger street art movement worldwide. I don't want to say he invented street art, because it has

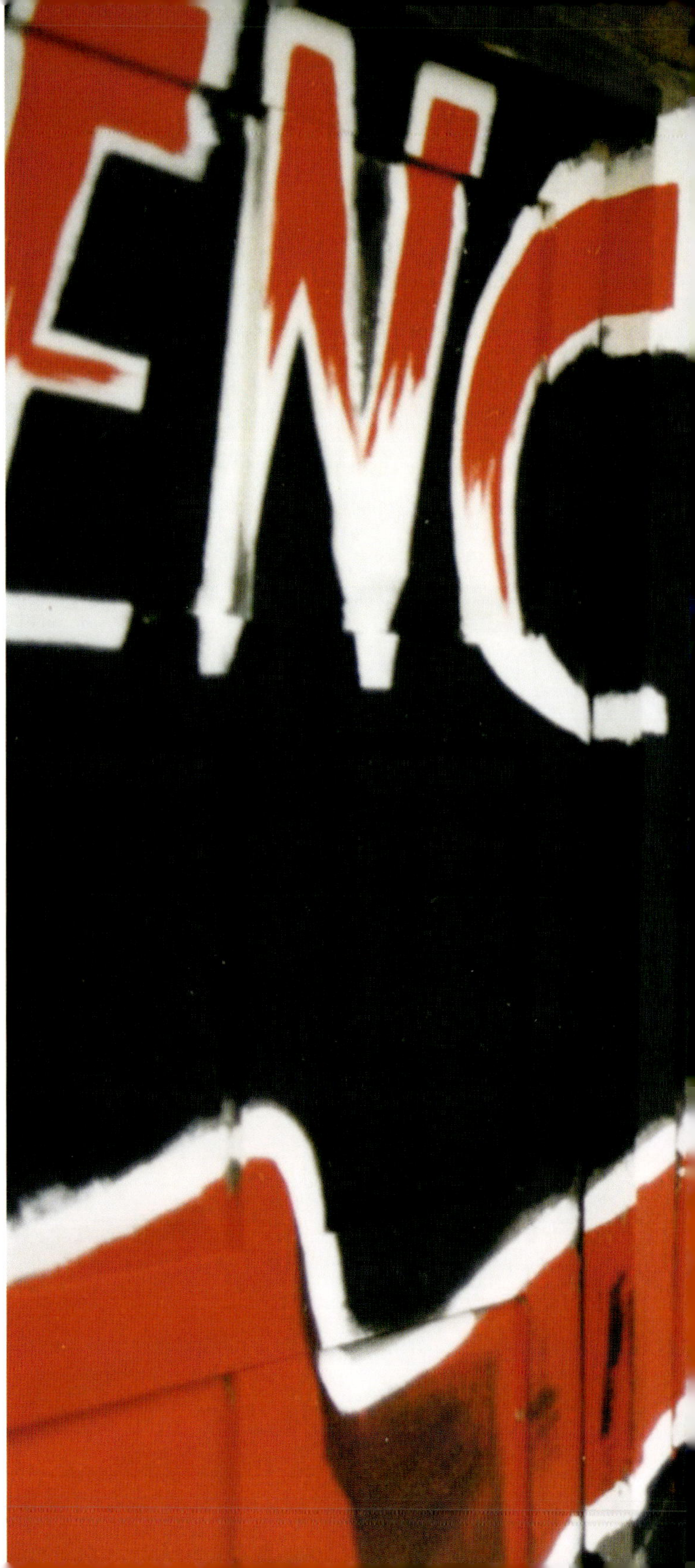

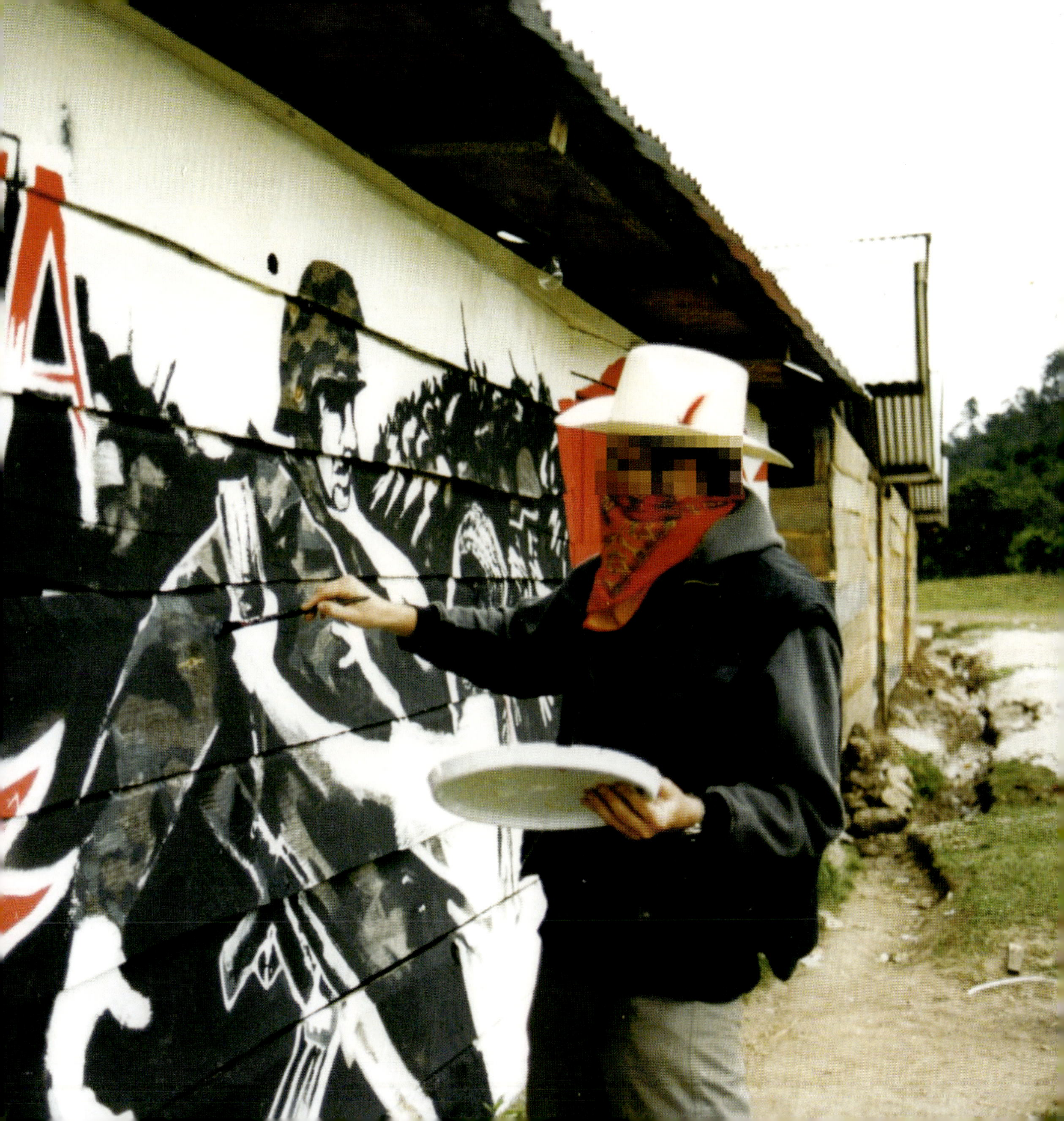

Some of the work from the Zapatista tour. The Ya Basta isn't Banksy.

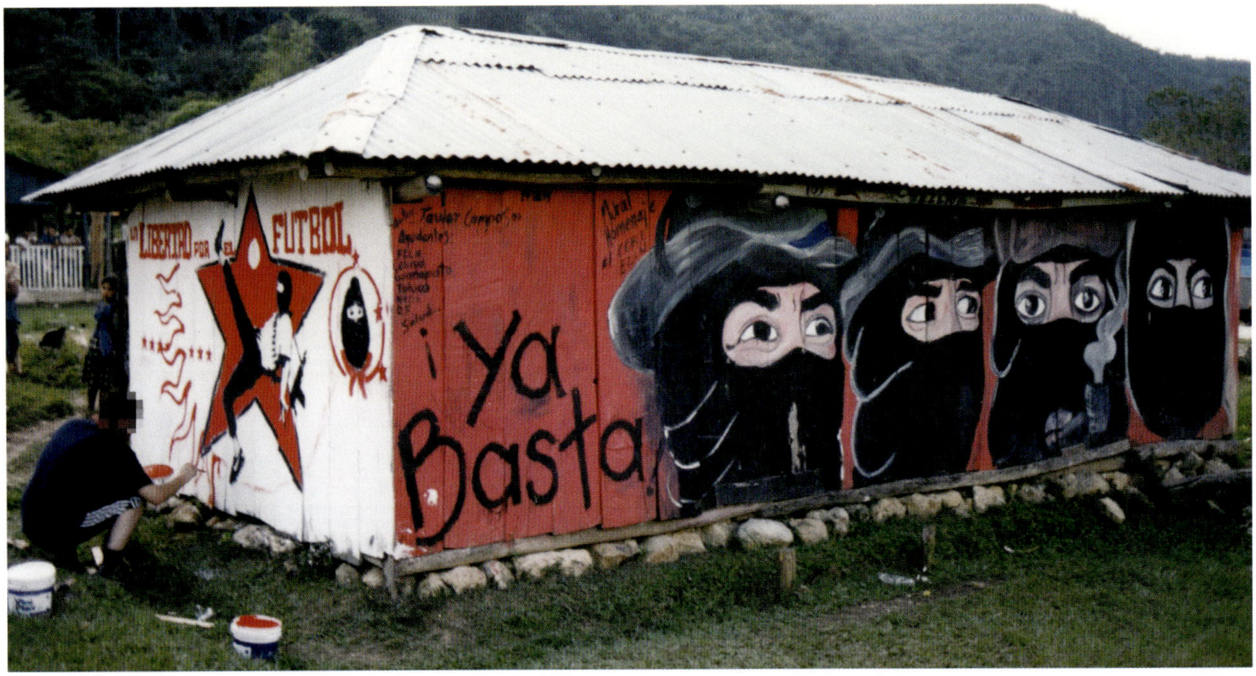

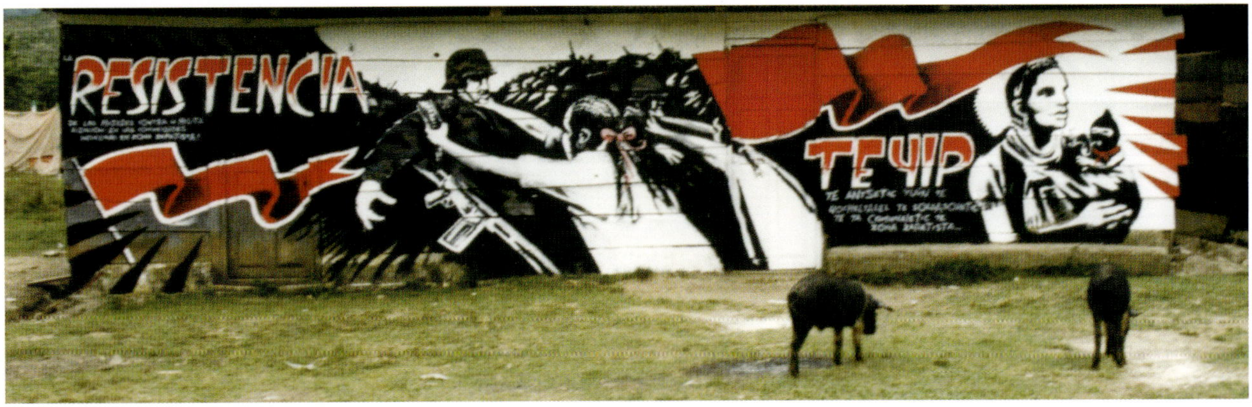

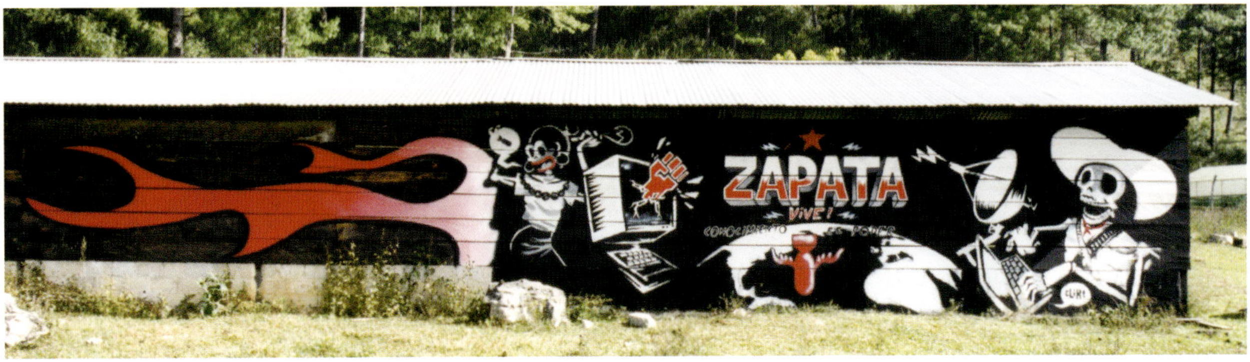

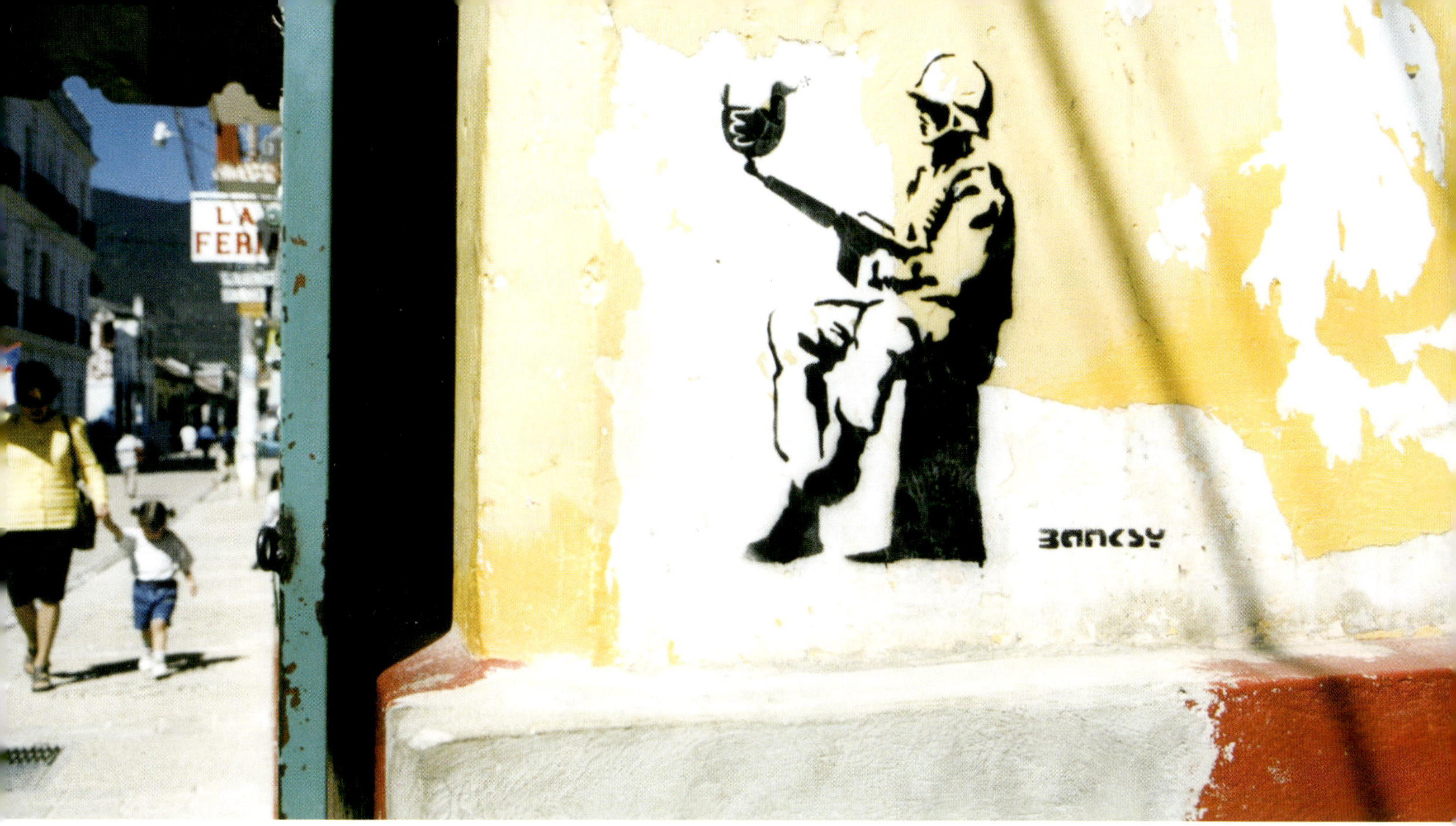

been around forever: but he is definitely one of those artists that come around once in a while, who propel the movement into the limelight. He managed to do the right thing in the right place at the right time. Much as people may want to criticise him, he's led the way with strong, thought-provoking ideas that spark an emotion in some way.

He has galvanised the scene in America. Like many Americans, I first heard of him via the internet, after Brad Pitt and Angelina Jolie paid big money for his artworks back in 2006. After that I started following his career – I learned about how he had gone into New York museums and galleries and placed his artworks on the walls. I thought that was very cool, very clever.

There is a mixed reaction to Banksy here. Hardcore graffiti artists don't buy into the whole stencil thing, they don't see that as true graffiti. They would say that it takes more guts to go out there with just a spraycan, than it does to go out with stencils – perhaps because the police will be more inclined to take a lenient view of stencil art, viewing it as more like art, less like vandalism, less intrusive somehow. So there is a division here between the stencil artists and the street bombers.

There are a bunch of Banksy imitators out here. There's a guy called Hanksy (tomhanksy.tumblr.com) who does Banksy-style stencils featuring the heads of Tom Hanks and other famous actors. And of course, before Banksy there were people doing similar things with stencil art – Blek le Rat, Nick Walker – who didn't achieve the same level of global fame.

What has taken Banksy further than those guys? He's been very clever about when and where he's placed his works to get maximum exposure – like painting the West Bank wall, for example. But I don't think there's any special formula – I don't think even Banksy would have anticipated the way things have turned out for him. I think his goal was just to get his work out there, like the rest of us.

More: tatscru.net

This page: One of the stencils that Banksy took with him to Mexico on the Easton Cowboys football tour.

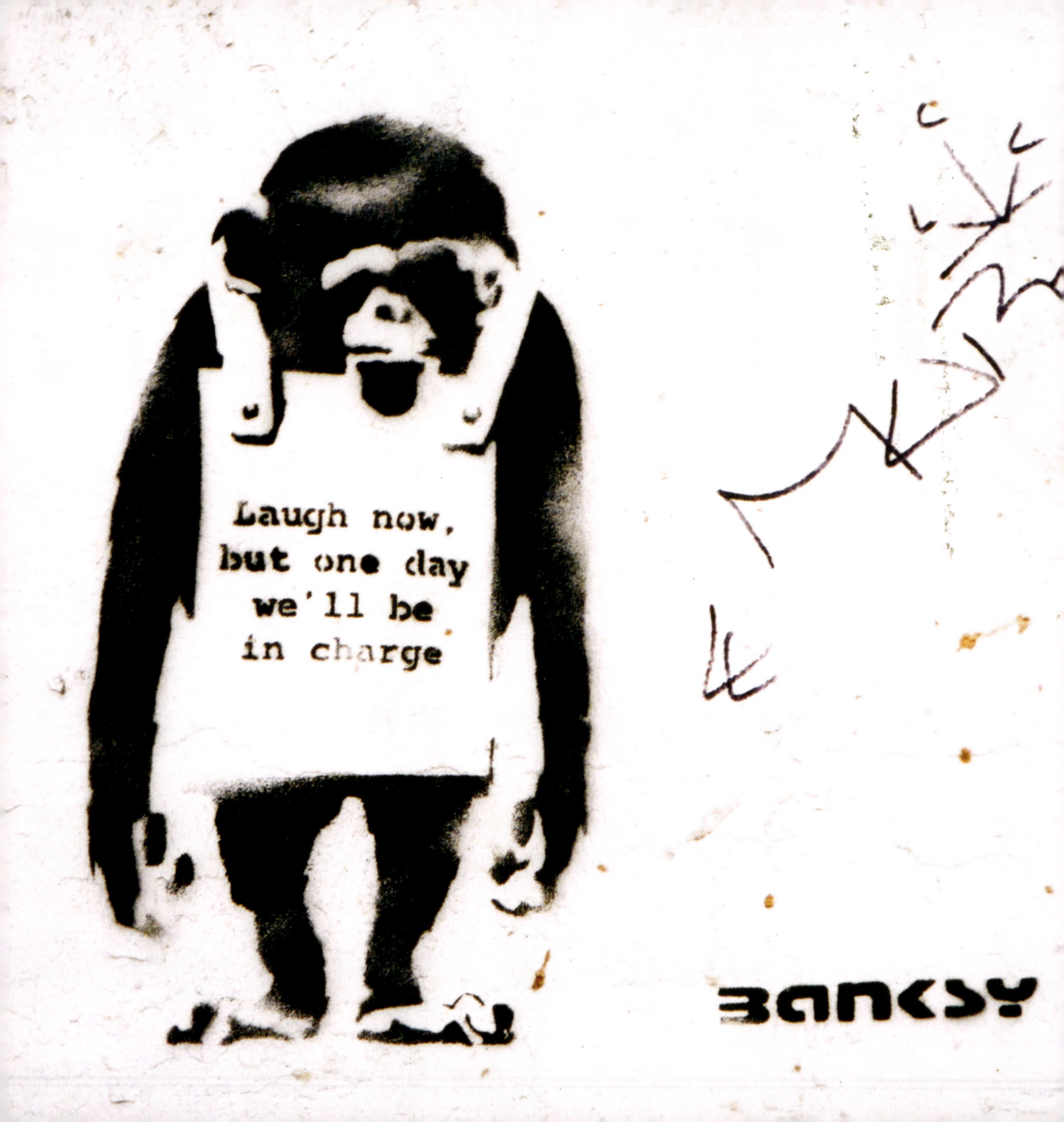
Laugh now,
but one day
we'll be
in charge
BANKSY

Making Art Work

So, where can we place Banksy in the art pantheon – and does it matter? If one of art's functions is to provoke reactions, to make you think, turn accepted notions on their head, and to do all this in as sharp and accessible way as possible, then you could easily argue for Banksy's place near the top of the tree.

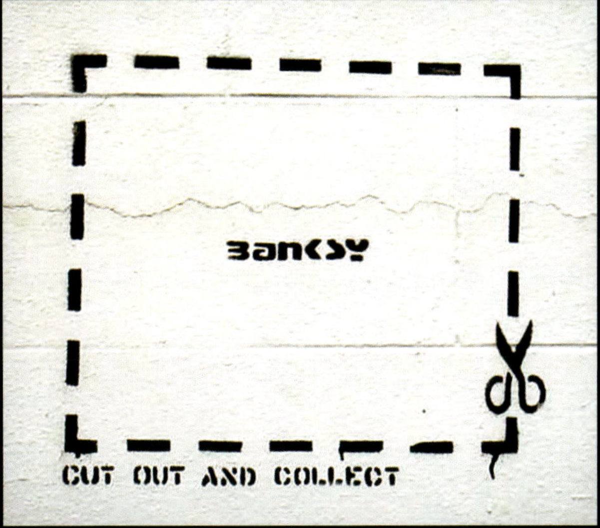

But is it art? The debate rages on about the merits of Banksy's work and the prices just keep on rising.

Banksy seems unconcerned about how the art world views him. "The art world is the biggest joke going," he said in *Swindle* magazine. "It's a rest home for the over privileged, the pretentious, and the weak. And modern art is a disgrace – never have so many people used so much stuff and taken so long to say so little. Still, the plus side is it's probably the easiest business in the world to walk into with no talent and make a few bucks."

In October 2005, speaking to *The Times* about his *Crude Oils* exhibition which featured 200 live rats roaming the gallery space, he justified the rodents' inclusion by claiming he would rather cross town to see 200 rats, than an exhibition of paintings.

Why is he so unimpressed with the art establishment? Largely, it seems, because he sees it as a self-sustaining, self-congratulating little coterie. He observed in *Wired* magazine in August 2005 that: "Art's the last of the great cartels. A handful of people make it, a handful buy it, and a handful show it. But the millions of people who go look at it don't have a say. I don't do proper gallery shows. I have a much more direct communication with the public."

He expands on the theme of democracy through art in his book *Wall and Piece*:

Art is not like any other culture because its success is not made by its audience. (…) The Art we look at is made by only a select few. A small group create, promote, purchase, exhibit and decide the success of art. Only a few hundred people in the world have any real say. When you go to an art gallery you are simply a tourist looking at the trophy cabinet of a few millionaires.

Just after his Bombing Middle England piece sold at Sotheby's for £102,000, an image appeared featuring an auctioneer holding court before a group of enthralled art buyers. The painting they were bidding on was a plain white canvas inscribed with the words 'I Can't Believe You Morons Actually Buy This Shit'.

It's the street, not the gallery, that resonates for Banksy – and for many others. "Every other type of art compared to graffiti is a step down," he said in *Swindle*. "Other art has less to offer people, it means less, and it's weaker. I make normal paintings if I have ideas that are too complex or too offensive to go out on the street, but if I ever stopped being a graffiti writer I would be gutted."

After sneaking his Warhol-esque painting of Tesco Value tomato soup cans into New York's Museum of Modern Art, Banksy recalls: "I took five minutes to see what happened next. A sea of people walked up, stared and moved on looking confused and slightly cheated. I felt like a true modern artist."

Bristol art collector Martin Roberts has known Banksy since the free party days of the Nineties. He admires the way in which the artist and his then agent, fellow Bristolian Steve Lazarides, played the art world through the LazInc website and the Lazarides gallery in Greek Street, Soho: "Banksy and Steve are like the Sex Pistols of the art world – they are not playing the art game, or the gallery system. They don't need Charles Saatchi, they're controlling the process in their own way."

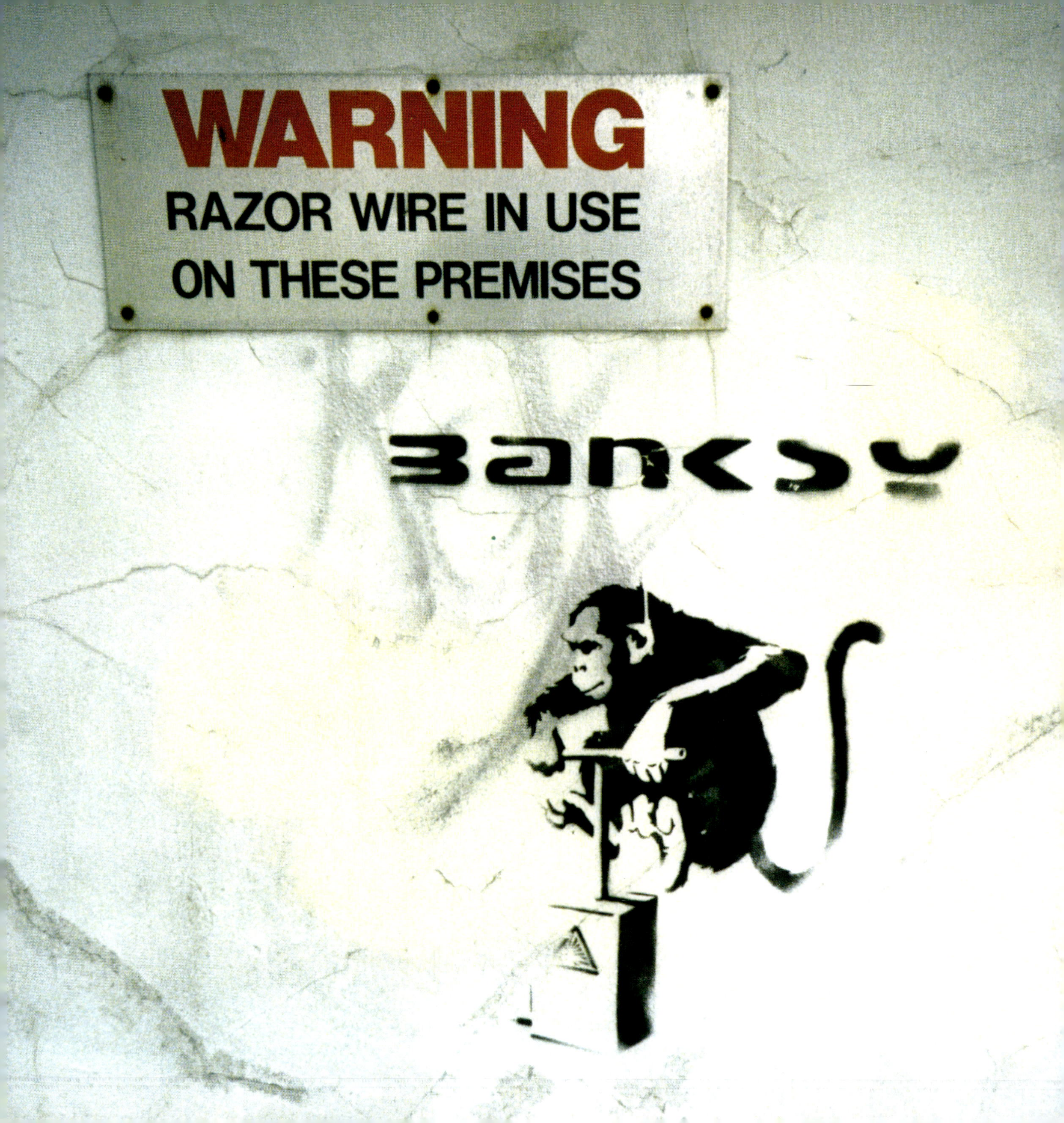
WARNING
RAZOR WIRE IN USE
ON THESE PREMISES
BANKSY

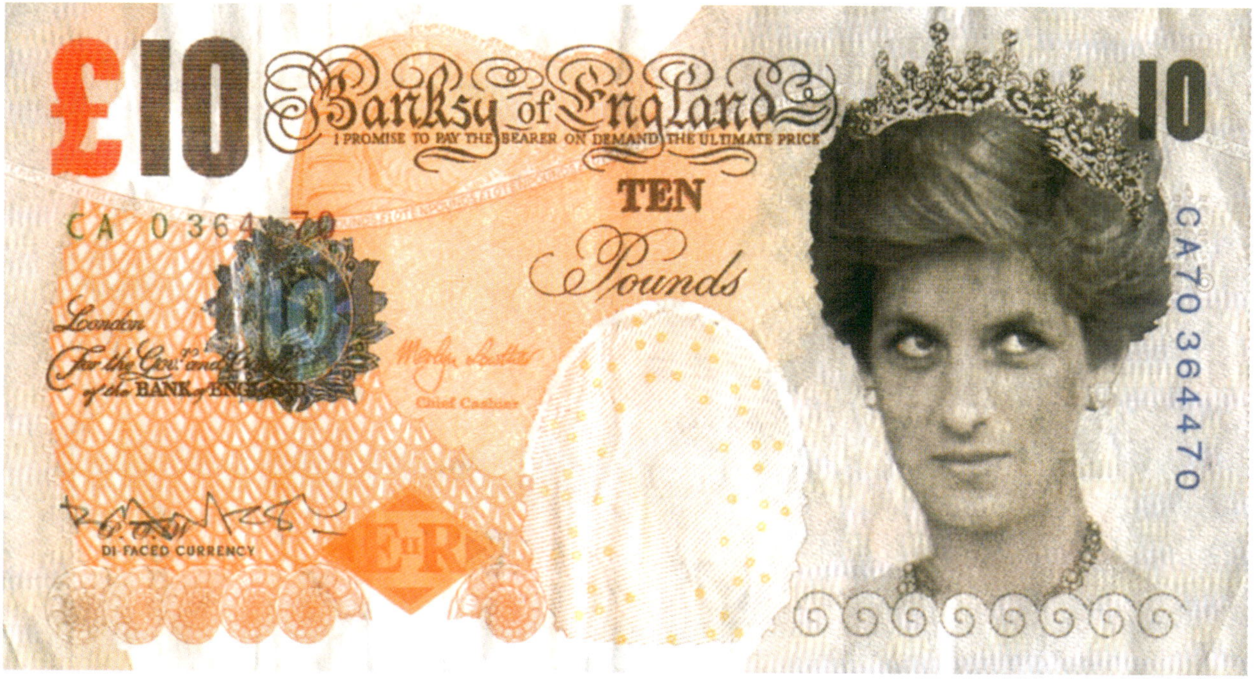

A Princess Di tenner from the Banksy of England.

In his book *Banging Your Head Against A Brick Wall*, Banksy observes that 'The quickest way to the top of your business is to turn it upside down': and that is, you can argue, exactly what he's done. "He could easily have sold out, and made a packet, doing interviews and commercial work," Roberts adds. "But he hasn't. He's carrying on purely for the love of his art, and that's quite a rarity."

The perfect example of turning the art world on its head, of course, was Banksy's infiltrations into various New York and London galleries and museums. Between March and May 2005, he snuck his way into four of New York's elite cultural institutions (the Metropolitan Museum of Art, the Museum of Modern Art, the American Museum of Natural History, and the Brooklyn Museum), plus London's British Museum, and stuck his own alternative artworks on the walls – an eighteenth-century debutante clad in a gasmask; an admiral clutching a spraycan in front of anti-war graffiti. Before that, in October 2003, he had made his way into Tate Britain and glued a painting – a classic eighteenth-century pastoral scene, altered to include police incident tape – to the wall. Banksy told the graffiti website www.woostercollective.com: "They're good enough to be in there, so I don't see why I should wait."

For sheer chutzpah, as well as the point they were making and the place they were making it, these museum 'stunts' rank as some of Banksy's finest. Yet, for all his shoulder-shrugging humour, his presence in these hallowed spaces meant something to him. In a telephone interview with the *Sunday Times*, he admitted to being flattered that the galleries he has infiltrated have left his pieces hanging. "I'm the only one from my generation there," he said. "In some of these places you are meant to be dead 200 years first."

He's showing us that art doesn't have to be produced by a self-perpetuating coterie of 'in' artists, nor consumed by someone with an art degree and a few lofty phrases. Some of the things he has done – those museum incursions but also some of his street interventions, like the wave of traffic cones apparently sinking into quicksand-like-tar on a London street – transform your whole idea of how public spaces look, what is normal reality, what assumptions we make about what we see around us.

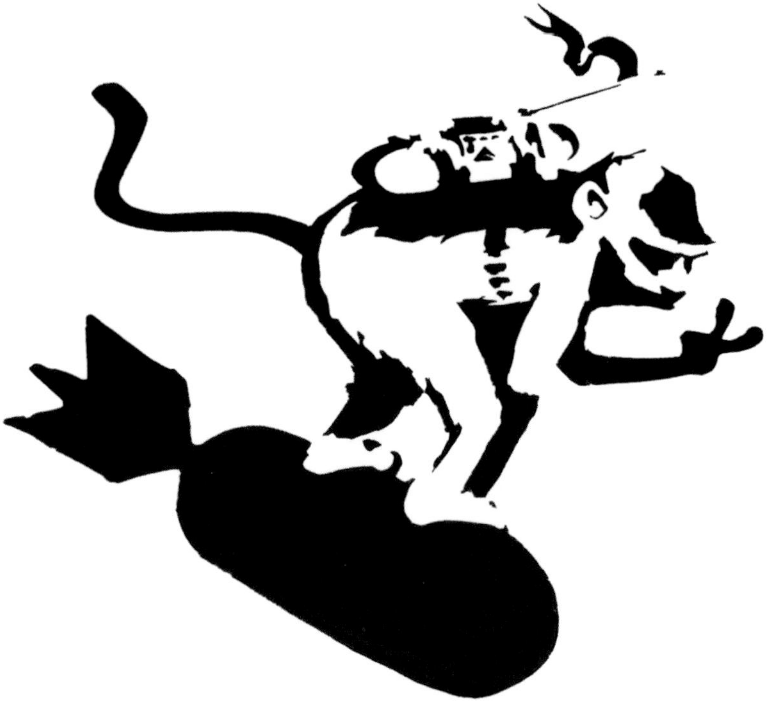

The way he goes about selling his art is also, largely, democratic and open to all. Pictures on Walls was set up as an online prints sales service featuring work by Banksy and other talented, graff-influenced artists. Banksy prints used to go on sale on the website (www.picturesonwalls.com) for under £500 – not bargain-basement prices, sure, but still relatively affordable in the modern art world, particularly when you consider the huge prices his work is now fetching. There seemed to be a philosophy of generosity, both of nurturing talented artists and of making their work affordable to many more than just those with a five-figure bank balance. "When we sell prints at below their true market value, that is done at the artist's request, not because we're stupid," says the POW website.

It also read: "Every POW edition print so far has sold out (eventually). They are always on eBay for more money. We genuinely set out to make art available to more than just tossers and gangsters." We've heard a rumour (which neither Banksy nor agent Steve Lazarides would confirm nor deny) that Pictures on Walls tries to discourage 'flipping' – buying artwork at cheap prices on the site and then flogging it on at huge profit on Amazon or eBay.

Anyone can have a go

"It's making art as affordable as possible to as many as possible," says Roberts. "The POW website also supports emerging artists, because the presence of Banksy's work on the site attracts huge traffic – visitors who then start browsing and buying work by other artists in the store."

And of course, the very medium that Banksy has chosen also means that he doesn't have to play by the same rules as the art establishment. Stencil art is by its nature relatively fast and easy to produce, meaning that he's been able both to produce and sell his pieces cheaply, and to encourage others to do the same. It's, in intention at least, the very opposite of a rigid art hierarchy. For his first London exhibition in 2001, Banksy simply whitewashed a tunnel at Rivington Street, Shoreditch, spraying 12 of his pieces (within 'frames') directly onto the white walls. Art surely doesn't come any faster or more accessible than that.

He made perhaps the ultimate statement of this DIY art when, in the summer of 2002, he allowed *Bizarre* magazine to give away a free stencil of one of his designs, featuring a rat smoking a cigarette and holding a shovel. 'This isn't just me', was the obvious message behind this unusual freebie. 'Anyone can have a go.' His books also feature advice for the would-be stenciller.

"He's changing the way we relate to art," says Roberts. "He's making it more accessible, no longer a rich man's painting club. It's pretty hard getting people hooked into art if you say, 'right, this is a Rembrandt – now you have a go!' That's not inspiring, because it doesn't feel achievable. Banksy, on the other hand, is quite explicit about how he produces his pieces and tells others how to make their own."

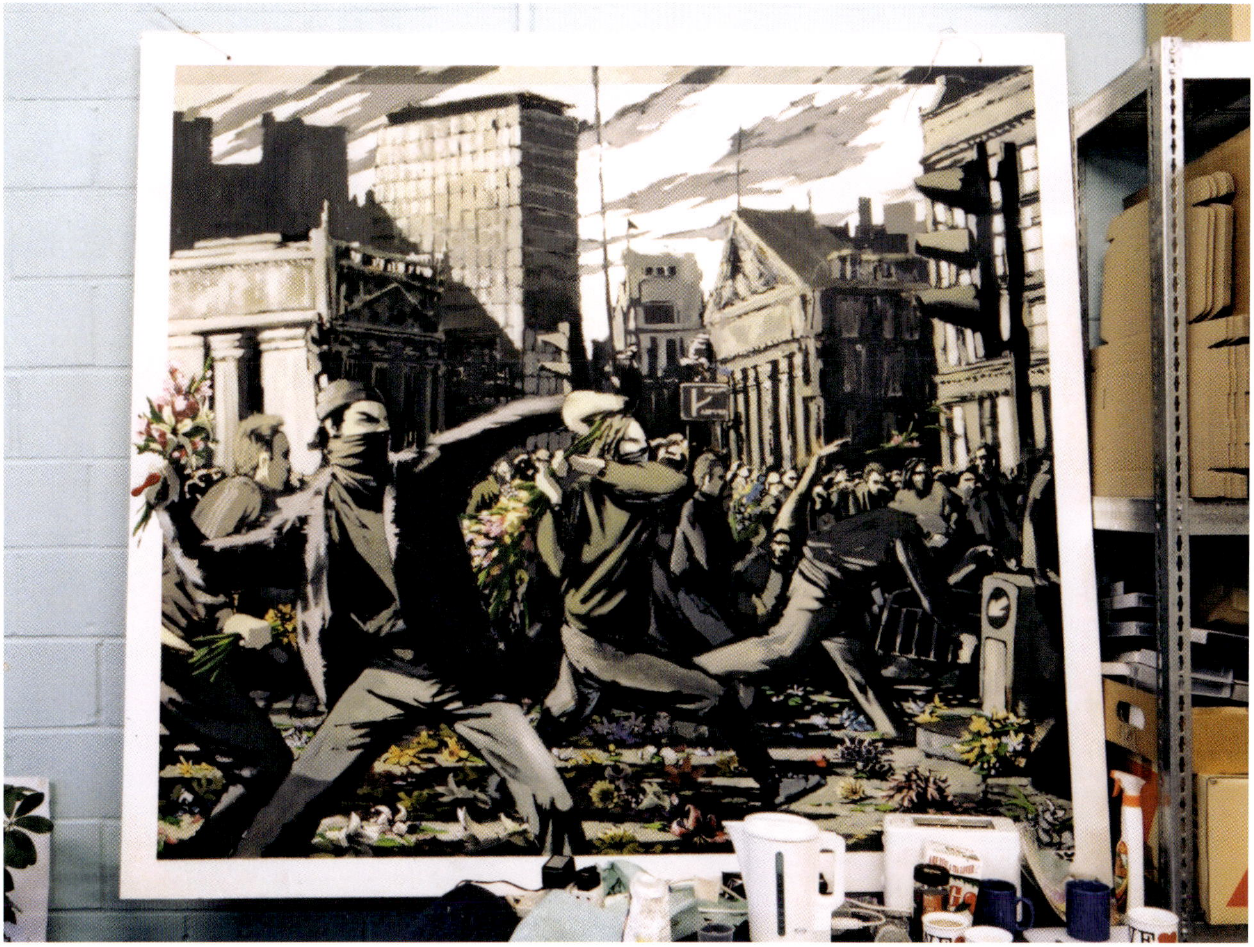

Flower Power being 'exhibited' in a garage in Easton.

Who's laughing now?

"The art world is the biggest joke going," says Banksy. So what does the joke make of him? Alan Bamberger is a US-based art consultant and author who shared these thoughts as Banksy was starting to make a major impact on the art world in 2007...

What's Banksy's future on the global art market?

I think the Banksy bubble will burst. Basically, he's unproven. What determines whether an artist ultimately goes on to sell for huge amounts of money, is whether that artist is able to produce gratifying work consistently over a long time, of equal or better quality than the art that's been produced up until then. And, with Banksy, the jury's still out on that. At the very least, you have to leave it a couple of decades: that's when the people who really count – the curators, the scholars, the people who actually have standing in the art business – take a look at this work and say, 'OK, is this for real? Or was it just a fad, a flash in the pan?' While it's happening, you don't really know.

What do you think of his stuff?

He has a very engaging take on urban art. His work actually makes you think. You're not just looking at a typical piece of graffiti: there's a story there, there's something happening, something to think about, a

The rat is a recurring image. At his Crude Oils show Banksy released 200 into the gallery.

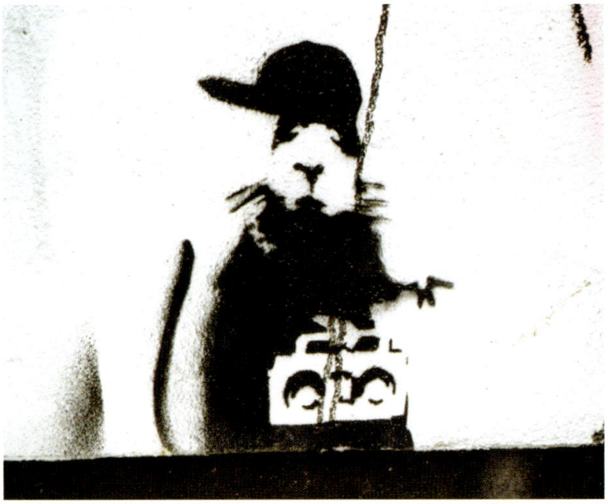

message. Even if the message is no message, there's something else happening, that extra intangibility that works so nicely. Plus, he's done some things to help himself, like placing these bogus pictures in museums – he's very good at garnering publicity for himself.

How might Banksy's legacy look?

Too many people confuse artists with athletes, like you draft them out of college and they're in their twenties and brilliant at some particular sport, but by the time they're 30 they're basically done. The opposite holds for an artist: they can come onto the scene and be brilliant and fresh, but will they still hold that attraction years down the road? Project yourself forward a few years, and imagine the hundredth time you see another Banksy stunt: will it be, 'OK, it's Banksy again, whatever', or is it going to fascinate you again and again? There's a crucial transition from fashionable to true greatness. But from where I see it now, he could definitely be looked on as someone who changed the art scene and made an impact.

But the current boom won't be sustained?

My guess is that the people paying these ridiculous amounts are not professional, experienced art collectors. I would guess that there's a money angle, they can see that his stuff is going up and up at the moment, but I don't think we have a really dedicated, moneyed fanbase to sustain this level of price increase. It makes no sense: how can something be worth $100,000 today and $200,000 in a month? How can that be?

Has he climbed too far too quickly?

He's under heavy, heavy pressure to perform. Is he able to take it, is he able to continue to produce, or is he just going to disappear?

Will Banksy survive in the long term?

He has all the raw ingredients to go on to be an important and influential artist: but we don't really know yet, and it's a very long game. At his L.A. show in 2006, Angelina Jolie spent some ridiculous amount of money on some of his pieces, and, of course, all that celebrity gossip gets people excited. But Angelina Jolie is not known as an art collector, she just has a lot of money. She doesn't carry any weight in the art world. It's like, OK, they're fetching these prices, but who's doing the buying here?

So, what's it worth?

Ralph Taylor from Sotheby's Contemporary Art department on Banksy's extraordinary journey

"Part of Banksy's impact has been because he has come from the whole urban/street art context, which had its roots in 1980s graffiti and hip hop culture. That has meant that he has appealed to a whole new generation who previously weren't buying art. His art is also accessible to all – you don't need to go to galleries or have the benefit of a rarefied artistic education to enjoy it – they are up on the streets for all to see. And perhaps most important of all is his gallows humour – his work is anti-establishment, but it uses laughter to get its point across. It is also, visually, very easy to understand – which means that it both catches the eye of the passer-by, and is also relevant across social and cultural boundaries. Grannies, kids, people from outside the UK: everyone 'gets' Banksy's work. But he's seen as dangerous, because of the illegal nature of his street work and because of his anti-establishment messages.

That danger adds to the excitement around him. People who are part of the establishment are buying strongly anti-establishment pieces, and I think there's a frisson of irony, of danger for them in that. It's a strange relationship, but one I think both sides get a lot out of.

"His impact has been phenomenal. To have reached his level of interest so quickly is extraordinary. It helps that he is part of a group of artists – including Antony Micallef, Adam Neate, Jamie Hewlett and Paul Insect – who often collaborate and feed interest into each other's work, which thus creates its own market.

"Banksy's proven to be extremely robust. At the beginning of 2007, there was a phenomenal demand for Banksy pieces, and people were paying incredible prices. It was a case of 'I want a Banksy, no matter what.' There was also a large supply available, because a lot of people bought Banksy pieces for, say, £200 in Bristol back in 2000. Being able to sell that for perhaps 100 times the original price was extremely enticing – show me a hedge fund manager who would ignore the potential of a 10,000 per cent return over just a few years, let alone regular guys from Bristol who bought because the message resonated with them! This is another secret to Banksy's commercial success; as art is developed as an alternative asset class, investors are always on the look out for the next big thing, which can explain some of the steepness of his curve.

Post-Berlin Wall zeitgeist. Eh?

"I think interest in his 'edition' canvases* and some of the more obscure images might plateau. But if we were to see, say, a really strong architectural piece (such as a stencil on a wall or piece of iron where the street context is still linked to the work), the sky's the limit. That's where the interest will come from, when he's creating something truly original. I also think that he is extremely significant art-historically – the Princess Diana £10 notes that he placed all over London are incredibly powerful and the murals on the Palestinian wall capture both a post-Berlin Wall zeitgeist as well as representing an act – he is not just saying something serious, by going on location he is doing it too. Damien Hirst's show *MurderMe* in 2006, which was the first public exhibition of (a small part of) Hirst's own collection, featured three or four Banksys. The cover for the exhibition catalogue, a tattoo design, was also by Banksy. So Banksy has been endorsed by the pre-eminent artist of our generation. If Damien Hirst, no less, thinks Banksy is the real deal, then you can understand new collectors saying, 'who are we to disagree?' Personally, I think it's important he continues to do his stunts and get his messages out there in the imaginative, absurd, unsettling ways he always has done. It's crucial that he maintains the integrity of doing things on the street, showing that it is still all about the message."

**An 'edition' canvas is where an artist uses the same stencil on a series of 5-15 identical canvases; each piece is the same but the artist's hand is still evident in each through the spray can – which is not the case with prints.*

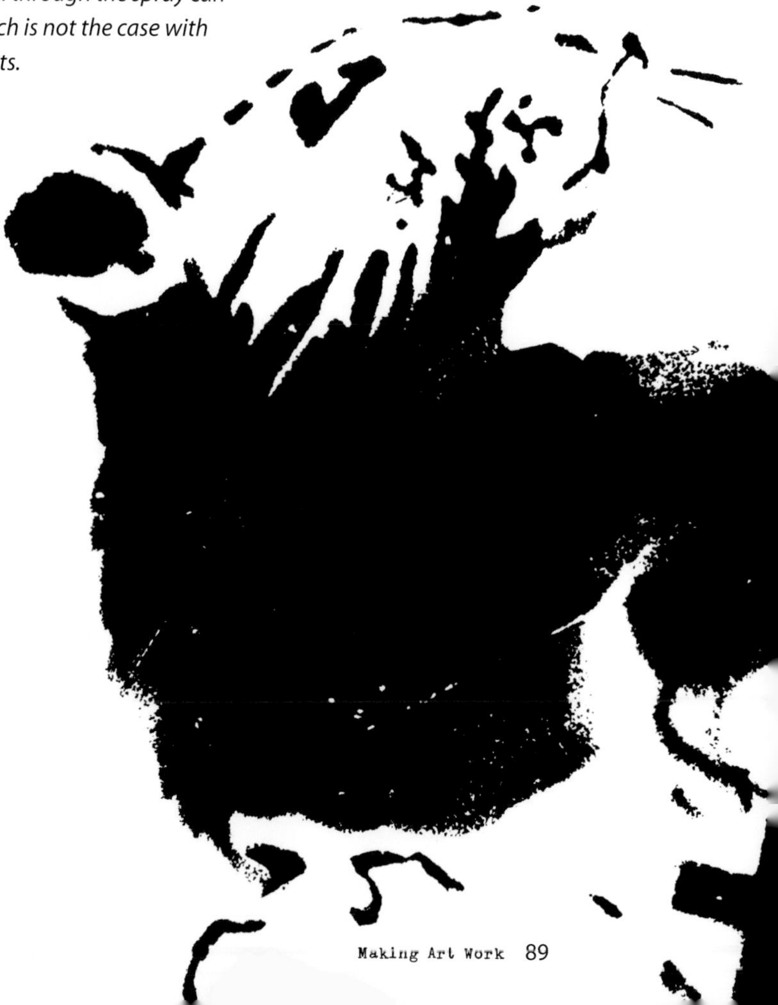

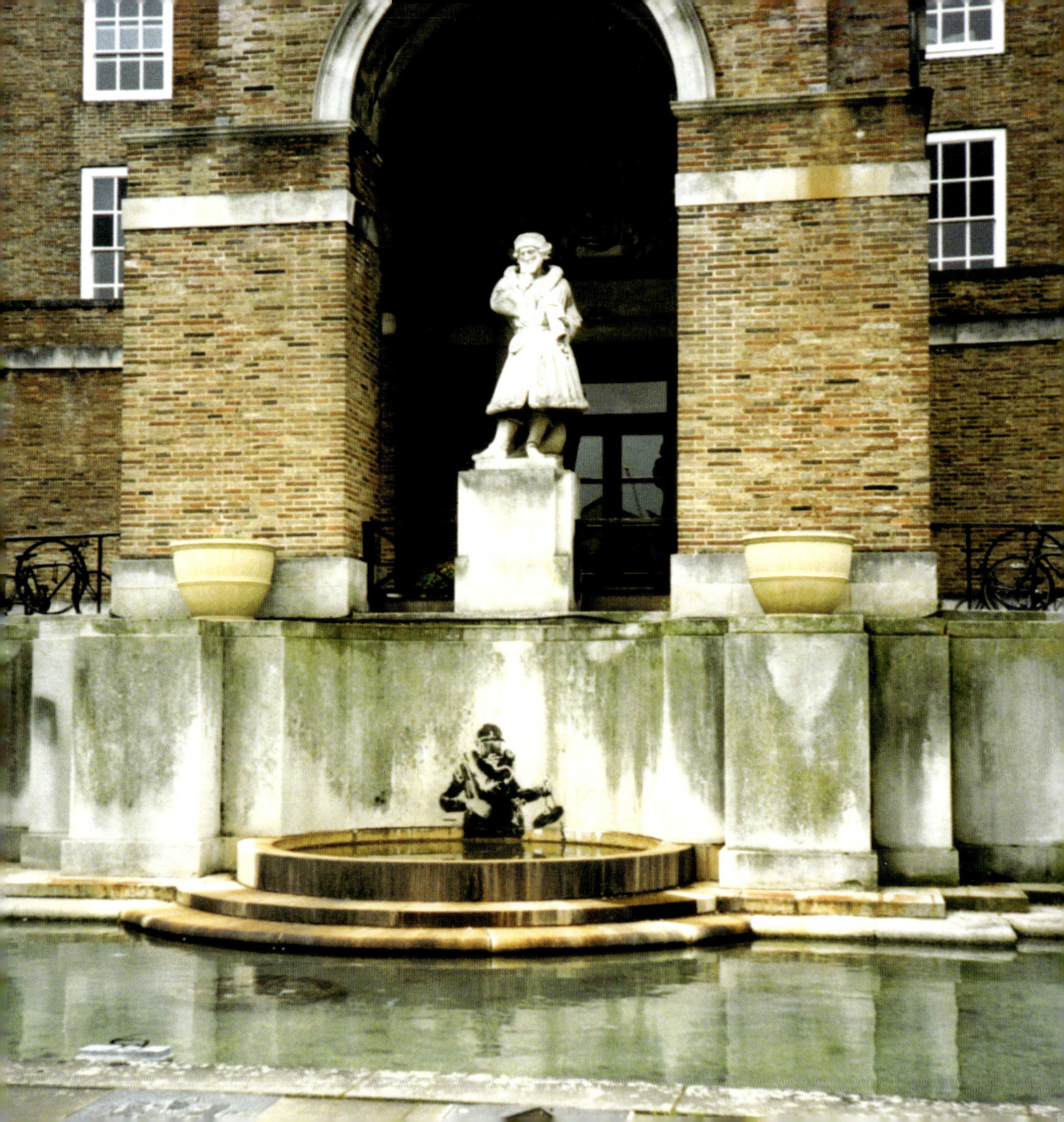

Home Sweet Home

One of the most fascinating parts of the Banksy story is how, in his native city, he's helped drive a massive public debate about graffiti – whether it's ever art or always just criminal damage, where we want to see it, and by whom. Of course, he hasn't been the only Bristol artist to change public perception. Graffiti writers such as FLX and Paris have also worked hard to change the public view of graffiti, encouraging local kids to get away from tagging and experiment with more inventive graffiti styles. But the debates around Banksy's Bristol pieces have been the most prominent.

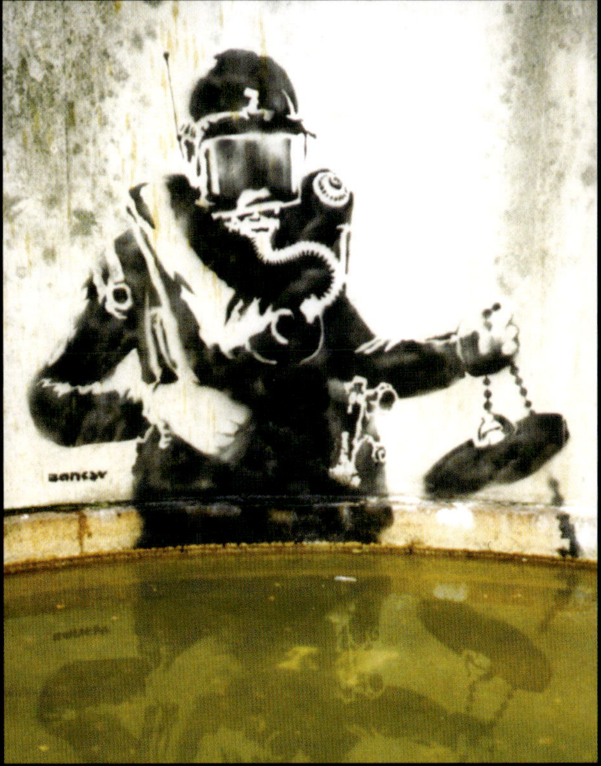

The diver pulling the plug on Bristol City Council was removed within hours, but now Banksy is featured on the Destination Bristol website.

Banksy and the City Council

August 1998

Inkie and Banksy collaborate at *Walls on Fire*, a weekend-long festival of street art with the blessing of the City Council. Top graffiti writers from across the UK paint a 400m stretch of hoardings running around the Bristol 2000 site – the future At-Bristol.

1999

Mild Mild West, perhaps Banksy's most iconic Bristol piece, goes up. It's still there. Originally, Banksy planned to paint a piece showing a building in flames with looters fleeing with shopping trolleys.

May 2003

Banksy's tag appears on the side of the Thekla floating nightclub in Bristol, sparking an 'art/vandalism' debate. The Thekla ask punters what to do with it, and they voted overwhelmingly to keep it, but BCC paint over it. The Thekla draws up legal proceedings for criminal damage against the Harbourmaster. Banksy returns and paints a grim reaper in the same spot, "In the hope we can lure him out and go for a full custodial sentence this time."

June/July 2006

The debate over Banksy's Frogmore Street piece begins. Spud Murphy, the Tory councillor for Avonmouth, tells Radio Bristol listeners that it's not art because Banksy used stencils and "I could have done that."

March 2007

A wall in Albion Road, Easton featuring a blue Banksy mural, one of his first, is painted over by council workers. The council says that it has specified that all Banksy works were to be protected, and announces an investigation into why the order was ignored. On the same day, residents turn out in force to prevent another Banksy piece, on the side of a house on the corner of Mivart Street, Easton, being painted over.

May 2007

Plans are announced to protect Banksy's iconic Mild Mild West in a glass atrium at the front of a new development

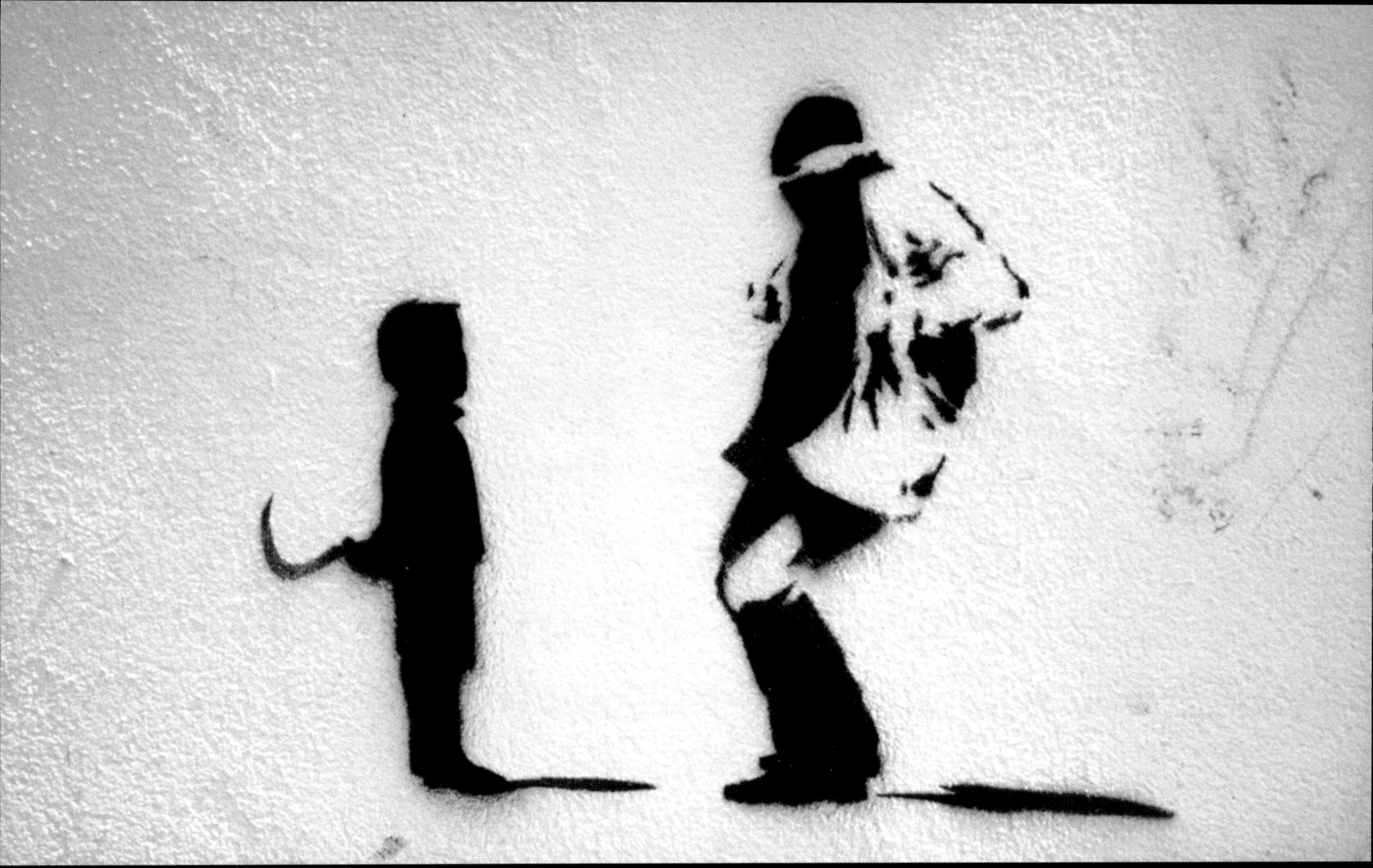

of flats, shops and offices. Officials say tagging and graffiti should be discouraged, but work of Banksy's quality ought to be 'recognised as a positive feature.'

"I think people assumed the worst when they heard about the development," explains Gavin Carpenter, of the building's owners Connolly and Callaghan. "They thought the mural would go. But Banksy is very much the man of the moment and this will bring some kudos to the development."

July 2007

Bristol City Council gives the go-ahead to the City's second legal graffiti site, the first in 20 years, off Junction 3 of the M32. (Dame Emily Park, Bedminster being the first). One Bristol graffiti blogger comments: "The fact that it has taken 20 years to get a second legal site in one of the most dynamic graffiti hot spots in England is somewhat mystifying, but it's here now and represents a positive move by Bristol City Council, who have to be seen to be hot on vandalism.

"This demonstrates a willingness by the Council to provide public spaces to artists where they can practise their art legally, and where anyone interested in street art can go and meet artists and learn about the culture. Bristol has been crying out for more space, and this is a welcome step in the right direction."

July 2009

Banksy vs Bristol Museum is an international phenomenon.

Banksy tales

Gez Smith worked for Bristol City Council and helped to push for a public debate about Banksy's Frogmore Street piece

"The Council were washing off stuff more indiscriminately a few years ago. Now they pause for reflection more often, which is good. They have been a bit contradictory about what is and what isn't good art. I actually think Spud Murphy had a point – what actually is graffiti and what isn't? I'd like it if the Council simply said, 'we'll take down graffiti if it's crap, but if it's a nice, well-thought out piece, and adds something to the area, then we'll leave it.'

"I love what PRSC, for example, are doing [the People's Republic of Stokes Croft, an organisation of artists and residents who, in 2007, started to decorate the Stokes Croft area of central Bristol with impromptu street art]. Because ultimately people, not the Council, own the streets.

"On the other hand, although it's a real shame that loads of Banksys have gone, that's what it is: it's street art, it's ephemeral. You wouldn't expect to be able to go to an original Pink Floyd concert any more, so why should you expect to see an original Banksy? Street art, like music, moves on..."

A railway cleaner's guide to art

In March 2007, workers employed by Network Rail to erase graffiti were given art lessons, to ensure that they didn't inadvertently erase any more of Banksy's work. The graffiti-cleaning teams were shown examples of Banksy's work after staff had painted over one of his murals (a monkey detonating a bunch of bananas) in Leake Street next to Waterloo station.

A Network Rail spokesman said: "We take a very tough line on graffiti, which is an anti-social crime affecting both passengers and staff, and costs the railway industry millions of pounds every year. Dealing with graffiti also diverts valuable resources away from improving the railway.

"However, given the possible value of some of Banksy's work, we have circulated examples to employees and contractors involved in cleaning up our property. If they see something they think could be by Banksy, then they are to notify their manager, who will come along to inspect. If feasible, we will consider the option of removing the graffiti and look into whether it can be auctioned for charity or donated to a local museum, gallery or other organisation."

These two were in Montpelier but have long since gone.

The lost Banksys

Countless Banksy pieces have been lost – erased by zealous council graffiti removal teams, or hacked away by opportunistic street-art thieves. Here are a few examples:

2006

Stencil of a rat bouncing a beach ball under a 'No Ball Games' sign is cut from a wall in Paddington, west London and auctioned on eBay for £20,000.

2006

Early Banksy stencil removed from outside wall of Full Moon pub in Stokes Croft. The piece fetched £26,000 at auction in 2013 with 50 per cent going to charity.

April 2007

A group of transport workers paint over Banksy's Pulp Fiction-inspired mural in Old Street, Shoreditch, London. Experts value the piece at £250,000. "You wouldn't paint over a Van Gogh, nor should you paint over a Banksy," comments an alleged friend of the artist.

2012

The Masked Gorilla on Fishponds Road, Bristol is painted over by the building's new owner.

2014

Bristol City Council remove the Banksy painted on railings at the Eastville Park roundabout.

Former *Venue* magazine publisher Dougal Templeton's lost Banksy tale

"*Venue* had been doing a lot of coverage of the graffiti scene and commissioned and helped young talent (including paying 3D to paint the side wall of our office in Jamaica Street, buying paint cans, commissioning Inkie and so forth). We gave Banksy a lot of coverage, and a mutual contact passed on a series of sketches from him for some of his best Bristol pieces, which we put together in a framed collage. That got abandoned in an office move because certain *Venue* staff thought they weren't worth putting in the van!"

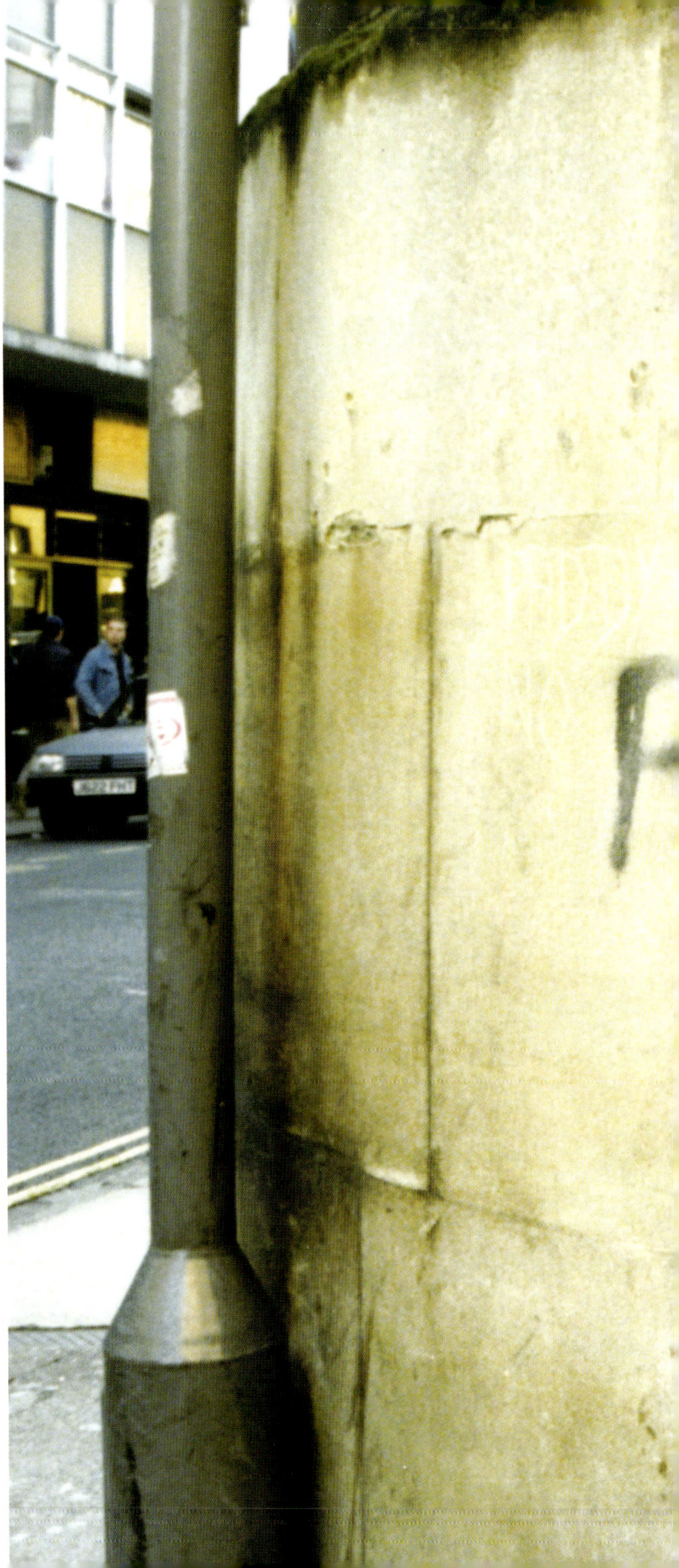

Context is important for Banksy. This lost Banksy was on the side of the Nelson Street police station in Broadmead.

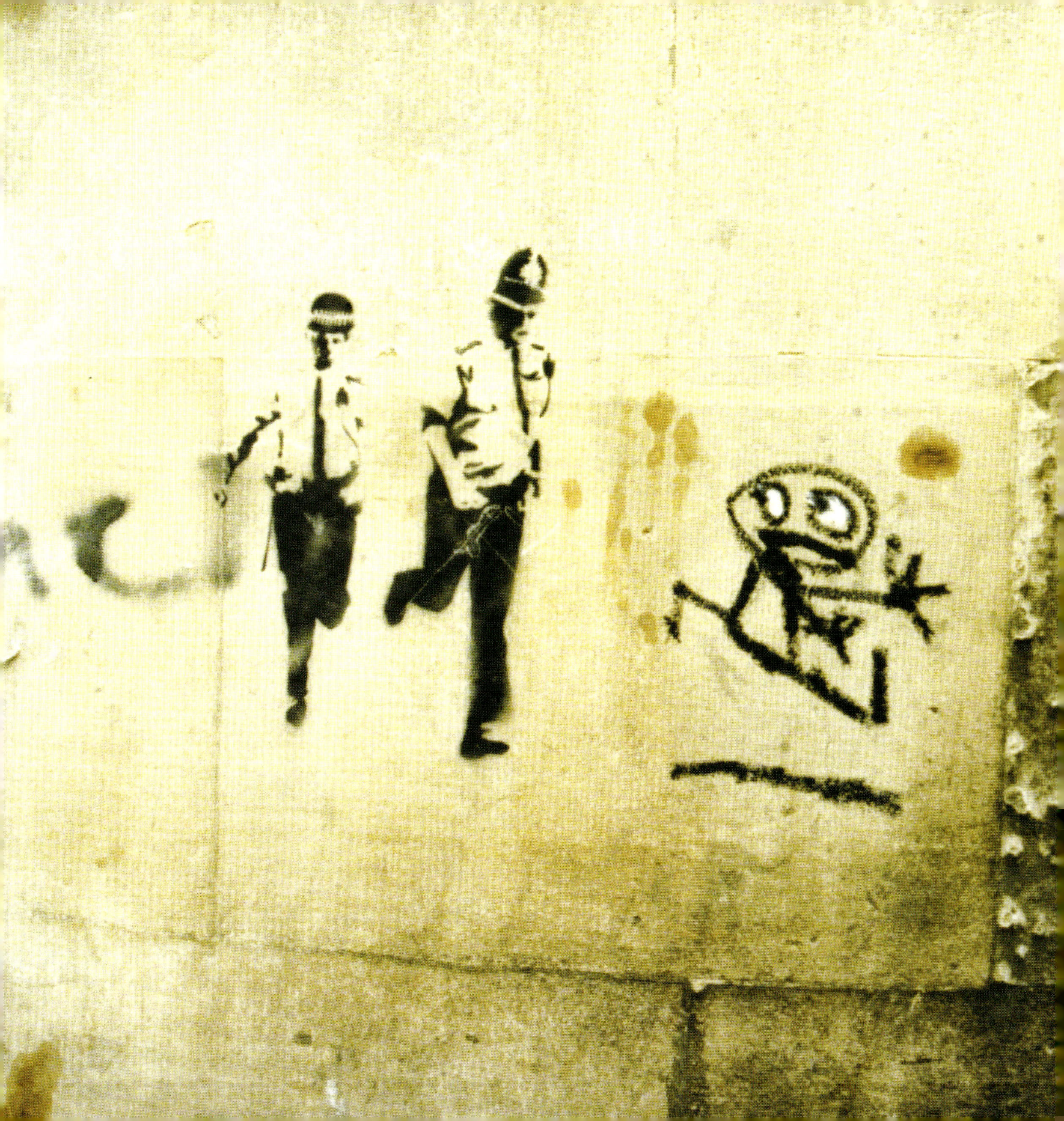

The police have been after Banksy for years.

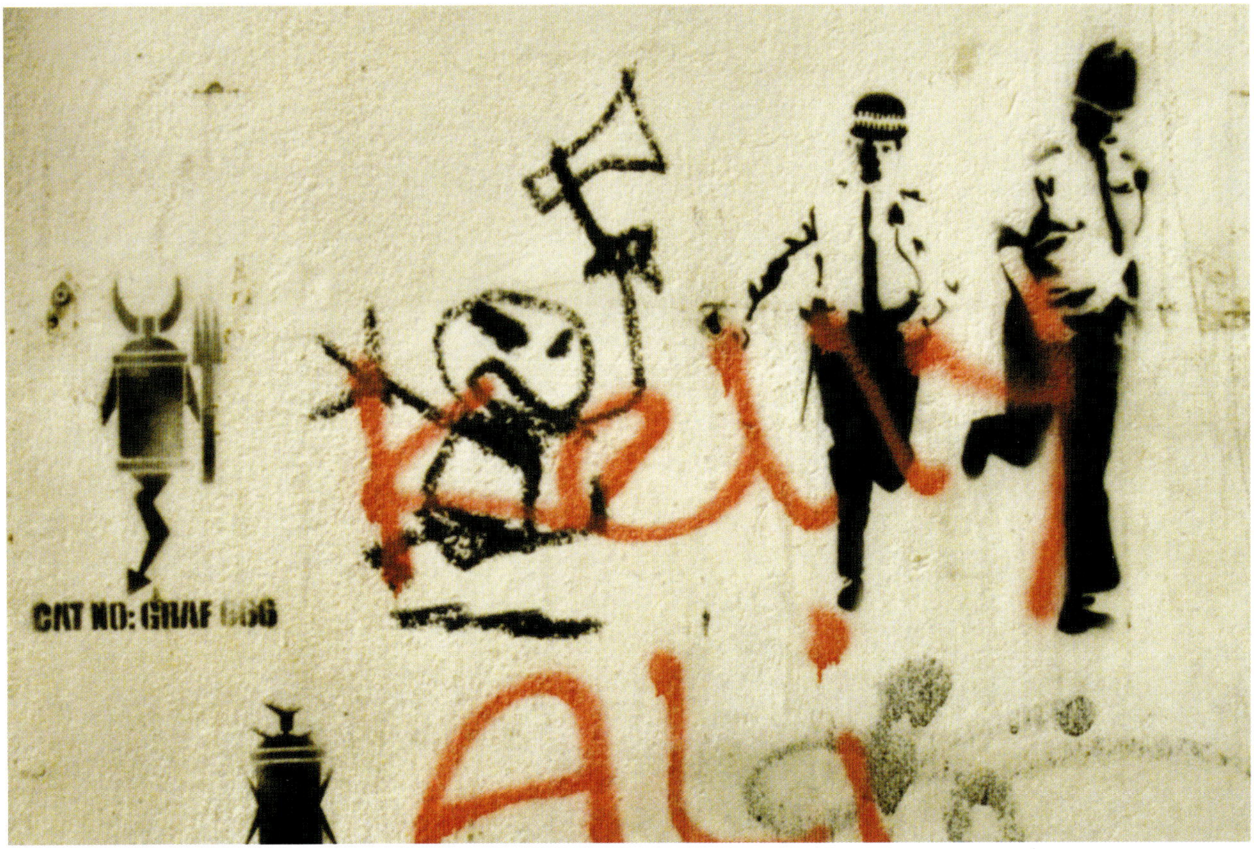

Banksy backlash

Colin Saysell, British Transport Police and Bristol anti-graffiti officer, who has spent years trying to track down Banksy

"What is one man's art is another man's unmade bed. The debate over whether what Banksy does is art is neither here nor there, because if it is done in a place without permission then it's criminal damage. Banksy is a self-confessed vandal, and that's why he goes to such lengths to keep his identity a secret. Those who support him support these criminal activities and that cannot be right. Why should people in Bristol or in London, or anywhere else, have to pay more council tax to clean it up?"

Veteran art critic Brian Sewell, by voicemail

"A long-delayed response to your letter. I don't know anything about Banksy, and I don't care tuppence about graffiti or street art. Sorry abut that. Talk to me about Michelangelo and I will willingly respond, but Banksy? No."

Jonathan Jones, *The Guardian,* on web blog

"I think there's some wit in Banksy's work, some cleverness – and a massive bucket of hot steaming hype."

Banksy, Bristol and the Lifestyle Effect

Eugene Byrne is a Bristol author and journalist

"I think Banksy's obviously a Jolly Good Thing as far as Bristol is concerned. He's given us a few iconic images (especially the Mild Mild West) and, when you add him into that MassiveHeadTrickySize Bristol sound, it adds to the city's cachet as somewhere cool and edgy. Obviously that whole thing is grossly exaggerated, but it doesn't do any harm.

"But I wonder about the economic benefits of the city's 'cool' image. When you talk about that, people tend to think of it in terms of tourism, but I think of it more in terms of demographics. One of the great mantras of economic development these days is so-called 'graduate retention', the idea that clever people with in-demand skills will move to a place, or stay in a place when they finish university.

"Bristol has very high concentrations of these, and those directing what passes for economic policy in the area know that this 'cool' image is useful (and is of course actually un-threatening – what a lot of graduates want, especially as they get older, is the appearance of rebellion with none of the inconvenient or expensive actuality).

"Now obviously it's more useful if the jobs are there, but for most people, particularly graduates, it's all about lifestyle as well. So one of the amusing ironies is that this street artist with the most impeccable anti-capitalist credentials, is actually adding economic value to Bristol. One of the sharpest examples of this irony is that Banksy's popular Mild Mild West mural is going to be preserved behind glass and shoved in the atrium of some upmarket flats for yuppies being developed on Stokes Croft."

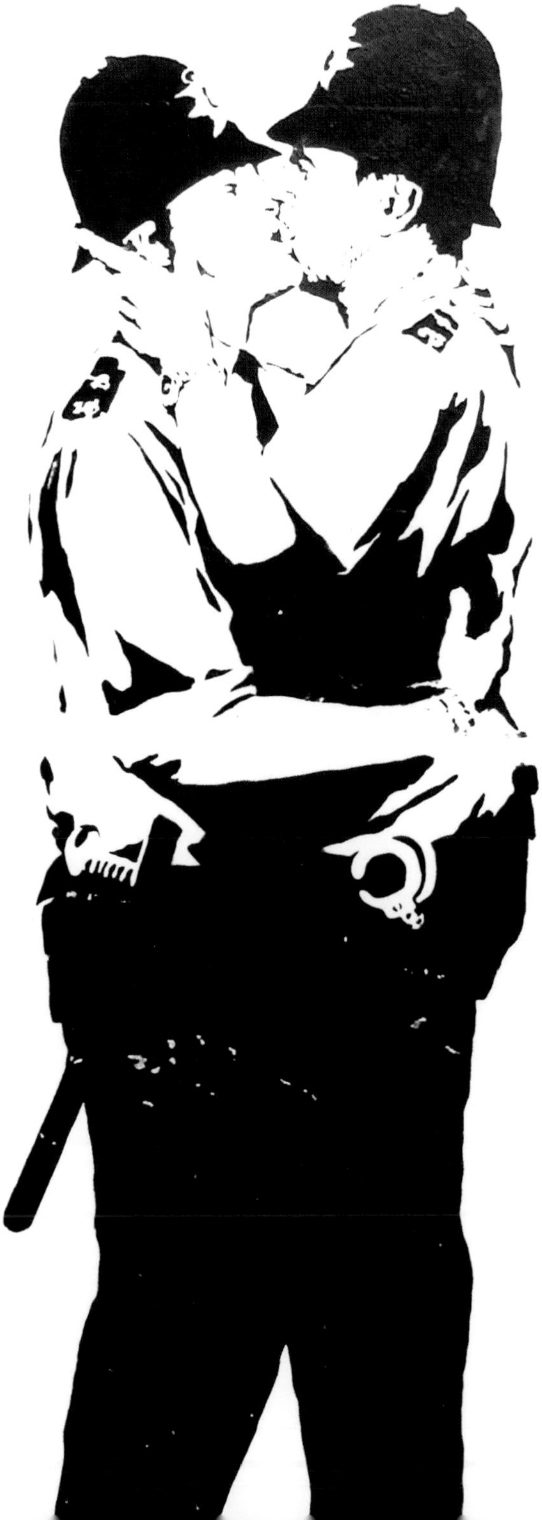

Little black books

A crucial part of the Banksy strategy was the release of his three 'little black books', *Banging Your Head Against a Brick Wall* (2001), *Existencilism* (2002) and *Cut It Out* (2004). Mixing musings with photos of his work to date, these little paperbacks were later collated into his mega-selling coffee-table book *Wall and Piece* (Century); but, before he was a household name, the books, which originally cost less than a fiver and are now selling at around £40 a piece on Amazon, pushed his name out there with some classic stealth marketing.

"The books were a piece of genius, because they were so accessible," says Banksy collector Martin Roberts. "The best way for him to influence people was to get them reading those books, understanding for themselves what he's about, making them feel they have a stake in the whole Banksy phenomenon. Just the same as with celebrity chefs, the books are a hugely important part of who they are and how they are known – suddenly they're in your homes, you can spend time thinking about them, feel you've got to know them better."

John Mitchell, former editor of *Venue*, agrees. "Until I'd read his books, I'd never realised how prolific, funny and creative his art was. I'd thought the whole Banksy phenomenon a bit overblown. Seeing how much he'd done – and how good it was – completely changed my opinion of him."

"I admire his business sense, he's been very shrewd," adds Ghostboy. "I remember seeing his little books in the bookshops, and I thought they were a masterstroke. They were £2 or £3 each, by the counter while you were waiting in the queue. You speak to people and they say, 'yeah, I've seen Banksy's work, and you say 'where?', and it turns out that they've seen the books. A lot of people got to know his work that way. People who, previously, had shown no interest in art had those books around their house."

For a guy who once admitted in an interview in *Venue* in March 2000 that his ideal night out in Bristol was: "Off your head on cider and ketamine spitting at things off the edge of the Suspension Bridge", Banksy clearly has an acute business sense.

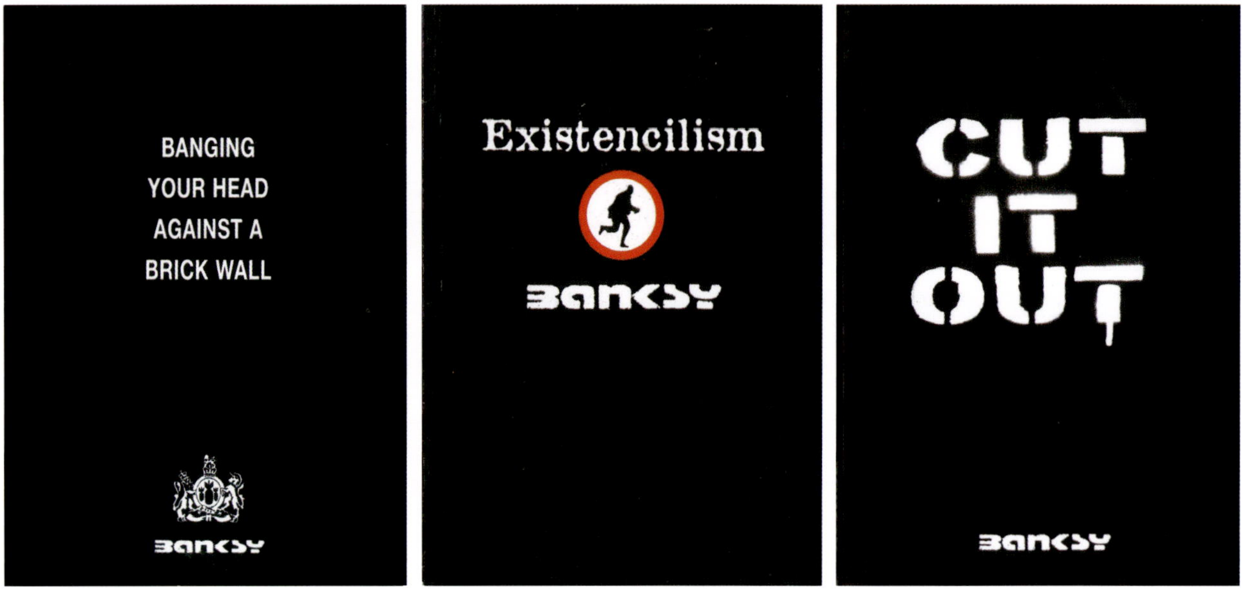

The three books sold for under a fiver. They go for £40 or more on eBay.

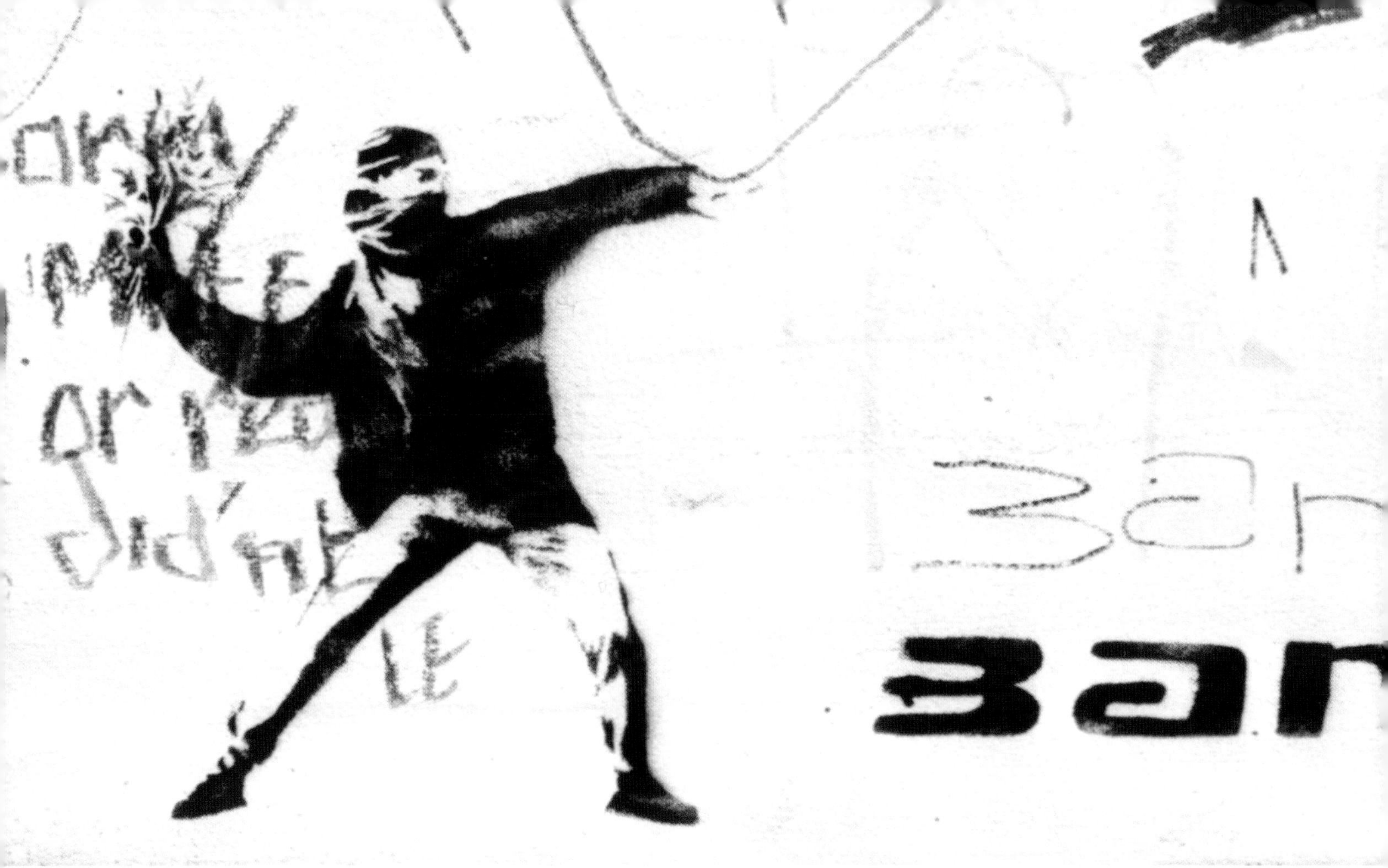

Cut it out

It's not always been possible to say for certain if a 'Banksy' is a Banksy, if you know what we mean. In April 2007, Bristol City Council announced that it planned to remove a mystery 'cut out coupon' (a familiar Banksy design) sprayed on a wall and pavement in Queens Road, Clifton after deciding it was not, in fact, from the hand of our elusive hero. The stencilled dotted black line with a pair of scissors was even accompanied by Banksy's trademark tag, but the council weren't convinced.

"He said it's not him, but he always says that," said Banksy's spokeswoman Jo Brooks mysteriously. The piece was duly removed. One reader promptly wrote in to the *Evening Post*: "Could someone explain to me why the 'cut out coupon' was 'art' when thought to be by Banksy – and, because it is by someone else, it is now graffiti?" Indeed.

A similar debate was triggered by the appearance of a 'Banksy' opposite the Children's Hospital in October 2007. The sniper with a child behind him about to burst a paper bag has all the hallmarks of Banksy's humour and the inclusion of a child (or animal) is a Banksy trademark. But it's not 'signed' which reopened the 'Is it only art if it says it's a Banksy?' issue. Councillor Gary Hopkins said that counterfeit 'Pranksys' should be allowed to remain depending on how 'funny' they are. This elicited an immediate and withering response from the Bristol Blogger: "Sorry there Leonardo, Turner, Cezanne and especially you Goya, I'm afraid you lot don't make the grade any more using Gary's new humour test for real art."

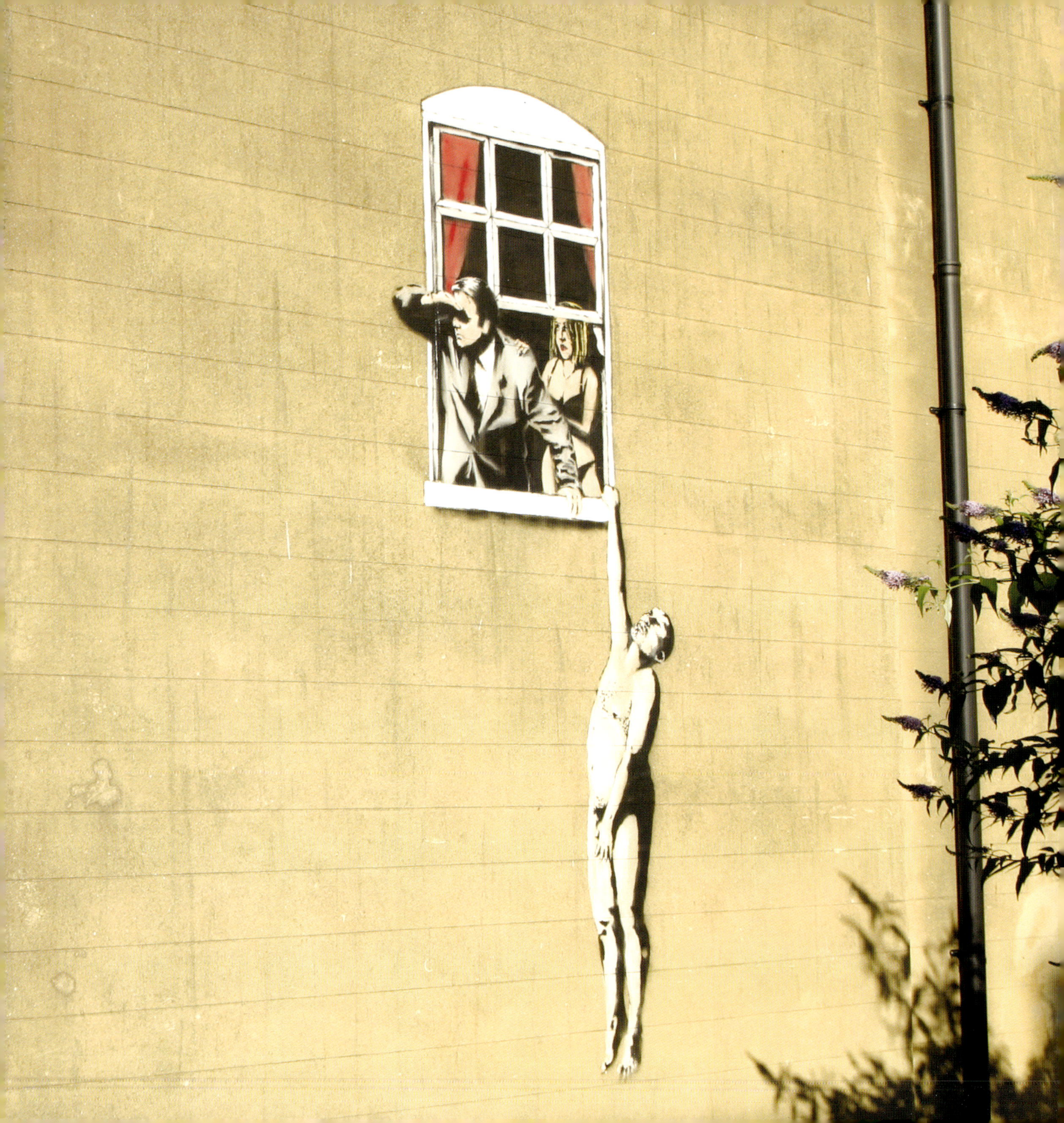

Keep the piece

The debate over the Frogmore Street Banksy...
Banksy famously returned to Bristol in June 2006 to paint a mural of a naked man hanging from a window on the side of a sexual health clinic in Frogmore Street, facing Park Street and City Hall. The piece, on the wall of the Brook Young People's Clinic, sparked a heated debate about whether it should be allowed to stay. Lib Dem Councillor Mark Wright said that the image had artistic qualities and launched a petition to save it, to which the local MP Stephen Williams signed up.

"The vast majority of people can see the difference between street art and vandalism," said Wright. "For as long as residents continue to support the Banksy artwork, it should stay. Why should the Council remove something, at significant expense, that most people enjoy and want to stay? What a waste of money that would be."

A Council spokesperson confirmed that "Bristol City Council has not received any complaints from the public about the 'Banksy' on Park Street."

The Council decided to put the question to the public via an online poll. Nearly 500 Bristolians voted, 97 per cent of them in favour of keeping the piece. Not everyone was happy, though – in particular Conservative Councillor Spud Murphy, who commented "It's ludicrous. The Council have gone mad", and warned that the move would encourage more acts of paint-based vandalism across Bristol. "It's absolutely stupid. They will have them all over the city now. They have given a licence for everybody in Bristol to do it. These graffiti artists all think they are better than each other and try to out-do each other."

"The council went through all manner of contortions over the fate of the bloke hanging-out-of-the-window picture," comments journalist Eugene Byrne. "I think it's a mark of his talent that he can spark off this huge storm-in-a-teacup debate about whether or not it should have been painted over."

One of those keenest to preserve the piece was Annie Evans, medical director of the Brook Young People's Clinic on which the image was painted. "We emailed Banksy to explain how wildly appropriate the subject matter was, bearing in mind we are a sexual health clinic. He replied saying he hadn't realised that and thought it was really funny. He said he hoped it wouldn't be removed straight away. I replied saying they would bulldoze it over my dead body!"

Banksy hired scaffolding with sheets around it and had it put up alongside the wall. Nobody thought to check why the scaffolding was there because it's such a common sight in city centres. Concealed by the sheets, Banksy painted the Well-Hung Man at his leisure in broad daylight and when it was finished, the scaffolding company removed the structure thus 'unveiling' Banksy's latest work.

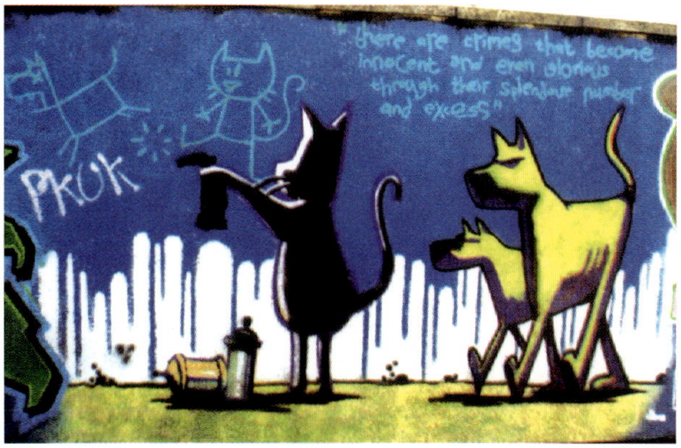

That page: Bristolians voted to keep the Well-Hung Man.

This page: An early Banksy on the walls of the Kebele anarchist centre in Easton.

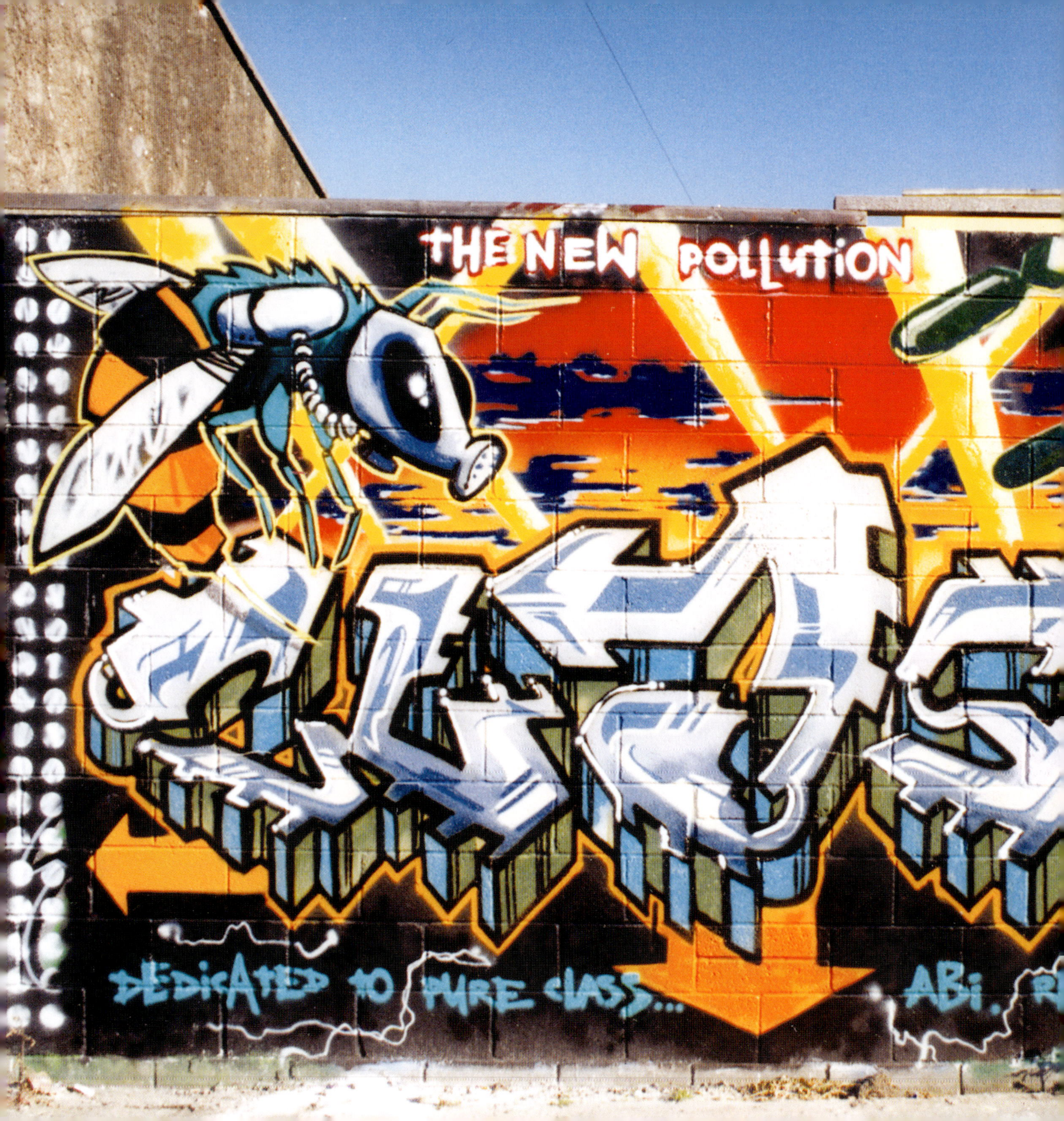
THE NEW POLLUTION
DEDICATED TO PURE CLASS...
ABI.

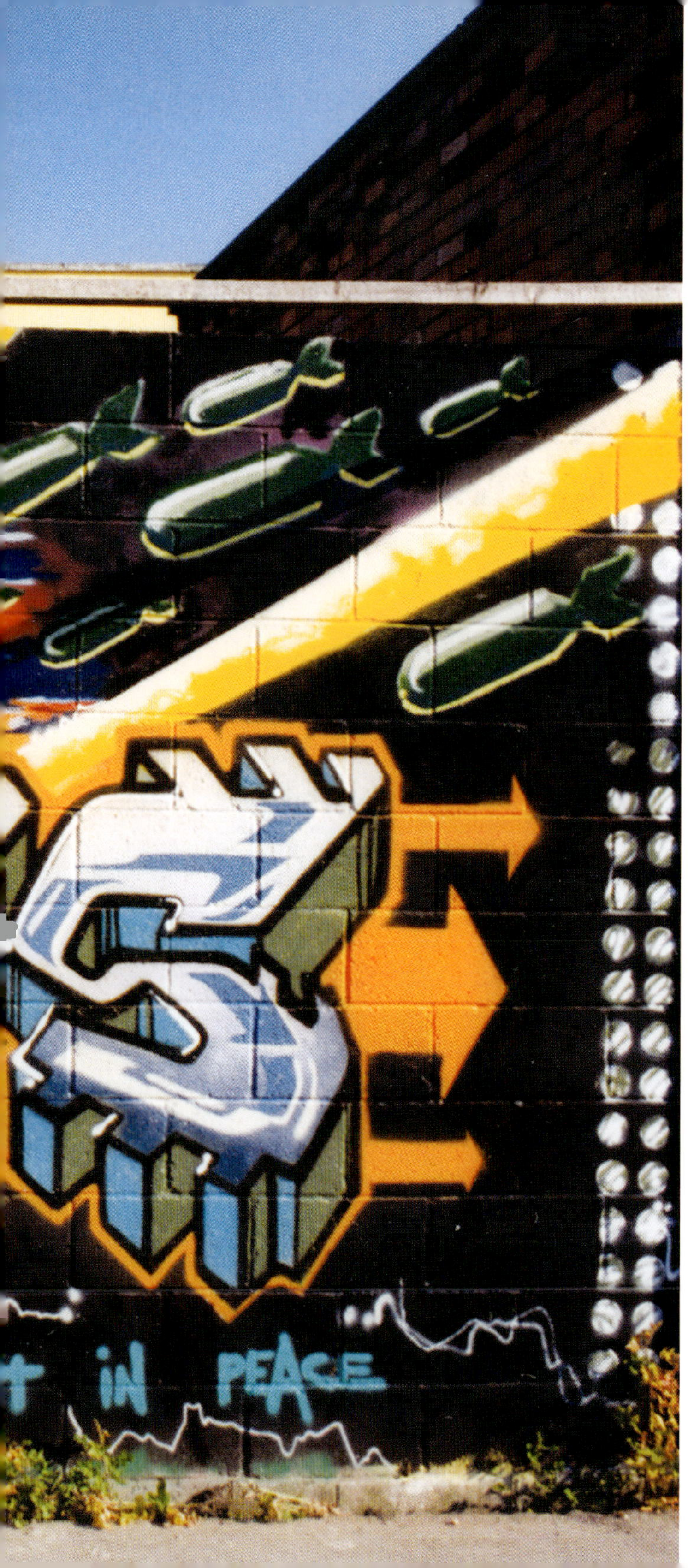

The New Pollution

At the end of 2006, there was much sadness in St Werburgh's, Bristol, over the demolition of a wall named 'Abi's Wall' which featured a Banksy piece titled The New Pollution. It was dedicated to Abi Clay, a young resident of Ashley Hill who died, aged 21, after suffering an asthma attack at the Thekla nightclub. Banksy, one of Abi's friends, designed the mural in early 1998, and other friends painted it.

The piece featured an image of an insect wearing a gas mask, a reference to Abi's asthma: it's thought that Banksy's common image of an angel wearing a gas mask is also a tribute to Abi. It was one of the relatively rare, early freehand (non-stencil) Banksys, and also one of Bristol's earliest pieces of spontaneously-produced community art. Many St Werburghians regard its removal – knocked down to make way for flats – as an act of vandalism.

When the piece was demolished, *The Times* contacted some auctioneers for a valuation of the lost piece. Answer? Difficult to quantify, apparently, but "without a doubt into six figures". David Friedman, managing director of developers Springdale, said: "I was talking to local agents about the value for the future flats, but no-one ever mentioned the sentimental value of the graffiti. If I'd known about it earlier I'd have done all I could to save it."

It seems a shame – when all sorts of public art is being expensively commissioned and the soon-to-open Museum of Bristol is looking for ideas of exhibits that best encapsulate the city – that free, spontaneous public art like this is lost.

Photographer Mark Simmons on The New Pollution

"I photographed this piece in May 1998 before I knew him. I love his pieces that get you thinking and make powerful social/political statements. This was dedicated to a special friend of his who died from asthma, making the piece all the more poignant. It was sited on a busy commuter traffic junction in Bristol, just a stone's throw from primary schools and a doctor's surgery. Powerful symbolism – the masked mutant bee, the attacking bombs and, of course, the irony of the location – it all works towards what he's saying."

There was widespread dismay when Abi's Wall was demolished to make way for new flats. After protests the flats were named Abi Clay Court as a mark of respect.

Banksy put this one up in Glastonbury while he was on his way to Pilton to create Boghenge for the 2007 festival.

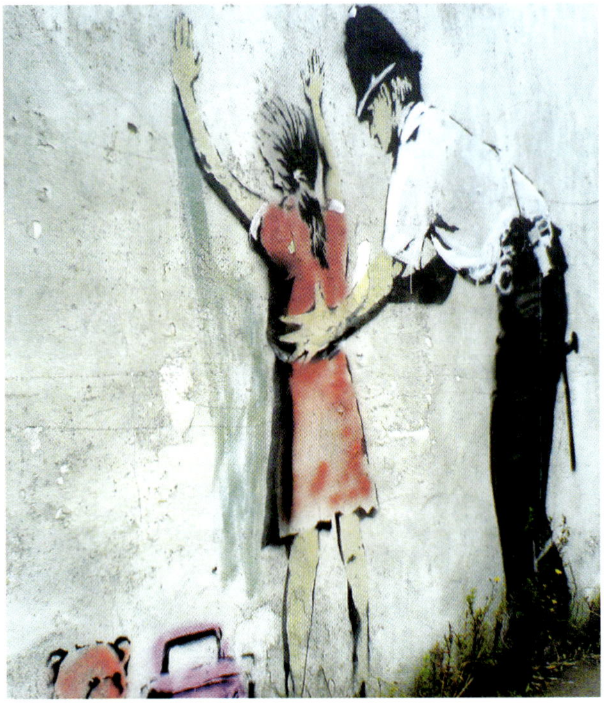

Bristol author Stephen Morris on the Banksy Effect

"Banksy's clever: he delivers great visual one-liners, poking fun at unfaithful wives and cuckolded husbands, grim reapers with smiley faces, buried treasure under Weston-super-Mare beach. No other graffiti artists do this in quite the same way. Some graffiti is very good, but none surprises you or makes you think or laugh like Banksy's.

"Is he a force for good? He is a tourist attraction, but exposure devalues his place in the counter-culture. He's one of several accomplished graffiti artists associated with Bristol, but perhaps the only one whose name and reputation is known outside of the city. His work doesn't just fill a gap and explore colour and form, it cuts to a message – political, punning, funny, satirical. In this way he's different. He doesn't make big claims for his work, but I think this is a bit disingenuous – nobody goes to Palestine and paints on the peace wall without a degree of political awareness and motivation.

"I don't think his work has great artistic merit, but (like Warhol's cans of soup), it has iconic status. Parody is the key to his work. He's not angry, he won't riot, but he does have a sideways look at hypocrisy and makes us laugh at ourselves and our circumstances."

Bone on Banksy

Ian Bone, founder of Anarchist group Class War, author of *Bash The Rich* and former editor of *The Bristolian* scandal sheet on Banksy

"The creative personality does not seek to shock or entertain the bourgeoisie but seeks to destroy them... Banksy is Captain Swing and General Ludd, Spartacus and the Scarlet Pimpernel, Spring Heeled Jack and the Angel of Mons. The Witchfinder Generals will open a thousand coffins, unbrick a thousand priest holes, disinter a princess, but Magwitch will be loping through the long grass of the salt marshes."

Wall-to-wall coverage

A prominent, anonymous Bristol graffer on the Banksy effect

"I respect the guy's work, but I think he is casting a giant shadow over the scene and has created [albeit unwittingly] a horrible state of affairs, where every art agent and dealer is looking out for the 'next Banksy' and the media are unable to focus on any other street artist. I've no interest in being labelled 'the next Banksy'.

"D*Face [another British street artist] is a case in point, an artist whose work panders unashamedly to media hype, often appropriating the same iconic images that Banksy has used – Warhol, £10 notes, and so on – and bringing nothing new to the scene.

"On the plus side, the huge profile and exposure given to Banksy's work has re-opened the debate on vandalism vs. graffiti and has seen Bristol City Council slowly starting to take its street artists more seriously."

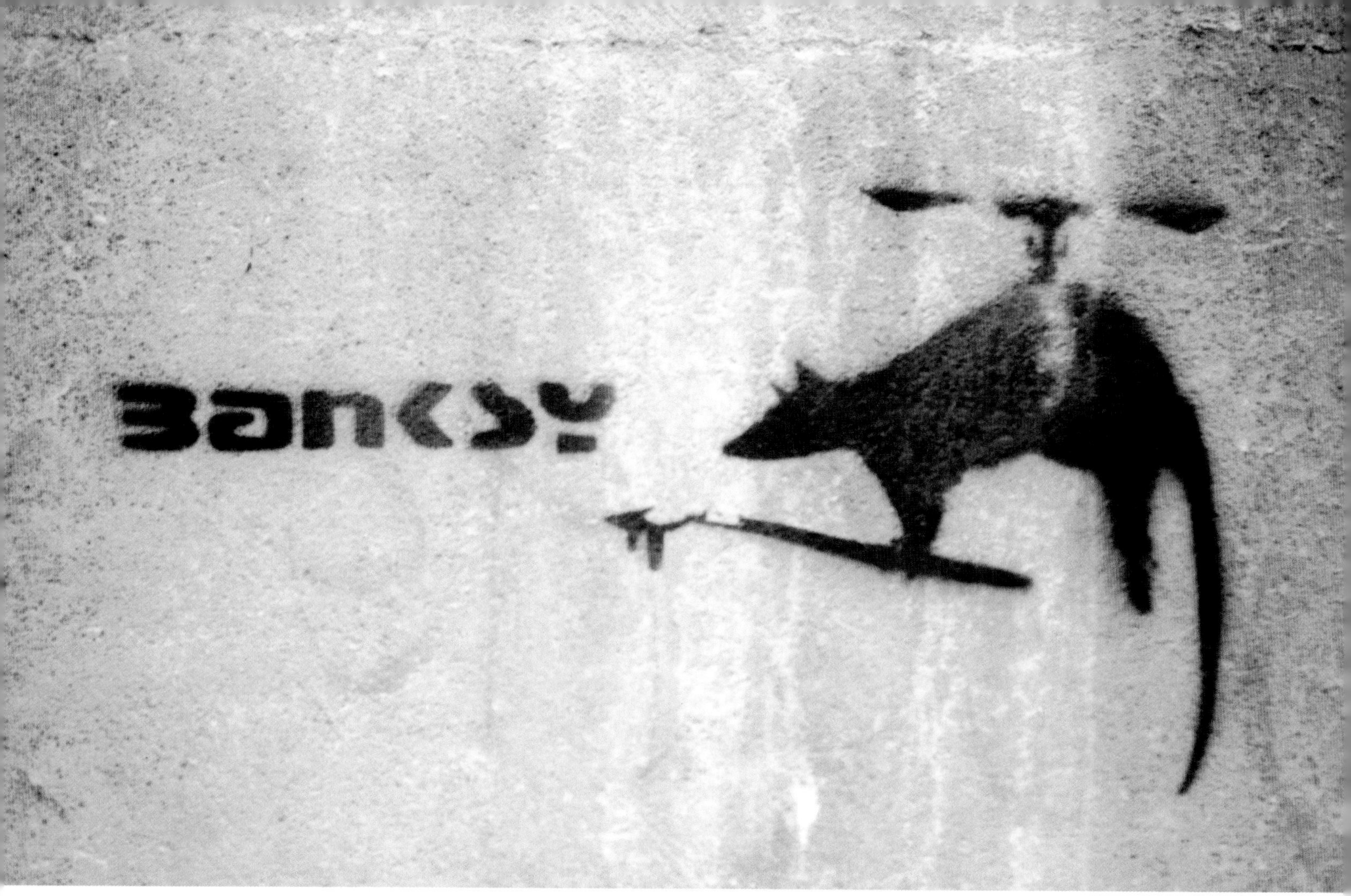

Banksy, by the Bristol Blogger

The Bristol Blogger is an anonymous satirical observer of Bristol's social and political scene who can be found at thebristolblogger.wordpress.com.

Does Banksy belong to a subversive Bristol tradition that runs from riots in Queen Square in 1831 to subvertising more recently?

"I find this whole idea of Bristol as a subversive place a bit of a joke, to be honest. It's a very, very conservative city, still run and dominated by a very, very conservative toff/mercantile alliance (The Merchant Venturers and their circle) who still set the social, political and cultural agenda in the city to a remarkable extent. These tossers crop up everywhere with their culturally conservative agenda eg. Watershed, Arnolfini, Old Vic, Bristol Post, City Council, voluntary sector etc.

"The reality is that Banksy had to go to London to make a name for himself as he was ignored in Bristol. He follows in a long line of talent such as [progressive nineteenth-century architect] Edward William Godwin and [playwright] Tom Stoppard, who have had to head for London to get noticed.

"Where's the evidence of this subversive culture the city's fostered? It's certainly not capable of supporting or promoting itself within the city, let alone nationally or

The creative personality does not seek to shock or to entertain the bourgeoisie but seeks to destroy them.

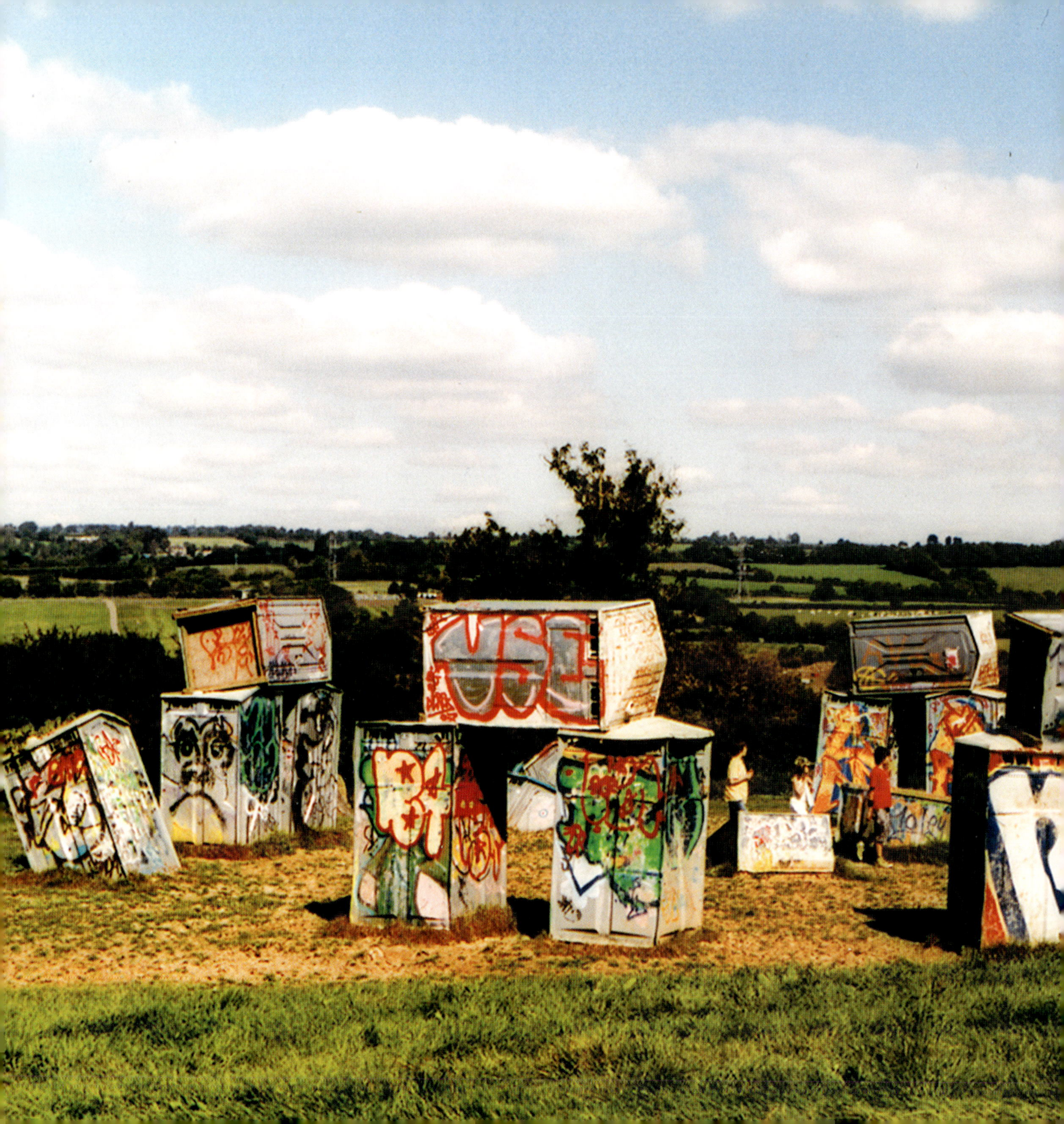

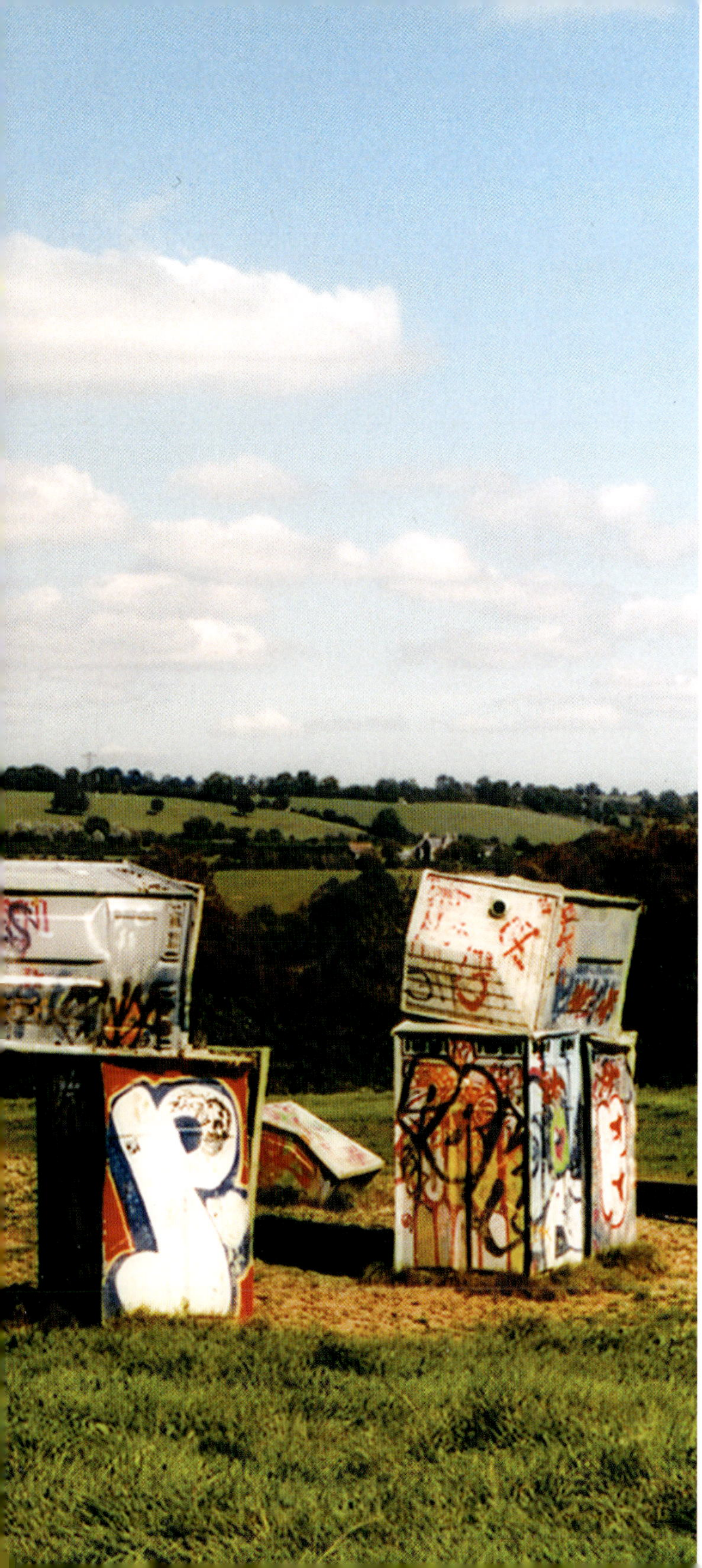

internationally. And the kind of institutions that might support such a culture (see above) do sod all. Arnolfini and Watershed particularly consistently spend their large budgets on out-of-towners and their ideas.

"And, by the way, I think Massive Attack are the exception rather than the rule in Bristol. It's also worth remembering that we're talking about a band who had their heyday years ago – although they do have a tangential relationship to Banksy through the hip hop/graf thing.

What do you make of Banksy's work?
Extremely well executed. He has that impressive ability to make what has clearly been well thought out and worked through extensively look like it's been thrown together. This gives it its 'street' feel. I'd put him up there with Peter Saville [graphic designer who produced, among others, record sleeves for Joy Division and New Order] and Neville Brody [former graphic designer for *The Face* and *Arena* magazines] in terms of graphic art. I do think if you have to ask the question: "But is it art?" The answer is invariably "no".

Bristol's establishment couldn't give a toss about Banksy's work. They just see a new marketing opportunity for the city (and by extension their businesses). Plus they're so tasteless and moronic that if London says something's good, they'll believe it regardless. Whereas if something under their noses is good, they'll ignore it unless they're told it's good by someone from *The Guardian*!

Is there some irony that Banksy, with his impeccable anti-capitalist credentials, is adding to Bristol's economic, tourist and property values?
It's not ironic. And his credentials aren't impeccable! You can't bring down capitalism through the art market – a pillar of capitalist accumulation. It was true then and it's true now. The purpose of entering the art market is to make money. What else is it for? Anybody who thinks they can spark a revolution, create the new Jerusalem, redistribute wealth or feed the starving via the art market is a twat.

Boghenge at Glastonbury Festival 2007.

Is the media too slavish in its admiration of Banksy?

Yes. It's well-crafted anti-capitalist agit prop FFS. It's interesting to note that most of the journalists writing about Banksy tend to be establishment news reporters, rock critics, Sunday supplement interviewers etc. who seem to have a romantic and uncritical approach to the whole 'street' thing. I think he's hooked into that big audience of male, white, middle-class, graduate Nathan Barleys who are on a black/working class/street/authenticity trip.

Has he been a force for good in Bristol?

Yes. He makes us look smart and streetwise.

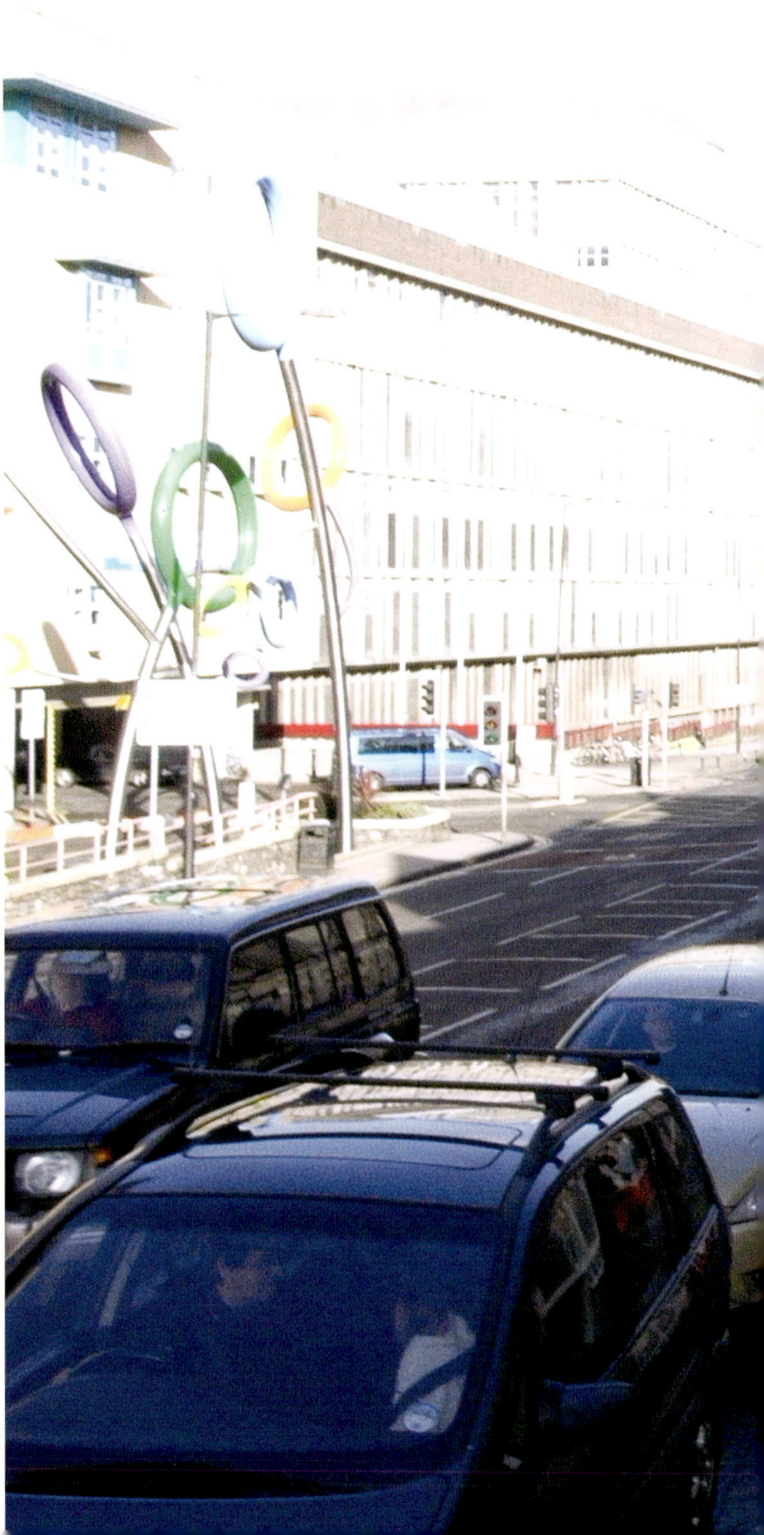

The lack of a tag on the October 2007 Banksy re-ignited the whole 'But is it art?' debate.

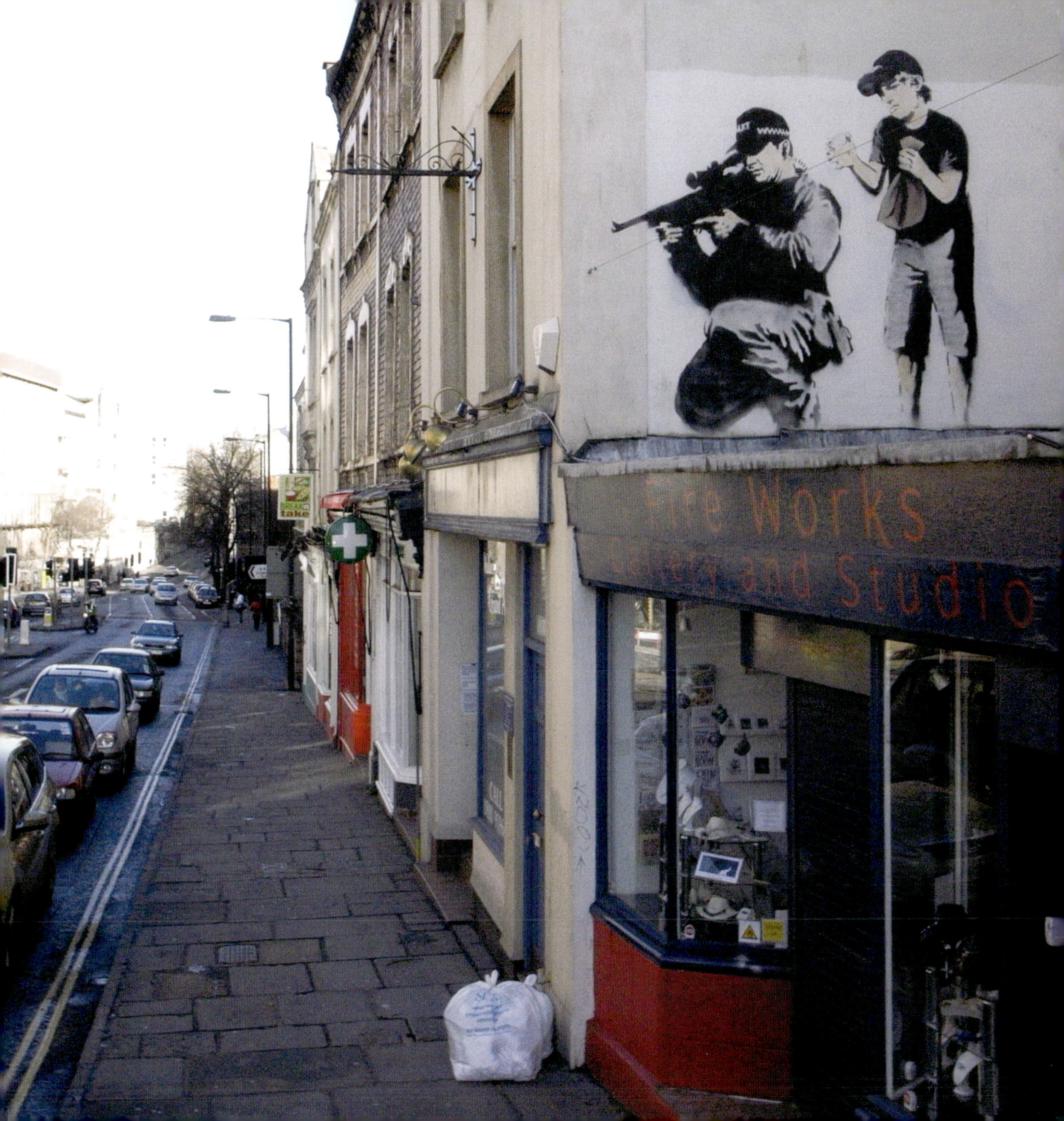
Fire Works
Gallery and Studio

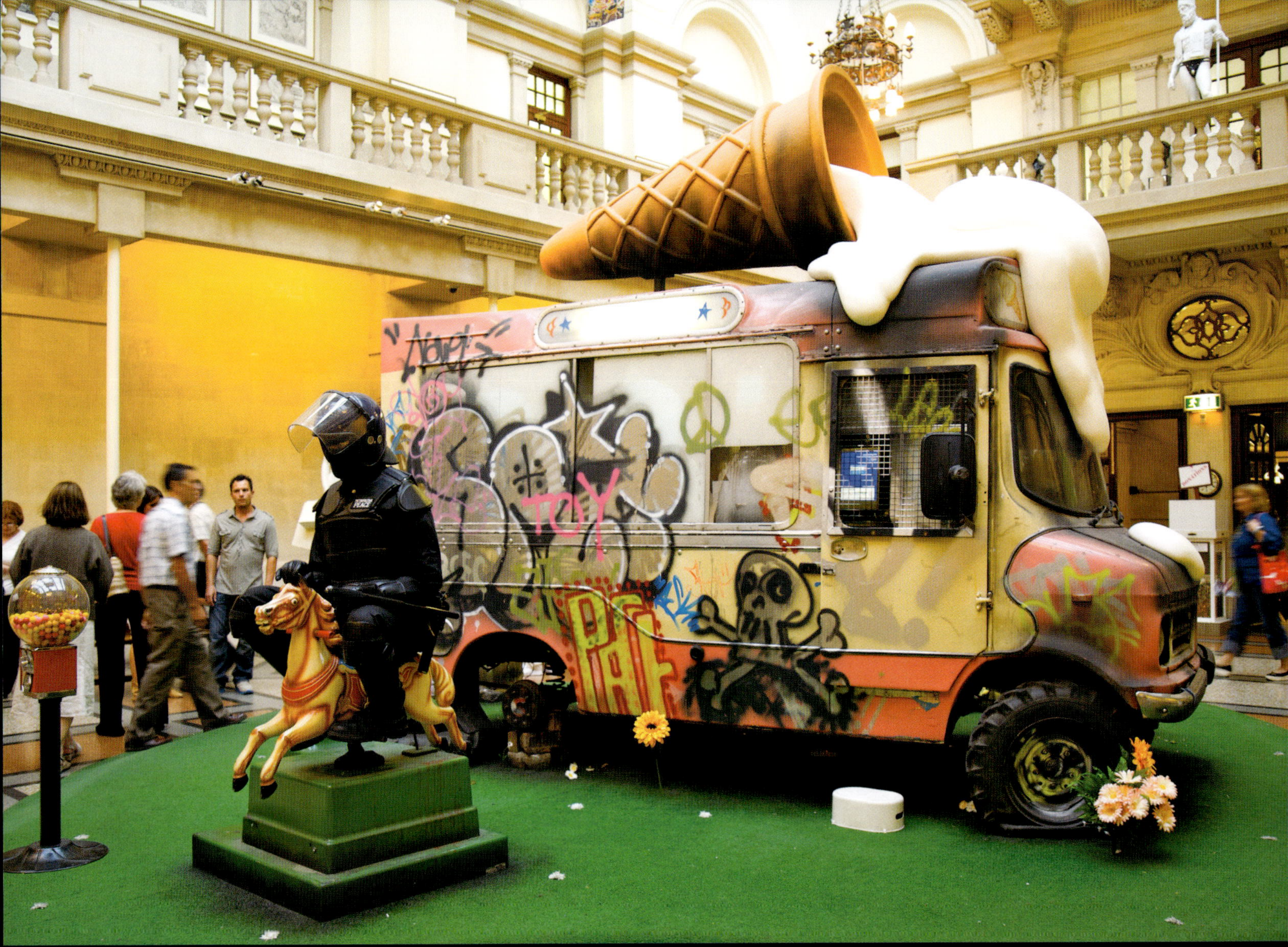

Banksy vs Bristol Museum

Renegade, subversive genius or half-baked hip art-

native Bristol is sharp, witty and often pretty bleak – but the most striking thing about it all, really, is the sheer fact and size of it.

Yep, the art's good, though it doesn't have the same incendiary impact and sense of place as a street piece maps of Olde Bristle and portraits of portly Victorian philanthropists are now an urban jungle of bombed-out ice-cream vans, tottering alabaster ladettes and mother-hen CCTV cameras tending to their babycam brood.

Yes, this is (morally) Bankrupt Britain, as seen through Banksy's unmistakably jaundiced lens: and it's plastered all over one of our great bastions of art, learning and culture. And the fact that he did all this under a cloak of secrecy, unbeknownst to all but a small cabal of intimates; that he's come back to honour his home town and remind his global fanbase where it all started; that he paid for the whole thing himself; and that nothing inside is for sale (delivering, for now, a robust rap over the knuckles to the 'Banksy = sellout' school of thought): these are the show's biggest draws.

Beside which, the works on show are... not half bad, actually. In the centre of it all, a life-size ice cream van sits forlornly in a no-man's land of battered oil drums and discarded tyres. The supersize cone on its roof is upended, its beaten-up panels are caked with layers of tagging and its faulty chime plays an endless, mournful dirge. Splendidly, it's also been transformed into the Museum's reception for the duration of the show. Yards away, Banksy's given us a Classical sculpture on a plinth, just where you'd expect to see one in this place – but this beauty, in pencil bra, kitten heels and microshorts, swigs from an alcopop and totters tipsily through a rubble of chips, fag packets and takeaway boxes.

Upstairs, Banksy has infiltrated a few of his own fine-art revisions onto the gallery walls. He's doctored Millet's famous pastoral 'Gleaners', for example, so that one of the French peasant women has sidestepped out of the frame for a quick fag. Elsewhere, the muted bucolic colours of Claude's 'Flight into Egypt' are trampled over by a garish hoarding boasting Easyjet's budget Cairo deals.

A lot of the visual humour is brilliant in its absurdity and its upending of everyday normality. Banksy's always given underdogs their day – see those cheeky-varmint rats that rule his world – and they're still on top here, like the statue of a satisfied-looking circus lion with blood-spattered mouth, whip in its teeth and the remains of its tamer's sports-casual clothing at its feet. These visual one-liners are everywhere: some are clever, humane, even touching, and some are underwhelming (hur hur, it's the House of Commons but they're all, like, apes, hur hur).

A lot of them arouse a bit more than laughter, too. Stare too long at these urban wastelands, animatronic Chicken McNuggets and nest-building CCTVS, and you can start to feel a bit queasy at the soulless, automated, concrete-clad alienation of it all. The apocalypse has come and all we can do is eat and spend money; everything in this new world is either rotten or mechanical. But if

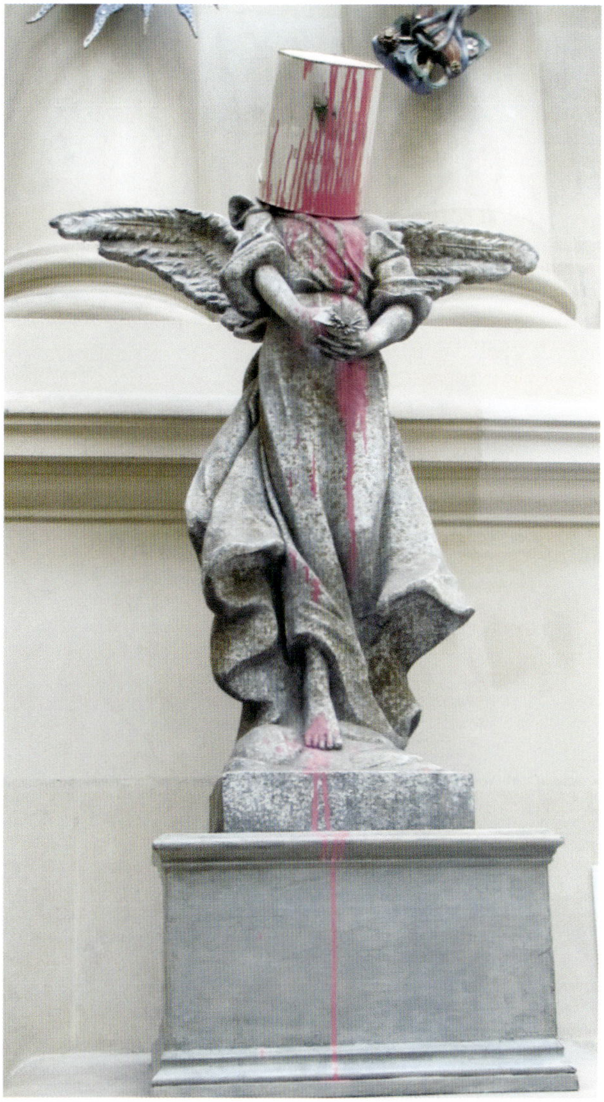

That page: This was the first sight that greeted visitors when they entered the museum.

This page: Paintpot Angel from the 2009 show is still on display at Bristol Museum and Art Gallery.

This page: Michael Jackson feels the force of Banksy's wit.

That page: Banksy's penchant for 'adapting' old masters was much in evidence at Bristol Museum.

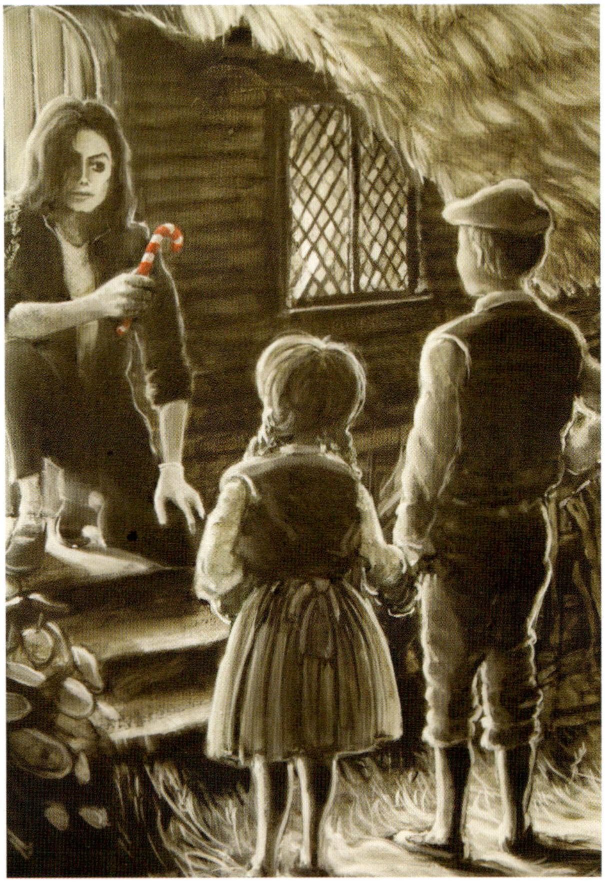

Banksy's vision of the future is bleak, it's astonishingly well-illustrated. And the fact that the laughter comes before the gag reflex is crucial to his appeal.

Is it art? I'm not sure that it is, because it doesn't have that sense of optimism, of portraying a slightly transformed, more edifying or just more interesting version of our own world, that much art has. It ruthlessly punctures our nice, clean view of things; it takes a dry, disaffected look at life and sees the small print in the dream everywhere. But it has a laugh, always, while doing so. It's a series of visual gags, many of them very similar in feel, and the joke may well wear thin someday. But for now, this show is instantly striking, funny and fairly memorable. And for the sheer courage of the thing, of taking over a pillar of the cultural Establishment and filling it with his images of Alienation Britain, we salute both Banksy and the City Museum.

Museum pieces

As the then Director of Museums, Galleries and Archives for Bristol City Council, Kate Brindley masterminded the Bristol Museum exhibition alongside Banksy and his team. Here she recalls the preparations for, and impact of, the most extraordinary show in Bristol Museum's history.

Banksy got in touch with us. He was keen to show at the museum. He could have exhibited anywhere in the world and he chose to come to Bristol. That was a real statement for him.

As Director, I took the decision that this was too good an opportunity to pass up. My job was to programme the Museum, not to go around asking people's permission. None of us understood the scale of what we were getting involved with, though – we didn't realise it would be one of the 10 most visited exhibitions in the world. You don't go around thinking like that.

We gave Banksy and his team free rein: we just stepped in to fulfil our legal and health and safety requirements. And the care of the collection was very important to us – it is, after all, property of the people of Bristol. So we had some lines we would not cross – and the Banksy team were very respectful of those. It was a different way of working for them, as normally they would infiltrate an institution rather than ask permission of it. But they were a slick operation.

His initial idea was much smaller than what we ended up with, but because both parties got very excited about the possibilities, it grew. He clearly knows the museum really well and had done a lot of thinking about what he wanted to do, which then needed quite a bit of testing and discussion.

He didn't ask for any fee, either for himself or his people; nothing at all. His technical team talked with us about the technical possibilities, because it was all quite a big deal for us. Blacking out the whole of the rear hall was no mean feat, for example. As far as I know, that had never happened before, but this evolving conversation about the philosophical, curatorial and technical issues made the whole process possible. Banksy was incredibly

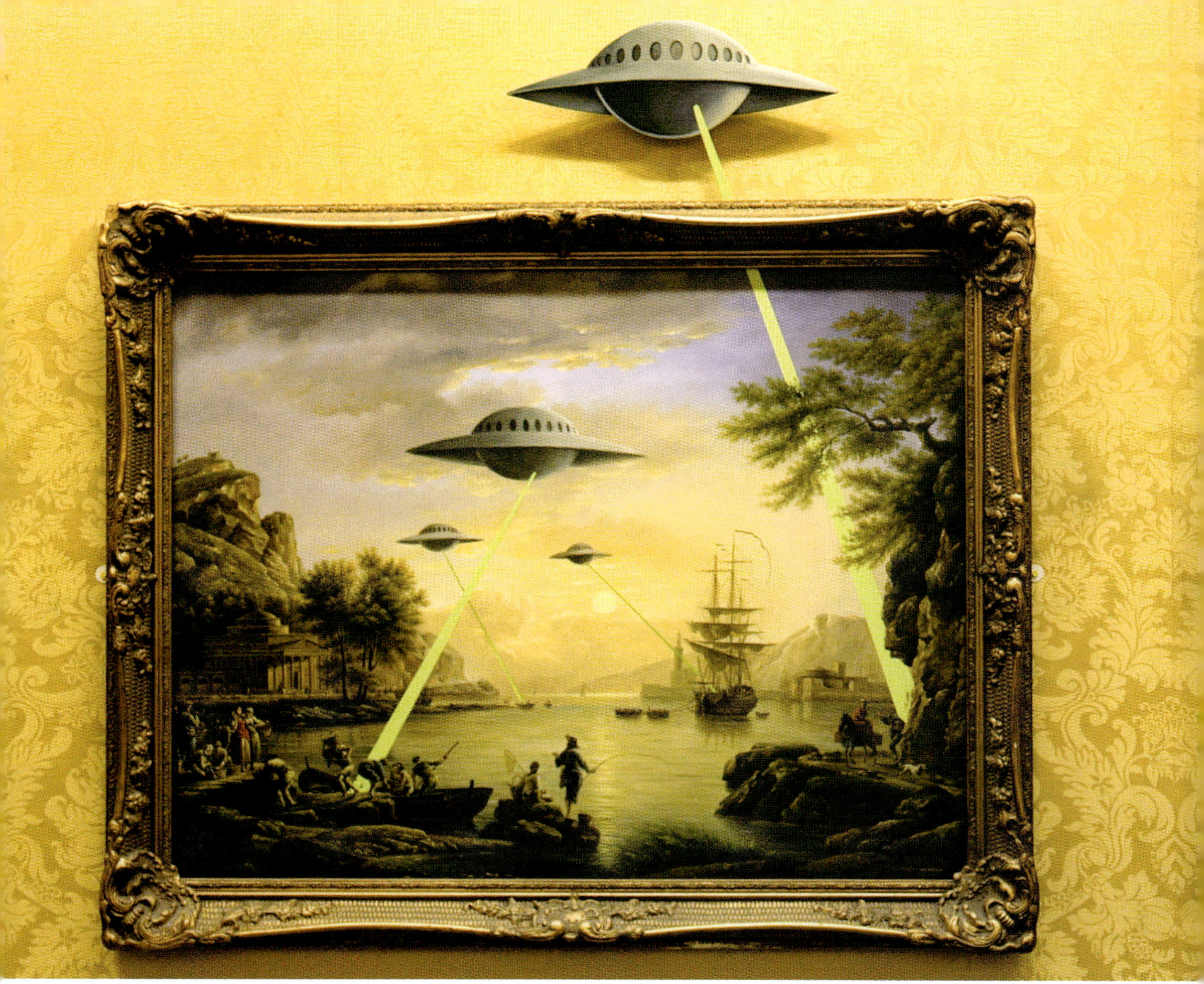

generous about all the costs: we put in no more than we would to a normal exhibition – less in fact, because he was so generous in paying for the changes. It was really a gift from him to the city; it says a lot about him and his loyalty to Bristol, in my view.

The show had to be kept secret, so a very small number of us, among the Museum's 150-odd staff, actually knew about it before the opening. That was quite a tough thing to manage. It's not the way we usually work, so it wasn't always that comfortable. But we knew that we had to do it that way, otherwise it would jeopardise the outcome of the show. And of course, all sorts of people, within and outside the Museum, were asking what we'd got planned for the summer months. I can't remember

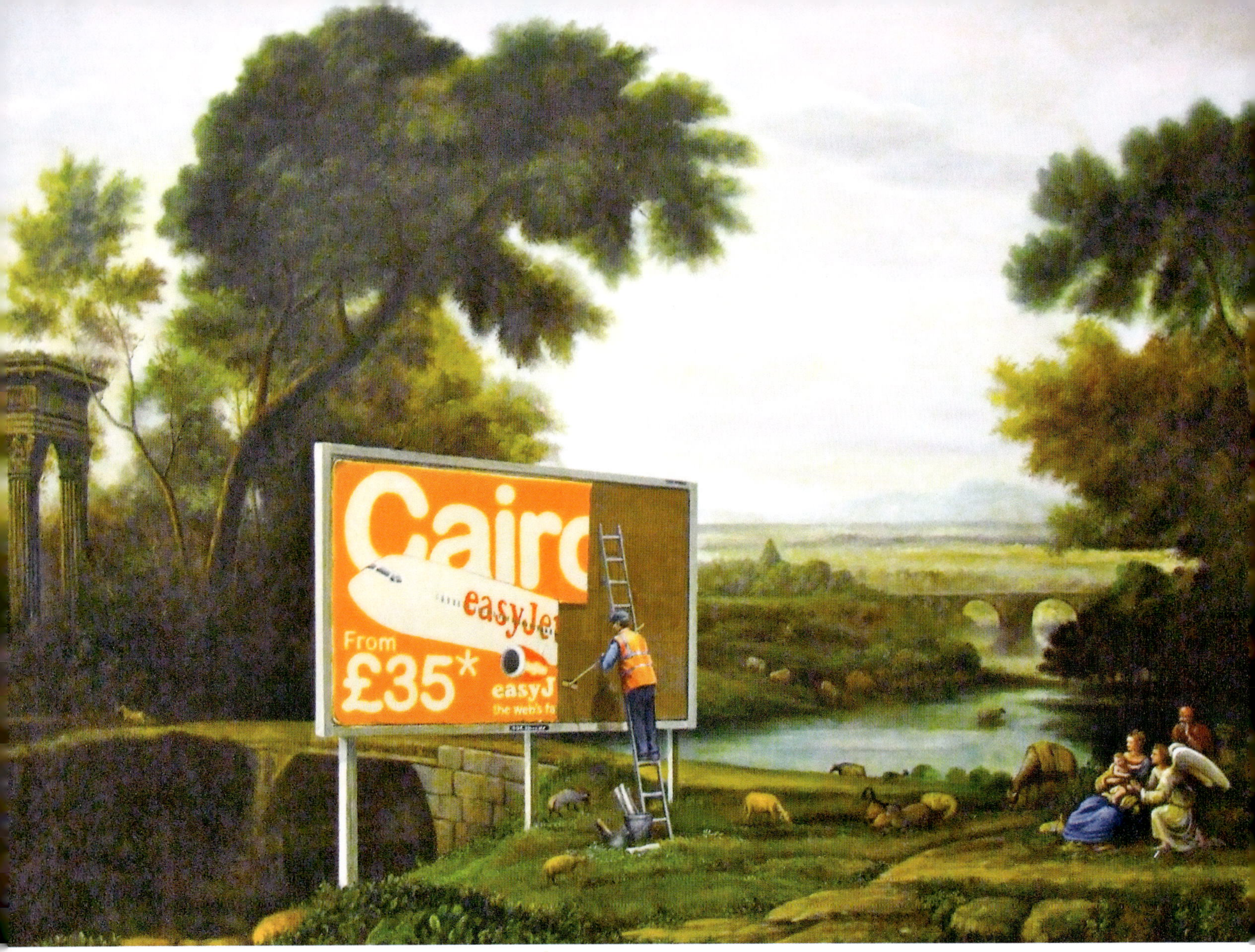

how we got round that – I think we told everyone that we had essential maintenance work to do over the summer.

The show was hugely popular, but Banksy didn't want it to run any longer than 31 August. He normally comes and goes in a few weeks at the most, or does his little 'pop-up' shows… Spontaneity is part of the whole persona.

Did I ever meet the man himself? No – or, if I did, I didn't know. And really, that seems immaterial, because the mystique is all part of the appeal with Banksy.

The impact of the exhibition on Bristol was phenomenal. It had huge popular appeal and publicity, and the city embraced it wholeheartedly. I think everyone felt part of it. It had immense economic value for Bristol too. And it gave another reason – if Bristol needed it – for the city to say, 'culture is really important to us, it's an essential part of the USP and lifeblood of this city'.

Of course, Bristol was already starting to realise that it needed to embrace street art. Events like 'Crimes of Passion' (a massive group street art exhibition, featuring dozens of well-known Bristol graffers both emerging and established] earlier that year had already helped to cement street art as part of Bristol's mainstream culture – something we wanted to embrace, not eradicate.

Now, street art is part of the Bristol landscape – but that wasn't the case back then. I had people ringing me directly after the show still with their fears about what to do with street art: 'how are we going to deal with the fact that it's going to become an acceptable practice?' And of course there is still a debate about where art begins and vandalism ends, but I think that debate is less pressing now – and this exhibition played a big part in that.

How did the serious art world react to the show? Banksy is not embraced by the serious art world. A lot of my peer group found it completely unacceptable. I don't mind that at all. It was the right thing to do at that moment, for that museum and for Bristol.

The art world – the curators, not the auction houses – will probably never accept Banksy, but I think the art world is always like that and Banksy himself plays with that. He is now one of the most commercially successful UK artists along with Damien Hirst. One of those two is acceptable, the other isn't – and is quite happy not to be. There is always debate in the art world about what is acceptable and what isn't, and there always will be.

Has the show had a long-term impact? It's been great to see the British Museum collaborating with Grayson Perry. Would they have done that in a world without the Banksy vs Bristol Museum exhibition? I think that the more open institutions are to challenge and dialogue, the better. And that openness to dialogue was a really important part of what drew me to Bristol. It's very important that the city continues to do that.

While we were planning the Banksy show, the same team was planning M Shed, the new Museum for Bristol. And the same principles applied there – being open to different voices, to dialogues about the city's history, embracing hidden histories and not just telling the stories of the big powerful men. Offering different, often controversial, often uncomfortable stories. Even though his forms of expression are humorous and tongue-in-cheek, the things Banksy has to say aren't always comfortable.

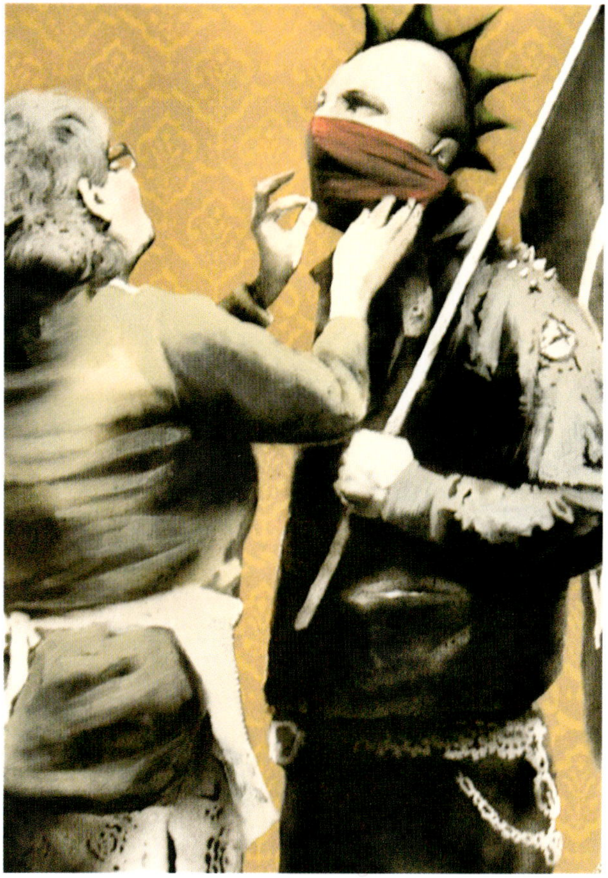

That page: The Flight To Egypt by Claude Derain gets the Banksy treatment.

This page: Even anarcho-punks have mums.

People will always associate me with that show. I was asked to speak at a conference at the British Museum about working with artists in museums with historic collections, and they said, 'we want you to talk about Banksy'. So he might not be acceptable to the art world on one level, but the art world is very interested in him. He was debated in that hall all day long: he is such a source of contention. Basically, people are very divided about whether he should be taken seriously. The show was so popular that it couldn't be ignored, but does that make it acceptable? Questions like that fascinate me.

I'm so happy to have been part of the show. It was an absolute, unique, once-in-a-career opportunity; you just couldn't not do it.

Exit Through the Gift Shop was billed as the first ever street art disaster movie (Pictures: Paranoid Pictures/ Revolver).

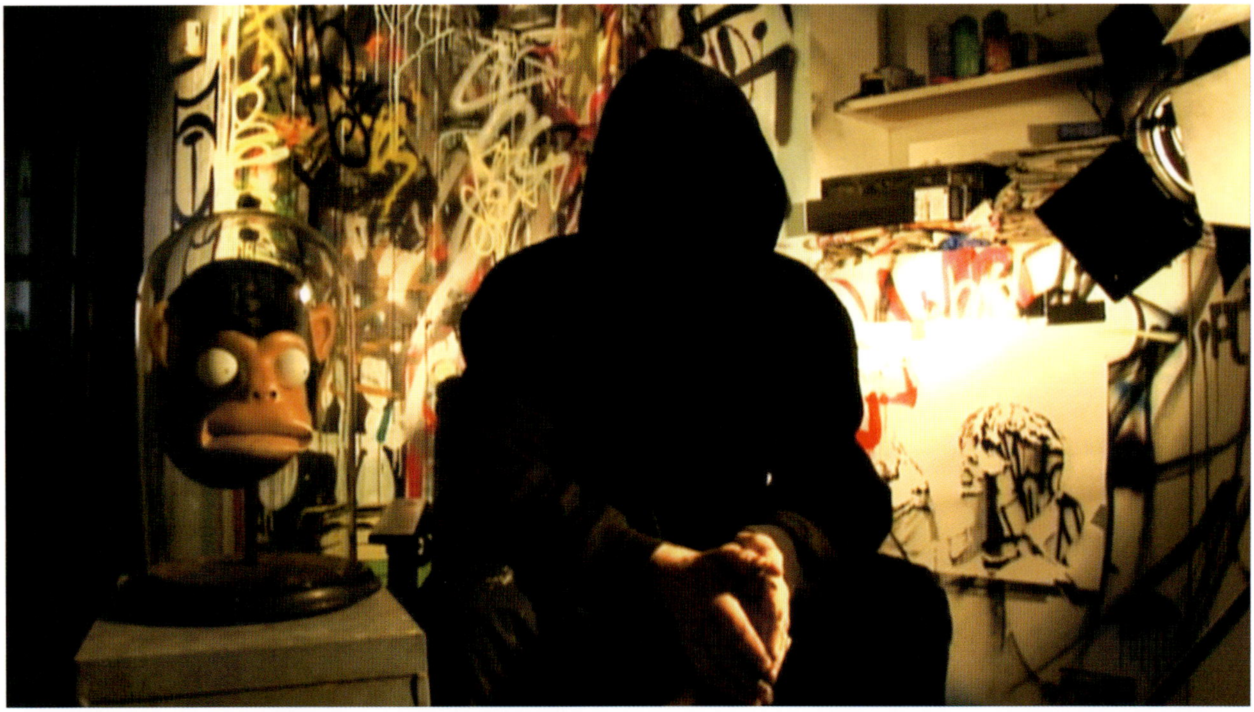

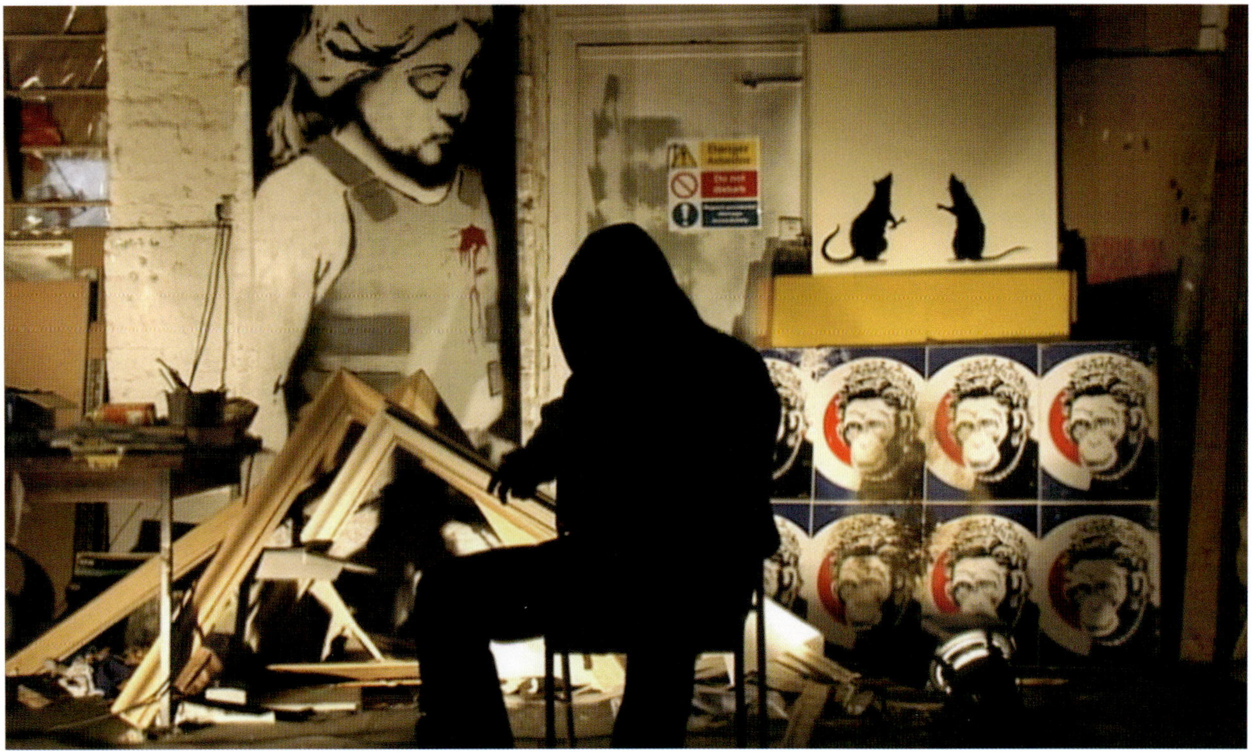

Exit Through The Gift Shop

The UK press show of Banksy's *Exit Through the Gift Shop* was never going to be a sober affair taking place in one of Soho's plush screening rooms. What the nation's film hacks weren't prepared for was the level of cloak and dagger secrecy surrounding the event. With just hours to go before the screening on Monday 22 February 2010, reviewers received a text message directing them to the Leake Street tunnels beneath Waterloo Station. This warren of disused railway arches had been converted into a pop-up cinema dubbed the Lambeth Palace. A scuzzy, grotesque parody of the grimiest fleapit, the 150-seat Palace was approached via a red carpet freshly painted on the road. Inside, journalists were greeted with a variety of tableaux: Banksy's burnt-out ice cream van, a simulated pyre of old masters, Her Maj and Prince Philip unveiling an anarchy symbol, and so on. On leaving, they were each handed a can of spray paint by a girl dressed as an usherette and invited to become complicit in the heinous crime of street art.

Billed as the first ever street art disaster movie, *Exit Through the Gift Shop* purports to tell the story of Thierry Guetta, a French immigrant to Los Angeles who met Banksy when the artist was preparing his Barely Legal show. An obsessive videographer, Guetta alleges he's constructing a documentary about the street art scene, but his tapes lie forlornly uncategorised and unedited. Banksy eventually turns the tables – and the camera – on Guetta, encouraging him to create art of his own. Little suspecting that he has spawned a monster, he keeps the camera rolling as Guetta re-brands himself 'Mr Brainwash' and employs a retinue of minions to churn out street/pop art on an industrial scale.

Few critics were prepared to take any of this at face value, possibly fearing that the joke may be on them. Was it, they wondered, another clever situationist prank transposed to a different medium? Was Banksy taking a snide swipe at his rivals and imitators? Or heaping scorn on those who admire or collect his art? Who is David Guetta/Mr. Brainwash, anyway? How much is he Banksy's own creation? Could he even be Banksy himself, hiding in plain sight with a funny French accent and a pair of stick-on sideburns? Maybe Banksy was demonstrating what would happen if he really was the 'sell-out' his detractors accused him of becoming. It's certainly striking that the scenes in which acolytes gush over Banksy's work at the Barely Legal show are interchangeable with the later ones where Mr Brainwash unveils his own chaotic exhibition.

On the other hand, perhaps all this speculation about motive is to miss the point, rather like those who have become obsessed with uncovering Banksy's real identity when there's no public appetite for him to be unmasked. Driven by Rhys Ifans' wry narration, *Exit Through the Gift Shop* is a hugely entertaining and frequently very funny film. There's also more than enough fascinating footage of Banksy going about his clandestine business – dumping a Guantanamo Bay 'prisoner' in Disneyland, creating his 'murdered phone box' piece in London with a team of helpers – to satisfy those who might otherwise feel short-changed by the focus on Guetta.

Exit Through the Gift Shop took a modest £310,000 at the UK box office, but earned more than $5 million worldwide. In January 2011, the film was nominated for an Oscar in the Best Documentary category. Its creator was refused permission to attend the ceremony incognito for fear that hordes of gate-crashing Banksys might show up, and the film eventually lost out to Charles Ferguson's excellent financial crisis documentary, *Inside Job*. This might have been the more deserving winner, but who wouldn't have wanted to hear a Banksy acceptance speech instead?

Robin Askew

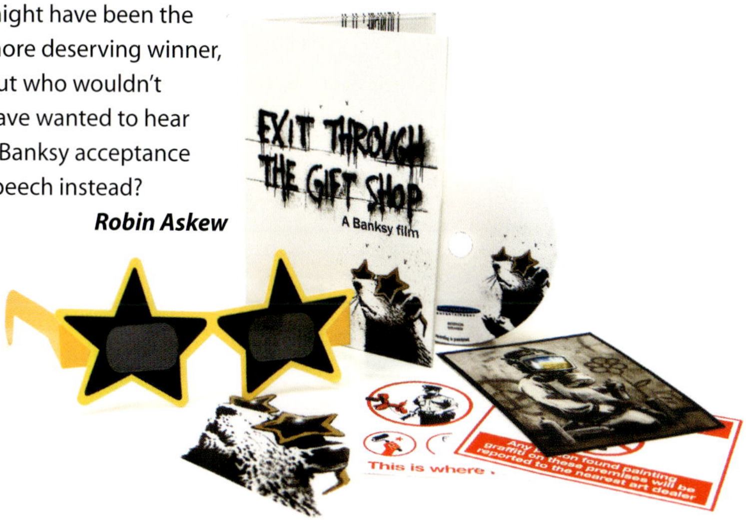

This page: 2,000 limited edition petrol bomb prints were sold for a fiver each at Bristol Anarchist Bookfair.

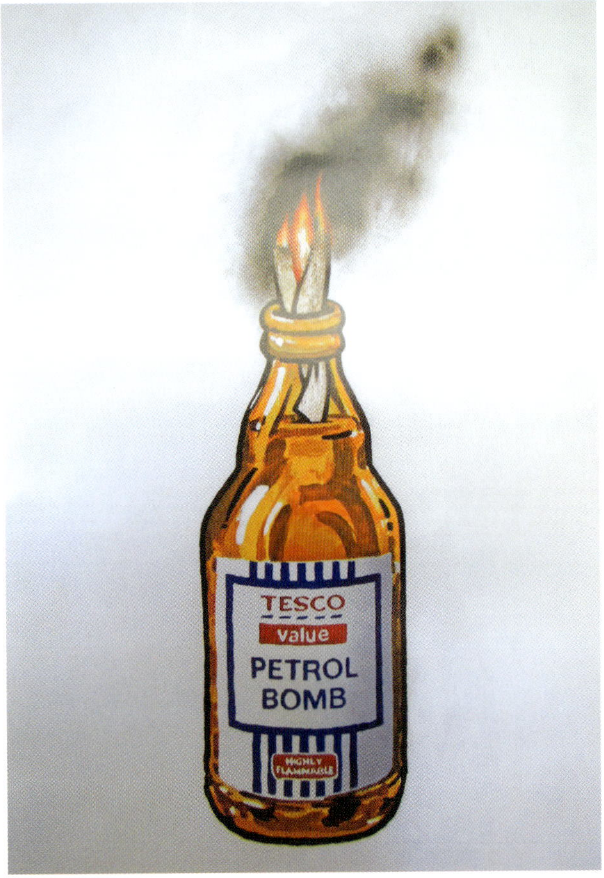

Tesco Value Petrol Bomb

It is undeniably the case that Banksy's work often has consequences – no more so than on the occasion of the Tesco Petrol Bomb being sold at the Bristol Anarchist Bookfair.

The Bookfair took place on May 7th, 2011 – a couple of weeks after the Stokes Croft riots resulted in the controversial Tesco store on Cheltenham Road being trashed by rioters after police were forced to retreat from the area. The riots were not related to the civil disobedience in the summer of 2011, but had a very specific cause. Police raided the Telepathic Heights squat opposite the Tesco store after allegedly being tipped off that someone in the building had made petrol bombs and was planning to use them in an attack on the Tesco store.

The police raid was a catalogue of errors. Riot cops, mostly from outside Bristol, stormed the building from riot vans early in the evening and within minutes a large crowd had gathered. The squatters fought back and according to many reports, police used heavy-handed tactics to try to clear the crowd outside. The onlooking crowd retaliated and within no time at all we had a riot The battle raged in Stokes Croft and through Montpellier and St Paul's until the early hours when the police were forced to retreat and Tesco was attacked.

There were fears that police might try to snatch people attending the Anarchist Bookfair who they suspected of being involved in the riot. Enter Banksy who, a couple of days before the Bookfair, revealed his limited-edition Tesco Value Petrol Bomb print which would only be sold at the Bookfair. The consequences of Banksy's action were twofold.

Firstly, a crowd of several thousand Banksy fans queued from early morning to buy their copy meaning that the police were unlikely to stage an operation against individuals at the Bookfair in the glare of all the public and media interest now surrounding it. Of course, it may well be the case that the police had no such plans and the rumours were a consequence of anarchist paranoia.

Secondly, money raised from the sale of the print was divided between the defence fund for the squatters, the People's Republic of Stokes Croft and Coexist who run Hamilton House where the Bookfair was held.

The whole affair also served to confuse and confound the Bristol establishment. Just a year earlier, Banksy had been the saviour of Bristol when his Museum show had injected tens of millions of pounds into the local economy.

Now Bristol City Council leader Barbara Janke said: "What a sad, sordid way to thank Bristol for providing this talented, privileged but misguided young man with a springboard for his career as a graffiti artist.

"This city has long been proud of his work, but the decent citizens of Bristol who have been disgusted with the violence and intimidatory tactics of the recent rioters will be rightly appalled by Banksy's apparent willingness not only to identify himself with their cause but to aid them in their cowardly attempts to evade justice."

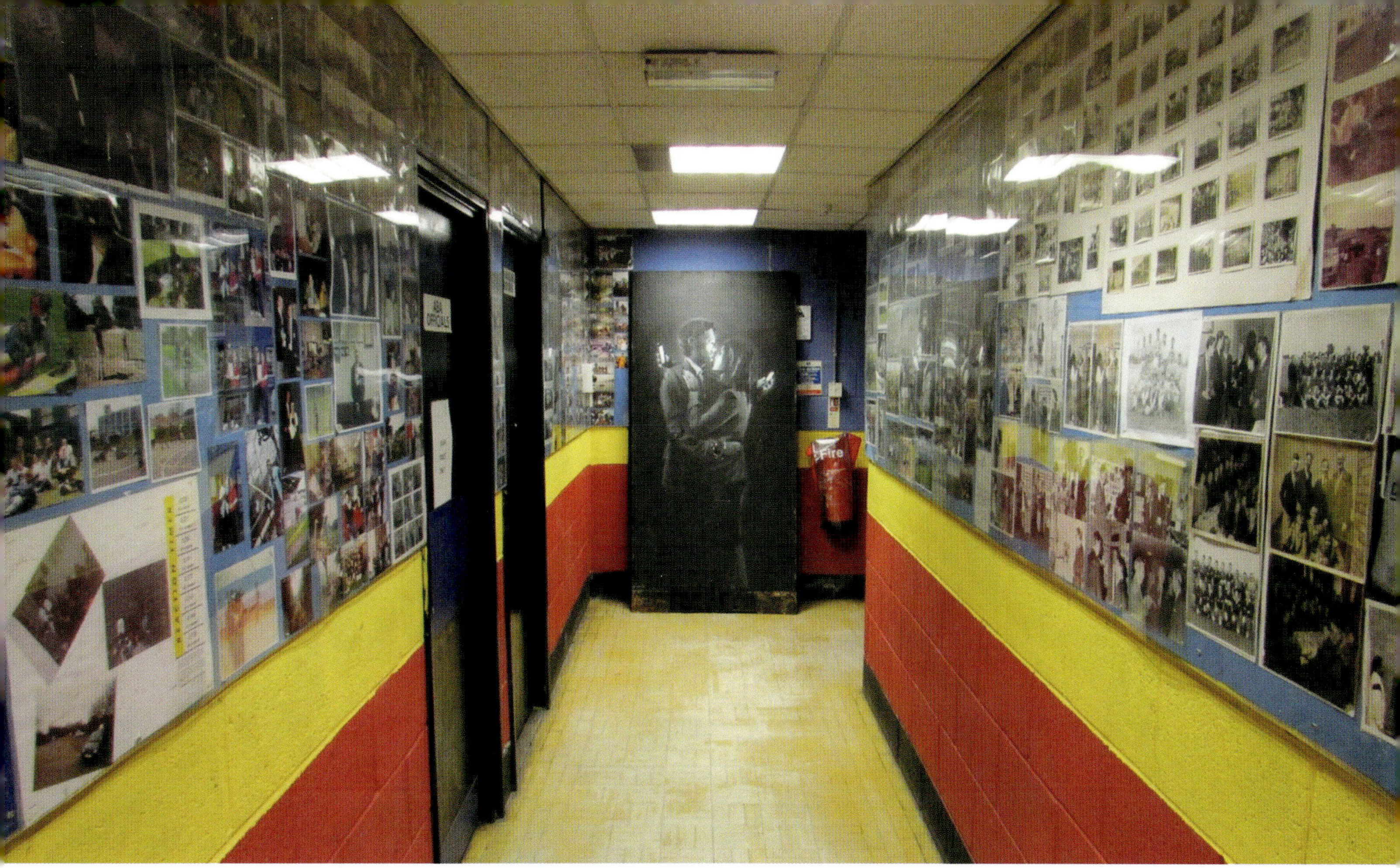

Mobile Lovers

The saga of Mobile Lovers began in the dead of night on the weekend of April 13, 2014, about the same time as the Surveillance piece appeared in Cheltenham. On Sunday 14th the Mobile Lovers image appeared on Banksy's website – his way of announcing new work – but with no indication of where it was.

On April 15, a tweeter called Sally (@BanksysTeddy) announced she had used Google Maps to locate the piece down a side road (Clement Street) directly outside Broad Plain Boys' Club in Bristol. You may find it suspicious that Sally joined Twitter in March 2014, and by mid May had posted 9 tweets.

However, Sally wasn't the first to spot Mobile Lovers. Dennis Stinchcombe (58) who runs Broad Plain Boys' Club noticed it on Sunday 14, thought it might be a Banksy, carefully crowbarred it off the wall and hauled it into the Boys' Club.

You may wonder why Banksy put the piece on easily-removed plywood and why Dennis was so sure it was a Banksy. Anyway, the piece is in the Boys' Club and Dennis begins charging donations for the cash-strapped Club for people to come in and take pictures.

Enter Bristol's elected Mayor George Ferguson who announces that because the City Council owns the tatty old bit of plywood on which the piece appeared, Mobile Lovers belongs to the Council. By this time Dennis has offers exceeding £100,000 from fancy London dealers to buy the piece.

It should be noted that one of the reasons that Broad Plain Boys' Club is cash strapped and threatened with

Mobile Lovers was brought into the Broad Plain club for safe keeping.

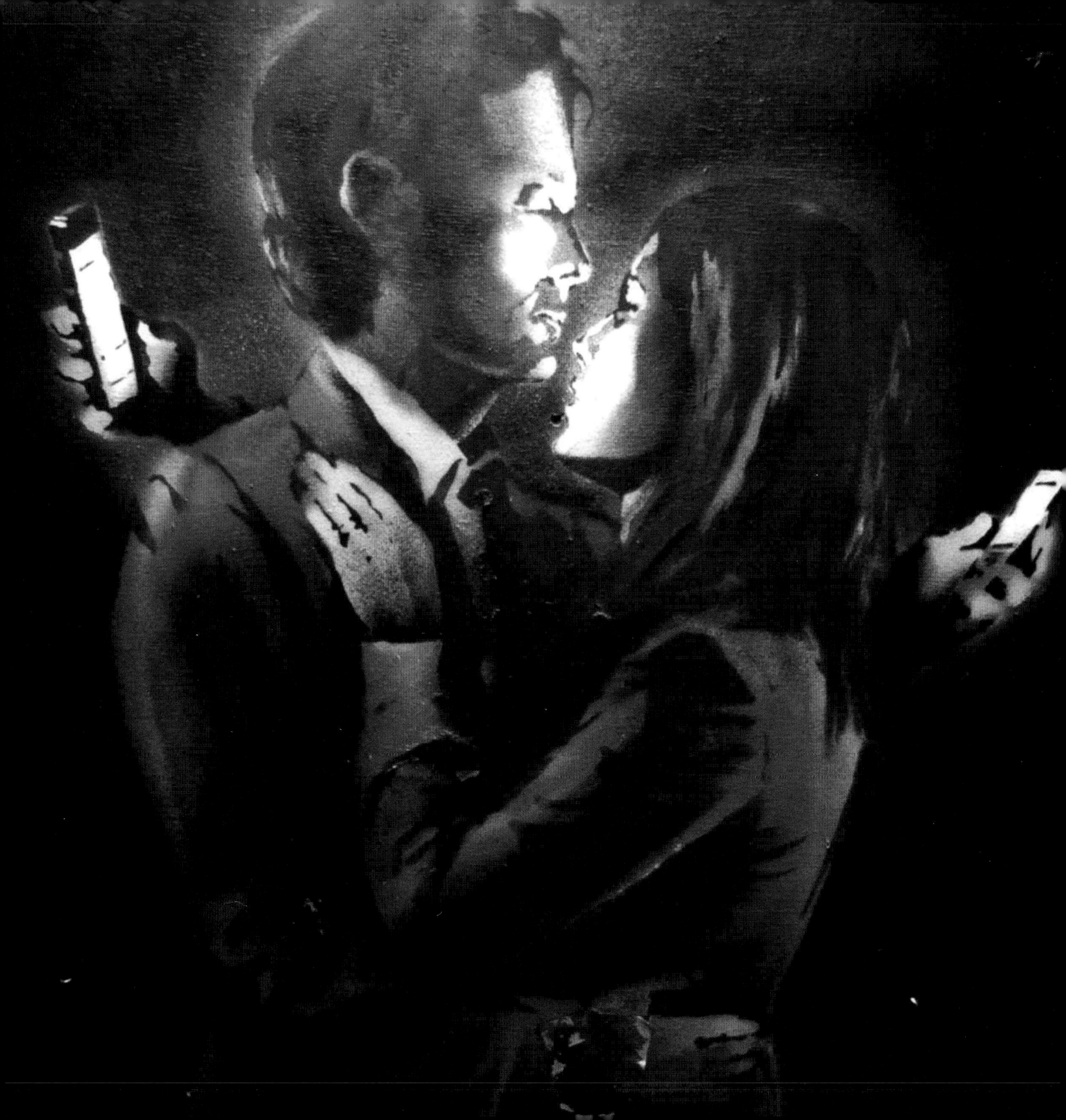

cuts or closure is because it is one of the many victims of Central Government cuts forced on Mayor Ferguson and the City by the ConDem Coalition.

Anyway... George announces his intention to reclaim Mobile Lovers, house it in the City Museum and presumably start knocking out postcards and prints and we have what is known as a stand-off played out in front of the national and international media. Dennis has the Banksy, George wants the Banksy. It should also be noted that Broad Plain is a boxing club. The odds would seem to favour Dennis.

Seconds out! Round two! It is agreed that the piece should be housed in the City Museum for safekeeping with visitors asked to make a donation to the Boys' Club while Banksy is contacted via his management so that his wishes are known. The options are that the piece stays in the Museum, is given back to the Boys' Club or is reinstated in its original position on the doorway presumably with some form of protective covering.

The police take the piece in for safe keeping before it is delivered to the City Museum. It is, of course, deeply ironic that after years if trying to identify Banksy and put him in the cells for criminal damage, the coppers are now protecting his work. It would be nice to think that they kept it in a cell overnight.

On May 8th, the Boys' Club released a letter from Banksy in which he made it clear that he wanted Mobile Lovers to go to the Boys' Club. The full text of the letter reads

Dear Dennis
I hope this finds you well. As you know I recently painted on a doorway near the club. This was meant to be a small visual gift for the area – but apparently a financial one would've been more useful.

I don't normally admit to committing criminal damage, but seeing as it looks like charges won't be brought any time soon you have my blessing to do what you feel right with the piece.

I'm a great admirer of the work done at the club and would be chuffed if this can help in some way. Your tenacity in the past few weeks has made for and entertaining spectator sport. I assume you're familiar with the quote attributed to Abraham Lincoln: 'Things may come to those who wait, but only the things left behind to those who hustle.'

That page: The piece eventually sold for £403,000.

The Boys' Club sold Mobile Lovers to a private collector in August for £403,000 – enough to safeguard the future of the club for the next generation of young people.

The following report appeared on www.bristolpost.co.uk in February 2014. Did Banksy read it?

The oldest boys' club in Bristol could be under threat of closure if it cannot find the money to stay open.

An appeal has been launched to raise £120,000 by the end of the year to keep Broad Plain Boys' Club, a registered charity, afloat.

Dennis Stinchcombe, who runs the club, said: "No different to any other youth club out there, we are desperately feeling the pressure of the recession and fear if we don't do something substantial fairly quickly we will end up running out of funds and eventually close. I think this would be disastrous for the young people of Bristol.

"We are the oldest youth group in Bristol and possibly the West Country, and I have been leader for 38 years, so we have always had continuity and offered young people a fantastic resource where they are able to nurture and develop, at their own pace, into upstanding young adults."

The club is based at Riverside Youth Project on Clement Street, Easton, and is used by hundreds of children and young adults. In the evenings, many go there for the expert boxing coaching.

Mr Stinchcombe, who is recovering from a triple heart bypass, added: "I want to make a request to members past and present, businessmen and women – in fact, anyone in Bristol who feels that we still have a lot to offer the young people of Bristol – to help us in our time of need."

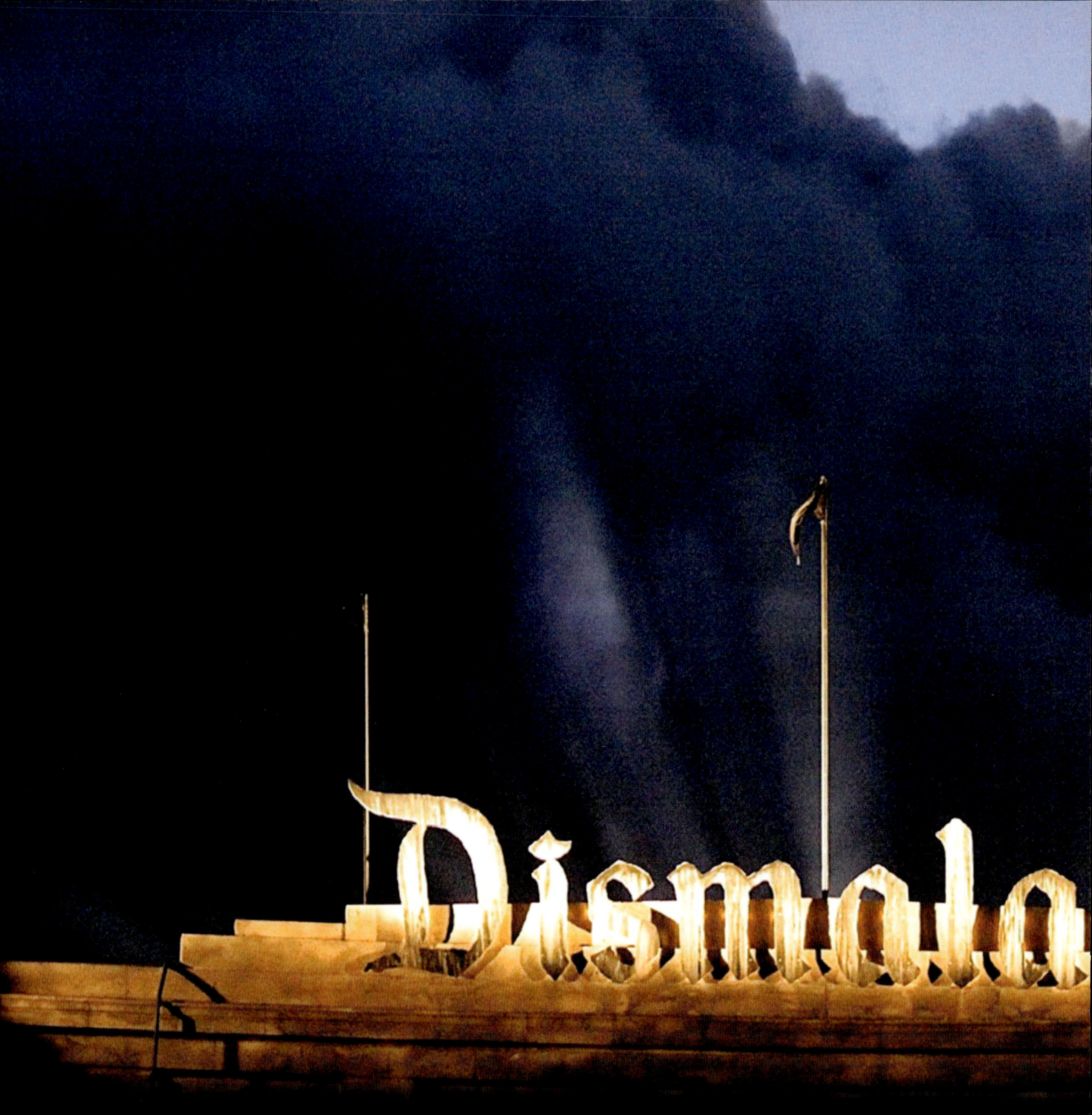
Dismala

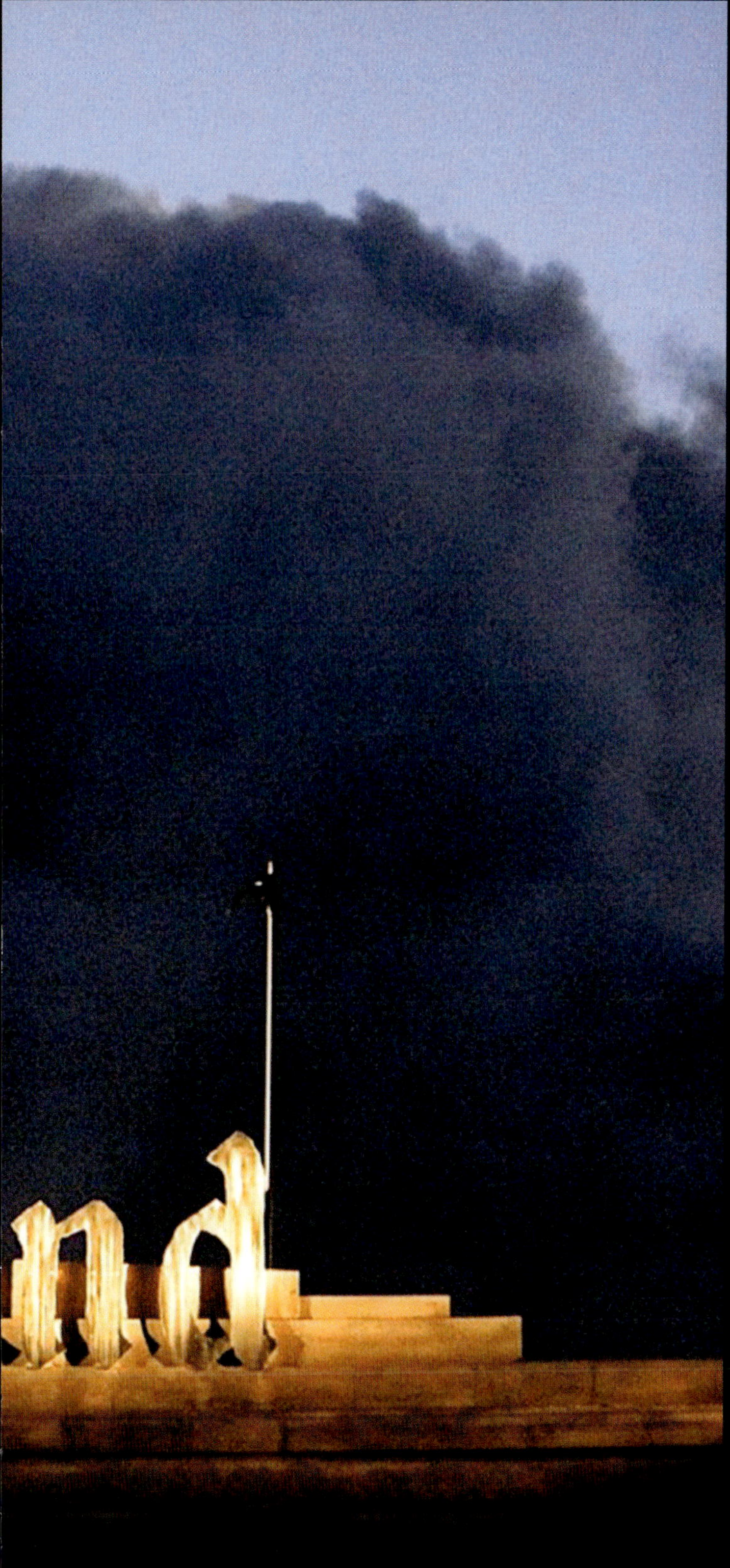

Dismaland

The street art community was rife with rumours of a major Banksy show in the Bristol area in 2015, but nobody anticipated an event of the scale, complexity or radical nature of Dismaland. And nobody predicted that Weston-super-Mare, not Bristol, would stage Banksy's most ambitious project to date.

Where do you start with Dismaland? Well, to begin at the beginning…

The Weston-super-Mare Lido was opened in 1937 (when it was also known as The Pool). It was an Art Deco construction built on the beach at the popular holiday resort, a couple of hundred yards from the Grand Pier. The outdoor pool, it was claimed, was the biggest in Europe measuring 950 square metres. The café and changing rooms were modern and stylish and the Art Deco diving platform was an architectural tour de force. The central concrete arch had three diving boards on either side with the 10-metre board (the highest in Europe) towering over the pool.

The pool itself sloped from paddling depth to 15-feet deep under the boards. Every afternoon throughout the summer, a team of five professional divers, including one woman, performed acrobatic feats "just for the kicks and the thrills" according to the holiday brochures. Pictures of the Lido show the synchronised team of divers flying through the air in formation.

Hundreds of thousands of holidaymakers visited the pool in the post-war years but by the 1970s visitors were looking for something more sophisticated – and warmer. The size of the pool meant it was impossible to heat the water. In 1981 the local council overturned the diving board's listed status and it was demolished as the Lido was rebranded as the Tropicana, complete with the introduction of plastic palms and large orange pineapple structures.

This is the Tropicana that Banksy would have experienced and like other teenage visitors from Bristol, he would have been aware of the threat of low-level Somerset violence from local youths. The Tropicana

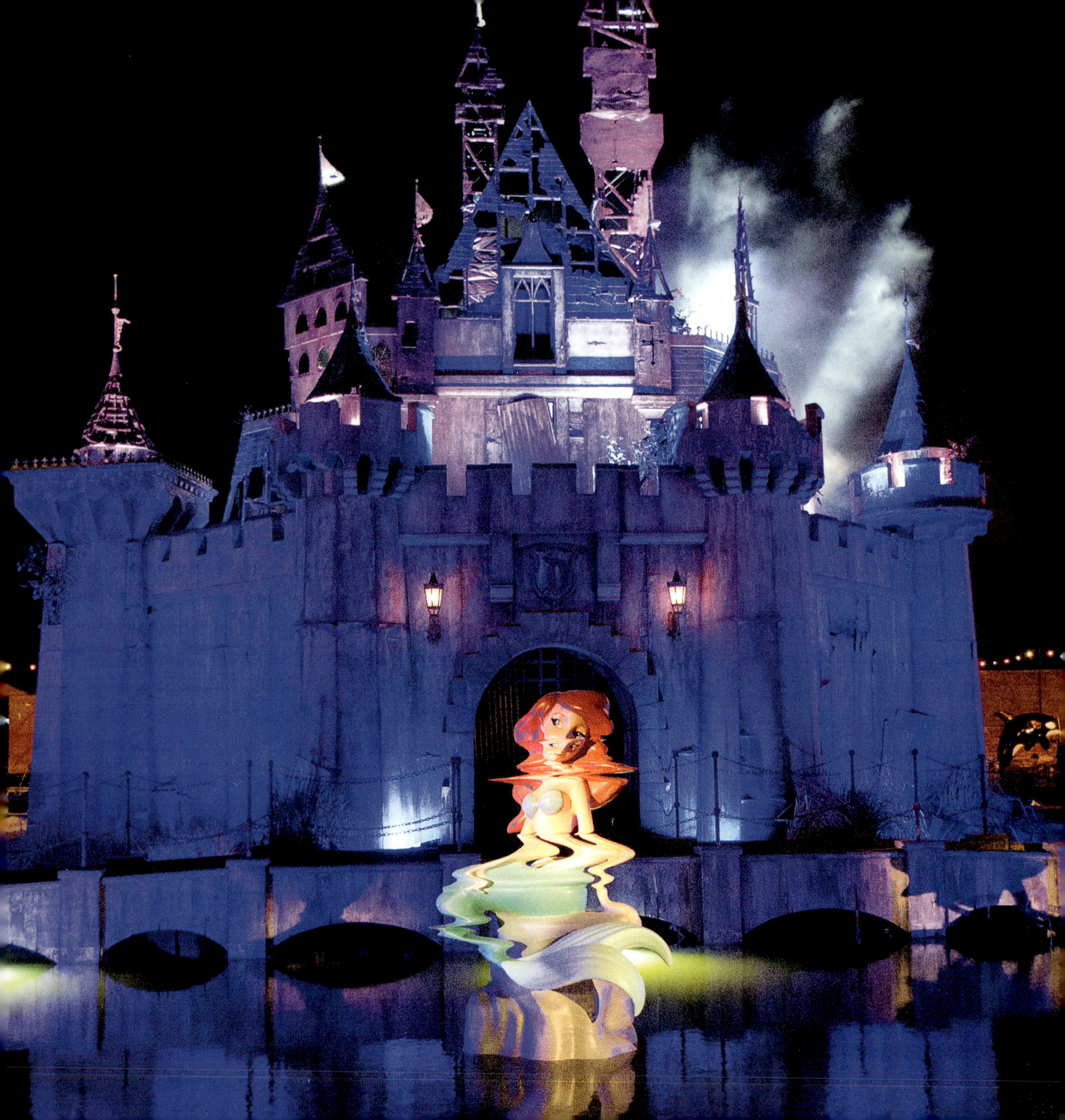

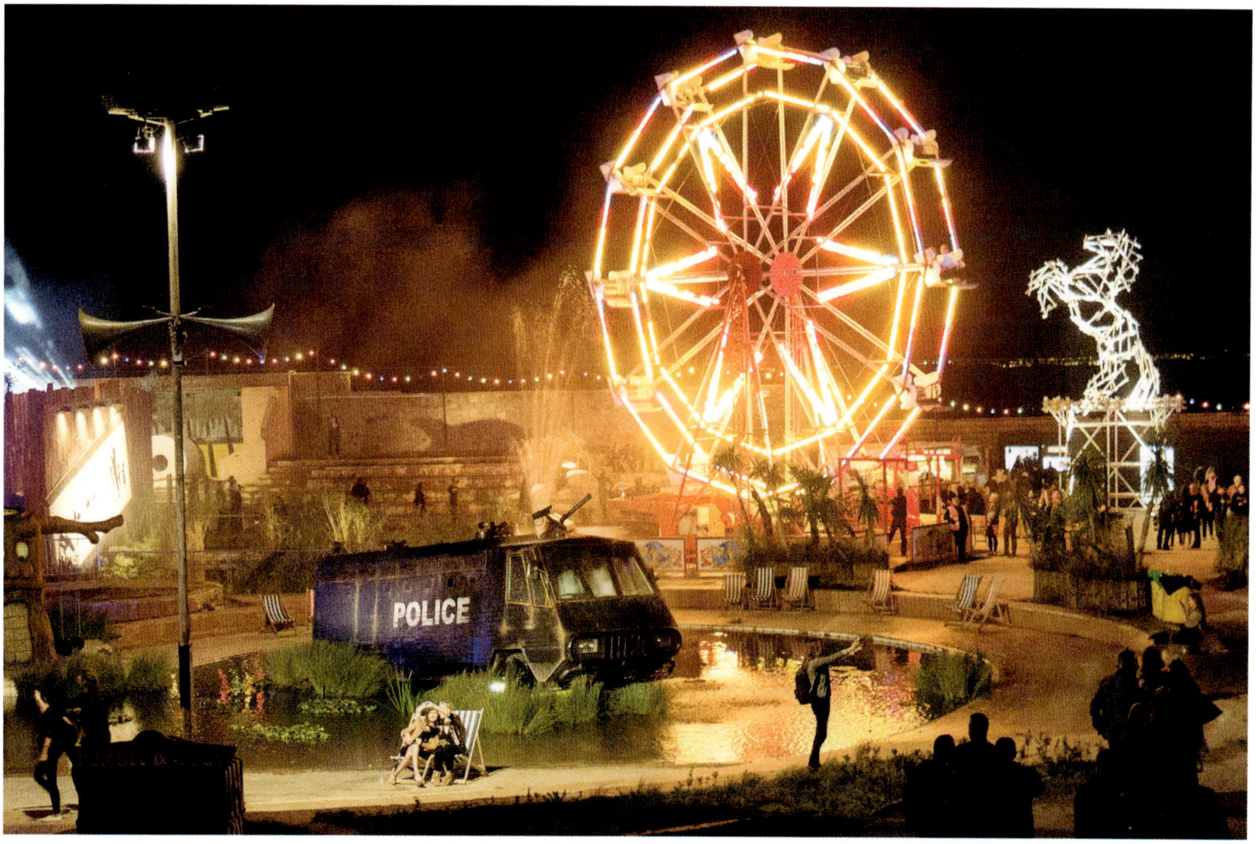

Dismaland at night.

closed in 2000 and gradually became derelict as various developers failed to deliver regeneration plans.

The 2.5 acre Tropicana site is a metaphor for the diminution of the British seaside resort in general and the alarming decline of Weston-super-Mare in particular.

Perhaps Banksy was being less than sincere when he told the Weston Mercury newspaper: 'I loved the Tropicana as a kid, so getting to throw these doors open again is a real honour.'

On Thursday, 20th August the press were invited and on Friday 21st August, more than 1,000 Weston-super-Mare residents who had cut out their coupon from The Mercury and brought it along to the sea front (with proof of address) became the first members of the public to experience the Dismaland Bemusement Park.

By the time Dismaland closed its doors for the last time on September 27th 2015 more than 150,000 people had paid £3 each to experience described by Banksy as 'The UK's most disappointing new visitor attraction.'

But what is a Bemusement Park?

Most critics didn't know what to make of Dismaland other than to state the bleedin' obvious about it being a parody of Disneyland. Even those who liked it failed to grasp the many facets of Banksy's most complex work to date.

Think of Dismaland as a festival – perhaps a mini Glastonbury Festival – but without the tents, and you'll begin to appreciate the Bemusement Park experience as a complete concept made up of many parts including visual art, music, sound, movement, satire, performance, spoken word, light, radical politics, humour, parody, food, entry level anarchism, alcohol and more.

Visitors entered Dismaland through a fake security installation constructed from cardboard by Californian

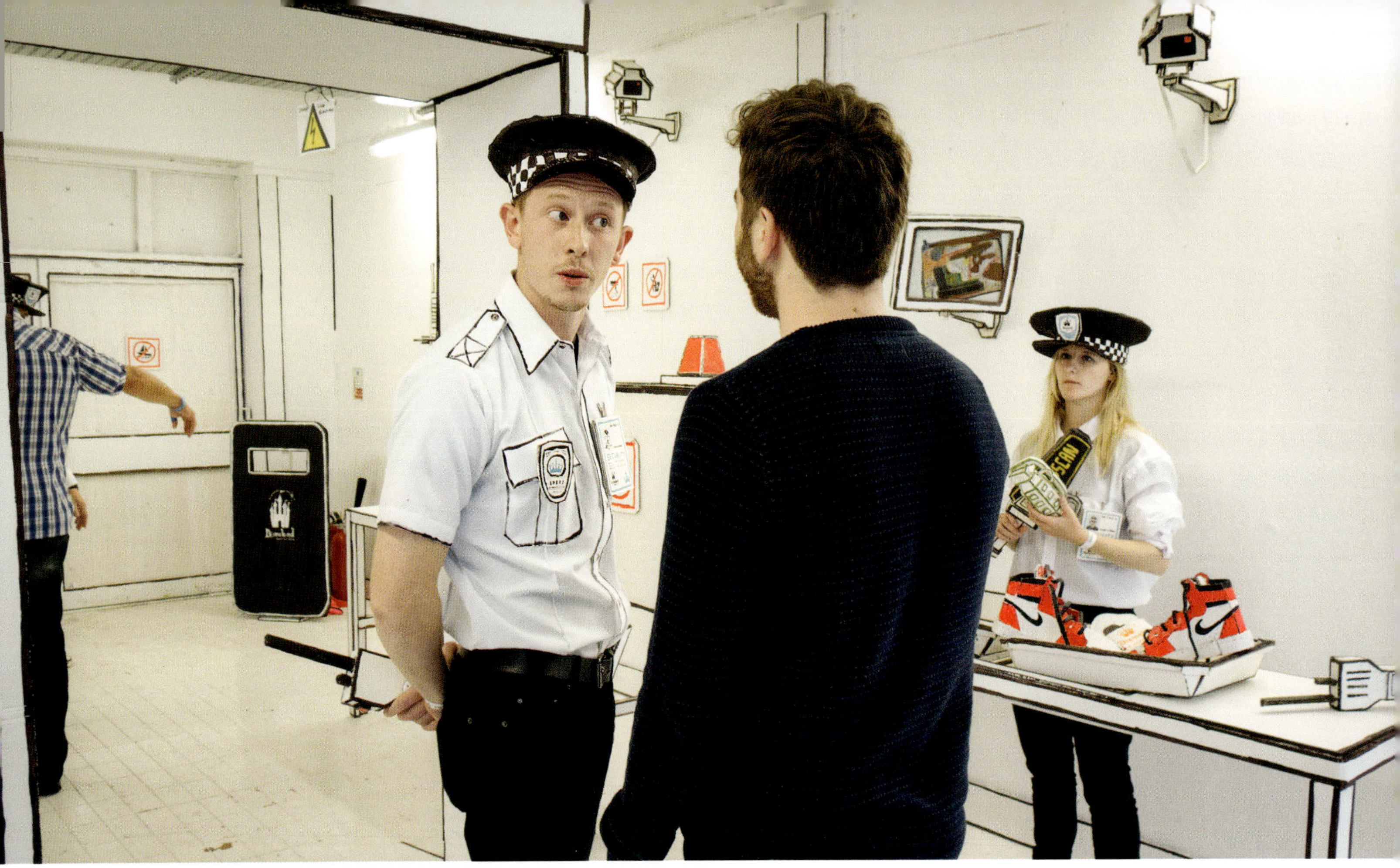

Mock security on the way into the Bemusement Park by Bill Barminski.

artist Bill Barminski. Apparently bored security guards ask routine questions but carry just enough menace to create a sense of unease. The performance element of Dismaland is pronounced from the start and if you'd gone straight to the burnt-out ice cream van to buy a programme, a sneering vendor would reluctantly push the programme your way and possibly screw up the notes in your change and flick them at you.

Looking back towards the entrance the Art Deco walls of the Tropicana are painted with ghostly figures and the word 'mediocre' in giant letters. Towards the art exhibition housed in the former Tropicana changing rooms and café there are scattered, rusting children's rides. It's a dystopian vision of the theme park experience that is remarkably similar to the reality of the Grand Pier and town centre just a few hundred yards away. Weston-super-Mare town centre has everything you could possible want – as long as it's from a charity shop or a phone shop, or it's an e-cigarette or a kebab.

Banksy's vision of the decline of Western capitalism as realised by a trip to the seaside is further confused with the reality of Weston when it's announced in the local paper that the main Tourist Information Office will be closed for good during the course of Dismaland because of lack of funds: 150,000 new visitors and global media interest? Let's close the Tourist Information Office.

Back to 'The UK's most disappointing new visitor attraction'… The art exhibition is a collection of work curated by Banksy by more than 50 contemporary artists – two turned him down. An ecological theme runs through much of the work.

Among the stand-out exhibits are the light

installations by James Joyce; Banksy's Grim Reaper on a dodgem car; Caroline McCarthy's plant pot and food packaging garden; Jessica Harrison's tattooed porcelain figurines; Amir Schiby's moving image of four Palestinian boys playing football on a beach who were killed by Israeli shelling, but most of all Jimmy Cauty's astonishing model city frozen in time after a period of civil unrest. It's called Aftermath Displacement Principle and the attention to detail is remarkable – mangled roadways, crashed cars, political graffiti 3,000 yellow-jacketed police, tower blocks with broken windows, searchlights beaming down from helicopters. It's an incredible piece of work.

Back outside the stage, which has music or comedy/ spoken word performances every Friday, is an outdoor cinema the rest of the time showing more than 20 short films from around the world on repeat. You're less than half way round and the ticket cost you £3.

This side of Dismaland is dominated by the Big Rig Jig giant truck sculpture by American artist Mike Ross and The Shove by Peter Kennard and Cat Phillips – a billboard of Prime Minister David Cameron sipping a glass of champagne in front of a cityscape being crumpled up by a person in a hoody. When Dismaland finished the 4-metre by 3-metre piece was put on eBay for 99p and eventually sold for £5,402.

The centrepiece of Dismaland is Banksy's fairy castle. It's set in a lake containing a warped Cinderella piece and an abandoned police riot van spraying a constant stream of water pointlessly in the air.

On entering the castle, you're asked to stand in front of a green screen to have your picture taken before walking through into the main, dark room where you can make out some crouching figures. As you grow accustomed to the gloom you slowly realise it's a group of paparazzi wearing crash helmets, scooters abandoned behind them, clicking away and, as you walk around them, their subject becomes apparent – a crashed Cinderella coach with the dead princess sprawled out of one of the windows.

It's a cleverly worked Banksy gag and most people's reaction was laughter as they realised the 'joke'. On the way out you can buy the green screen pic of you peering over the paps' shoulders.

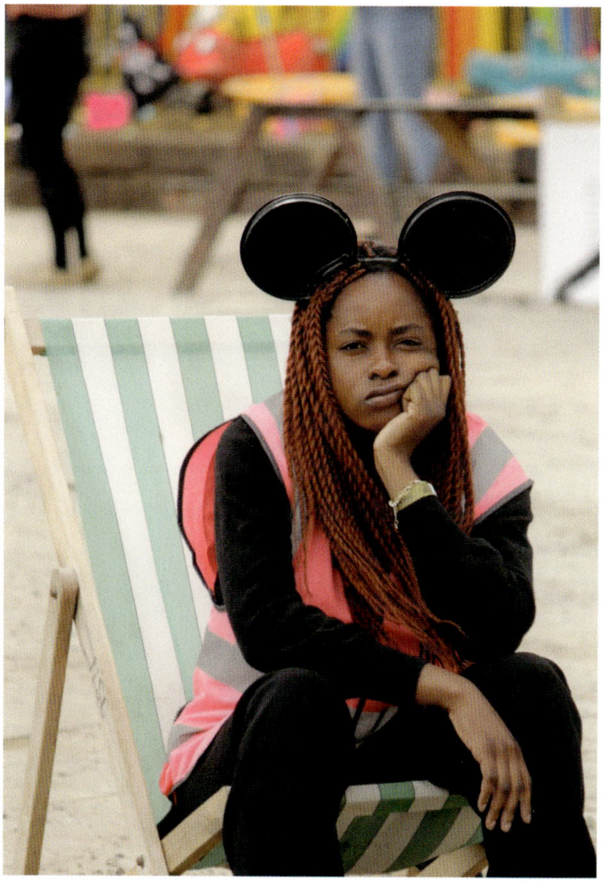

Everything is too much effort for the Dismaland stewards.

On exiting the castle, pass Michael Beitz's bog roll bench, Banksy's whale jumping through a hoop, the big wheel, and Ben Long's giant horse made out of scaffolding poles and you're in the political and satirical bit – that £3 is sure going a long way.

This is where humour and Banksy's 'entry level anarchism' collide with startling affect. In the library one of the highlighted books is Ian 'Class War' Bone's Bash The Rich, but it's not there. Has someone really nicked it, or is this a subtle Banksy joke about one of the nation's most stolen books?

The Museum of Cruel Objects curated by art historian Dr Gavin Grindon is a harrowing exhibition of things that were made to hurt people and animals, including guns, surveillance devices, restraints, rubber bullets and anti-sitting spikes.

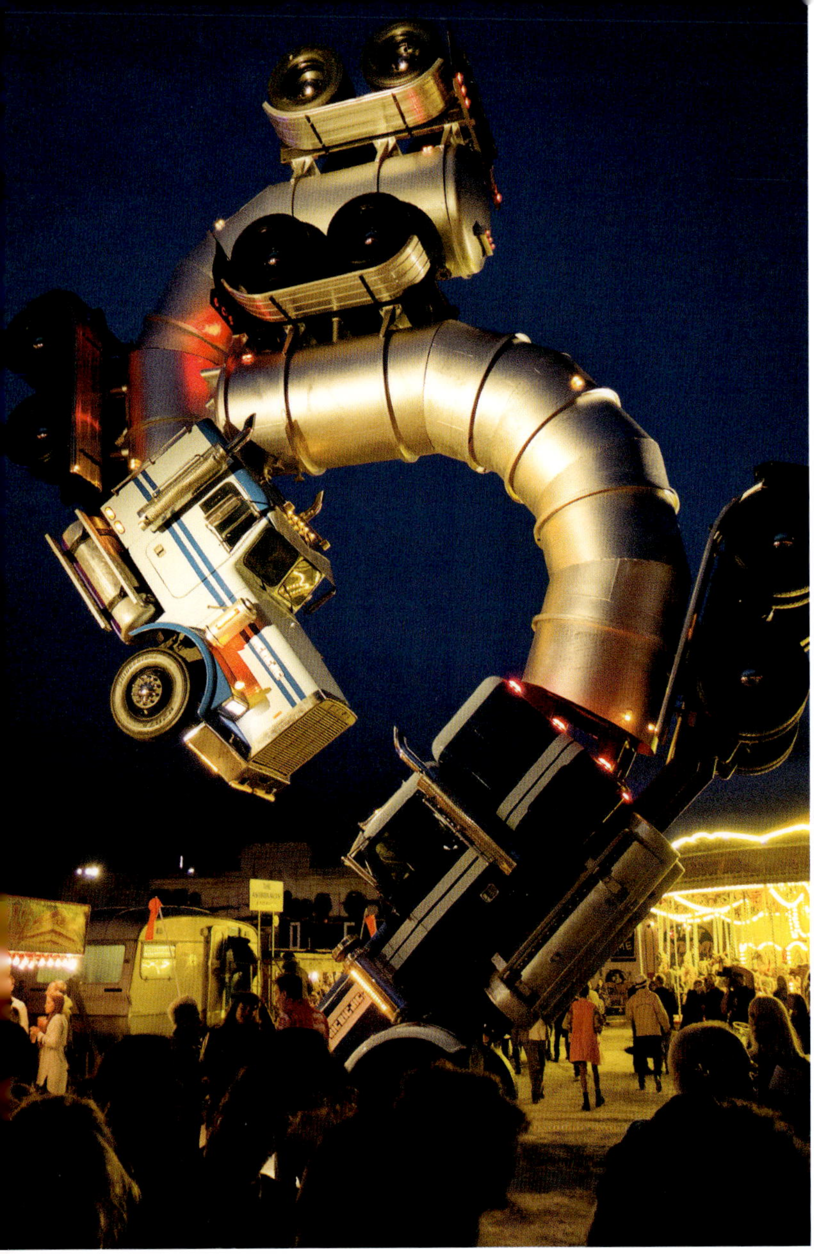

The Big Rig Jig by Mike Ross.

Next door is the Comrades Advice Bureau housing pressure groups invited to Dismaland by Banksy, including the Independent Workers Union of Great Britain, Occupy Design and Acorn (the housing direct action pressure group). The best-selling item here seems to be the Adbusters Ad Space Hack Pack – a couple of Allen keys and box spanner and a set of instructions. It's all you need to spring open bus shelter advertising stands in order to replace a corporate message with one of your own.

It's rumoured that the tube and bus shelter subvertising blitz against the London Arms Fair was organised from Dismaland. The poster campaign against the Defence and Security Equipment International Arms Fair broke open advertising stands on the London Underground and bus network and inserted posters with the message:

"This September, a swarm of arms dealers will be descending on the DLR. These visitors make huge amounts of money from weapons and equipment that kill people in wars all over the world.

"Your taxes help pay for it. Customers are requested to help stop the arms fair."

One of the most striking areas of Dismaland is the dome tent featuring the work of banner maker Ed Hall who has supplied banners to trade unions and protest groups for 40 years. The fusion of art and political message is both fascinating and moving.

Darren Cullen's Pocket Money Loans shop is a razor-sharp parody of the pay-day loan culture with its 'Get Out Of Debt With a Loan' message. 'I'm especially interested in the point where the terrible requirements of our system collide with the innocence of childhood,' says Cullen.

So that's what your £3 gets you and we haven't even mentioned the refugee boats, the Wasted Rita messages dotted around the site, the mock fairground stalls, the roundabout, the Astronauts' Caravan, the Freak Show tent, the crazy golf, the ritual burning of Jeffrey Archer books every evening, Julie Burchill's Punch and Judy show, the giant sandcastle and more.

All of this is delivered to a backdrop of warped Hawaiian guitar music and the occasional indecipherable child's voice making a Tannoy announcement.

There are three bars on site, cheap-eats vegetarian pizza and falafel with salads from the Bristol-based Severn Project, a farm working with recovering addicts. All of this is overseen by an army of pink jacketed, mouse-eared Dismal Staff and it is the 100 or so Dismal People who add yet another dimension to the Dismaland experience.

The Dismalfolk were given stage school training in how to be miserable by acting expert Pat Welsh who spent four days coaching 100 recruits on being 'dismal and aloof'

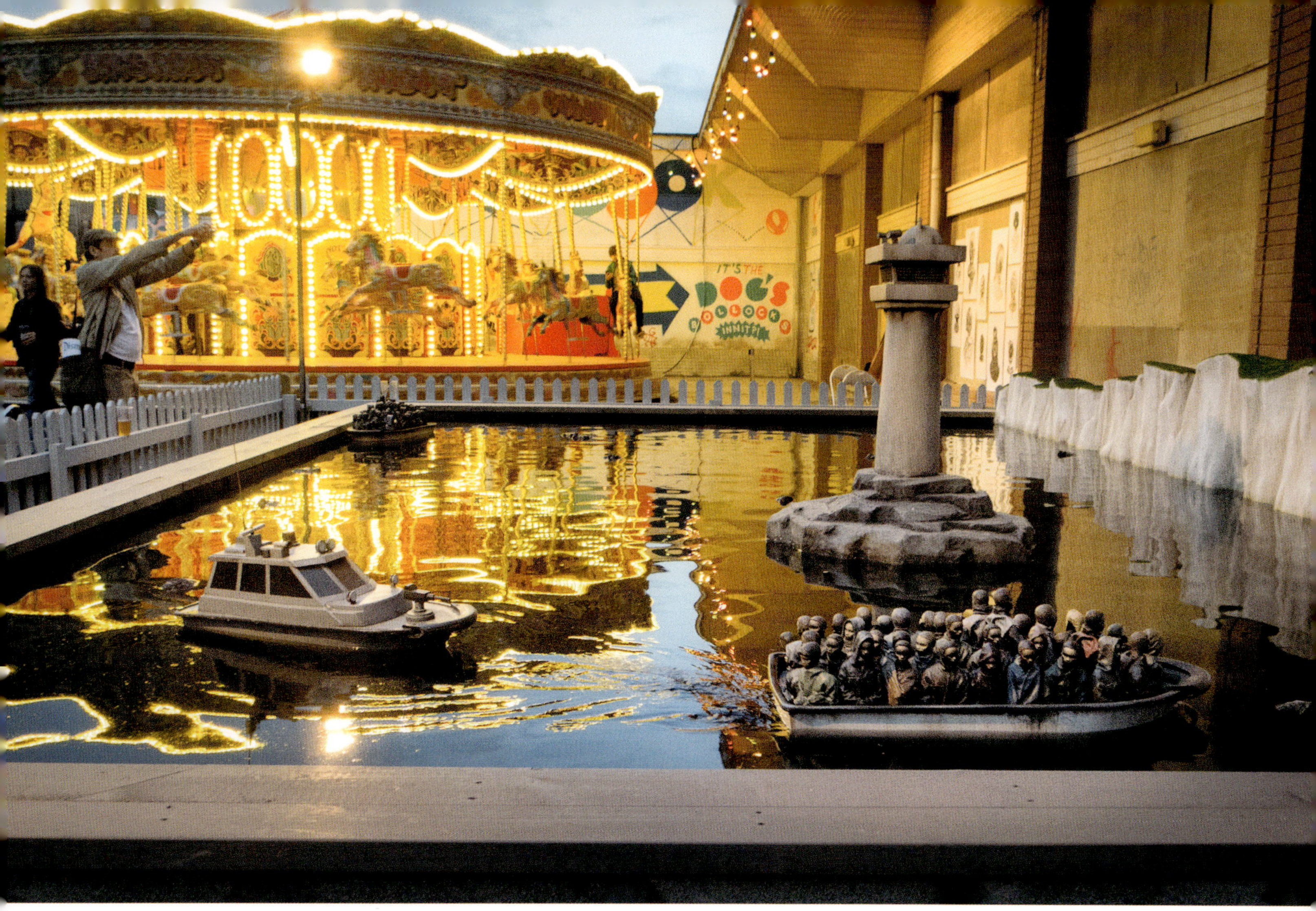

as part of the artist's vision for his creation.

The workers were also taught how to be as unhelpful as possible to visitors during the drama workshops.

Applicants were initially told they would be extras in a film who had been recruited by a fictitious studio to avoid suspicion.

It was only at the end of the course that they discovered they would actually be working at the Banksy theme park.

Pat, a senior lecturer in acting, said: "The challenge of developing the performance skills of inexperienced and sometimes reluctant actors was exacerbated by the necessity to limit the details of the ultimate role to the bare minimum.

"It was a tough brief to have to teach someone to act deadpan, not to laugh and not to over-act, after all the stewards were there to add to the overall dismal experience but not to outshine the amazing artworks on display.

"Once the stewards were on location they soon embraced the concept and the feedback on their consistently negative outlook has been universally positive."

Pat, who taught acting for ten years at Bath Spa University, said he never had any 'direct communication' with Banksy over the project.

Banksy's boat pond highlighted the plight of refugees crossing the Mediterranean.

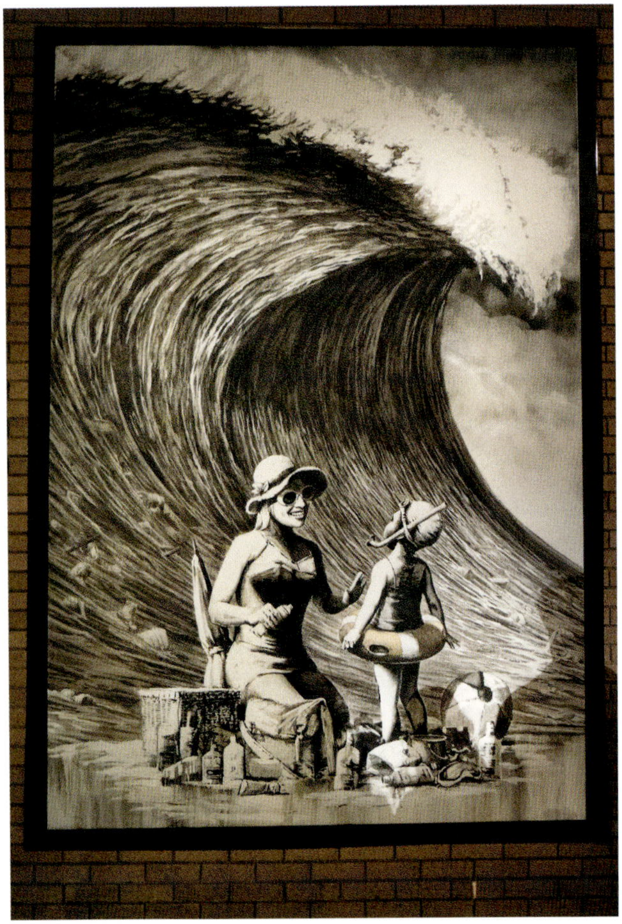
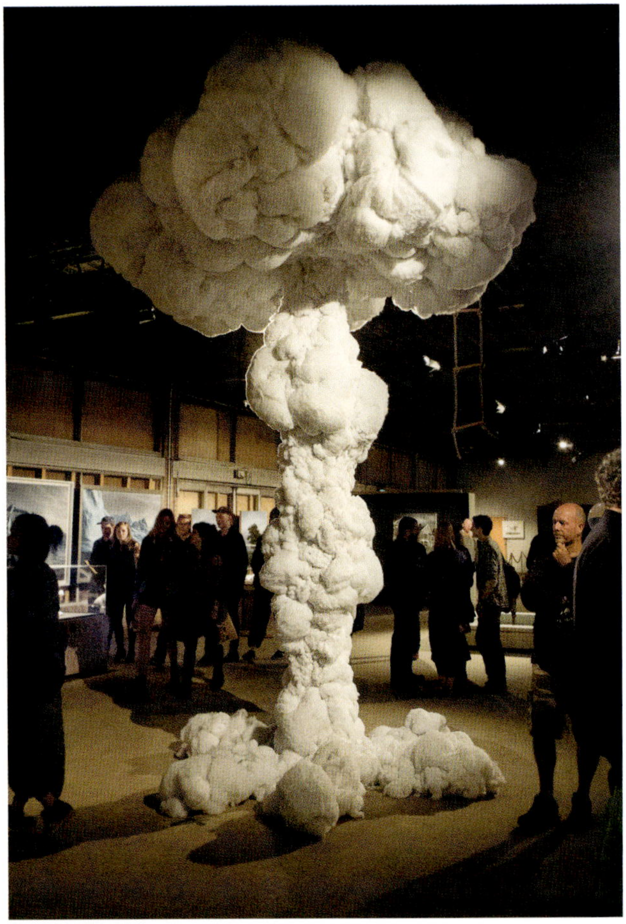

Banksy's Tsunami and the mushroom cloud tree house by Dietrich Wegner.

The Dismalfolk grew into the role, becoming increasingly influential in the overall atmosphere at Dismaland. Towards the end they were instructed to only sell I Am An Imbecile balloons to children or parents with a kid in tow. This led to the hugely amusing sight of lone adults demanding to buy a balloon labelling them an imbecile as the vendors turned their backs on the fiver-waving grown-ups.

So, like a festival, Dismaland was a different experience for different people, depending on whether you had to queue for a long time in the rain or whether you got in quickly on a sunny day. Perhaps the Dismalfolk amused you, maybe they annoyed you, maybe you were there on a day when the Notional Trust were doing their street theatre, perhaps you bumped into old friends or went on an evening when there was live music. If you were lucky enough to attend the opening night, you might have seen Richard Hawley deliver an outstanding set followed by an astonishing firework display on Weston-super-Mare beach. Some of the art will have pleased you, some of it less so. If you knew the Tropicana and are familiar with Weston-super-Mare, the parody element of Dismaland will have had greater resonance than if you don't know the area.

Perhaps you went more than once and found that Dismaland was actually just a fascinating place to hang out, eat pizza and people watch.

But whatever your Dismaland experience, you were part of the show because even 'the UK's most disappointing new visitor attraction' needs a crowd.

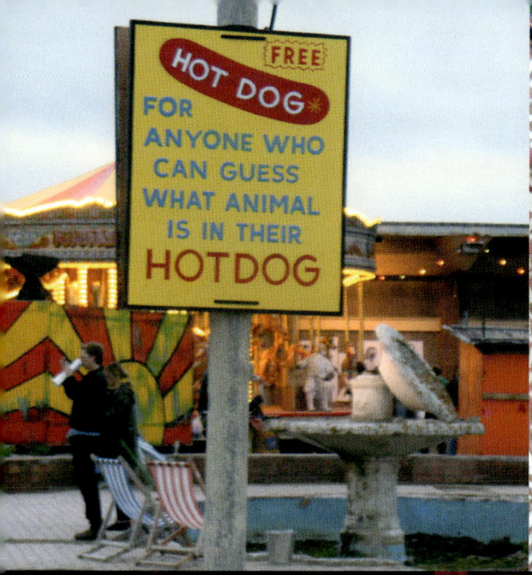
FREE
HOT DOG
FOR
ANYONE WHO
CAN GUESS
WHAT ANIMAL
IS IN THEIR
HOTDOG

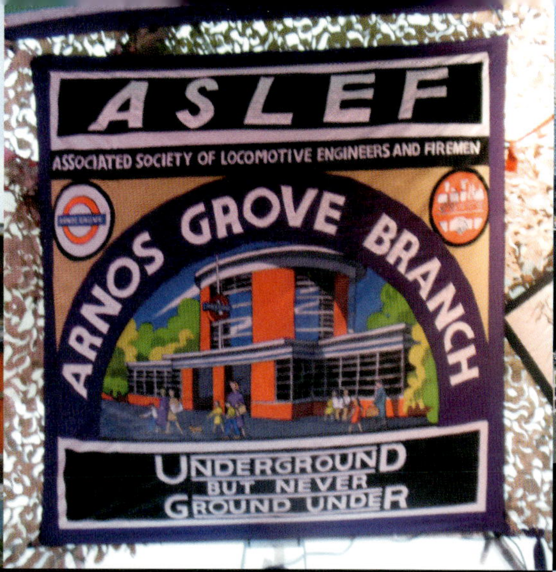
ASLEF
ASSOCIATED SOCIETY OF LOCOMOTIVE ENGINEERS AND FIREMEN
ARNOS GROVE BRANCH
UNDERGROUND
BUT NEVER
GROUND UNDER

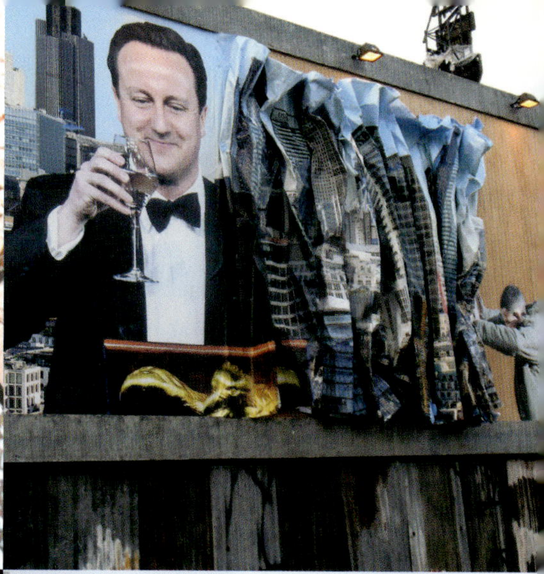

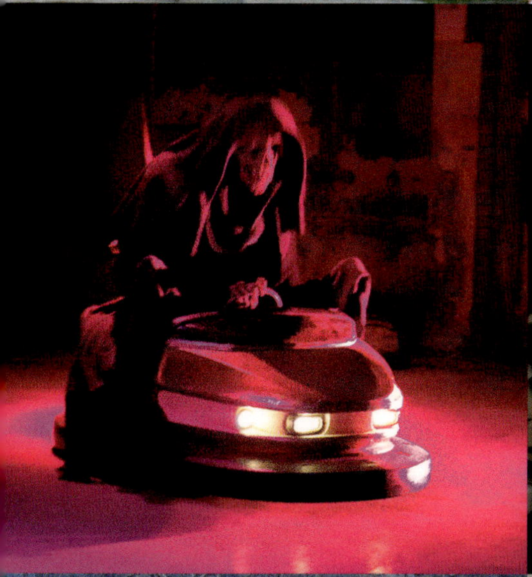

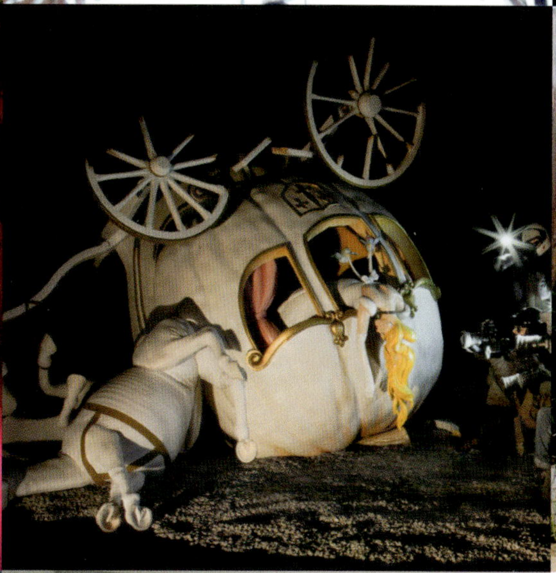

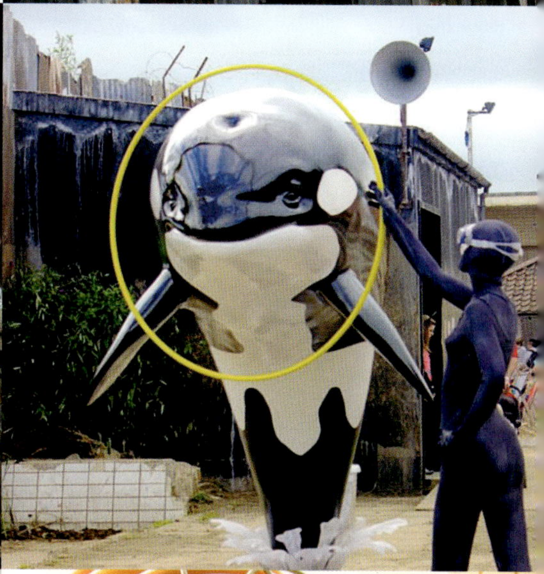

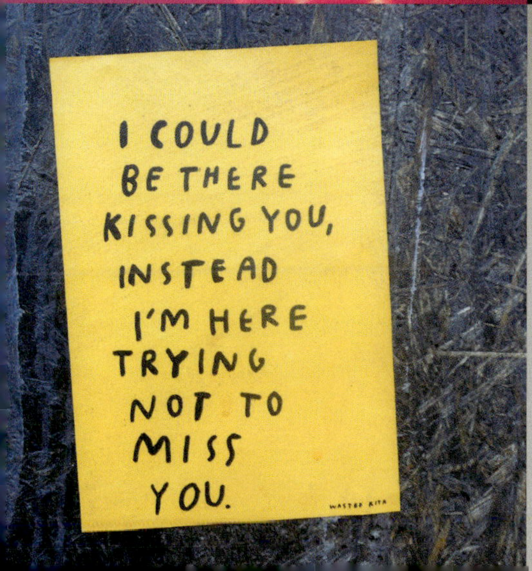
I COULD
BE THERE
KISSING YOU,
INSTEAD
I'M HERE
TRYING
NOT TO
MISS
YOU.

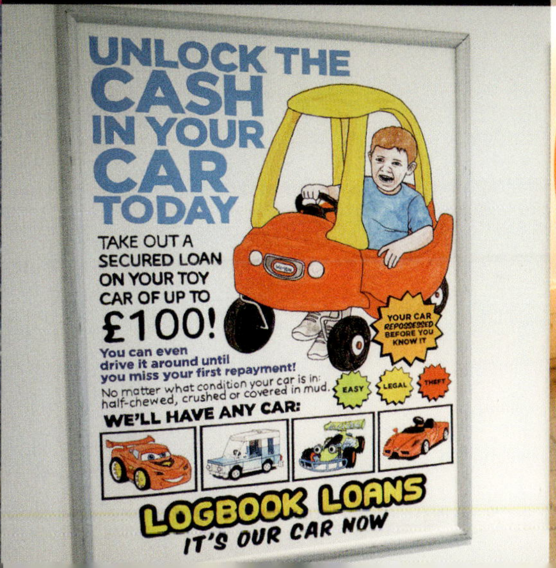
UNLOCK THE
CASH
IN YOUR
CAR
TODAY
TAKE OUT A
SECURED LOAN
ON YOUR TOY
CAR OF UP TO
£100!
You can even
drive it around until
you miss your first repayment!
No matter what condition your car is in:
half-chewed, crushed or covered in mud.
EASY
LEGAL
THEFT
WE'LL HAVE ANY CAR:
LOGBOOK LOANS
IT'S OUR CAR NOW

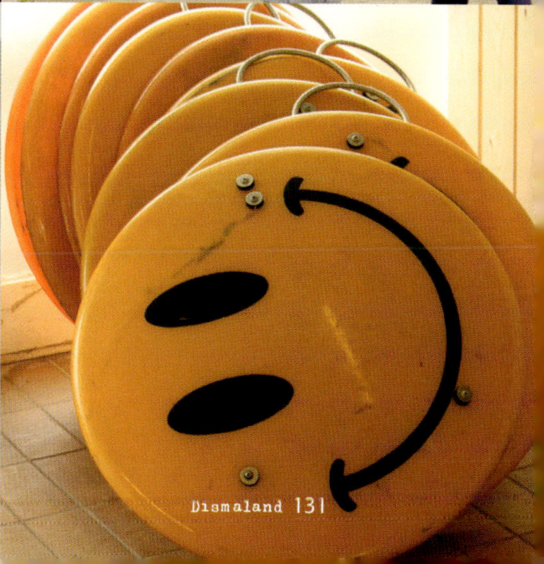

Enter Dismaland through the 'Gates of Mediocrity'.

Banksy on Dismaland

In his introduction to the Dismaland programme, Banksy says:

Bertolt Brecht once said 'Art is not a mirror held up to reality, but a hammer with which to shape it'. Which is fine, but what if you're in a hall of mirrors and the giant hammer is made of foam? This is the question raised by Dismaland Bemusement Park.

It's with great pleasure we throw open the doors of the Tropicana once again, I've dreamed of installing a theme park on this site ever since I walked past the building six months ago and peered through a gap in the fence. But this is not your average sugar-coated fantasyland selling scrapings from the Hollywood floor. No, we couldn't afford the licence for that.

Instead this is an attempt to build a different kind of family day out – one that sends a more appropriate message to the next generation – sorry kids. Sorry about the lack of meaningful jobs, global injustice and Channel 5. The fairytale is over, the world is sleepwalking towards climate catastrophe, maybe all that escapism will have to wait.

Here you'll find work by more than 50 artists from 17 nations who all toil under the darkening clouds. They hail from a wide variety of backgrounds and disciplines – one was awarded the gold medal at the Venice Biennale, one burnt a million pounds and one has spent 40 years making banners in his shed.

This event is so much more than just an art show, well, two things more. It's got a bar and a cinema. Think of this as a fairground that embraces brutality and low level criminality – so a fairground then. Here you're encouraged to consider, not just consume, to look, not just spectate and most of all – be aware of uneven floor surfaces.

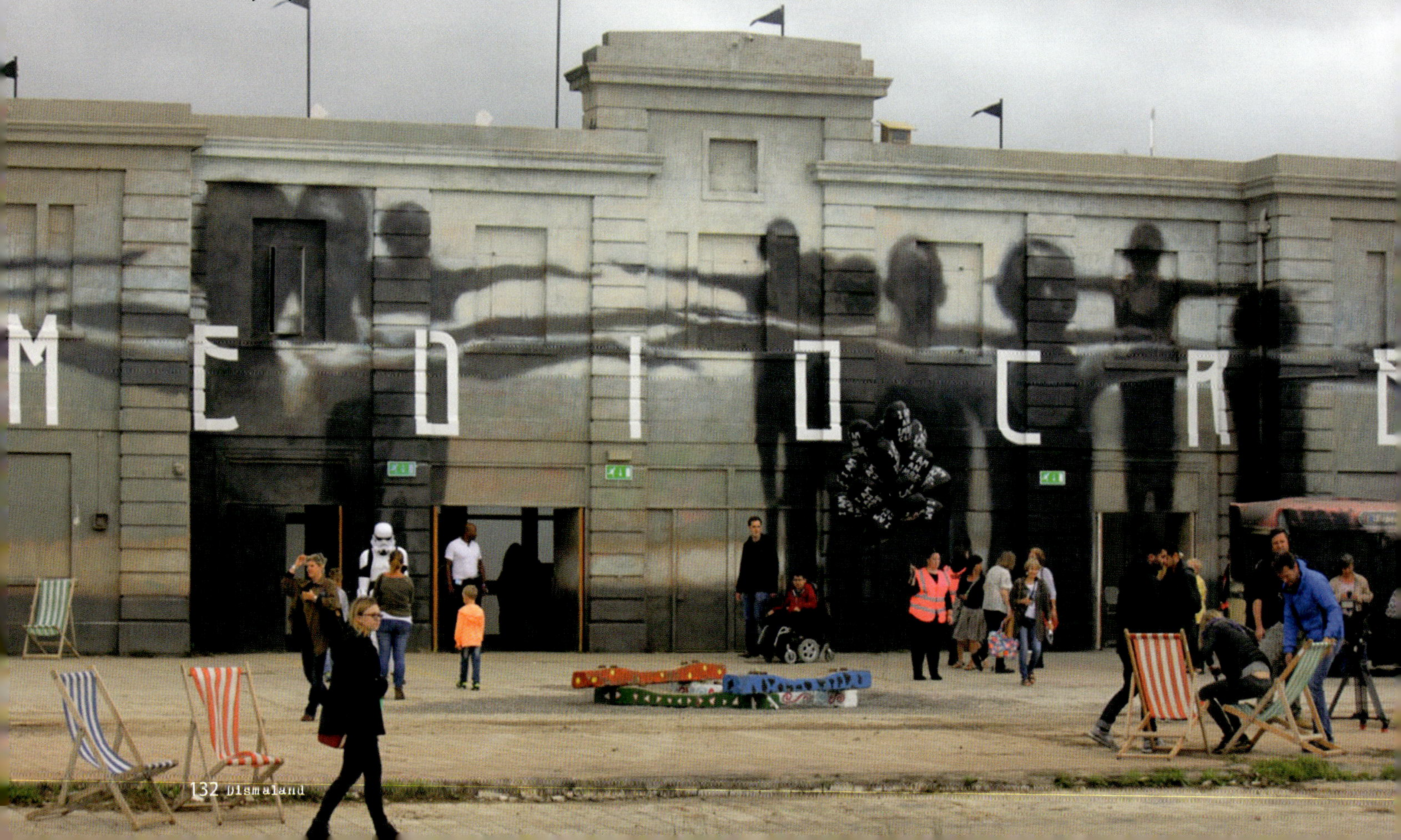

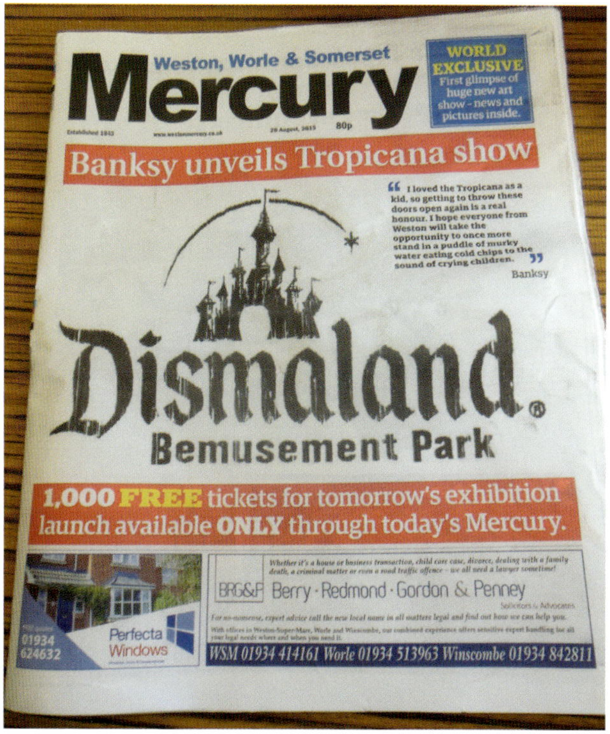

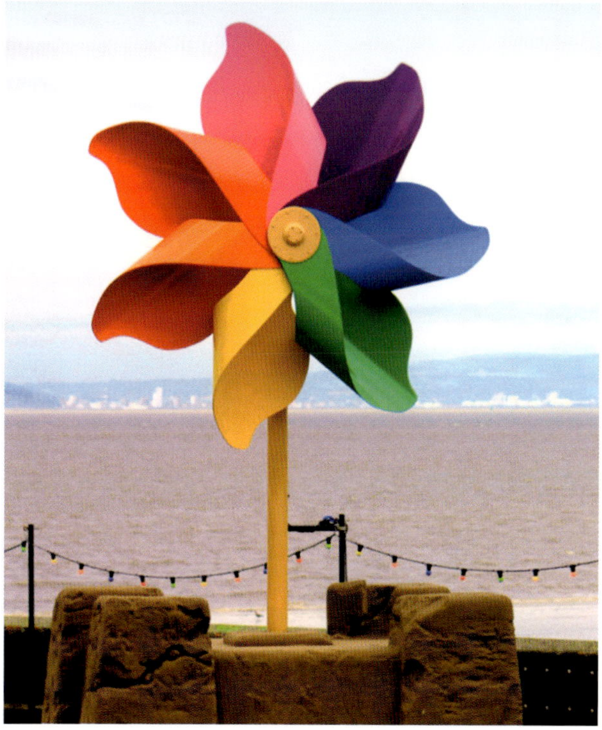

The Weston Mercury claimed a World Exclusive for their Dismaland special edition.

The windmill and giant sand castle at Dismaland.

Dismal stewards top poll

■ A poll of Weston Mercury readers who visited Dismaland revealed what the townsfolk enjoyed most about Banksy's Bemusement Park experience.

45% The Dismal Stewards
11% Dietrich Wegner's Mushroom Cloud installation
6% Cinderella, indoor gallery, Grim Reaper
5% Going to the Tropicana, Banksy's seagull attack
4% Banksy's castle, Jimmy Cauty's 'riot village'.

■ Only four people at North Somerset Council knew about the Dismaland project, one of those was its Tory leader, Nigel Ashton. "I gave it a lot of deep thought... for about two and a half seconds. For a second I thought, 'who is behind the wind up?' because you don't get that lucky. But how do you say no?"

■ A survey by Visit Somerset estimated that Dismaland was directly responsible for an injection of at least £20 million into the local economy. Train journeys between London and Weston almost doubled during Dismaland.

■ Visitor numbers at the nearby Grand Pier were up by 9,000 during Dismaland.

■ The Sunfold Hotel opposite Dismaland reported its busiest September ever.

■ Jo Burgon and Tallulah Belle from Weston camped overnight to become the first people to enter Dismaland.

■ A press release was circulated in early July 2015 claiming the Tropicana site was being used as the set for a crime-thriller film called Grey Fox between August and October.

■ Material from Dismaland was used to create shelters for migrants in the Calais 'Jungle' refugee camp.

■ Simon Christie-Irwin and Rachel Summerson-Wright cancelled their honeymoon in Cuba so they could be married at Dismaland.

■ A slice of Dismaland pizza sold on eBay for £1.66 plus £7.10 postage.

■ When the Dismaland ticket website crashed due to high demand, it was reported that this was a deliberate ploy to reinforce the miserable experience of visiting 'The UK's most disappointing new visitor attraction'.

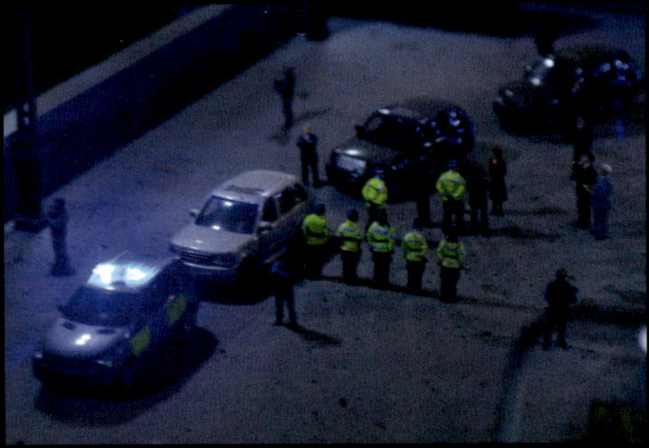

Jimmy Cauty's Aftermath Displacement Principle: a city frozen in the moments after a huge period of civil unrest.

What the papers said...

- Dismaland received mixed reviews from critics. Mark Hudson of *The Telegraph* gave the event a highly positive review – he 'loved it' and admired Banksy's use of the 'most potent image-making skills to convey a deadly serious message'.
- Prospero in *The Economist* admired the political and subversive nature of the Bemusement Park: 'Above all Dismaland appeals because it remains a fun "family day out". For all his protests, Banksy is a showbizman.'
- Mike Nudelman of *The Business Insider UK*, on the other hand, felt that Dismaland was merely an example of 'art about nothing', before describing Banksy as the 'Michael Bay' of 'socially and politically conscious art', implying that, much like Michael Bay's films, there was no actual substance behind the grand spectacles of the installation.
- Ben Luke of *The Evening Standard* only enjoyed the works of other artists, praising Jimmy Cauty's miniature city-scape as 'a corner of sincere radical politics.'
- *Vice* magazine really didn't like Dismaland: 'It felt hackneyed and was lost on me, and was the sort of gag a smug sixth former would make while bullies kicked him around the common room floor and rubbed apple cores in his face,' wrote Joe Bish.
- *The Guardian*'s Jonathan Jones is well known for his dislike of Banksy's work and Dismaland did nothing to change his mind: 'Dismaland does not offer the energy and danger that real theme parks do. Instead, it brings together a lot of bad art by the seaside.'
- The incident that caused the most controversy was the artist's invitation to celebrities such as Brad Pitt to privately experience the exhibition. However, Banksy claimed that the appearance of celebrity faces at the park would have brought 'a bit too much glamour' to what was intended to be a 'thoroughly depressing visit'. Dismaland was supposed to depict a 'fairground that embraces brutality and low level criminality'.
- Matt Selman, an executive producer of *The Simpsons*, seemed unimpressed by Banksy's showcase, commenting on Twitter, 'Have we ruled out that Dismaland is a meta-prank designed to expose those who think it clever as comedically feeble?'.

This is not the first time Banksy has received criticism from personnel at the show. In 2010, Banksy wrote the opening titles and couch gag for the Simpsons episode 'MoneyBart', which featured images of a Korean sweatshop producing merchandise of the show. According to Banksy, the sequence was 'inspired by reports that Simpsons characters are animated in Seoul, South Korea'; he also claimed that the animation process 'led to delays and a threatened walk out by the animation department'.

Al Jean, an executive producer at the show, has denied that this happened, although the animators did consider the couch gag to be 'excessive and offending'.

Sol Wilkinson

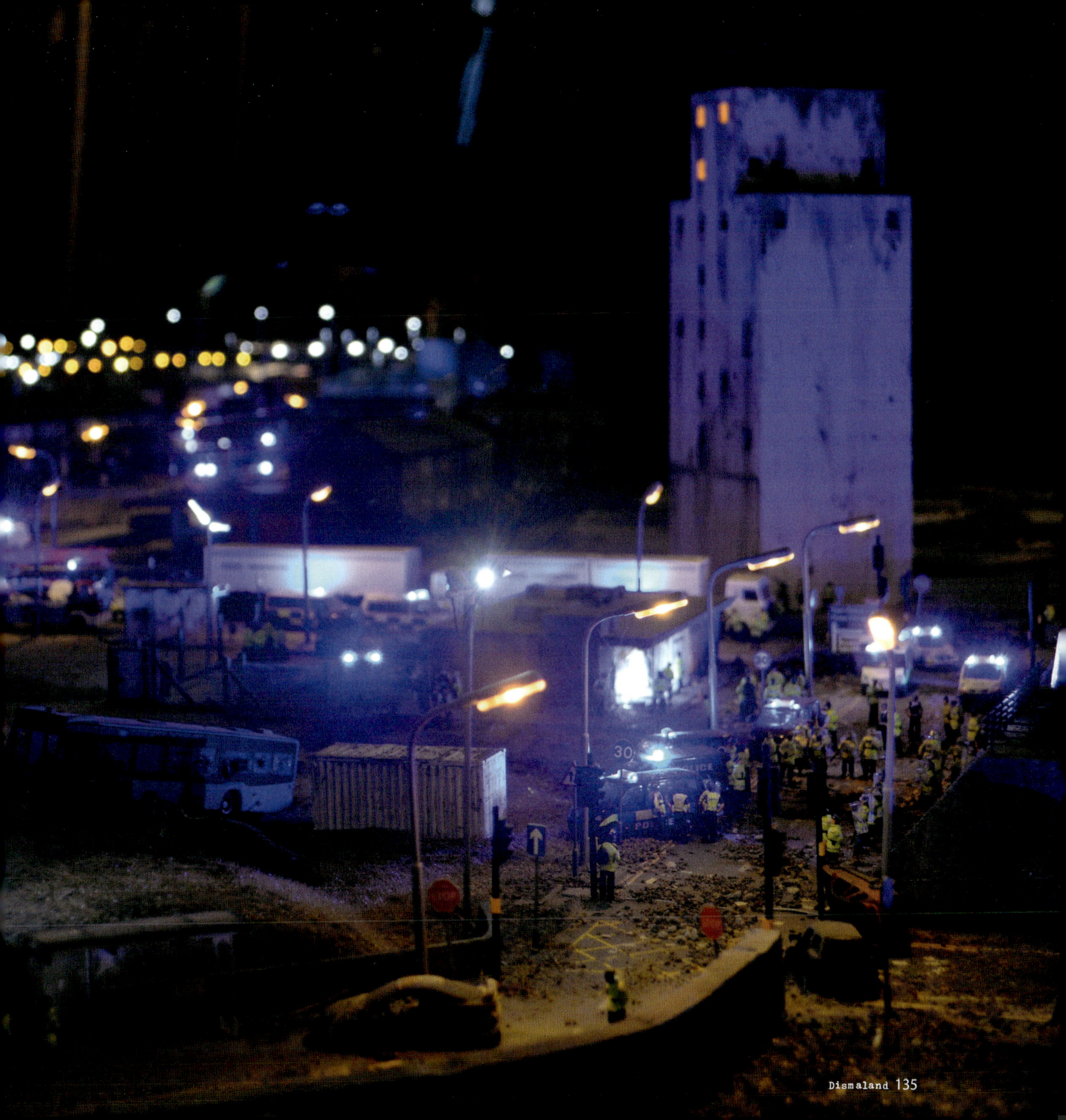

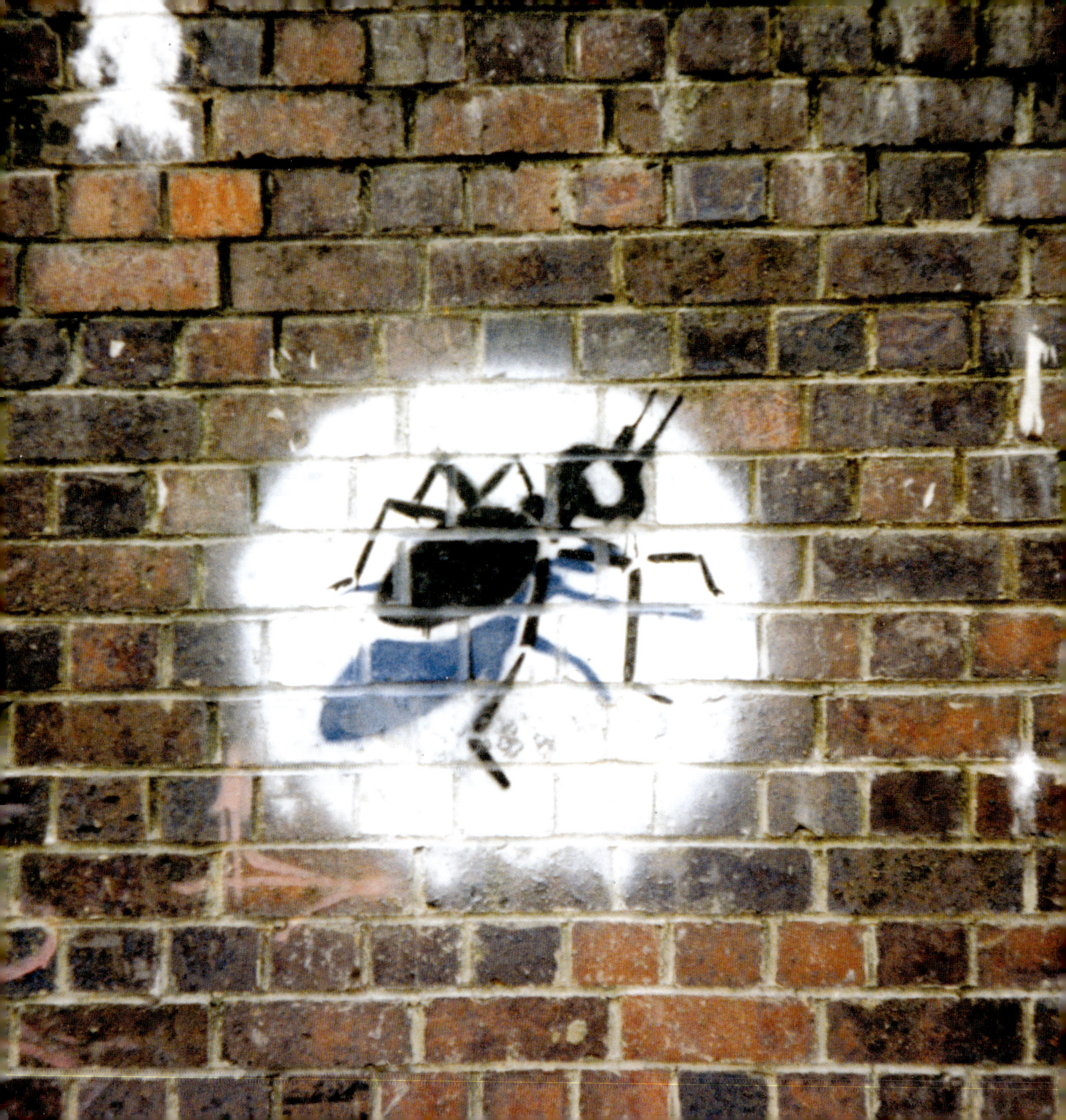

A Banksy Timeline

1974
Born in Bristol area.

1989
MARCH: At 6am on Monday 20 March, the joint forces of Avon and Somerset Police and British Transport Police raid the houses of 72 individuals in Bristol, Bath, Exeter and Cardiff in the Operation Anderson crack down on graffiti. Many of the writers frequented the Barton Hill Youth Club run by John Nation. The young Banksy was on the fringes of the Barton Hill scene, but was hugely influenced by it.

1990–91
After Operation Anderson many graffiti writers decide to 'go straight', but a small nucleus continue to paint illegally and harder than ever to keep the Bristol scene alive. Among them are the DryBreadZ Crew (DBZ) from Kingswood whose members include Lokey, Soker, Kato, Tes, Sorse and a young writer called Robin Banx, soon to become Banksy. His tag appears on DBZ pieces until about 1997.

Mid 90s
Banksy's first stencil – the insect in a spotlight (pictured left) appears on a wall in Windmill Hill, south Bristol.

1998
JULY: Paints a piece with Inkie beside the main stage at St Paul's Carnival.

AUGUST: Collaborates with Inkie and others for the *Walls On Fire* graffiti festival at Bristol Harbourside in which leading graffers paint the hoardings around the future At-Bristol site. Banksy's pieces are said by many to be among the best at the festival – but they're stolen shortly after.

1999
Banksy, Inkie and Mode2 paint Take The Money And Run mural, opposite the Old England pub in Montpelier.

Mild Mild West goes up on Stokes Croft.

JULY: Spraypaints van at Ashton Court Festival and leaves his tag on the golf course. Departs Bristol for London.

2000
JANUARY: Back to Bristol, to decorate the casket of local club legend Lez Hutchinson.

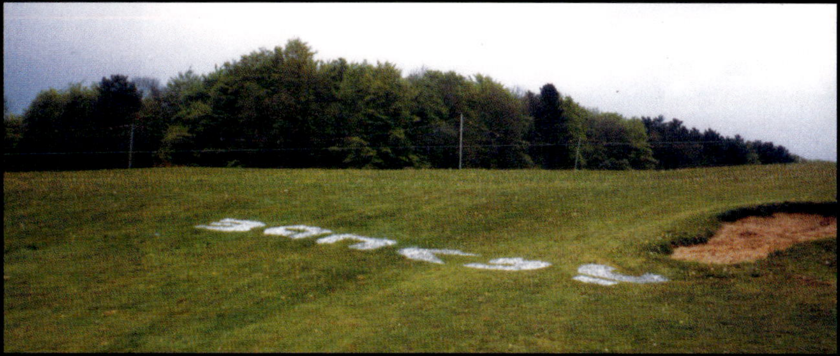

FEBRUARY-APRIL: Solo show at Severnshed restaurant with the theme, he tells *Venue* magazine, of 'punk fuckin' rock'. All but three of his paintings, priced from £89 to £2,000, sell on the first day.

JUNE: Collaborates with artist Paul Insect on artwork for the *Do Community Service* LP by Bristol trip-hop outfit Monk & Canatella.

OCTOBER: Exhibits at urban clothes shop Alterior, Park Street, Bristol. His paintings, which fetch prices between £150 and £899, are bought within three days of going on display. "I put his work up on the Saturday of the Ashton Court festival because the shop was so quiet and by Tuesday I had sold the whole lot," says Alterior's Justin McCarthy.

2001
First (unofficial) London exhibition, spraypainting 12 works (over a number of weeks) including Riot and Tiger Economics onto the whitewashed walls of a tunnel at Rivington Street, Shoreditch, above the title Speak Softly. But Carry a Big Can Of Paint.

NOVEMBER: Sprays (legitimately) the walls of the Swiss Embassy, London.

NOVEMBER: *Banging Your*

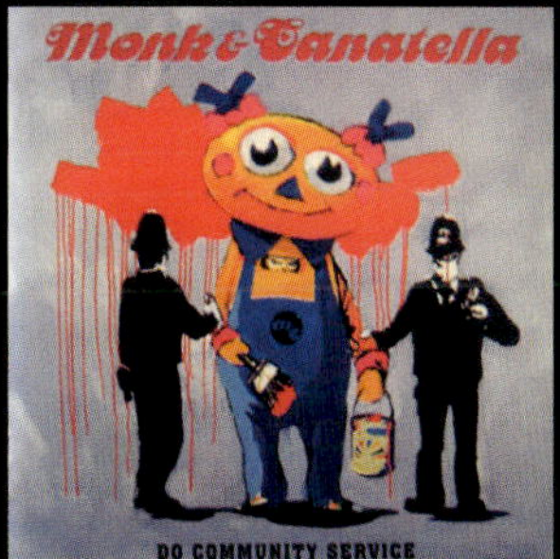

Above: Banksy leaves his mark at Ashton Court in 1999.

Below: Artwork for Monk & Canatella LP in 2000.

The original Banksy tag on the side of the Thekla in 2003.

Head Against A Brick Wall, the first of Banksy's little black books, is published by Weapons of Mass Disruption.

2002

MAY: Weapons of Mass Disruption publishes *Existencilism*, Banksy's second little black book. It is dedicated to 'All people with a vicious disregard for common sense.'

SUMMER: A Banksy stencil – featuring a rat smoking a cigarette and holding a shovel – is given away free with *Bizarre* magazine.

JULY: Does artwork for St Paul's carnival again.

SEPTEMBER: Shows at a London exhibition presenting an alternative view of the Queen's Golden Jubilee, alongside Throbbing Gristle's Genesis P-Orridge and Jamie Reid, sleeve-designer for the Sex Pistols. "At once calling for the abolition of the monarch, this show and gallery celebrate the spirit of punk, of bondage, of do-it-yourself cut and paste cultures that create opposition and will not tolerate conformity and the status quo," says a spokesman for the show.

2003

MAY: Hands out signs reading 'I Don't Believe In Anything. I'm Just Here For The Violence' at a May Day demonstration, London.

MAY: Banksy tags the side of the Thekla floating nightclub. On the Thekla website, customers vote overwhelmingly to keep it, but Bristol City Council paints over it – graffiti is seen as detrimental to the harbourside's image. Banksy returns to the same place soon after, and stencils an image of the Grim Reaper in a jollyboat.

JULY: Spraypaints animals from a farm in Somerset, for the exhibition Turf War in Shoreditch, London. The show includes a cow covered in Warhol portraits, sheep stencilled with the striped pyjamas of Holocaust victims and a pig bearing the chequered stripes of the Metropolitan Police. Animal rights activist Debbie Young chains herself to railings surrounding a Warhol cow.

"The cattle are show cattle donated by a farmer and he was happy to lend them," says a spokeswoman for the exhibition. "The RSPCA and the council checked it all out and they think it is fine to have the animals in the exhibition – if a little unusual." The exhibition is later called off because hot weather is distressing the animals.

OCTOBER: Slips into Tate Britain and glues a painting – a pastoral scene with police incident tape painted over it – to the wall. Only discovered when it crashes to the floor later.

NOVEMBER: Seen at the demonstration against the Iraq War that culminates at Trafalgar Square. Banksy hands out flyers that read 'Warning: Americans Working Overhead', with his helicopter stencil.

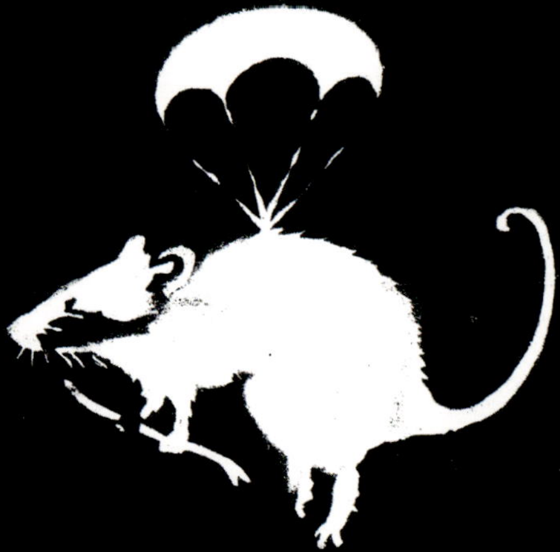

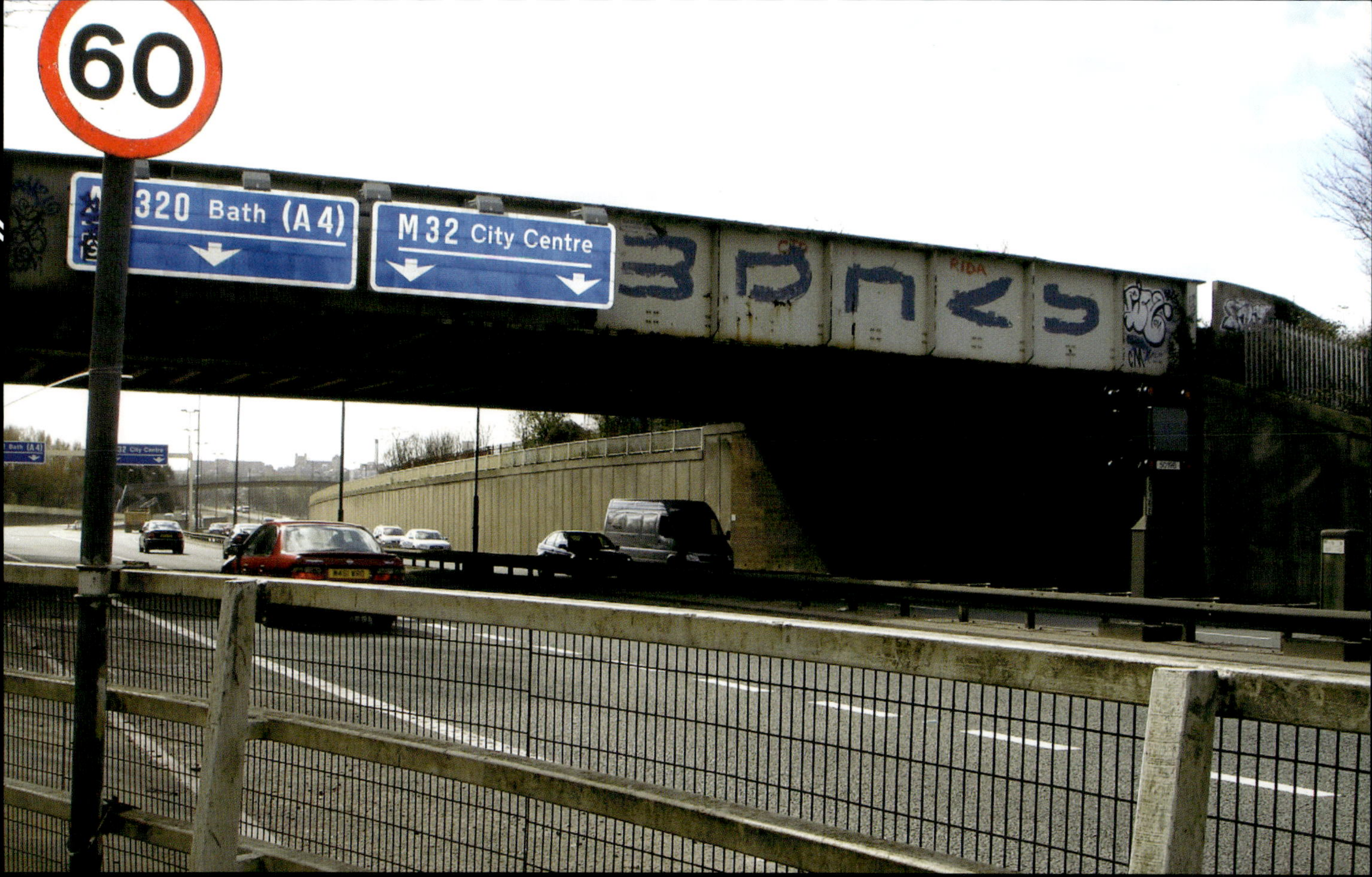

Banksy is 'shocked and saddened' by M32 'inferior work' in 2004.

2004

JANUARY: Advertising industry journal *Campaign* reports that Charles Saatchi is a big Banksy fan. Banksy's riposte: "I wouldn't knowingly sell a painting to Saatchi."

APRIL: Banksy, disguised as a museum employee, smuggles a dead rat in a glass-fronted box into the Natural History Museum, London. The rat wears wraparound sunglasses and carries a rucksack, a microphone and a miniature spraycan. And it's just sprayed, on the wall behind it, the message 'Our time will come.'

APRIL: He's being hunted by police after a large 'Banksy' tag is painted onto a railway bridge over the M32 in Easton, Bristol, causing a £20,000 clean-up bill. Banksy originally denies doing the piece. In a statement faxed to the Bristol *Evening Post*, he says: "I am shocked and saddened to see my name being used in vain on the M32 train bridge. The painting, which appears to say 'Bonsky', is not something I would want to put my name to. The lettering is not in proportion or even straight.

"I take my job as a professional vandal extremely seriously and consider this to be an inferior piece of work. I wish the relevant authorities all the best in returning the bridge to its former flat, grey, colour."

Despite his denials, the piece features in Banksy's book *Wall And Piece*. "The M32 bridge was definitely him," confirms an anonymous Bristol graffer and close Banksy associate. "He told me he was well pissed, so was pretty embarrassed by it!"

JULY: *Beyond Banksy* exhibition at Northern Lights gallery, Bristol. Includes work by Nick Walker and Ghostboy.

JULY: The *Evening Post* 'reveals' Banksy's identity. In fact, it's a picture of a man in a balaclava, and beside it the paper says that Banksy is 'thought to be 28' and that his 'real name is

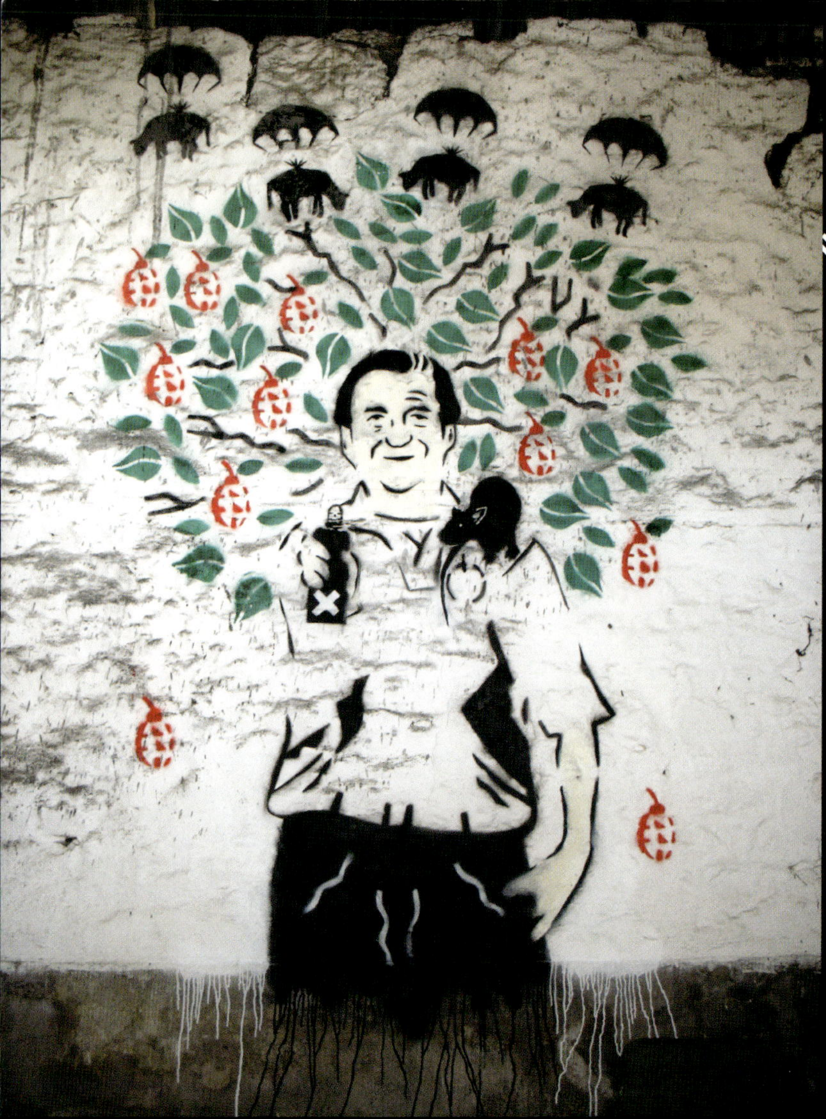

Banksy imitators at work in Roger Wilkins' Somerset cider barn in 2006.

understood to be Robert Banks'.

DECEMBER: Banksy publishes *Cut It Out*, the third and final little black book. Greenleaf Bookshop in Bristol is selling Banksy prints for £40-£80.

2005

MARCH: Enters, and hangs his work in, four world-famous New York museums and art galleries (Museum of Modern Art, Metropolitan Museum of Art, Brooklyn Museum, American Museum of Natural History). "This historic occasion has less to do with finally being embraced by the fine-art establishment and is more about the judicious use of a fake beard and some high-strength glue," Banksy comments to the graffiti website www.woostercollective.com "I've wandered round a lot of art galleries thinking 'I could have done that', so it seemed only right that I should try. These galleries are just trophy cabinets for a handful of millionaires. The public never has any real say in what art they see."

MAY: Another museum infiltration – this time at the British Museum, where he places a cave painting of a primitive man pushing a supermarket trolley. The piece is entitled Early Man Goes to Market, and captioned 'This finely preserved example of primitive art dates from the Post-Catatonic era and is thought to depict early man venturing towards the out-of-town hunting grounds. 'The artist responsible is known to have created a substantial body of work across the South East of England under the moniker Banksymus Maximus, but little else is known about him.' The British Museum adds the piece to its permanent collection.

MAY/JUNE: On the strength of his recent museum incursions, Banksy is put forward by the public (though later not shortlisted) for the Turner Prize.

JUNE: Sticks a shark's fin among the mudslides at Glastonbury Festival.

JUNE: Banksy is nominated for the South Bank Show Awards, but loses out to landscape painter John Virtue.

AUGUST: Decorates the West Bank segregation wall in Palestine with various scenes including a trompe-l'oeil of a hole in the concrete barrier, revealing an idyllic, unspoilt tropical beach on the other side.

OCTOBER: New exhibition *Crude Oils* features 200 live rats, plus 20 versions of classic oil paintings, retouched in Banksy's distinctive style. The rats are allowed to run free around the gallery at 100 Westbourne Grove, London.

2006

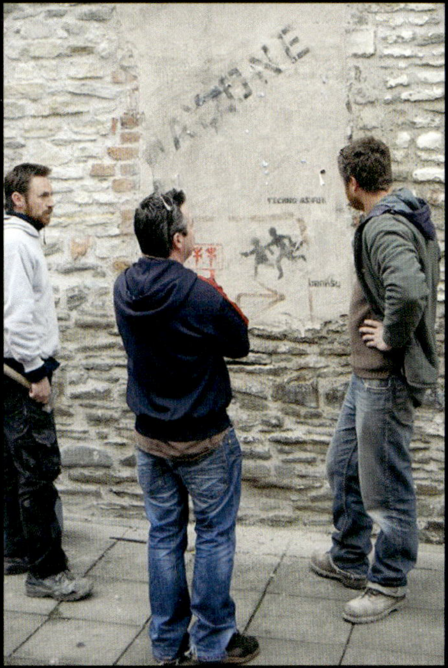

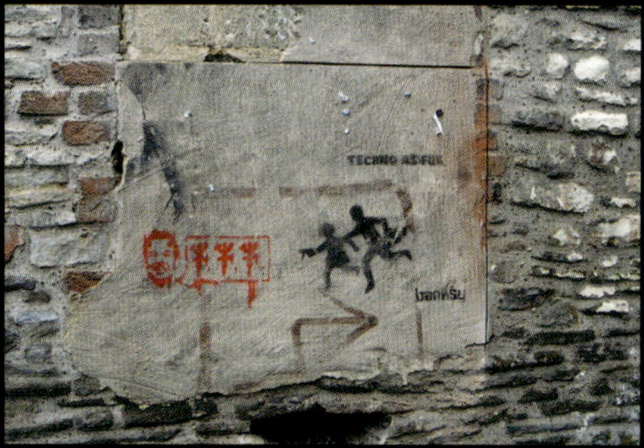

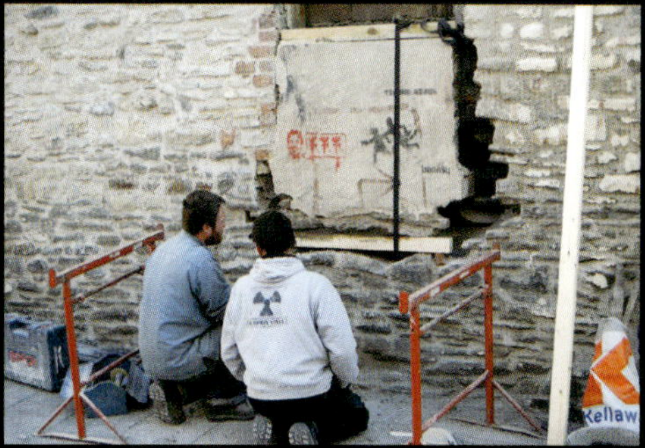

An early Banksy stencil is removed from the wall of the Full Moon in Stokes Croft in 2006.

MAY: Landlord JJ Gorman removes an early Banksy stencil from the outside wall of the Full Moon pub in Stokes Croft, Bristol after several attempts to 'steal' it.

JUNE: Paints Well-Hung Man, the window-hanging nude lover mural on Frogmore St, Bristol facing Bristol City Council's HQ.

JUNE: Visitors to Roger Wilkins' cider barn in Mudgley, Somerset notice a new piece of artwork in the 'lounge' area. Although there is no indication it is by Banksy, the parachuting cows remind some observers of stencils used on the Easton Rockers piece some years earlier. Banksy denies it is his work.

JULY: The Well Hung Man piece is allowed to stay after overwhelming support from people in the city. Nearly 500 Bristolians respond to the council survey, with 97 per cent voting to keep it.

JULY: While in London, Christina Aguilera pays £25,000 for a Banksy painting depicting Queen Victoria in a lesbian act.

AUGUST: Spraypaints his signature on five pigs on a farm near Glastonbury, which are to appear in *Pig Boy*, a comedy horror film by a Glastonbury-based film company. Farmer Andrew Wear: "I think that it is great. The pigs do not seem to have noticed much."

AUGUST/SEPTEMBER: Banksy swaps shop copies of Paris Hilton's latest CD with his own fake version, featuring his own takes of her music and new cover artwork. Hilton appears topless on the cover; the amended song titles include *Why Am I Famous?* and *What Am I For?*'

SEPTEMBER: Dresses an inflatable doll as a Guantanamo Bay prisoner and places it within the Big Thunder Mountain Railroad ride at the Disneyland theme park, California. The piece remains for 90 minutes before the ride is halted and the figure pulled down. A spokeswoman for Banksy confirms that the stunt is intended to highlight the detention of suspects at the controversial camp in Cuba.

SEPTEMBER: A wall on Sevier Street, St Werburgh's, Bristol, featuring a mural by Banksy (and others) is torn down to make way for flats. A block from the mural with Banksy's tag is auctioned on eBay, fetching more than £400.

2006–10

2007: A rare Banksy freehand piece in Easton is painted over by council contractors despite orders to leave it alone.

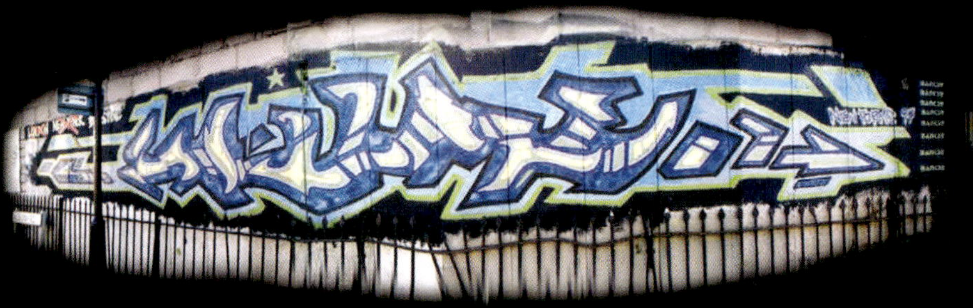

SEPTEMBER: *Barely Legal* exhibition in LA, featuring live 'elephant in the room'. Brad Pitt, Angelina Jolie, Jude Law, Keanu Reeves and Joni Mitchell are in attendance at the VIP preview. Jolie spends £200,000 on three pieces, including a portrait of a man hit on the head with a custard pie.

DECEMBER: Banksy's new print Flag goes on sale at Workshop, Park Row, Bristol, at £100. Only one print per person. Proceeds of the sale go to Sightsavers International, an international charity working to combat blindness in developing countries. The 100 prints sell out within two hours.

2007

FEBRUARY: Easton, Bristol: Owners of a house with a Banksy mural on the side decide to sell the house through an art gallery, after offers fall through because the prospective buyers want to remove the mural. The house is then listed for sale as a mural with a house attached. The mural itself is later defaced and the house withdrawn from the market.

MARCH: An early freehand Banksy is painted over by Council graffiti-removal contractors in Albion Road, Easton.

APRIL: Familiar stencil of a cut-out coupon appears off the Triangle, Clifton. Later removed because the Council doesn't think it's a Banksy.

APRIL: A new Banksy record is set: £288,000 for Space Girl And Bird, at Bonhams.

MAY: Gains the award for Art's Greatest Living Briton (ITV, *Greatest Britons 2007*), beating Antony Gormley and Sam Mendes. Other winners: David Beckham, Ricky Gervais, Amy Winehouse, Dame Helen Mirren, the Queen. He doesn't turn up to accept his gong.

MAY: Banksy's iconic Mild Mild West mural in Stokes Croft wins BBC Radio Bristol's public poll to find an Alternative Landmark for the city. The mural gets 47 per cent of the vote – more than double its nearest rival, the old industrial chimney stack at Troopers Hill in St George.

JUNE: Banksy erects his Boghenge sculpture at Glastonbury Festival. The piece features several portable chemical toilets piled on top of each other, Stonehenge-fashion. A statement from Banksy said: "A lot of monuments can be a bit rubbish. But this really is a pile of crap." 54 per cent of voters to a poll at www.efestivals.co.uk judge the piece 'bad'. A spokesman for the festival says: "The Henge will come down at some point but it still belongs to Banksy and it will then be up to him to decide what he wants to do with it."

JUNE: A YouGov poll to find art heroes among the under-25s puts Banksy third, after Walt Disney and Peter Kay but ahead of Leonardo da Vinci.

OCTOBER: Banksy features, for the first time, in the uber-prestigious Evening Sale at Sotheby's.

OCTOBER: Returns to Bristol to paint a piece opposite the Children's Hospital. The image shows a police marksman preparing to fire, with a small child behind him about to burst a paper bag next to his head.

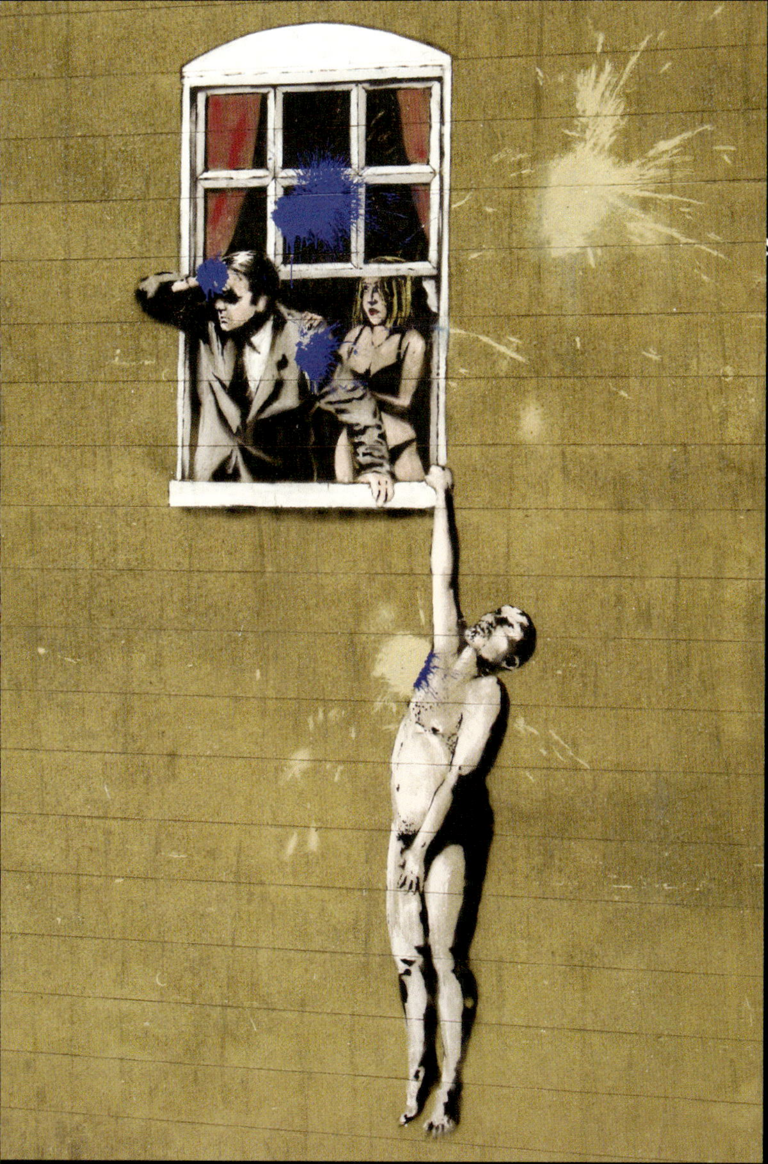

OCTOBER: First official exhibition in New York City. It's called The Village Pet Store And Charcoal Grill and features a series of animatronic pets in the store window.

2009

JULY: It had been rumoured since the beginning of the year that Banksy was planning a major stunt in his home town in the summer of 2009. But even those close the Banksy camp had no idea where or exactly what was going to happen until a couple of days before the event and the vast majority of Bristolians were entirely unaware that anything was going on until the morning of June 12 when the *Evening Post* informed them that Banksy had taken over the City Museum for

speculation that the act was perpetrated by Bristol Rovers fans who were unhappy with Banksy's alleged comment that Rovers play 'a dire form of the beautiful game.'

2010

JANUARY: *Exit Through The Gift Shop* is premiered at the Sundance Festival. There are many commendable aspects of Banksy's first foray into feature films, but perhaps its true genius is that it takes a Banksy gag (so evident in all his finest artwork) and translates it into 90-minutes of cinema. Audiences leave the film confused about whether Mr Brainwash is entirely a front for Banksy or whether the film is indeed a documentary charting the rise of Thierry Guetta from maverick street art watcher

Bristol Rovers fans are blamed for paintballing the Well-Hung Man in 2009.

Banksy releases Tesco Value Petrol Bomb at Bristol Anarchist Bookfair in 2011.

Right: Who was responsible for this piece opposite the Bristol Royal Infirmary in 2012?

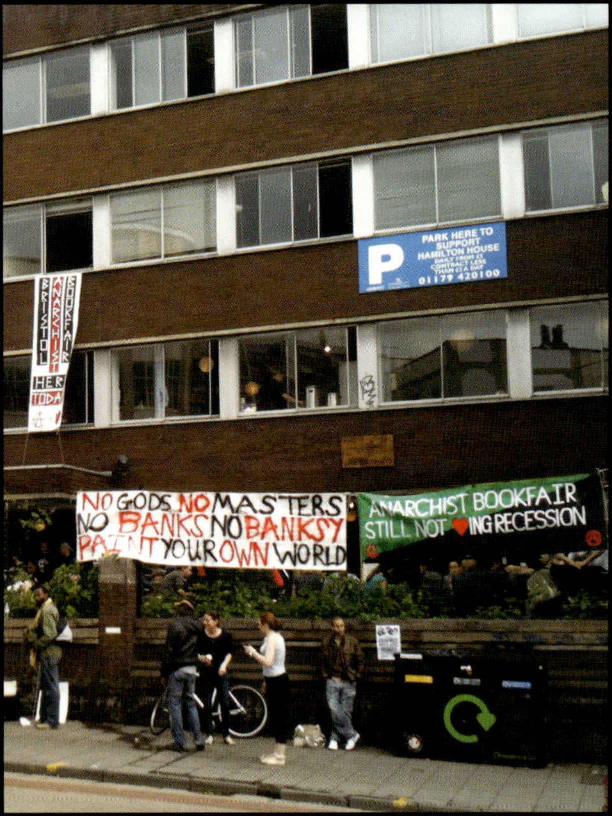

Bay prisoner at the bottom of a water ride.

AUGUST: A Barcode Leopard stencil is lost from the wall of a house in Pembroke Road, Clifton when it is demolished and rebuilt. There is speculation that the piece is still there, but 'buried' under the new house.

OCTOBER: Banksy becomes the first artist to create an intro for *The Simpsons*. But is this further proof of the artist selling out or an audacious attack at the very heart of Murdoch's global media empire? Who knows, but his detractors choose the former and his admirers the latter option. The intro starts with Banksy's tag scrawled across the town of Springfield. It closes with a minute-long sequence showing dozens of sweatshop workers and animals making Simpsons merchandise. The episode, called MoneyBart, is shown in the UK on October 21, 2010 and is apparently inspired by reports the show outsources animation to a company in South Korea.

2011

MAY: Banksy releases a limited edition print of a Tesco Value Petrol Bomb to raise money for the defence fund for the squatters arrested in the 'Tesco Riots' that followed a raid on the Telepathic Heights squat in Stokes Croft. The 2000-edition print is sold at the Bristol Anarchist Book Fair for £5. The proceeds are split three ways between the defence fund, the People's Republic of Stokes Croft and Coexist who run the Hamilton House project in Stokes Croft where the Bookfair took place.

2012

JUNE: A picture of The Queen as David Bowie appears on the wall where the Banksy Sniper was for five years. The Sniper was defaced in a feud with supporters of rival artist King Robbo and shortly afterwards the new piece appeared, marking the Queen's 60th anniversary as monarch and the 40th anniversary of David Bowie's album *The Rise And Fall Of Ziggy Stardust And The Spiders From Mars*. But is it a Banksy? There's no tag and it has never been claimed but the word on the street is that the piece was produced in mysterious circumstances.

If the rumours are to be believed, a Bristol street artist or artists received precise instructions to collect stencils and put up the piece and it was duly created. But who was issuing the instructions?

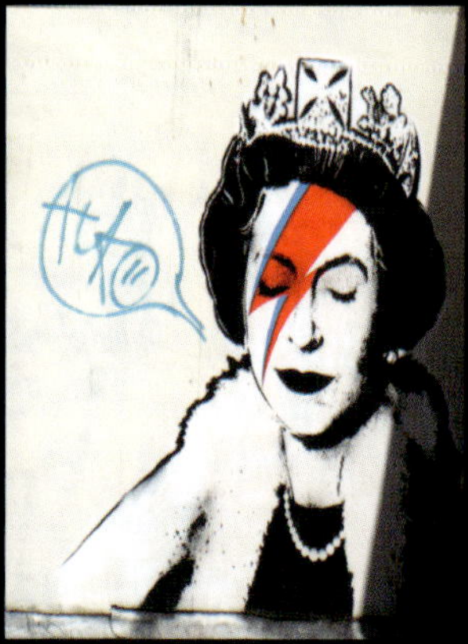

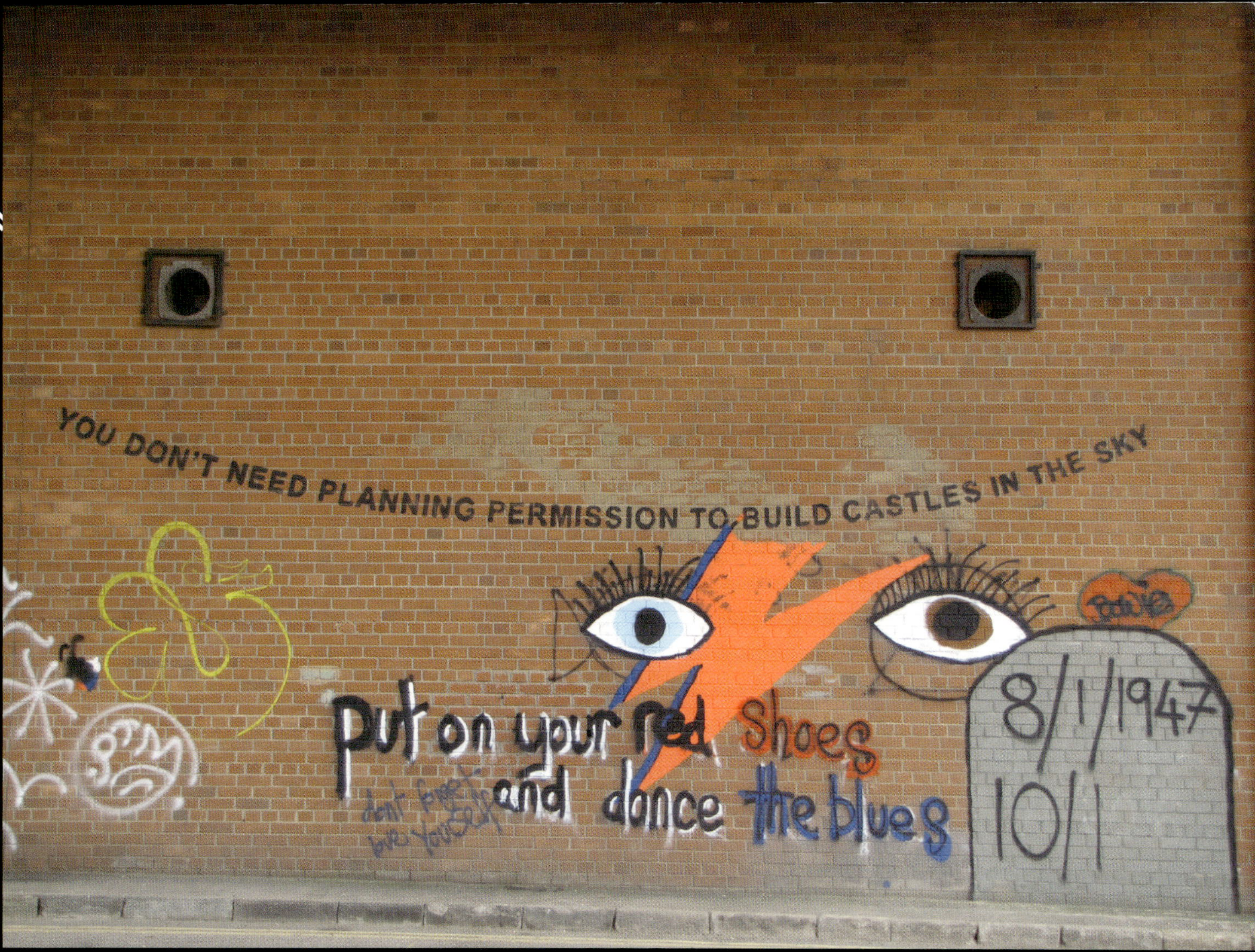

The Gorilla on Fishponds Road is painted over by the new owner of the building. Attempts to restore it are only partially successful.

JULY: An unclaimed piece appears at the back of Bristol Central Library The wording makes a smiley face between two extractor fans: 'You don't need planning permission to build castles in the sky.'

The piece appears on Banksy's website which is the accepted way of the artist claiming ownership of the work in the absence of a tag.

2013

OCTOBER: Banksy launches his *Better Out Than In* 'residency' in New York in which he unveils a piece, installation or video every day for a month. At a press

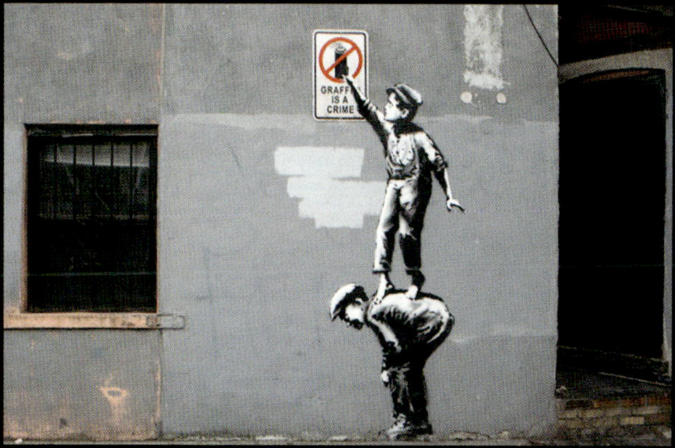

Above: Castles In The Sky from 2012.

Left: Better Out Than In - New York 2013.

2013-14

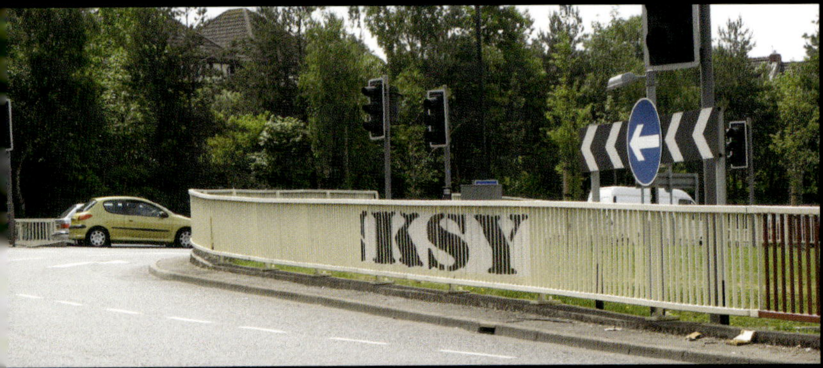

Above: Bristol City Council removes this highly unusual Banksy piece in 2014.

Right: The Grim Reaper is removed from the Thekla in 2014.

conference, New York City Mayor Michael Bloomberg says:"Graffiti does ruin people's property and is a sign of decay and loss of control." The New York work includes a video of Jihadist militants shooting down an animated Dumbo the Elephant, travelling installations including a slaughterhouse delivery truck full of stuffed toy animals, and a modified painting donated to a charity shop which was later sold in an online auction for $615,000.

DECEMBER: The stencil removed by landlord JJ Gorman from the wall of the Full Moon in Stokes Croft (see 2006) is sold for £26,000 at the Smile Britannia auction at the House Of Commons. Half the money goes to the Bristol-based Temwa charity that supports people in northern Malawi and the other half goes towards renovation at the Full Moon.

2014

APRIL: The Spy Booth piece appears on the side of a house in Cheltenham where the Government's GCHQ intelligence and security headquarters is based.

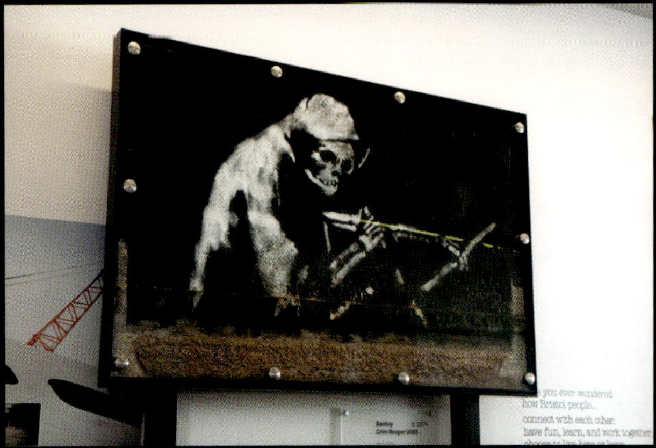

APRIL: Mobile Lovers appears on a wall outside Broad Plain Boys' Club. Some of the lads arrive early at the club and realise the piece may be valuable so remove it and take it inside. It is rumoured that they were about to put the piece on eBay when youth workers arrive and realise it is a Banksy.

AUGUST: Mobile Lovers is sold to a private collector for £403,000.

AUGUST: The Grim Reaper is removed from the Thekla when the boat goes into dry dock for repairs.

SEPTEMBER: The 'lost' Barcode Leopard from Pembroke Road, Clifton (see 2010) is 'found' when it goes on display at an open evening at Nailsea School. The architect husband of a textile teacher at the school removed the stencil from the wall with the owner's permission and it spent four years stored under a bed.

SEPTEMBER: Bristol City Council removes the KSY lenticular piece on railings at the Eastville Park roundabout. Although it was never claimed by Banksy, those in the know say it was definitely his work.

OCTOBER: Girl With A Pierced Eardrum appears on a wall at the back of a recording studio near Spike Island on Bristol's Floating Harbour. It parodies the famous Girl With A Pearl Earring by Johannes Vermeer, replacing the earring with an alarm box fixed to the wall. The piece is vandalised within hours with a splatter of dark paint.

OCTOBER: A hoax story about Banksy being arrested is published by satirical US website *National Report*: the article claims Banksy's identity had finally been revealed by the Metropolitan Police, holding him "on charges of vandalism, conspiracy, racketeering and counterfeiting".

2015

FEBRUARY: Banksy publishes a 2-minute video entitled 'Make This The Year **You** Discover A New Destination' about his trip to the Gaza Strip. During his visit he paints various pieces. In a statement to the *New York Times*, Banksy says: 'I don't want to take sides. But when you see entire suburban neighborhoods reduced to rubble with no hope of a future – what you're really looking at is a vast outdoor recruitment center for terrorists. And we should probably address this for all our sakes.'

JUNE: The Grim Reaper from the Thekla goes on display at the nearby M Shed museum. The piece is on long-term loan from the Thekla.

AUGUST: Dismaland opens at the Tropicana in Weston-super-Mare. The event is Banksy's most ambitious project to date and he claims to have completed it in six months after walking past the abandoned Tropicana site and looking inside through a gap in the fence. Banksy's team create a gallery for an impressive collection of contemporary art, featuring more than 50 artists from around the world. The exhibition is curated by Banksy but two unnamed artists decline his offer to show their work. The rest of the 2.5-acre site is given over to a dystopian funfair or Bemusement Park. Banksy labels the Tropicana event as 'The UK's Most Disappointing New Visitor Attraction.' The ticket website crashes under the weight of demand although many claim the malfunction is deliberate to add to the dismal experience.

SEPTEMBER: A major subvertising campaign takes place in London against the The Defence And Security Equipment International Arms Fair at the ExCeL. Scores of bus stop advertising sites are broken into and protest posters appear there and across the tube network. The campaign is organised from Dismaland where an Adbusters team are selling Ad Space Hack Pack kits and explaining how to use them. Dismaland closes on

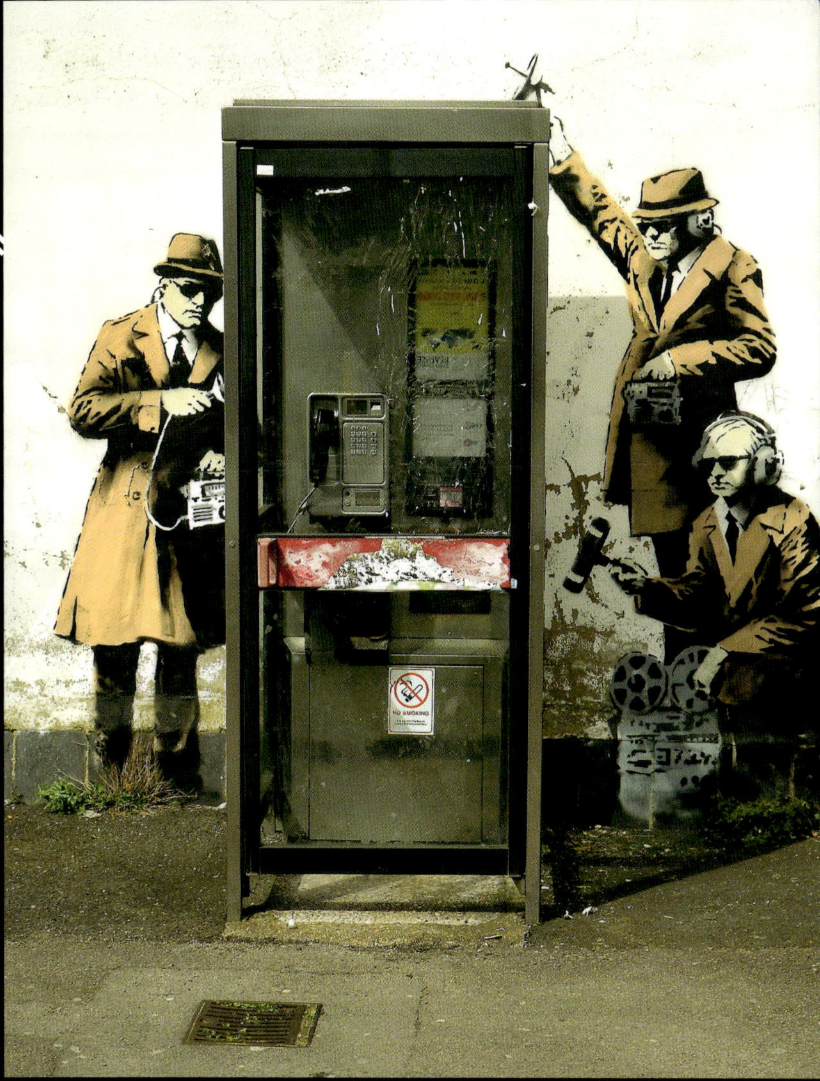

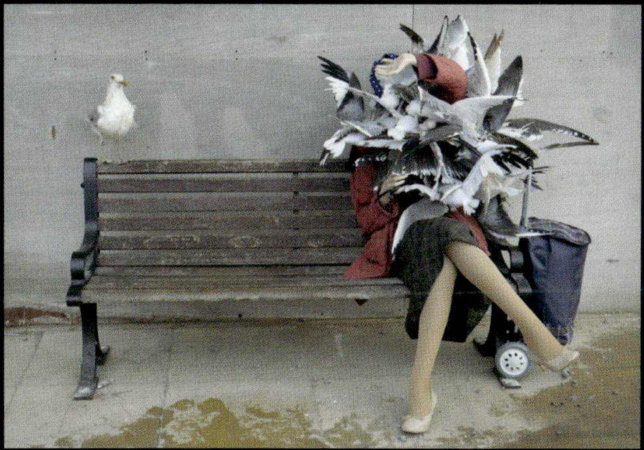

Above: Spy Booth in Cheltenham appears at the same time as Mobile Lovers in Bristol in 2014.

Left: Banksy's Seagull Attack at Dismaland.

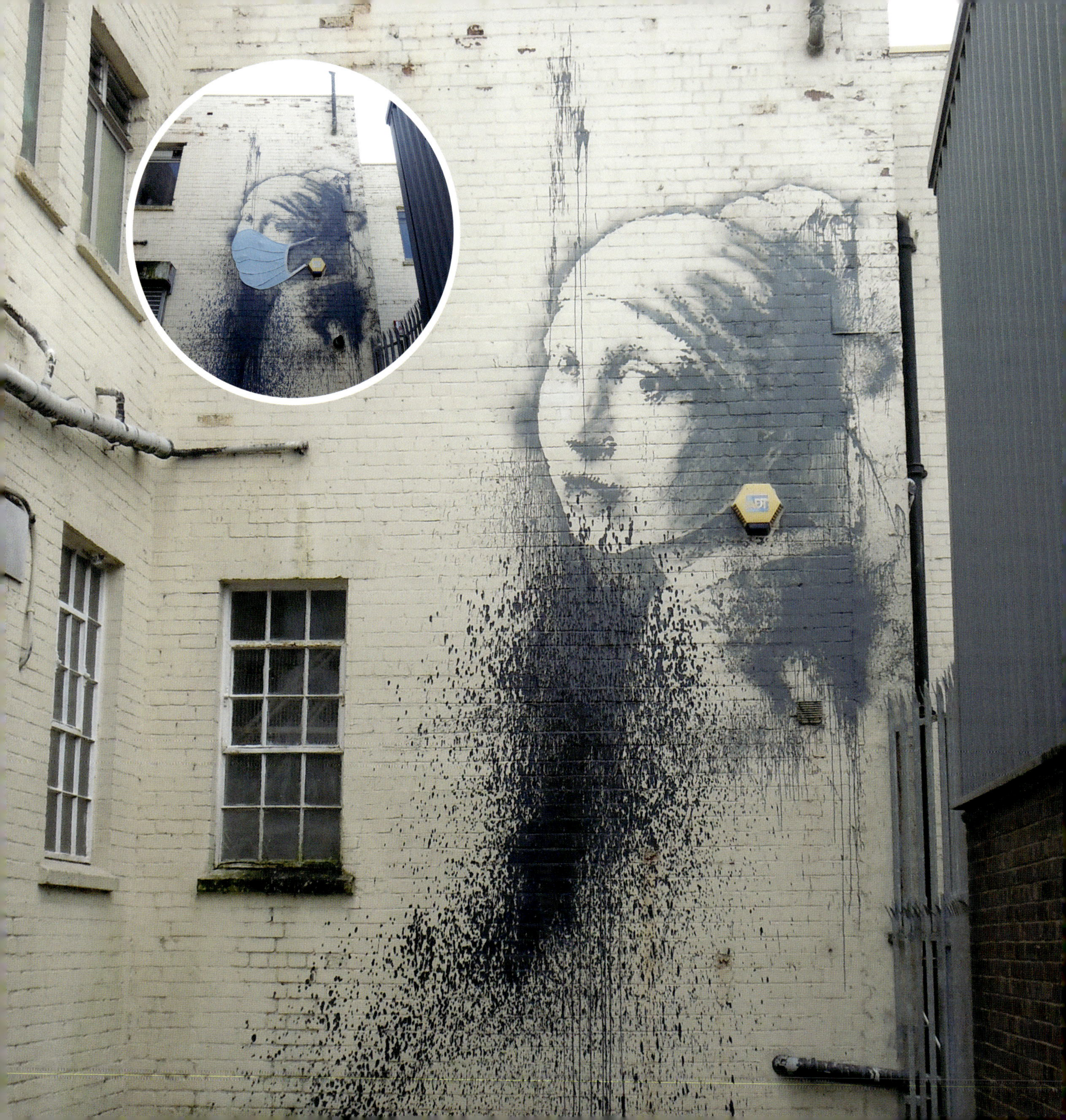

September 25. It generates at least £25 million for Weston-super-Mare. More than 150,000 people visit Dismaland.

OCTOBER: Materials from Dismaland are used to create shelters for refugees in The Jungle camp in Calais. The project is called Dismalaid. Banksy puts up several pieces in Calais and in The Jungle.

DECEMBER: At a ceremony held at the New Inn, Wedmore, Somerset, the annual Turnip Prize was awarded to Bristol artist Bonksy for his work entitled "Dismal And".

2016

JANUARY: A stencil depicting Steve Jobs as a Syrian refugee is defaced in The Jungle. Protective glass is smashed and giant letters reading 'London Calling' are painted across the artwork with Jobs used as a substitute for the letter 'I'.

JANUARY: Artwork by Banksy criticising the use of tear gas in The Jungle appears on the side of the French Embassy in London. The artwork depicts a young girl from the film and musical *Les Misérables* with tears in her eyes as CS gas billows towards her. For the first time Banksy uses a QR code. It links to a video of a police raid on the camp.

JUNE: Nobody, apart from Banksy, really knows whether Mobile Lovers (p119) was intended as a gift to Broad Plain Boys' Club, but there's no doubt that Girl With A Burning Tyre was painted as a 'thank you' to the pupils at Bridge Farm Primary School in Whitchurch in south Bristol.

The youngsters wrote to Banksy before Easter 2016 to tell him they had renamed one of their school houses in his honour. The other houses are named after Brunel (suspension bridge), Cabot (discovered America) and Blackbeard (the greatest ever pirate). On Monday June 6 at 6am the school is contacted by Jo Brookes, Banksy's PR, who says Banksy has left a present and she hopes the school has a liberal head teacher.

When site manager Jason Brady arrives at the school he discovers the piece depicting a scribbly school girl bowling a burning tyre along a 14ft wall in the manner of the Victorian stick and hoop children's game. Banksy also leaves a note for the school:

> *'Dear Bridge Farm School. Thanks for your letter and naming a house after me.*
>
> *'Please have a picture. If you don't like it feel free to add stuff. I'm sure the teachers won't mind. Remember – it's always easier to get forgiveness than permission.*
>
> *Much love, Banksy.'*

The Bridge Farm piece is unusual in several respects. It's the first time that Banksy has publicly responded to an approach and it's the first time in almost a decade that he has authenticated a piece with his tag – or more specifically his signature which is sprayed on the bottom-left of the piece.

So, what's it worth? Mobile Lovers and the accompanying letter was sold for £403,000, but was unsigned. In theory the Bridge Farm piece should be worth more than this because it's signed. But the initial reaction from Bridge Farm head teacher Geoff Mason is that the school has no plans to sell it, and regard it as "inspirational and aspirational" for the pupils.

That page: Girl With A Pierced Eardrum, 2014. The mask is added during the Covid-19 pandemic in 2020.

Below: Banksy's gift to Bridge Farm Primary School in 2016.

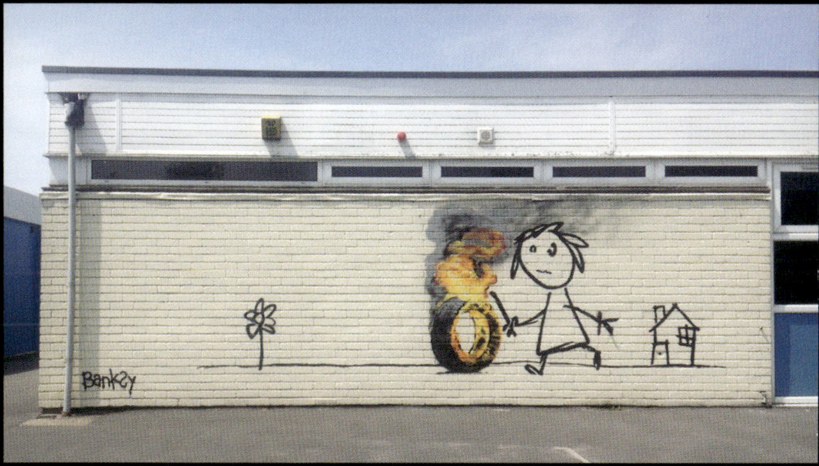

2018-20

Right: Banksy returns to Barton Hill in 2020.

Below: Was Banksy behind the display at the Star And Garter pub?

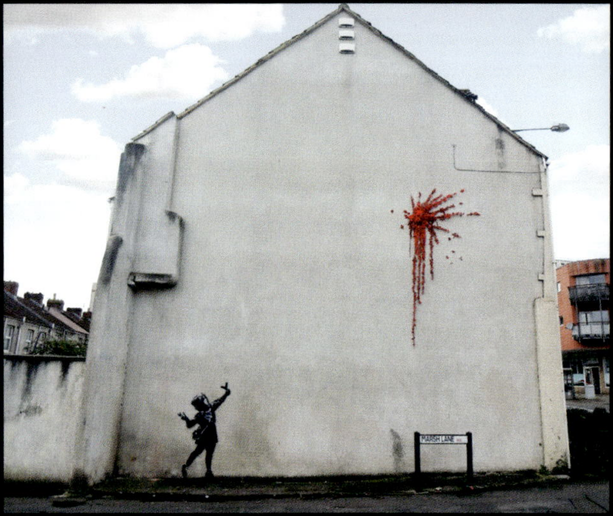

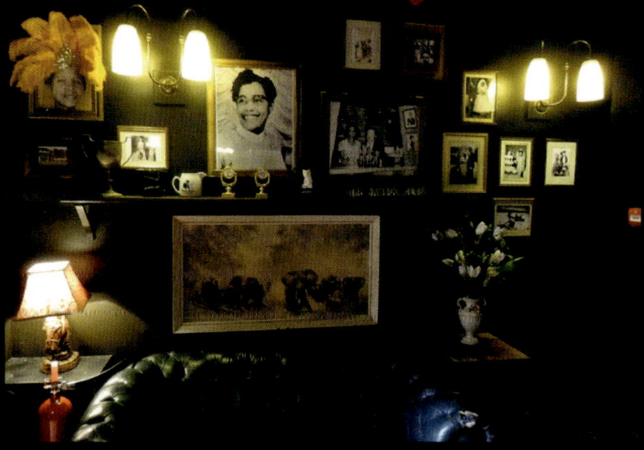

2018

JULY: Bristol's elected Mayor, Marvin Rees, reveals in a Bristol City Council Cabinet meeting that Banksy has offered to help keep Bristol libraries open. Faced with Tory austerity cuts, the council is considering closing libraries. Rees said :"He has come forward and talked about supporting us and we will see how that plays itself out. There is nothing signed and delivered and so far it is just a conversation that we had."

OCTOBER: Banksy plays one of the most audacious stunts in art history, when he arranges for one of his best-known works to self-destruct after being sold at auction for just over £1m.

Girl With Balloon is the final item in an auction at Sotheby's in London and its sale price equals the artist's previous auction record of £1.04m. Shortly after the hammer came down on the item, however, the canvas begins to pass through a shredder installed in the frame.

2019

MARCH: Devolved Parliament goes on display in the front hall of Bristol Museum And Art Gallery from March to September. The piece is loaned by a private collector 10 years after the Banksy vs Bristol Museum exhibition. Banksy said it is a comment on the parliamentary debates over Brexit.

The painting, which is four metres wide, is the artist's largest work on canvas. After being taken down from the Museum, it sells for £9.9 million during a record-breaking sale at Sotherby's on October 3. Its guide price is between £1.5-2 million. The sale comfortably beats the previous auction record for a Banksy, which is thought to be the 1.8 million US dollars (£1.4 million) paid for Keep It Spotless.

JUNE: One of Banksy's favourite Bristol pubs re-opens two years after the death of its long-time landlord Dutty Ken. The Star And Garter on Brook Road between St Paul's and Montpelier is taken over by music promoter Malcolm Haynes, an old friend of Banksy. Banksy is rumoured to have backed the pub refit along with Daddy G from Massive Attack and Roni Size. The interior of the pub is a fascinating display of ephemera celebrating the local black community and Bristol's black music history. It is widely thought that Banksy designed the brilliant display.

2020

FEBRUARY: Flower Girl appears on the side of a house in Marsh Lane, just yards from Barton Hill Youth Club where John

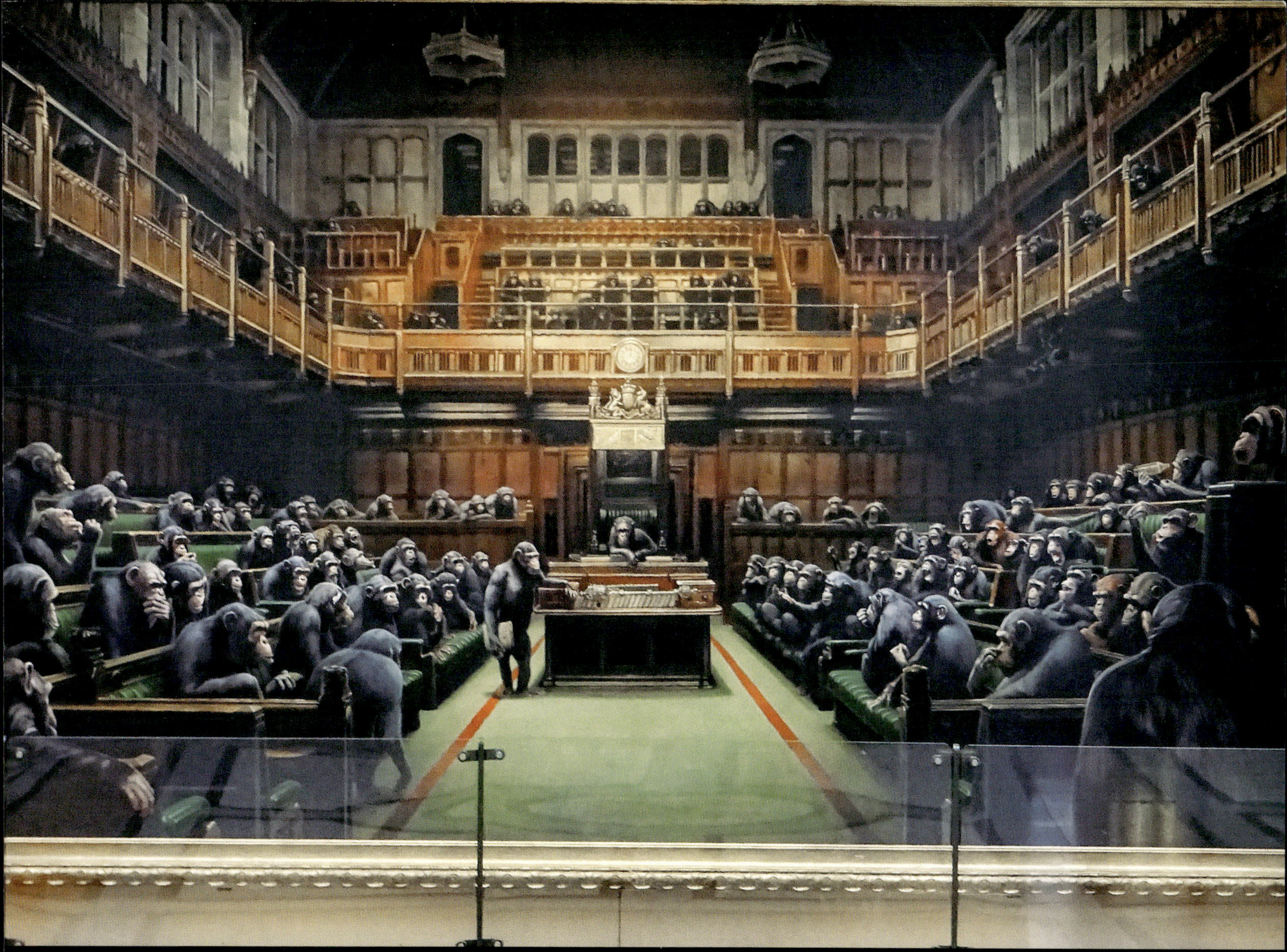

Nation fostered the first generation of Bristol graffiti writers in the mid-80s. The piece appears just before Valentine's Day and is defaced within 48 hours when someone paints a pink heart and the words 'BCC Wankers'.

The house is owned by Edwin Simons, 67, and the piece appears on his birthday. Mr Simons boards over the work in order to prevent any further damage.

Banksy claims in a tongue-in-cheek Instagram post that he is "kind of glad" that the piece in Barton Hill got vandalised. "The initial sketch was a lot better," he adds.

APRIL: A medical face mask is added to the Girl With The Pierced Ear Drum in Hanover Place behind Spike Island – a clear reference to the Covid-19 pandemic. The addition bears all the hallmarks of Banksy's work, but the artist does not claim responsibility for it.

Above: Devolved Parliament returns to Bristol Museum And Art Gallery in 2019.

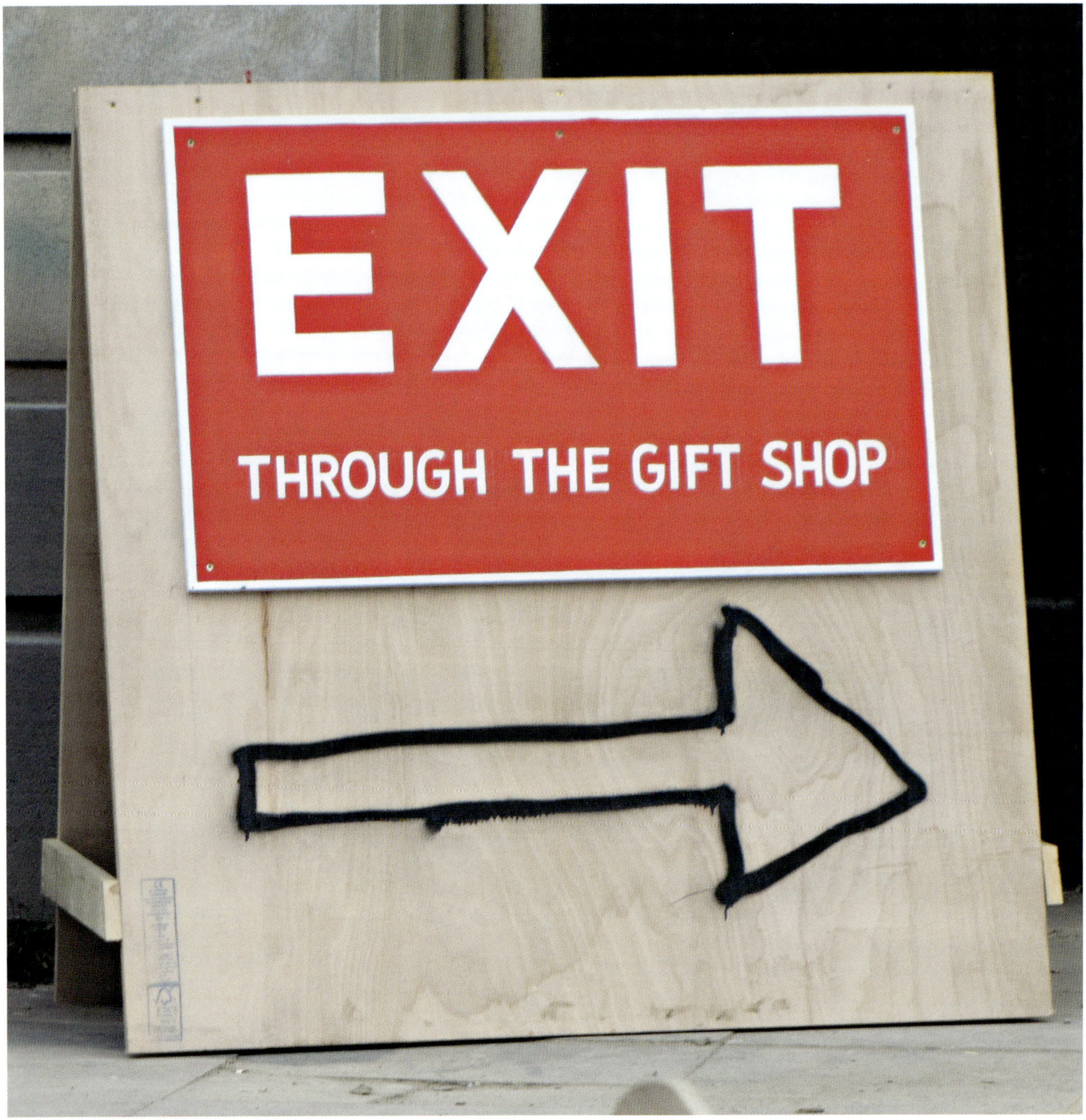
EXIT
THROUGH THE GIFT SHOP

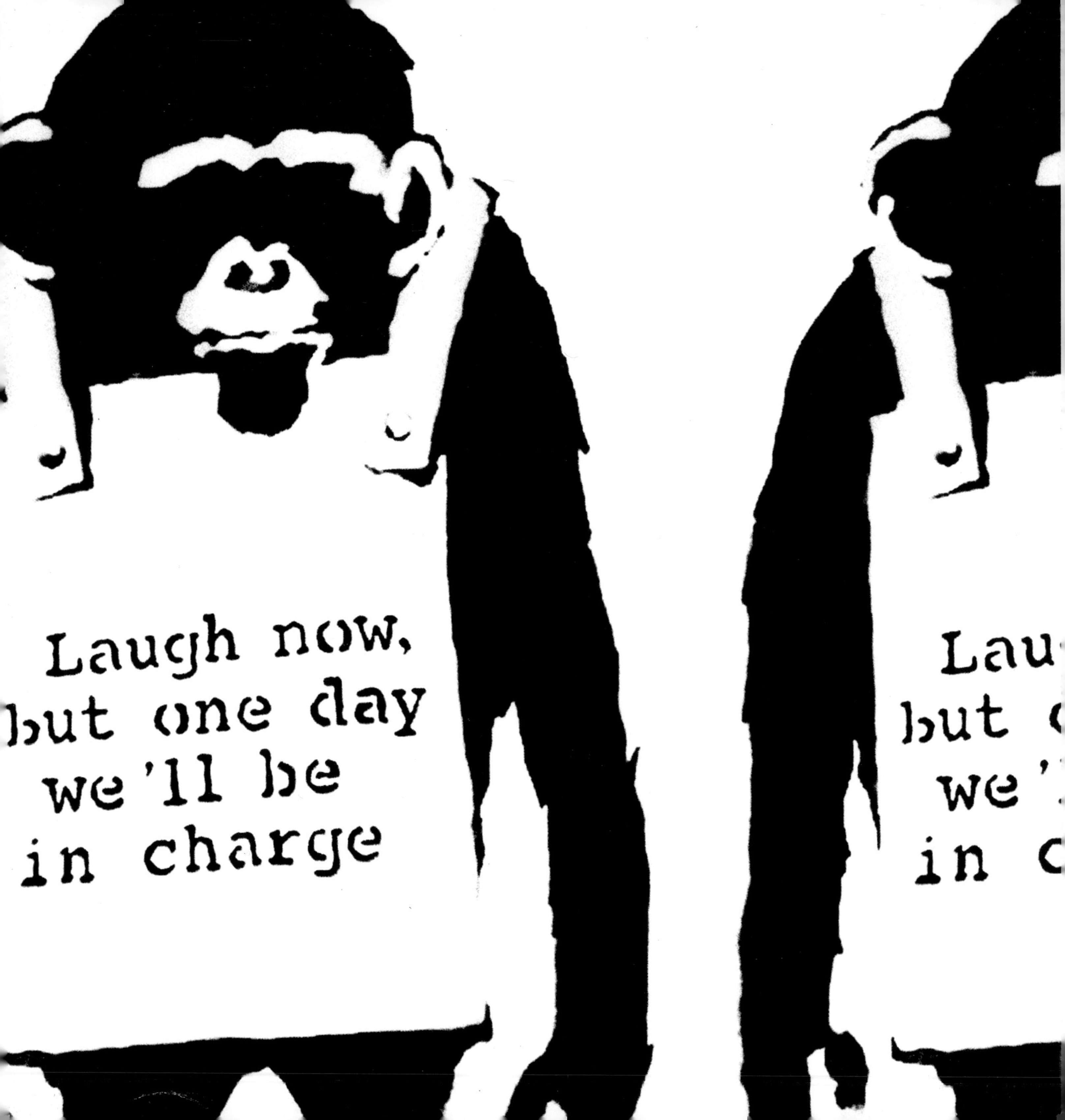
Laugh now,
but one day
we'll be
in charge